JUVENILE CRIME
JUVENILE JUSTICE

Panel on Juvenile Crime: Prevention, Treatment, and Control

Joan McCord, Cathy Spatz Widom, and Nancy A. Crowell, *Editors*

Committee on Law and Justice
and
Board on Children, Youth, and Families

Commission on Behavioral and Social Sciences and Education
National Research Council
and
Institute of Medicine

NATIONAL ACADEMY PRESS
Washington, DC

NATIONAL ACADEMY PRESS   2101 Constitution Avenue, N.W.   Washington, D.C. 20418

NOTICE: The project that is the subject of this report was approved by the Governing Board of the National Research Council, whose members are drawn from the councils of the National Academy of Sciences, the National Academy of Engineering, and the Institute of Medicine. The members of the committee responsible for the report were chosen for their special competences and with regard for appropriate balance.

This study was supported by Grant No. 97-JN-FX-0020 between the National Academy of Sciences and the U.S. Departments of Justice and Education, and grants from the John D. and Catherine T. MacArthur Foundation and the Harry F. Guggenheim Foundation. Any opinions, findings, conclusions, or recommendations expressed in this publication are those of the author(s) and do not necessarily reflect the view of the organizations or agencies that provided support for this project.

Library of Congress Cataloging-in-Publication Data

Juvenile crime, juvenile justice / Joan McCord, Cathy Spatz Widom, and Nancy A. Crowell, editors.
   p. cm.
  Includes bibliographical references and index.
  ISBN 0-309-06842-8 (hardcover)
  1. Juvenile delinquency—United States. 2. Juvenile justice,
Administration of—United States.   I. McCord, Joan. II. Widom, Cathy
Spatz, 1945- . III. Crowell, Nancy A.
  HV9104 .J832 2001
  364.36'0973—dc21
                  2001001248

Suggested citation: National Research Council and Institute of Medicine (2001) *Juvenile Crime, Juvenile Justice*. Panel on Juvenile Crime: Prevention, Treatment, and Control. Joan McCord, Cathy Spatz Widom, and Nancy A. Crowell, eds. Committee on Law and Justice and Board on Children, Youth, and Families. Washington, DC: National Academy Press.

Additional copies of this report are available from:

National Academy Press, 2101 Constitution Avenue, N.W., Washington, D.C. 20418; (800) 624-6242 or (202) 334-3313 (in the Washington Metropolitan Area). This report is also available on line at http://www.nap.edu.

THE NATIONAL ACADEMIES

National Academy of Sciences
National Academy of Engineering
Institute of Medicine
National Research Council

The **National Academy of Sciences** is a private, nonprofit, self-perpetuating society of distinguished scholars engaged in scientific and engineering research, dedicated to the furtherance of science and technology and to their use for the general welfare. Upon the authority of the charter granted to it by the Congress in 1863, the Academy has a mandate that requires it to advise the federal government on scientific and technical matters. Dr. Bruce M. Alberts is president of the National Academy of Sciences.

The **National Academy of Engineering** was established in 1964, under the charter of the National Academy of Sciences, as a parallel organization of outstanding engineers. It is autonomous in its administration and in the selection of its members, sharing with the National Academy of Sciences the responsibility for advising the federal government. The National Academy of Engineering also sponsors engineering programs aimed at meeting national needs, encourages education and research, and recognizes the superior achievements of engineers. Dr. William A. Wulf is president of the National Academy of Engineering.

The **Institute of Medicine** was established in 1970 by the National Academy of Sciences to secure the services of eminent members of appropriate professions in the examination of policy matters pertaining to the health of the public. The Institute acts under the responsibility given to the National Academy of Sciences by its congressional charter to be an adviser to the federal government and, upon its own initiative, to identify issues of medical care, research, and education. Dr. Kenneth I. Shine is president of the Institute of Medicine.

The **National Research Council** was organized by the National Academy of Sciences in 1916 to associate the broad community of science and technology with the Academy's purposes of furthering knowledge and advising the federal government. Functioning in accordance with general policies determined by the Academy, the Council has become the principal operating agency of both the National Academy of Sciences and the National Academy of Engineering in providing services to the government, the public, and the scientific and engineering communities. The Council is administered jointly by both Academies and the Institute of Medicine. Dr. Bruce M. Alberts and Dr. William A. Wulf are chairman and vice chairman, respectively, of the National Research Council.

Preface

When this project was in its planning stages, the violent juvenile crime rate was rising and some criminologists were predicting a coming wave of violent juvenile "superpredators." Policy makers at the state and federal levels responded by imposing tougher sanctions on juveniles and facilitating the move of younger juveniles into the adult system for a broad range of offenses. Over the course of this panel study, rates of juvenile violence have dropped considerably, but policies continue to increase the number of young people who become involved in the juvenile justice and adult criminal justice systems, at the same time that prevention programs are being cut back.

The Panel on Juvenile Crime: Prevention, Treatment and Control was established by the National Research Council under the aegis of the Committee on Law and Justice, in the Commission on Behavioral and Social Sciences and Education. The task this panel undertook was a large one—analyzing data on trends in juvenile crime and juvenile justice system processing; reviewing both the literature on individual, familial, social, and community factors that contribute to juvenile crime and that on prevention and treatment programs; and examining information that could shed light on the effects of mandates of the Office of Juvenile Justice and Delinquency Prevention. When we began the study, we were aware that other reports on juvenile crime had recently appeared and that others would appear during the course of our work. By assembling a panel with diverse backgrounds and perspectives, our goal was to take a fresh look at the research on juvenile crime in order to point the way toward more effective policies based on empirical evidence and to highlight areas in need of more research. Our ultimate goal is to assist youth in leading constructive lives and to protect the public from juvenile crime.

The panel met six times over the course of the study, with active deliberations both during and between meetings. The panel also heard from many experts, visited juvenile detention and correctional facilities, analyzed available data, reviewed numerous articles and books, and commissioned several papers as part of its work. The researchers and agency personnel who provided input into the process are listed by name and affiliation in the Acknowledgments.

Joan McCord, Cochair
Cathy Spatz Widom, Cochair
Panel on Juvenile Crime:
Prevention, Treatment and Control

Acknowledgments

The panel gratefully acknowledges the sponsorship of this study by the Office of Juvenile Justice and Delinquency Prevention of the U.S. Department of Justice, the Safe and Drug-Free Schools Program of the U.S. Department of Education, the John D. and Catherine T. MacArthur Foundation, and the Harry Frank Guggenheim Foundation. Much assistance in shaping this project was provided by staff at these organizations, in particular: Charlotte Kerr, Betty Chemers, and Shay Bilchik, Office of Juvenile Justice and Delinquency Prevention, U.S. Department of Justice; Ann Weinheimer, Safe and Drug-Free Schools Program, U.S. Department of Education; Laurie Garduque, John D. and Catherine T. MacArthur Foundation; and Karen Colvard, Harry Frank Guggenheim Foundation.

The panel drew on the expertise of many people during the course of its information gathering. The panel extends its thanks to Elmar G.M. Weitekamp, Hans-Juergen Kerner, and Gernot Trueg of the Institute of Criminology, University of Tuebingen, Germany, for a background paper on international comparisons of juvenile justice systems; Robert Worden and Stephanie Myers of the Department of Criminal Justice, University at Albany, for providing the panel with a background paper on police encounters with juveniles; and Patricia L. McCall of North Carolina State University, for assisting panel member Kenneth Land with the paper on crime forecasting that appears in Appendix B of this report; Gary Gates of Carnegie Mellon University, who assisted panel member Steven Schlossman in analyzing historical data on juvenile delinquency and involvement in the adult criminal and juvenile justice systems; and Amie Schuck and Jorge Chavez of The University at Albany for assisting panel cochair Cathy Spatz Widom with an analysis of data on racial disproportionality in the juvenile justice system. Special thanks are also extended to Howard Snyder, of the National Center for Juvenile Justice, for sharing some of his analyses of juvenile arrest data; Rolf Loeber, of the University of Pittsburgh Medical Center, for providing the committee with materials presented to the OJJDP Study Group on Very Young Offenders and for sharing the literature review from his grant application to NIMH on the development of conduct disorders in girls; and to Linda Teplin, Northwestern University, for sharing the literature review from her grant application to the National Institute on Mental Health on mental health problems among incarcerated female juveniles.

The panel would also like to acknowledge the following people for giving presentations at panel workshops and meetings:

David Altschuler, Institute for Policy Studies, The Johns Hopkins University

Mark Berends, RAND Corporation, Washington, DC

Donna Bishop, Department of Criminal Justice and Legal Studies, University of Central Florida

Hon. Jay Blitzman, Juvenile Court Department, Watertown, Massachusetts

George Bridges, Offfice of Undergraduate Education, University of Washington

Ted Chiricos, School of Criminology and Criminal Justice, Florida State University

Philip Cook, Terry Sanford School of Public Policy, Duke University

John Devine, School of Education, New York University

Mary Didier, United States Sentencing Commission, Washington, DC

Thomas Dishion, Department of Psychology, University of Oregon

Carol Dweck, Department of Psychology, Columbia University

Delbert Elliott, Institute of Behavioral Science, University of Colorado Boulder

Doris Entwisle, Department of Sociology, The Johns Hopkins University

Jeffrey Fagan, Schools of Law and Public Health, Columbia University

Barry Feld, School of Law, University of Minnesota

Lawrence Greenfeld, Bureau of Justice Statistics, U.S. Department of Justice, Washington, DC

David Harris, College of Law, University of Toledo

Philip Harris, Department of Criminal Justice, Temple University

Kimberly Kempf-Leonard, Department of Criminology and Criminal Justice, University of Missouri, St. Louis

David Kennedy, John F. Kennedy School of Government, Harvard University

Mark Lepper, Department of Psychology, Stanford University

Mark Lipsey, Institute for Public Policy Studies, Vanderbilt University

Rolf Loeber, Western Psychiatric Clinic, University of Pittsburgh Medical Center

Holly MacKay, United States Sentencing Commission, Washington, DC

Ellen Markman, Department of Psychology, Stanford University

Ken Maton, Department of Psychology, University of Maryland Baltimore County

Steven Messner, Department of Sociology, The University at Albany

Gale Morrison, Graduate School of Education, University of California, Riverside

Stephanie Myers, School of Criminal Justice, The University at Albany

William Oliver, Department of Criminal Justice, Indiana University

Daphna Oyserman, Institute for Social Research, University of Michigan

Howard Pinderhughes, Social and Behavioral Sciences, University of California, San Francisco

Gregory Pettit, Department of Human Development and Family Studies, Auburn University

Ira Schwartz, School of Social Work, University of Pennsylvania

Laurie Schwede, Census Bureau, U.S. Department of Commerce, Washington, DC

Margaret Beale Spencer, Graduate School of Education, University of Pennsylvania

Howard Snyder, National Center for Juvenile Justice, Pittsburgh, PA

Laurence Steinberg, Department of Psychology, Temple University

Cynthia Stifter, Human Development and Family Studies, Pennsylvania State University

Kenneth Trump, National School Safety and Security Services, Cleveland, Ohio

Lee Underwood, The Pines Residential Treatment Center, Portsmouth, Virginia

Robert Worden, School of Criminal Justice, The University at Albany

The panel is grateful to the following individuals who hosted site visits and shared their firsthand experience with juvenile justice system programs with panel members and staff:

Nancy Arrigona, Criminal Justice Policy Council, Austin, Texas

Judy Briscoe, Texas Youth Commission

Thomas Chapmond, Community Initiatives for Program Development, Texas Department of Protective and Regulatory Services

Stan DeGerolami, Giddings State School, Giddings, Texas

Hon. John K. Dietz, Travis County Juvenile Board, Austin, Texas

Mike Griffiths, Dallas County Juvenile Probation Department, Dallas, Texas

Dawn Heikkila, Criminal Justice Policy Council, Austin, Texas

Laura King, Southeast Austin Community Youth Development program

Vance McMahan, Governor's Policy Office, Austin, Texas

Estela Medina, Travis County Juvenile Probation Department, Austin, Texas

David Montague, Tarrant County Chief Juvenile District Attorney, Fort Worth, Texas

Ron Quiros, Travis County Juvenile Justice Alternative Education Program, Austin, Texas

David Riley, Bexar County Juvenile Probation Department, San Antonio, Texas

Linda Smith, Giddings State School, Giddings, Texas

Vicky Spriggs, Texas Juvenile Probation Commission

Johnny Sutton, Governor's Policy Office, Austin, Texas

Don Willett, Governor's Policy Office, Austin, Texas

Thanks and acknowledgment are due to the members of the study panel, all of whom gave generously of their time. Tony Fabelo graciously arranged a site visit to various juvenile detention and correctional facilities in Texas, as well as setting up meetings with a number of juvenile justice system officials. Patricia Cohen arranged a site visit to a correctional facility in New York state. Several members took primary responsibility for drafting sections of the report. We wish to thank Jane Costello for her contributions to the compound risk analysis in Chapter 6; Sandra Graham for her contributions to the section on school-related factors in Chapter 3 and school-based prevention programs in Chapter 4; Darnell Hawkins for his assistance with Chapter 6; Steven Schlossman for his analyses of historical data that appear throughout the report; Mercer Sullivan for his contributions to the section on community factors in Chapter 3; Richard Tremblay for his contributions to individual developmental factors in Chapter 3 and prevention programs in Chapter 4. Finally, we would like to thank the National Research Council staff for valuable assistance with this project: project assistant Glenda Tyson and senior project assistant Karen Autrey, for facilitating the panel's meetings; project assistant Lecia Henderson, for preparing the manuscript for publication; research assistant Brenda McLaughlin, for assisting in gathering materials for response to review; research associate Melissa Bamba, for helping to organize workshops and pulling together research materials for the panel; study director Nancy Crowell for analyzing crime data and turning the panel's writing contributions into a coherent whole; and CBASSE editor Christine McShane, whose editing of this report made it much more readable.

This report has been reviewed in draft form by individuals chosen for their diverse perspectives and technical expertise, in accordance with procedures approved by the Report Review Committee of the National Research Council (NRC). The purpose of this independent review is to provide candid and critical comments that will assist the institution in making the published report as sound as possible and to ensure that the report meets institutional standards for objectivity, evidence, and responsiveness to the study charge. The review comments and draft manuscript remain confidential to protect the integrity of the deliberative process.

We thank the following individuals for their participation in the review of this report: Donald Cohen, Yale-New Haven Children's Hospital, Yale University; David Farrington, Institute of Criminology, Cambridge, England; Barry C. Feld, Law School, University of Minnesota; Peter W. Greenwood, RAND, Santa Monica, California; Richard Jessor, Institute of Behavioral Science, University of Colorado; Mark Lipsey, Institute of Public Policy Studies, Vanderbilt University; Rebecca Maynard, Graduate School of Education, University of Pennsylvania; N. Dickon Reppucci, Department of Psychology, University of Virginia; and Richard Rosenfeld, Department of Criminology and Criminal Justice, University of Missouri-St. Louis.

Although the reviewers listed above have provided many constructive comments and suggestions, they were not asked to endorse the conclusions or recommendations nor did they see the final draft of the report before its release. The review of this report was overseen by Mark H. Moore, John F. Kennedy School of Government, Harvard University, and Henry W. Riecken, University of Pennsylvania School of Medicine (emeritus). Appointed by the National Research Council, they were responsible for making certain that an independent examination of this report was carried out in accordance with institutional procedures and that all review comments were carefully considered. Responsibility for the final content of this report rests entirely with the authoring panel and the institution.

While the individuals listed above have provided constructive comments and suggestions, it must be emphasized that responsibility for the final content of this report rests entirely with the authoring committee and the institution.

Contents

xvii

JUVENILE CRIME
JUVENILE JUSTICE

Executive Summary

The dramatic rise in juvenile violence, particularly homicides, which began in the mid- to late 1980s and peaked in the early 1990s, generated considerable fear and concern among the public and led to policy changes by federal, state, and local governments. For example, in response to the rise in juvenile violence and predictions of an upcoming wave of increasingly violent youth, most states stiffened their laws relating to juvenile justice, including measures that allow, or in many cases mandate, youngsters to be transferred to the adult system at younger ages and for a greater variety of offenses.

A large body of research, developed over the past two decades, has begun to identify factors that may increase the risk of juvenile crime. The research has also led to the design and evaluation of programs to prevent it. These developments led the Office of Juvenile Justice and Delinquency Prevention of the U.S. Department of Justice, the Safe and Drug-Free Schools Program of the U.S. Department of Education, the John D. and Catherine T. MacArthur Foundation, and the Harry Frank Guggenheim Foundation to sponsor a National Research Council panel to examine what is known about juvenile crime and its prevention, treatment, and control.

CHARGE TO THE PANEL

The Panel on Juvenile Crime: Prevention, Treatment, and Control was asked to identify and analyze the full range of research studies and datasets that bear on the nature of juvenile crime, highlighting key issues and data sources that can provide evidence of prevalence and seriousness; race, gender, and class bias in the juvenile justice system; and impacts of deterrence, punishment, and prevention strategies. The panel was further asked to analyze the factors that contribute to delinquent behavior, including a review of the knowledge on child and adolescent development and its implications for prevention and control; to assess the current practices of the juvenile justice system, including the implementation of constitutional safeguards; to examine adjudication, detention, and waiver practices; to explore the role of community and institutional settings; to assess the quality of data sources on the clients of both public and private juvenile justice facilities; and to assess the impact of the deinstitutionalization mandates of the Juvenile Justice and Delinquency Prevention Act of 1974 on delinquency and community safety.

JUVENILE CRIME TRENDS

Based on public concern and legislative actions about juvenile violence, one would think that it was continually increasing. Juvenile violent crime rates, however, have been declining for at least the past 5 years. The panel conducted a review of data on juvenile crime rates, including arrests, victim reports of crime, and self-reports by juveniles. Although there are many weaknesses in each of these data sources, the panel drew a number of conclusions about juvenile crime trends.

- Most juveniles break laws, such as shoplifting or minor vandalism, but only a small proportion commits serious crimes. In 1998, only 4 percent of juvenile arrests were for the violent crimes of homicide, rape, robbery, or aggravated assault and less than one-tenth of one percent of juvenile arrests were for homicide.
- There was, however, a surge in serious juvenile crime rates beginning in the late 1980s through the early 1990s. The juvenile arrest rate for violent crimes began decreasing in 1994 almost as rapidly as it had increased and, by 1999, was back to the rate of the late 1980s.
- The cause of the sudden rise and fall in juvenile violent crime rates in the United States, which also occurred among youth and adults in other countries, remains uncertain, although a number of theories have been put forth. Most if not all of the increase in U.S. youth homicides from 1987 to 1993 involved homicides committed with guns. Some of the rise in arrest rates for other violent crimes seem to have been a result of changes in police policies regarding whether to consider specific types of assault as aggravated assaults rather than simple assaults and an increased willingness to arrest for assault.

• Blacks are disproportionately represented among juveniles arrested for crimes committed in the United States. Moreover, while not the major focus of this report's discussion of race and crime, bias in the wider society, which distributes opportunities and resources to youth as they grow up, contributes to the risks of minority youth involvement in the juvenile justice system.

• Forecasts of juvenile crime based on the spike in homicide rates have proven to be misleading and inaccurate and highlight the caution with which predictions of future juvenile crime trends must be made.

THE DEVELOPMENT OF DELINQUENCY

Although a large proportion of adolescents gets arrested and an even larger proportion commits illegal acts, only a small proportion commits serious crimes. Furthermore, most of those who engage in illegal behavior as adolescents do not become adult criminals.

Risk factors for delinquency can be identified when studying individuals, social environments, and communities. Although more should be learned about interactions among risk factors, recent research has contributed to understanding who is at risk and why. The panel noted that predictions are no more accurate in identifying who will become a criminal than medical predictions are for identifying who will have a heart attack or develop lung cancer. In both domains, however, knowledge about risk factors can enhance preventive actions.

Early developmental factors have been shown to be related to adolescent delinquent behavior. Recent research suggests that prenatal and perinatal disadvantages (such as exposure to drugs, low birthweight, and trauma) become risks for delinquency. New studies suggest that poor language development and lack of empathy may be consequences of parental neglect. Deficiencies in language put a child at risk for school difficulties and delinquency. Children who do not learn to inhibit normal early physically aggressive behavior by about 3 years of age or who are highly physically aggressive are at high risk of becoming involved in juvenile crime, as are children with conduct disorder and oppositional defiant disorder. The risk for later juvenile crime may be exacerbated by abusive parenting, poor parenting practices, or disorganized family and neighborhood environments.

Although single-parent families have been widely held responsible for juvenile crime, a considerable amount of evidence indicates that if the remaining parent provides consistent and strong guidance, children in single-parent families are no more likely to commit criminal acts than are children in two-parent families. Studies continue to show that how parents treat their children has an important impact on whether or not their children become criminal delinquents. Parental conflict and harsh, erratic discipline have been shown to contribute to juvenile crime. Abused children are also at high risk of becoming involved in crime. Households that provide safety, emotional warmth, and guidance foster the development of noncriminal young people even in neighborhoods at high risk for crime. During early adolescence, peers begin to take on increasing importance. Those who associate with delinquent companions are likely to increase their misbehavior when spending time with those companions.

Contrary to their intentions, schools appear to foster problems among misbehaving children and adolescents through such common practices as tracking, grade retention, suspension, and expulsion. The panel took special note of apparent racial and ethnic biases in the administration of these practices.

Where families live affects the opportunities and resources available to them. Children who grow up in neighborhoods with high joblessness, poverty, and crime may see criminal behavior as an acceptable alternative when other opportunities are lacking. The negative impact of poor parenting is also stronger in disrupted neighborhoods (see Chapter 3).

RESPONSES TO JUVENILE CRIME

During the past decade, juvenile crime legislation and policy have become more punitive and have blurred the lines between juvenile and adult justice systems. Movement in this direction is continuing, despite indications from research on recidivism and deterrence that it may be counterproductive to treat juveniles as if they were adults. More and more juveniles are being detained and incarcerated, even though there is evidence that most juveniles can be treated equally or more effectively in the community than in secure confinement, without jeopardizing community safety.

Responding to juvenile crime requires the establishment of programs to prevent its development as well as programs to deal with young people who have committed criminal acts. These programs may be found in a variety of institutional settings, including schools, community-based organizations, religious organizations, mental health settings, and the formal juvenile justice and adult criminal justice systems.

Prevention

Our review of attempts at prevention has turned up very few programs that have credible evaluations. The most effective crime prevention programs, the panel concludes, address a range of difficulties. Approaches that appear successful in reducing delinquency, based on well-designed evaluations, include multiple components for parents, youngsters, and the environment (school or community) and target multiple behaviors. These types of programs appear to be more beneficial than narrowly focused programs. Several widely used and well-evaluated intervention strategies have been found to increase delinquency (see Chapters 4 and 5). Many such programs rest on drawing young misbehaving adolescents together, a practice that seems to reinforce their antisocial behaviors.

The Juvenile Justice System

A juvenile justice system separate from the adult justice system was established in the United States about 100 years ago with the goal of diverting youthful offenders from the destructive punishments of criminal courts and encouraging rehabilitation based on the individual juvenile's needs. In practice, there was always a tension between social welfare and social control—that is, focusing on the best interests of the individual child versus focusing on punishment, incapacitation, and protecting society from certain offenses. This tension has shifted over time and has varied significantly from jurisdiction to jurisdiction, and it remains today.

It is important to remember that the United States has at least 51 different juvenile justice systems, not one. Given the local nature of juvenile justice in the United States, there has never been a single dominant vision of how to deal with delinquent children in law or in practice. The trend during the past decade, however, has been toward stiffening the laws dealing with juveniles. Every state made changes in its laws and policies governing juvenile justice during the 1990s. These changes include easier waivers to adult court, excluding certain offenses from juvenile court jurisdiction, blended juvenile and adult sentences, increased authority for prosecutors to decide to file cases in adult court, and more frequent custodial placement of adjudicated delinquents. The great majority of recent changes in juvenile justice law and practice have not been evaluated. Research to date shows that juveniles placed in secure detention or incarceration suffer a wide range of negative effects and those transferred to adult court may be more likely to reoffend than those who remain under juvenile court jurisdiction (see Chapter 5).

Increasing numbers of young people are placed in secure detention, which disrupts young people's lives and has negative effects on behavior and future developmental trajectories. Incarcerated juveniles have higher rates of physical injury and mental health problems, and they have poorer educational outcomes, than do their counterparts who are treated in the community. Incarceration also causes severe and long-term problems with future employment, leaving ex-offenders with few economic alternatives to crime. Recent research also demonstrates that many serious as well as nonserious offenders can be treated in the community without endangering public safety.

Information about the number of juveniles in custody—in detention centers, jails, juvenile correctional facilities, or adult correctional facilities—is very poor. Data on the conditions under which juveniles are incarcerated and the types of services available to them are minimal. From the few available data, it appears that the rate of juveniles placed in custodial institutions has increased substantially in the past two decades, leading to widespread overcrowding in detention and other correctional facilities.

RACIAL DISPARITY IN THE JUVENILE JUSTICE SYSTEM

The proportion of black juveniles under the supervision of the juvenile or adult criminal justice systems is more than double their proportion in the general population, and these discrepancies exist at most points in justice system processing. The existence of disproportionate racial representation in the juvenile justice system raises questions about fundamental fairness and equality of treatment of these youth by the police, courts, and other personnel connected with the juvenile justice system. Furthermore, what happens to youth in their dealings (or lack of dealings) with the juvenile justice system may have substantial consequences for subsequent development and prospects for the future.

Studies of self-reported offending find that black juveniles report more delinquent behavior than whites, but the difference is not nearly as large as the difference in arrest rates. The question remains of *why* black juveniles should be more likely to engage in criminal behavior than whites. Such overrepresentation may be at least partially explained by considering how exposure to risk factors affects the probability of engaging in criminal behavior. More minority children, and black children in particular, are subject to risk factors associated with crime, such as living in communities characterized by concentrated poverty and social disorganization.

Differences in behavior cannot explain all the disproportionate representation of blacks in the juvenile justice system. Some research has documented apparent bias at various points, such as likelihood of arrest, pretrial detention, or formal processing. Disproportionate involvement of some minorities in the juvenile and adult justice system cannot be explained without considering the larger society as well as differential behavior and biases in the justice system.

RECOMMENDATIONS

Being placed in secure detention disrupts a young person's life and increases the juvenile's likelihood of receiving formal processing and punitive sanctions. Correctional facilities have become increasingly crowded, impairing their ability to provide adequate services to their heterogeneous populations. Overcrowded conditions also increase the risk of injury to both staff and juveniles. Research on alternatives to secure detention and confinement have found them to pose no greater risks to the public than secure detention or confinement. In addition, alternatives to detention or confinement tend to be less costly.

Recommendation: The federal government should assist the states through federal funding and incentives to reduce the use of secure detention and secure confinement by developing community-based alternatives. The effectiveness of such programs, both for the protection of the community and the benefit of the youth in their charge, should be monitored.

Public policy on juvenile crime, particularly the trend toward more punitive sanctions, appears to have been influenced in part by predictions of future crime rates—predictions that have proven notoriously inaccurate. Although short-term forecasts are necessary for allocating resources at the local, state, and federal levels, the committee finds long-term forecasts of behavior, such as the prediction of a future violent crime wave involving superpredators, to be fraught with uncertainty.

Recommendation: Because of the inaccuracies inherent in long-range predictions of behavior, public policy should not be based on the assumption that any specific forecast will be true. The periods over which crime forecasts are made should be as short as possible and the forecasts should be reviewed frequently. (For specific suggestions for improving forecasts, see Chapter 2 and Appendix B.)

Research has shown that treating most juvenile offenders within the community does not compromise public safety and may even improve it through reduced recidivism. Considering the negative effects of detention and incarceration, community-based treatment should be expanded. Evaluation components should be built into program delivery with the goal of improving services, expanding the use of programs that work, and ending support for programs that are shown to be ineffective. Replication studies of programs that have been found successful, such as treatment foster care or multisystemic therapy, is particularly important to advancing knowledge about what works and for whom.

Recommendation: Federal and state funding should be provided to replicate successful research-based, community-based treatment programs for all types of offenders with continuing evaluations to ensure their safety and efficacy under the specific circumstances of their application.

Overrepresentation of blacks, Hispanics, and American Indians in the juvenile justice system requires immediate attention. The existence of disproportional racial representation in the juvenile justice system raises concerns about differential exposure to risks and the fairness and equal treatment of youth by the police, courts, and other players in the juvenile justice system. Given the importance of the problem of race, crime, and juvenile justice in the United States, the scant research attention that has been paid to understanding the factors contributing to racial disparities in the juvenile justice system is shocking.

Recommendation: The panel recommends that a comprehensive, systematic, and long-term agenda for acquiring empirical knowledge to understand and meaningfully reduce problems of unwarranted racial disparity in the juvenile justice system is a critical priority and that new funding should be set aside for this effort.

Prevention and Treatment

Although evaluation research has resulted in some information about what types of programs may be effective in preventing delinquency, much remains to be known. At what age is it best to intervene? Is there an ideal length of program delivery? Are some programs more effective for certain types of children or families or at certain ages? Which programs are counterproductive? Some relatively well-evaluated programs, such as D.A.R.E. and shock incarceration programs, have been shown to have little impact on the targeted behavior and even to have counterproductive impacts among some populations. Until aspects of programs are systematically varied and well evaluated, these questions will remain.

Recommendation: All publicly supported intervention programs should be evaluated for both safety and efficacy using scientifically credible methods for doing so. Adequate funding for such evaluations should be included in the public support of intervention programs. Funding for programs whose effectiveness is shown to be limited should be discontinued.

Delinquency is associated with poor school performance, truancy, and leaving school at a young age. Some pedagogical practices may exacerbate these problems. The available research on grade retention and tracking and the disciplinary practices of suspension and expulsion reveal that such policies have more negative than positive effects. For students already experiencing academic difficulty, tracking and grade retention have been found to further impair their academic performance. Furthermore, tracking does not appear to improve the academic performance of students in high tracks compared with similar students in schools that do not use tracking. Suspension and expulsion deny education in the name of discipline, yet these practices have not been shown to be effective in reducing school misbehavior. Little is known about the effects of these policies on other students in the school. Given the fact that the policies have been found to interfere with attachment to school and to disproportionately affect minorities, they may impede the opportunity to learn, unintentionally reinforce negative stereotypes, and contribute to long-term harm with regard to future educational achievement and involvement in crime.

> **Recommendation: Federal programs should be developed to promote alternatives to grade retention and tracking in schools.**

Placing one or two antisocial juveniles in a group of primarily prosocial young people can decrease their antisocial behavior and increase their prosocial behavior without negatively influencing the prosocial youngsters. Some well-designed evaluations of treatments for at-risk juveniles found, however, that placing such youngsters together in groups, even under careful adult supervision, had the undesired outcome of increasing their antisocial behavior.

> **Recommendation: Federal and state funds should be used to develop treatments for misbehaving youngsters that do not group aggressive or antisocial youth together.**

Prenatal exposure to alcohol, cocaine, heroin, and nicotine is associated with hyperactivity, attention deficit, and impulsiveness, which are risk factors for later antisocial behavior and delinquency. Biological harms suffered during the prenatal period may have some devastating effects on development. Consequently, preventive efforts during the prenatal period, such as preventing fetal exposure to alcohol and drugs, may have great benefits. Reducing alcohol and drug abuse among expectant parents may also improve their ability to parent, thus reducing family-related risk factors for delinquency.

> **Recommendation: Federal, state, and local governments should act to provide treatment for drug abuse (including alcohol and tobacco use) among pregnant women, particularly adolescents.**

Research and Data Needs

Data to track or monitor crime committed by juveniles are inadequate. The data from the Uniform Crime Reports do not lend themselves to analyses of specific crimes in relation to the ages of juveniles who are arrested. We therefore do not know, for example, whether changes in policies on violent crimes or on drugs and guns have led to changes in the age of juveniles being arrested. Because of the known high level of co-offending among juveniles, neither arrests nor self-reporting of offenses can currently be used to measure the impact of policies on social order.

Recommendation: Incentives should be established to encourage all police agencies to report data to the Federal Bureau of Investigation (FBI). In addition, a monitoring system should be established to oversee the accuracy and completeness of the information received by the FBI for the Uniform Crime Reports and the National Incident Based Reporting System.

The Office of Juvenile Justice and Delinquency Prevention sponsors a biennial Census of Juveniles in Residential Placement that provides only minimal information. This instrument identifies juveniles in custody on the specific date of the survey and therefore oversamples juveniles in long-term confinement. Furthermore, neither this instrument nor the newly designed Juvenile Residential Facility Census (begun in October 2000), yields information about children or youth housed in jails, adult institutions, or mental hospital facilities. The Office of Juvenile Justice and Delinquency Prevention is planning a Survey of Youth in Residential Placement that will help to inform the public about conditions of confinement. It should be a matter of public accountability for all facilities that hold juveniles in secure confinement to report regularly on the conditions under which those juveniles are kept and the types of services provided.

Recommendation: The Congress should provide adequate funds to the Office of Juvenile Justice and Delinquency Prevention and the Bureau of Justice Statistics in order to ensure proper data collection about conditions of confinement as well as new funds to develop national data collection systems to measure the number and characteristics of children and adolescents outside juvenile jurisdictions, those transferred to criminal court, and those held in adult prisons or jails.

Research has shown that the greater the number of risk factors present, the higher the likelihood of delinquency. It is not clear, however, whether certain risk factors or combinations of risk factors are more important than others in the development of delinquency. Furthermore, the timing, severity, and duration of risk factors, in interaction with the age, sex, and the environment in which the individual lives, undoubtedly affect the behavioral outcomes. A better understanding of how risk factors interact is important for the development of prevention efforts, especially efforts in communities in which risk factors are concentrated.

Recommendation: Research on risk factors for delinquency should focus on the effects of interactions among various risk factors. In particular, research on the effects of differences in neighborhoods and their interactions with individual and family conditions should be expanded. (For details of needed research areas, see Chapter 3.)

Research on delinquency has traditionally focused on boys. Although boys are more likely to be arrested than girls, the rate of increase in arrest and incarceration has been much larger in recent years for girls than boys, and the seriousness of the crimes committed by girls has increased.

Recommendation: The Department of Justice should develop and fund a systematic research program on female juvenile offending. (For details of needed research areas, see Chapter 3.)

Despite the large amount of descriptive literature about the juvenile justice system, little research has identified how different laws regarding juvenile crime or different practices in confinement affect those in the juvenile justice system. For example, do behavioral modification programs used in secure facilities have an influence on behavior of juveniles after release? Are there long-term effects of isolation used as punishment for disobedient juveniles in confinement? Are there special benefits for particular educational programs carried out in juvenile institutions? Evaluation studies of a variety of policies and practices should be undertaken. Emphasis should be placed on measuring psychological, educational, and physical effects on the juveniles, as well as measures of recidivism.

Recommendation: The federal government should assist the states in evaluating the effects of correctional policies and practices, such as the use of behavior modification programs, physical restraints, and isolation on incarcerated juveniles, as well as determining the effectiveness of educational and psychological programming in correctional facilities.

The panel also recommends a number of other areas in which funding of research is needed, including:
- Improving the quality of existing information on juvenile crime and developing alternative sources of information (see Chapter 2);
- Reviewing the effects of school policies and practices, such as grade

retention, tracking, suspension, and expulsion on delinquency, educational attainment, and school atmosphere and environment (see Chapter 3);

• Using prospective longitudinal studies to increase understanding of the role of factors in prenatal, perinatal, and early infant development on mechanisms that increase the likelihood of healthy development, as well as the development of antisocial behavior (see Chapter 3);

• Studying long-term outcomes of well-designed interventions that have shown short-term promise for reducing delinquency (see Chapter 4);

• Evaluating the adequacy of standards for juvenile detention and correctional facilities (see Chapter 5); and

• Developing a research agenda on juvenile justice system practices and their effects, including the extent, systemic effects, costs, and cost-effectiveness of the various possible dispositions of juvenile cases, and the long-term effects of transferring juveniles to adult court and incarcerating them in adult facilities (see Chapter 5).

1

Introduction

Juvenile crime is one of the nation's serious problems. Concern about it is widely shared by federal, state, and local government officials and by the public. In recent years, this concern has grown with the dramatic rise in juvenile violence that began in the mid-1980s and peaked in the early 1990s. Although juvenile crime rates appear to have fallen since the mid-1990s, this decrease has not alleviated the concern. Many states began taking a tougher legislative stance toward juveniles in the late 1970s and early 1980s, a period during which juvenile crime rates were stable or falling slightly, and federal reformers were urging prevention and less punitive measures. Some of the dissonance between the federal agenda and what was happening in the states at that time may have been caused by significant changes in legal procedures that made juvenile court processes more similar—though not identical—to those in criminal (adult) court. The main response to the most recent spike in violent juvenile crime has been enactment of laws that further blur distinctions between juvenile courts and adult courts. States continued to toughen their juvenile crime laws in recent years, making sentencing more punitive, expanding allowable transfers to criminal (adult) court, or doing away with some of the confidentiality safeguards of juvenile court. Many such changes were enacted after the juvenile violent crime rate had already begun to fall. The rehabilitative model embodied in the Juvenile Justice and Delinquency Prevention Act of 1974, focusing on the needs of the young offender, has lost ever more ground over the past 20 years to punitive models that focus mainly on the offense committed. These punitive policies have had a disproportionate impact on some minority groups, particularly black youngsters, an important issue that is explored in depth in Chapter 6.

Crime policies in the United States have been moving in the direction of treating juveniles as adults, even though many young people continue to grow up in settings that "fail to provide the resources, the supports, and the opportunities essential to a healthy development and reasonable preparation for productive adulthood" (National Research Council, 1993a:2)—settings that put young people at high risk for delinquency. In 1997, 40 percent of all those living below the poverty level in the United States were under the age of 18 (Snyder and Sickmund, 1999). Structural changes in society, including fewer two-parent homes and more maternal employment, have contributed to a lack of resources for the supervision of children's and adolescents' free time.

Government policy on juvenile delinquency must often struggle with the appropriate balance of concern over the healthy development of children and adolescents who violate the law and a public desire to punish criminals. This tension between rehabilitation and punishment when dealing with children and adolescents who commit crimes results in an ambivalent orientation toward young offenders. Criminal acts must be suppressed, condemned, and punished. Nevertheless, children and adolescents who commit criminal acts must be educated and supported in a growth process that should be the objective of government policy for all young people, including young offenders.

A number of cognitive and social features of childhood and adolescence influence the content of juvenile crime policy. Historically, children under the age of seven have been considered below the age of reason, and therefore unable to formulate the criminal intent necessary to be held accountable for criminal offenses. In practice, children younger than age 10 are rarely involved in the juvenile justice system. Arrests of those younger than 10 years old account for less than 2 percent of all juvenile arrests. By the age of 16 or 17, most adolescents are deemed to have sufficient cognitive capacity and life experience to be held accountable for intended wrongful acts. How to deal appropriately with those who commit crimes between the ages of 10 and 17 is the issue faced in juvenile crime policy. Adolescence is a period of dating, driving, and expanding social networks—all choices that can produce positive or negative consequences for the adolescent and the community. Public policies in the areas of education, medical care, alcoholic beverage control, and juvenile crime reflect beliefs that adolescents have not acquired the abilities or capacities necessary for adult status. Creating the appropriate public policy for a period of semiautonomy is no small task (Zimring, 1982). To further complicate the matter, crime rates peak in mid- to late adolescence, making policy toward young offenders of special importance.

To best answer the questions of how to deal with young offenders requires knowledge of factors in the individual, family, social settings, and community that influence the development of delinquent behavior; of the types of offenses committed by young people; and of the types of interventions that can most efficiently and effectively prevent offending in the first place or prevent its recurrence. This study reviews literature in all of these areas to provide an objective view of juvenile crime and the juvenile justice system in the United States.

CHILD AND ADOLESCENT DEVELOPMENT: NOT JUST LITTLE ADULTS

What is often missing from discussions of juvenile crime today is recognition that children and adolescents are not just little adults, nor is the world in which they live the world of adults. Physical, emotional, and cognitive development continue throughout adolescence. Although young people can approach decisions in a manner similar to adults under some circumstances, many decisions that children and adolescents make are under precisely the conditions that are hardest for adults—unfamiliar tasks, choices with uncertain outcomes, and ambiguous situations (see, for example, Beyth-Marom and Fischhoff, 1997; Cohn et al., 1995). Further complicating the matter for children and adolescents is that they often face deciding whether or not to engage in a risky behavior, such as taking drugs, shoplifting, or getting into a fight, in situations involving emotions, stress, peer pressure, and little time for reflection.

Young people are liable to overestimate their own understanding of a situation, underestimate the probability of negative outcomes, and make judgments based on incorrect or incomplete information (Quadrel et al., 1993). Although adults are also prone to the same misperceptions, children's and adolescents' lack of experience increases their vulnerability. Quadrel et al. (1993) found that high-risk adolescents (with legal and substance abuse problems, recruited from group homes) were more likely than middle-class youngsters to have incorrect information about risks, while being extremely confident in their information.

Emotions can affect decision making for both adolescents and adults. When people are experiencing positive emotions, such as excitement, happiness, love (as adolescents often do when with groups of their peers), they tend to underestimate the possibility of negative consequences to their actions. When experiencing negative emotions, such as anger, jealousy, sadness, people tend to focus on the near term and lose sight of the big picture. This is particularly relevant for adolescents, who have been found to experience wider and more rapid mood swings than adults (Larson et al., 1980; Larson and Lampman-Petraitis, 1989; Larson and Richards, 1994).

Studies of young people's understanding of legal processing and the consequences of various legal choices, such as forfeiting the right to remain silent or to have an attorney, show differences between those younger and older than about 15 years (Grisso, 1997). Those under age 15 often misunderstand the concept of a right, in general, and of Miranda rights, in particular. They foresee fewer alternative courses of action in legal proceedings and tend to concentrate on short-term rather than long-term consequences (Grisso, 1980; 1981). For example, younger youth often misconstrue the right to remain silent, believing it means they should be quiet until they are told to talk. Nor do they completely understand the right to have an attorney present, without charge, before they talk (Abramovitch et al., 1995; Grisso, 1981). These misunderstandings raise concerns about children's and young adolescents' competence to stand trial in adult court. Children and adolescents from disadvantaged socio-economic backgrounds and those with low IQs fare worse in understanding the legal process and their rights than do other children and adolescents of comparable ages (Grisso, 1997). Furthermore, experience with the justice system does not ensure that young people fully understand the process, their rights, or the implications of the decisions they make. Both Grisso (1981) and Lawrence (1983) have found that adolescent delinquents had much poorer understanding of their rights than did adult defendants.

Emerging research using magnetic resonance imaging of the brain demonstrates the cognitive and emotional differences between adolescents and adults. Children and adolescents process emotionally charged information in the part of the brain responsible for instinct and gut reactions. Adults process such information in the "rational" frontal section of the brain (Baird et al., 1999). Children and adolescents may be physiologically less capable than adults of reasoning logically in the face of particularly strong emotions. In a recent study, Thompson et al. (2000) found that the brain continues to develop and change through at least midadolescence, with the most active parts of the brain changing during development. These new insights on brain development may have implications for holding children and adolescents criminally responsible in the same way as adults and raise concerns about initiatives to transfer younger and younger defendants to adult courts.

INTERNATIONAL PERSPECTIVE[1]

Looking at the policies of other countries provides some perspective on criminal justice in the United States. An international study of 15 countries—Australia, Austria, Belgium, Denmark, England and Wales, France, Germany, Hungary, Italy, Japan, The Netherlands, New Zealand, Russia, Sweden, and Switzerland—notes that all have special provisions for young criminals in their justice systems, although some (such as Denmark, Russia, and Sweden) have no special courts for juveniles. Table 1-1 depicts some of the differences among countries, showing the range in variability for the minimum age of criminal responsibility, the age at which full responsibility as an adult can be assumed, the type of court that handles young people committing crimes, whether such young people can be tried in courts that also try adults, the maximum length of sentencing for a juvenile, and policies regarding incarcerating juveniles with adults.

The United States was not alone in seeing a dramatic increase in violent crime by juveniles in the 1980s and early 1990s. Many European countries and Canada experienced increases in their rates of violent crime, particularly among juveniles (Hagan and Foster, 2000; Pfeiffer, 1998). It is difficult to compare rates across countries, because legal definitions of crime vary from country to country. For example, in Germany, assault is counted as a violent crime only if a weapon is used during the commission of the crime, whereas in England and Wales, the degree of injury to the victim determines whether or not an assault counts as a violent crime. Crime is also measured differently in each country. For example, the United States commonly relies on numbers of arrests to measure crime. In Germany, Austria, and Italy, among other countries, crime is measured by the number of cases solved by police (even if the offender has been apprehended) (Pfeiffer, 1998). Nevertheless, trends in juvenile violent crime appeared similar in many developed countries in the 1980s and early 1990s,[2] although the rates were different.

The United States has a high violent crime rate—particularly for homicide—in comparison to other countries, although property crime rates, particularly burglary, are higher than U.S. rates in Canada, England and Wales, and The Netherlands (Hagan and Foster, 2000; Mayhew and White, 1997). In 1994, the violent crime arrest rate (includes homicide, aggravated assault, robbery, and rape) for 13- to 17-year-olds in the United

---

[1]The panel is indebted to Elmar Weitekamp, Hans-Juergen Kerner, and Gernot Trueg, from whose commissioned paper this material is drawn.

[2]Data from other countries after 1995 were not available to the panel at the time this report was written, so no comparisons for the latter half of the 1990s were possible.

TABLE 1-1 International Comparisons of Juvenile Justice Systems

Country	Minimum Age of Criminal Responsibility	Age of Adult Criminal Responsibility	Court That Handles Juveniles
Australia	10[a]	16-17[b]	Children's courts, which are part of the criminal justice system and deal with juveniles charged with a crime
Austria	14	19	Special sections in local and regional courts; youth courts
Belgium	16-18	18	Special juvenile courts
Denmark	15	18	No juvenile court
England and Wales	10	18	Youth courts
France	13 (unofficial)	18	Children's tribunals; youth courts of assizes
Germany	14	18	Single sitting judge; juvenile court; juvenile chamber
Hungary	14	18	Special sections of regular courts
Italy	14	18	Separate juvenile courts
Japan	14	20	Family courts
The Netherlands	12	18	Special juvenile courts
New Zealand	14; 10 for murder and manslaughter	18	Youth courts
Russia	16; 14 for certain crimes	18	No juvenile court
Sweden	15	18	No juvenile court
Switzerland	7	18	Special juvenile courts and/or juvenile prosecutors

SOURCE: Weitekamp et al. (1999).

[a]The lower age limit is 7 in Tasmania.
[b]Age of full criminal responsibility differs by state

Transfer to Adult Court Allowable?	Maximum Length of Sentence for a Juvenile	Separation of Incarcerated Juveniles from Adults
Yes, for serious felonies	2 to 7 years	Not mandatory, generally separated in practice
No	1/2 adult sentence	Yes
Yes	No juvenile incarceration	Not mandatory, generally separated in practice
N/A	8 years	Yes
Yes	2 years	Yes
No	1/2 adult sentence	Yes
Yes	10 years	Yes
No	15 years	Yes
No	1/3 adult sentence	Yes
Yes	Lifetime sentence	Yes
Yes	Lifetime sentence	Yes
Yes	No juvenile incarceration	No (some exceptions)
N/A	10 years	Yes
N/A	No lifetime sentence	Yes
No	One year	Yes

States was nearly 800 per 100,000 (Federal Bureau of Investigation, 1995). In England and Wales, about 600 per 100,000 14- to 16-year-olds were convicted or cautioned by the police for violent crimes (homicide, assault, robbery, and rape) in 1994. In Germany, 650 per 100,000 14- to 17-year-olds and in The Netherlands 450 per 100,000 12- to 17-year-olds were suspects of violent crime in 1994 (Pfeiffer, 1998).

Comparing how different countries deal with juvenile offenders is equally challenging. Countries differ in the ages of young people considered legal juveniles, in how juvenile courts are organized, and in the types of institution used to sanction juvenile offenders. As Table 1-1 shows, the minimum age for being considered criminally responsible varies from 7 years (in Switzerland and the Australian state of Tasmania) to 16 (in Belgium and Russia). The age of full criminal responsibility (i.e., the age at which an offender is automatically handled as an adult) is 18 in most of the countries studied by Weitekamp et al. (1999), but is as low as 16 in some Australian states and is 20 in Japan. In the United States, both minimum and maximum ages of juvenile court jurisdiction vary by state, with most states having no minimum age (although in practice, children younger than 10 are seldom seen in juvenile courts). The maximum age of juvenile court jurisdiction is younger in many U.S. states than in the other countries studied, with 3 states having a maximum age of 15, 10 of 16, and the remaining states having a maximum age of 17.

At the same time that states and the federal government in the United States have been moving toward treating juvenile offenders more like adult criminals, many other countries retain a strong rehabilitative stance. The 1988 Youth Court Law of Austria, for example, describes juvenile offending as a normal step in development for which restorative justice, not punishment, is the appropriate response. The Belgium Youth Court Protection Act specifies that the only measures that can be imposed on a juvenile are for his or her care, protection, and education. In New Zealand, since 1989, Family Group Conferences have been used to replace or supplement youth courts for most of the serious criminal cases. In the early 1980s, England and Wales moved toward community-based sanctions for young offenders and away from institutional placements. This trend was reversed in the 1990s, however, when England and Wales reacted to the upswing in juvenile violence in a manner similar to the United States, focusing on the offense, rather than the offender. The U.K. Criminal Justice and Public Order Act of 1994 made it easier to place offenders younger than 15 years in juvenile correctional facilities and extended the maximum length of allowable sentences. The U.K. Crime and Disorder Act of 1998 moved the English juvenile justice system even further toward a punitive, offense-based model.

Neither Sweden nor Denmark uses a separate juvenile court, but youthful immaturity is considered a mitigating factor in deciding their criminal responsibility. In Denmark, maximum punishments well below those available for adults are specified in law for juveniles 15 and older; juveniles under the age of 15 may not be punished, but may be referred to a social welfare agency. In Sweden, imprisonment may only be imposed on juveniles under exceptional circumstances, and even then, the sentences imposed are shorter than for adults.

The United States has a very high overall rate of incarceration. At 645 per 100,000, the U.S. incarceration rate is second only to that of Russia at 685 per 100,000 (Walmsley, 1999). Although adequate juvenile incarceration figures do not exist in the United States, the incarceration rate for homicides committed by juveniles is illustrative of the difference in incarceration rates. In 1992, 12.5 people per 100,000 were incarcerated in the United States for homicides committed as juveniles. Comparable numbers in other countries are 2.3 per 100,000 in The Netherlands, 1.6 per 100,000 in Italy, and 1.3 per 100,000 in Germany (Pfeiffer, 1998). Some of the differences in juvenile homicide incarceration rates are likely to be due to differences in homicide commission rates. In none of the 15 countries surveyed by Weitekamp et al. (1999) can a juvenile who commits a crime be executed, whereas this practice is allowed in the United States.

CHARGE TO THE PANEL

The Panel on Juvenile Crime: Prevention, Treatment, and Control was asked to identify and analyze the full range of research studies and datasets that bear on the nature of juvenile crime, highlighting key issues and data sources that can provide evidence of prevalence and seriousness; race, gender, and class bias; and impacts of deterrence, punishment, and prevention strategies. The panel was further asked to analyze the factors that contribute to delinquent behavior, including a review of the knowledge on child and adolescent development and its implications for prevention and control; to assess the current practices of the juvenile justice system, including the implementation of constitutional safeguards; to examine adjudication, detention and waiver practices; to explore the role of community and institutional settings; to assess the quality of data sources on the clients of both public and private juvenile justice facilities; and to assess the impact of the deinstitutionalization mandates of the Juvenile Justice and Delinquency Prevention Act of 1974 on delinquency and community safety.

To meet this charge, the study panel and staff gathered information in a number of ways. Relevant research studies were identified through targeted searches of UnCover, Medline, Educational Resources Information Center (ERIC), and the National Criminal Justice Research Service (NCJRS). The panel met six times between June 1998 and October 1999 to discuss data availability and research findings, identify critical issues, analyze the data and issues, seek additional information on specific concerns, formulate conclusions and recommendations, and develop this report. Four of these meetings were preceded by workshops at which experts presented information on selected topics and engaged in discussions with panel members. Workshops were held on education and delinquency, juvenile justice system issues, developmental issues relevant to delinquency, and racial disparity in the juvenile justice system. (See Appendix E for workshop agendas.) In addition to the workshops, Howard Snyder, research director of the National Center for Juvenile Justice, spent part of one meeting discussing relevant datasets with the panel members. The panel commissioned three papers: "International Comparison of Juvenile Justice Systems" by Elmar Weitekamp, Hans-Juergen Kerner, and Gernot Trueg; "Police Encounters with Juvenile Suspects" by Robert Worden and Stephanie Myers; and "The Indeterminancy of Forecasts of Crime Rates and Juvenile Offenses" by Kenneth Land and Patricia McCall. Several members of the panel made site visits to juvenile detention and correctional facilities in Texas and New York. Study panel members and staff also consulted informally with various experts between meetings.

The charge to the panel was extremely broad, covering many topics that merit books unto themselves, and indeed some of the areas have been the subject of more than one recent book. The panel chose to provide a broad overview of juvenile crime and the juvenile justice system, touching on all the topics in its charge, but going into various levels of depth depending on the amount and quality of data available. In organizing its plan for the study, the panel focused on answering several questions:

1. What have been the major trends in juvenile crime over the past 20 to 30 years, and what can be predicted about future trends?

2. What is the role of developmental factors in delinquent behavior and how do families, peers, communities, and social influences contribute to or inhibit that behavior?

3. What responses are in place to deal with juvenile crime today, are they developmentally appropriate, and do they work?

This report reviews the data and research available to answer these questions, suggests areas that require additional research, and makes recommendations about policies for dealing with child and adolescent offenders.

DEFINITIONS USED IN THIS REPORT

The terms *juvenile* and *delinquency* (or *delinquent*) have specific legal meanings in state and federal law. In this report, however, the panel uses the term *juvenile*[3] in its general sense, referring to anyone under the age of 18, unless otherwise specified. The terms *young person, youngster, youth,* and *child and adolescent* are used synonymously with juvenile. For many of the analyses of crime trends in Chapter 2, *juvenile* refers to those between the ages of 10 and 17, because those under the age of 10 are seldom arrested. We use the term *adolescent* to refer specifically to young people between the ages of 13 and 17.

The term *delinquency*[4] in this report refers to acts by a juvenile that would be considered a crime if committed by an adult, as well as to actions that are illegal only because of the age of the offender. The report uses the term *criminal delinquency* to refer specifically to the former and *status delinquency* to refer specifically to the latter. Criminal delinquency offenses include, for example, homicide, robbery, assault, burglary, and theft. The term *juvenile crime* is used synonymously with criminal delinquency. Status delinquency offenses include truancy, running away from home, incorrigibility (i.e., habitually disobeying reasonable and lawful commands of a parent, guardian, or custodian; also referred to in various statutes as unruly, uncontrollable, or ungovernable behavior), and liquor law violations. In some states, status delinquents are referred to the child welfare or social service systems, while in others status delinquents are dealt with in the juvenile justice system.

PLAN OF THE REPORT

Following this introduction, Chapter 2 discusses the datasets commonly used to measure juvenile crime rates, examining the relative strengths and weaknesses of each. The chapter then discusses the trends in juvenile crime rates over the past several decades and how trends differ depending on the dataset employed. Differences in crime rates and

---

[3]In the context of crime, juveniles are defined as those under a specified age, which differs from state to state, who are not subject to criminal sanctions when they commit behavior that would be considered criminal for someone over that age. Depending on the state, the age at which a young person is considered a juvenile may end at 15, 16, or 17. This makes the legal use of the term *juvenile* difficult when discussing multiple jurisdictions.

[4]The use of the term *delinquency* differs from state to state. In some states it refers only to offenses that would be criminal if committed by an adult; in others it also includes status offenses.

types of offense by sex and race are noted. The chapter ends with a discussion of forecasting juvenile crime rates.

Chapter 3 examines factors related to the development of antisocial behavior and delinquency. Several other recent reports (Loeber et al., 1998; Rutter et al., 1998) have extensively reviewed the research on many of these factors, particularly as they relate to the development of serious, violent offending. In this report we have attempted to supplement these other reports rather than duplicate their literature reviews. In addition, this report does not confine its discussion to serious, violent offending.

Chapters 4 and 5 cover responses to the problem of youth crime. Chapter 4 focuses on preventive interventions aimed at individuals, peer groups, and families, interventions delivered in schools, and community-based interventions. Chapter 5 describes the juvenile justice system process in the United States and discusses treatment and intervention programs delivered through the juvenile justice system.

Chapter 6 examines the issue of racial disparity in the juvenile justice system, discussing explanations that have been put forth to explain that disparity and the research support for those explanations.

The panel's conclusions and recommendations for research and policy can be found at the end of each chapter.

2

Patterns and Trends in Juvenile Crime and Juvenile Justice

Since the late 1980s, there has been growing concern about crimes committed by young people. News accounts of serious crimes committed by children and adolescents and criminologists' warnings of a coming tide of vicious juveniles—sometimes referred to as superpredators (see, e.g., Bennett et al., 1996)—have encouraged a general belief that young people are increasingly violent and uncontrollable and that the response of the juvenile justice system has been inadequate. Reacting to evidence of increases in juvenile violence, state and federal legislators have proposed, and most states have passed, laws that make the juvenile system more punitive and that allow younger children and adolescents to be transferred to the adult system for a greater variety of offenses and in a greater variety of ways (discussed in Chapter 5). Data about juvenile crime, in particular violent crime, and statistics about the size and characteristics of the juvenile population have played an important part in the policy debates (Zimring, 1998).

Are young people today actually committing more crimes than they did two decades ago? Are those crimes more violent? Are the trends the same or different for various offenses? Do those trends differ from trends in adult crime rates? How much of juvenile crime is concentrated in the nation's inner cities and among disadvantaged minorities? Because this type of information influences attitudes and government policy, it is important to have accurate answers to these questions. This chapter discusses the sources of data available for studying delinquency as well as the weaknesses of those data sources, summarizes what is known about

25

the trends in delinquency over the past several decades, and considers what forecasts can be made about juvenile crime.

SOURCES OF DATA

Three ways in which crime is often measured are arrest statistics, victim reports of crimes, and self-reports of offenses. These sources may yield different crime rates and trends. Each source has advantages and drawbacks, and each alone gives an incomplete picture of crime. In this section, we discuss these sources of data and their strengths and weaknesses.

Arrest Data

A common way of measuring crime is to use the Uniform Crime Reports (UCR), which are compiled from data on crimes known to the police and on arrests that are reported annually to the Federal Bureau of Investigation (FBI) by police agencies around the country. Data have been collected by the FBI since 1930, allowing the study of crime and arrest trends over time. The UCR provide crime counts for the United States as a whole, as well as for regions, states, counties, cities, and towns. In addition, the UCR provide data on, among other things, crimes known to the police, crimes cleared by arrest, and characteristics of persons arrested. However, UCR reporting is voluntary, and the total number of reporting police agencies varies from year to year. The accuracy and completeness of the data are affected by the voluntary nature of UCR reporting (Maltz, 1999). In some years, data from one or more entire states have been unavailable. For example, from 1988 to 1991, no usable data were obtained from either Florida or Kentucky (Federal Bureau of Investigation, 1998). Coverage within states also varies from year to year. The FBI imputes information when none has been reported. Because many of the tables in the published UCR, including the breakdown by age, are based on whichever agencies report in a given year and not on a nationally representative sample, caution must be used in making generalizations to all young people in the United States based on UCR data. This is particularly true with regard to analyses regarding race, because the racial makeup of the areas covered by reporting agencies may not reflect the racial makeup of the country.

Data in the UCR are reported by offense for 28 different offenses (for definitions of offenses used in the UCR, see Appendix A). The most information is reported on what are termed index (or part I) crimes— eight crimes that make up the crime index, which is used "to gauge fluctuations in the overall volume and rate of crime reported to law enforcement" (Federal Bureau of Investigation, 1998:5). The crime index includes the violent offenses of murder and nonnegligent homicide, forcible rape, robbery, aggravated assault, and the property offenses of burglary, larceny theft, motor vehicle theft, and arson.

There are drawbacks to using arrest data as a measure of crime. Arrest statistics do not reflect the number of different people arrested each year, because an unknown number of people may be arrested more than once in a year. For some crimes, no arrests are made. For others, there may be multiple arrests. Furthermore, not everyone who is arrested has committed the crime for which he or she was arrested. Arrests also depend on a number of factors other than overall crime levels, including policies of particular police agencies, the cooperation of victims, the skill of the perpetrator, and the age, sex, race, and social class of the suspect (Cook and Laub, 1998; McCord, 1997c).

Nor should arrest statistics be confused with the number of crimes committed, because in some cases, the arrest of one person may account for a series of crimes, and in others several people may be arrested for one crime. This is particularly true for young people, who are more likely than adults to commit crimes in a group (McCord, 1990; Reiss, 1986; Reiss and Farrington, 1991; Zimring, 1981). Snyder (1998) contends that this tendency to offend in groups makes arrest statistics an inappropriate measure of the relative proportion of crime attributed to young people. Checking on Snyder's position, McCord and Conway (2000) analyzed a random sample of juvenile offenders in Philadelphia. They found that the number of crimes accounted for by juveniles would be reduced by approximately 40 percent with an adjustment for co-offending. Rather, arrest statistics measure the flow of young people into the juvenile justice system or the criminal justice system. For this reason, the number of crimes known to police is often a preferred measure of crime (Cook and Laub, 1998). The UCR provide information on all crimes known to reporting police agencies, whether or not an arrest has been made. There is no information on age of the perpetrator, however, in the data on crimes known to police; thus even if they are a more accurate crime measure, the number of crimes known to police cannot be used to analyze juvenile crime.

Arrest clearance statistics, which measure the proportion of reported crime cleared by arrest (or other exceptional means, such as death of the offender), may more accurately portray the proportion of crime committed by young people, according to Snyder (1998). But even clearance statistics may overestimate juvenile crime. For example, if young people are more easily apprehended than adults, the proportion of their crimes cleared by arrest would be higher than the proportion of all crimes for which they were responsible (Snyder, 1998). The proportion of young people arrested consistently exceeds the proportion of crimes cleared by the arrest of young people for all crimes and across time, indicating that the use of arrest statistics may make it appear that juveniles account for more crime than they actually do. Likewise, Reiss and Farrington (1991) showed that offending appears less common in the teenage years if the rate is based on the number of offenses (which takes into account co-offending) committed by juveniles rather than on the number of juvenile offenders.

Another problem with the UCR as a measure of crime is that, regardless of the number of offenses that occur in an incident leading to arrest, only one offense—the most serious—is counted (for a detailed discussion of gaps in the UCR see Maltz, 1999). This procedure results in less serious crimes being undercounted by arrest statistics and a lack of information on the circumstances surrounding the crime. For example, if a homicide occurs during a robbery, only the homicide is counted. As Maltz (1999) points out, this masks the nature of the circumstances surrounding the homicide.

The UCR statistical system is summary-based. That is, each reporting agency reports *totals* of crimes known to police, of arrests, and of other information. Although summary-based statistics are important, there is a lot of information they cannot provide. For example, it is impossible to determine from such data the number of crimes committed by multiple rather than single offenders or the relationship of the victim to the offender from such data (Maxfield, 1999).

In the mid-1980s, in order to overcome some of these deficiencies in the UCR, the FBI began to implement a new reporting system, the National Incident-Based Reporting System (NIBRS). This system reports information by incident instead of by totals for an agency. NIBRS includes up to 10 different offense types per incident and provides details about all of the offenders and victims, as well as the situational context of the incident. Although NIBRS may have many advantages for researchers and federal agencies, its adoption by states and law enforcement agencies has been slow. Roberts (1997) reported that cost of implementing the new system was the most common concern cited as an obstacle to the adoption of NIBRS. Other obstacles noted by Roberts include uncertain benefits of NIBRS to the reporting agencies; concern that NIBRS reporting would be too time-consuming for officers; and concern that reporting all offenses in an incident may give the appearance of an increase in crime. Whatever the reason, only 18 states were NIBRS-certified by the end of 1999 (Federal Bureau of Investigation, 1999), and fewer than that have fully implemented NIBRS reporting. As Maxfield (1999) noted, it took over 30 years to develop the UCR program, and it may take decades to complete the implementation of NIBRS.

NIBRS may one day provide much useful information about juvenile crime that is currently not available from the UCR, but it is not problem free. NIBRS continues to rely on police to make decisions about how to classify offenses and what information to report. "Criminologists have long been cautious about accepting police reports as valid and reliable measures of even crimes known to the police. All police reports represent interpretations of events that are usually not witnessed by officials. Because of this, police records are best viewed as social constructions based on reports by witnesses and victims, together with physical evidence" (Maxfield, 1999:142).

Experience with UCR Supplemental Homicide Reports may provide some hints about the types of errors and omissions that may arise with NIBRS data. In addition to reporting totals of homicides, reporting agencies currently must fill out incident-based Supplemental Homicide Reports (SHR) detailing information about each homicide. Researchers have found inconsistencies between SHR data and police agency records (Loftin, 1986) and inappropriate classifications of murders as motivated by robbery (Cook, 1987). Supplemental Homicide Reports may be completed and archived before all the evidence has been gathered, calling into question their validity (National Research Council, 1993b). There is also variation among agencies and over time in how homicide circumstances are recorded (Maxfield, 1989). These types of problems may be even greater in NIBRS, which requires detailed information on crimes for which fewer police resources are dedicated than for homicides. Nevertheless, NIBRS promises to provide much information that cannot be obtained from the UCR.

Victim Reports

Information about crimes committed is also available from surveys of crime victims. The National Crime Victimization Survey (NCVS), begun in 1973, collects data annually on crime victimization from a nationally representative sample of approximately 43,000 households. Persons over the age of 12 in these households are asked about their experience with crime. The NCVS includes crimes whether or not they were reported to the police. Detailed information is collected on the frequency and nature of the crimes of rape, sexual assault, personal robbery, aggravated and simple assault, household burglary, theft, and motor vehicle theft (Bureau of Justice Statistics, 2000). Victims' perception of the age of the offender for violent crimes is included in the data collected. Because offenders' age may be difficult for a victim to estimate accurately, caution must be exercised in using NCVS to estimate juvenile crime. The NCVS does not ask about offenders in property crimes because victims of property offenses generally have no contact with the offenders.

The NCVS underestimates crimes because it omits crimes to businesses (e.g., shoplifting, employee theft). It also omits crimes against victims under the age of 12. Nor is information about homicides gathered in the NCVS. Because the sampling unit is a household, transient and homeless people—populations at substantially great risk of victimization—are not represented (National Research Council, 1993b).

Other aspects of the NCVS methods may inflate crime rates. Households are in the sample for three years and are interviewed every six months. Studies that rely on victim reports show that people tend to recall events of the distant past as though they happened more recently. Without a "bounding interview," respondents report more crime than has actually occurred within the period of time to which it is attributed. When households first enter the NCVS, a bounding interview is therefore conducted. Information gathered at this interview is not used except as a corrective for the subsequent interviews. However, households are kept in the survey even if the occupants change. No new bounding interview is done when the household contains new residents. Hence, in these households, there is a greater likelihood that reported victimizations would have occurred outside the six-month survey interval, thereby inflating official crime rates.

There has also been a shift in data collection methods over the years, away from face-to-face interviews to telephone and proxy interviews. The latter interview methods result in fewer victimizations being reported than in face-to-face and victim respondent interviews (Steffensmeier and Harer, 1999). Nevertheless, the NCVS provides another source of information to compare with UCR arrest data when looking at trends in juvenile violent crime.

Self-Report Data

Data on the commission of delinquent acts and crimes are also available from surveys of young people. Self-report data include crimes not known to the police, but they have their own set of drawbacks. Some self-report surveys that are frequently used for examining juvenile crime (e.g., Monitoring the Future and the Youth Risk Behavior Surveillance system) are conducted in schools. Missing from these data are students who are absent from school when the survey is taken, those who have dropped out of school, and homeless juveniles who are not attending school. In particular, school dropouts have higher rates of delinquency than those who remain in school. There may be an implicit bias inherent in which schools are selected to be included in the study. In addition, the behaviors covered in large surveys are often not directly comparable to criminal behavior that would result in arrest. National cross-sectional or longitudinal studies that are population-based rather than school-based may provide more valid samples for estimating juvenile crime.

Another problem with self-report data is accuracy of the information provided. Surveys generally indicate higher levels of delinquency than indicated by offenses known to police or arrests. Because police do not know about all offenses, it is difficult to verify the accuracy of the self-report offending data. However, in general, a high proportion of offenses known to the police are reported by respondents, although there is variation by offense (Huizinga and Elliott, 1986).

Some researchers have found the validity of self-report data to vary by race and by gender. For example, some researchers found that black or nonwhite respondents are less likely to report offenses already known to officials than are whites (Hindelang et al., 1981; Hirschi, 1969; Lab and Allen, 1984; Tracy, 1987). It is not known whether the self-reports or the official records are more accurate. More recently, Farrington et al. (1996) found no significant difference in the validity of self-report measures by race. In other research (Maxfield et al., 2000), race differences in the congruence between self-reports and official reports of arrests were sharply reduced in three situations: among those with recorded convictions, among those with both juvenile and adult arrests, and among those with five or more arrests. Maxfield and colleagues (2000) suggested that subjects with more recorded official contacts (e.g., multiple arrests, arrest plus conviction) more often self-reported arrests, regardless of race. Less is known about the effect of gender on self-reports of offending. Some studies have found that self-reports by males and females are equally valid, whereas others have found that females are less likely to report being arrested, even when they were convicted (Maxfield et al., 2000). It may be that girls and women experience more social stigma concerning their criminal behavior than do boys and men and are therefore less willing to report it to interviewers. Males, in contrast, have been found less willing than females to report a history of childhood sexual abuse (Widom and Morris, 1997). Maxfield et al. (2000) suggest that studies relying on self-reports may need to take social desirability into account when males and females have different response patterns.

Each type of data for analyzing crime trends has advantages and disadvantages. It is important to keep the weaknesses of the various types of data in mind whenever crime rates are discussed. In the following sections, trends in juvenile crime, based on the three different datasets, are discussed and compared.

CRIME TRENDS

Overall arrest rates in the United States have increased over the past three decades for all age groups (Figure 2-1). In 1998, arrest rates were 28 percent higher than in 1970. The increase in arrest rates does not necessarily mean that crime had grown by 28 percent. The arrest rate can be influenced by changes in policy, in police practices, and in the number of offenders arrested per crime. In fact, victim reports of overall crime indicate fairly consistent decreases since the early 1970s. The picture of crime becomes more complicated when broken down by age and offense.

Official crime rates are based on data reported by police agencies to the FBI about the index crimes of homicide, rape, robbery, and aggravated assault—which make up the violent crime index—and burglary, larceny and theft, auto theft, and arson—which make up the property crime index. In 1998, there were a total estimated 12,475,634 index crimes (both violent and property) known to police, 2,481,500 arrests for index crimes, and 14,528,300 arrests for all crimes (including status offenses) in the United States (Federal Bureau of Investigation, 1999). The vast major-

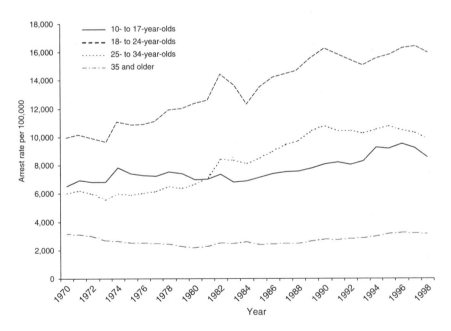

FIGURE 2-1 Arrest rates for all crimes. Source: Arrest data from Federal Bureau of Investigation (1971-1999). Population data from Bureau of the Census (1982) and online at http://www.census.gov/population/estimates.

ity of these arrests—82 percent—were arrests of adults. Arrests of those ages 10 to 17 accounted for 17.7 percent, or about 2.6 million arrests. In 1998, when those ages 10 to 17 were 11 percent of the population, 16.4 percent of all arrests for violent index crimes and 32 percent of all arrests for property index crimes were arrests of those ages 10 to 17.

Not only do young people account for a small percentage of all arrests, but also the vast majority of arrests of those ages 10 to17 are for nonindex crimes (73 percent of arrests in 1998), which are less serious than index crimes (see Table 2-1). In 1998, only 4 percent of juvenile arrests were for index violent crimes and less than one-tenth of one percent of their arrests were for homicide. Even in 1993, at the height of the violent crime wave that began in the mid to late 1980s, only about 6 percent of all juvenile arrests were for violent crimes and about two-tenths of one percent were for homicide. Young people are much more likely to be arrested for property crimes than for violent crimes. Over the past 30 years, between one-quarter and one-third of all juvenile arrests were for the index property crimes of burglary, larceny/theft, motor vehicle theft, and arson. In comparison, in 1998, about 5 percent of arrests of those over age 18 were

TABLE 2-1 Percentage of Arrests of Those Ages 10-17, by Offense

	1970	1980	1990	1993	1997	1998
Murder	0.08	0.09	0.15	0.17	0.09	0.08
Rape	0.20	0.22	0.27	0.26	0.19	0.20
Robbery	1.81	2.11	1.91	2.18	1.44	1.27
Aggravated Assault	1.27	1.90	2.93	3.37	2.68	2.76
Index violent crime	3.36	4.32	5.26	5.98	4.40	4.31
Burglary	8.82	10.61	6.35	5.71	4.55	4.37
Larceny	18.34	20.49	20.96	19.32	17.52	16.10
Motor Vehicle Theft	4.49	2.97	4.25	3.80	2.38	2.09
Arson	0.28	0.35	0.32	0.36	0.31	0.31
Index property crime	31.92	34.42	31.89	29.18	24.76	22.87
Other assaults	3.13	4.02	6.76	7.73	8.43	9.00
Vandalism	4.31	5.40	5.64	5.72	4.63	4.72
Weapons	1.05	1.21	1.85	2.62	1.85	1.74
Drug abuse violations	4.90	5.10	3.77	4.71	7.90	7.99
Disorderly Conduct	7.48	5.96	5.49	6.04	7.59	7.17
Curfew and loitering	6.56	3.36	3.75	4.30	6.59	7.41
Runaways	10.99	7.11	7.95	7.61	6.95	6.32
Other Offenses	26.29	29.11	27.64	26.12	26.90	28.46
Nonindex crime	64.72	61.26	62.85	64.84	70.84	72.81
Total	100.00	100.00	100.00	100.00	100.00	100.00

Source: Data from Federal Bureau of Investigation, 1971 to 1999.

for index violent crimes, 0.13 percent for homicides, 10 percent for index property crimes, and 85 percent for nonindex crimes. (See Appendix A for UCR definitions of various offenses.)

The likelihood of arrest differs by race, gender, and area of the country. For young people under 18, blacks and males have consistently higher arrest rates than whites and females, respectively, for both violent crimes and property crimes. In 1998, males accounted for 83 percent of arrests of those under 18 for violent crimes and 72 percent of arrests for property crimes.[1] As for race, black juveniles are disproportionately arrested in comparison to their proportion of the population. In 1998, only 15 percent of those under age 18 in the United States were black (whites made up 79 percent and other races were 6 percent of the juvenile population), yet blacks made up 42.3 percent of juvenile arrests for violent crime, whites 55.3 percent, and others 2.4 percent.[2] The UCR do not provide estimates for Hispanic juveniles.[3] For property crime arrests of juveniles, blacks accounted for 26.6 percent, whites 70.1 percent, and others 3.3 percent. Distributions for adults are similar, with blacks accounting for a disproportionate 40 percent of violent crime arrests and 35 percent of property crime arrests, compared with whites at 58 percent for violent crimes and 63 percent for property crimes, and others at 2 percent for both violent crimes and property crimes. (A more thorough discussion of racial disproportionality and possible reasons for it appears in Chapter 6.)

Violent Crime

The concern in recent years over juvenile crime has centered on violent crime. Indeed, it appears that there was a significant upswing in violence among juveniles and adults. As can be seen in Figure 2-2, beginning in the mid- to late 1980s, there was a large increase in arrests for violent crimes not only among juveniles (10- to 17-year-olds), but also among adults ages 18 to 24 and 25 to 34. Arrests for violent crimes of those 35 and older also increased, but more gradually and not nearly as much as for the younger groups. Since the mid-1990s, arrest rates for violent crimes have dropped dramatically for all age groups and are approaching the rates of the early 1980s.

---

[1]The UCR do not provide data by race for individual ages, but rather for those under 18 and for those 18 and older.

[2]The UCR report crimes for two groups besides blacks and whites: American Indian or Alaskan Native and Asian or Pacific Islander.

[3]Note that for federal data collection purposes, Hispanic is not considered to be a race, but rather an ethnicity. Hispanics are included in both black and white counts.

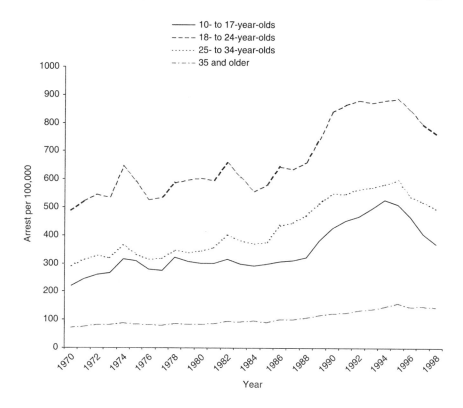

FIGURE 2-2 Arrest rates for violent index crimes. Source: Arrest data from Federal Bureau of Investigation (1971-1999). Population data from Bureau of the Census (1982) and online at http://www.census.gov/population/estimates.

Victim reports of violent crimes in which the perpetrator was thought to be under the age of 18 show somewhat different trends, although both indicate increases beginning in the late 1980s through the early 1990s and declines at the end of the century. The juvenile violent crime rate based on victim reports remained fairly flat from 1973 to 1989, then increased between 1989 and 1993 (see Figure 2-3). By 1995, when arrest rates according to the FBI were close to their peak, the victimization rate had returned to the level of the 1989 rate. Victim reports of serious violent crimes by adults, however, show a fairly steady decline, dropping and staying below 1973 rates since 1983, with an increase almost back to 1973 levels in 1993, then dropping again. Victim reports indicate a much higher rate of violent offending by young people and by adults than do arrest rates.

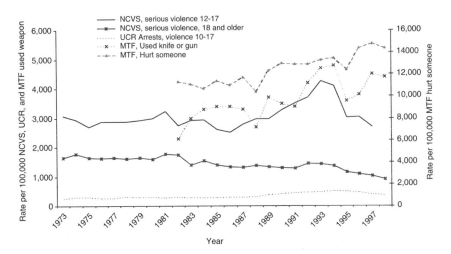

FIGURE 2-3 Rate of juvenile offending: Comparison of arrests, victim reports, and self-reports. Source: Arrest data from Federal Bureau of Investigation (1974-1999); self-report data from Maguire and Pastore (1994-1998); National Crime Victimization Survey data from Snyder and Sickmund (1999).

Self-reports of violent behavior by juveniles produce even higher rates of offending, but the questions used in such surveys as Monitoring the Future[4] may measure less serious behavior than that which results in arrest or victim reports. For example, the data shown in Figure 2-3 for Monitoring the Future are the results of high school seniors who answered at least once to the following two questions: "During the last 12 months, how often have you hurt someone badly enough to need bandages or a doctor?" "During the last 12 months, how often have you used a knife or a gun or some other thing (like a club) to get something from a person?" Other self-report surveys also yield rates of violent behavior much higher than arrest rates. For example, the 1997 National Longitudinal Survey of Youth, which interviewed a representative sample of 9,000 youngsters between the ages of 12 and 16 in 1996, found a prior-year assault rate of 12,000 per 100,000 (Snyder and Sickmund, 1999). The NLSY97 rate is lower than the 14,400 per 100,000 from Monitoring the Future in 1996. The samples in the two surveys are different, with Moni-

---

[4]Monitoring the Future is an annual school-based survey of high school seniors that has been conducted since 1976.

toring the Future including only high school seniors[5] while NLSY97 included 12- to 16-year-olds. The question in the NLSY97—"Have you ever attacked someone with the idea of seriously hurting them or have had a situation end up in a serious fight or assault of some kind?"—may elicit more serious incidents of assault than do those in Monitoring the Future. The differences in both the samples and questions may account for the difference in reported rates.

Violence encompasses a wide range of acts, from the threat of harm to assault and homicide. It is instructive to look separately at the various offenses that make up the FBI violence index. Figure 2-4 shows the arrest rates by age group for the violent crimes of homicide, rape, robbery, and aggravated assault (the four crimes that make up the FBI violent crime index) since 1970. (Note that the scales on the y-axes differ for each offense.) There are distinctly different patterns for each of the violent index crimes. Arrest rates for juveniles are lower than the rates for 18- to 24-year-olds for all four violent crimes and lower than the rates for 25- to 34-year-olds for homicide, rape, and aggravated assault.

Figure 2-5 shows the change in arrest rates for the violent index crimes since 1970 by age group. The increase in arrests of 10- to 17-year-olds for violent crimes is most pronounced in arrests for aggravated assault and homicide. Arrests for aggravated assault peaked in 1995 at 3.5 times the 1970 rate, and homicide peaked in 1994 at 2.5 times the 1970 rate, before both started declining. Rape and robbery increased less, peaking at 1.7 times the 1970 rate in 1991 and 1994, respectively. The increase in juvenile arrest rates for homicide and aggravated assault was not only larger than for rape and robbery, but also much larger among juveniles than among the older age groups. Thus, although juvenile arrest rates for each of the violent crimes were lower than rates for 18- to 24-year-olds throughout the period, the increase in arrest rates for 10- to 17-year-olds was greater than the increase for 18- to 24-year-olds for both homicide and aggravated assault.

Homicide arrest rates for 10- to 17-year-olds and 18- to 24-year-olds rose sharply beginning in the mid-1980s, peaked in 1993, and then began to decline steeply (see Figure 2-4). The homicide arrest rates for 25- to 34-year-olds paralleled rates for the younger groups until the mid-1980s, after which the older group's rates gradually declined.

Data sources other than arrest statistics are available for studying homicide, and those sources may be somewhat more accurate than arrest data. Supplemental Homicide Reports are compiled by the FBI and

---

[5]Recently, 8th and 10th grade samples were added to Monitoring the Future. We have used only the 12th grade sample to have the longer time trend.

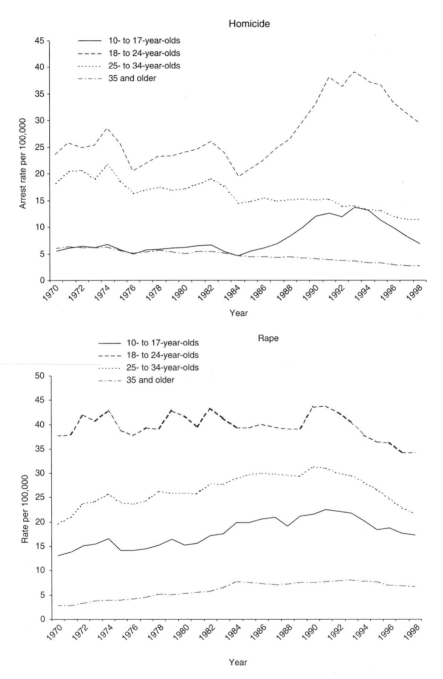

FIGURE 2-4 Arrest rates for violent index crimes by age group. Source: Arrest data from Federal Bureau of Investigation (1971-1999).

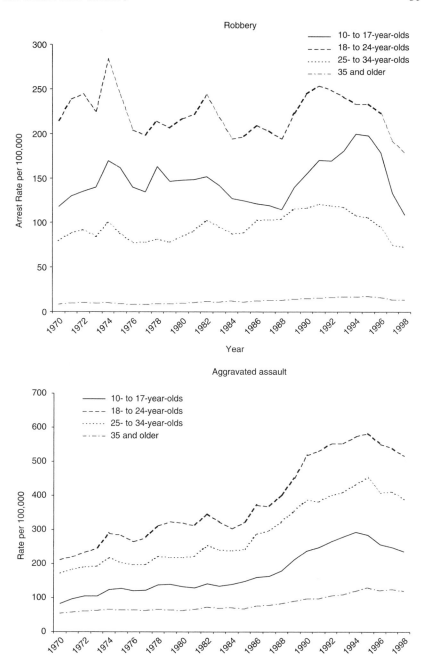

FIGURE 2-4 Continued

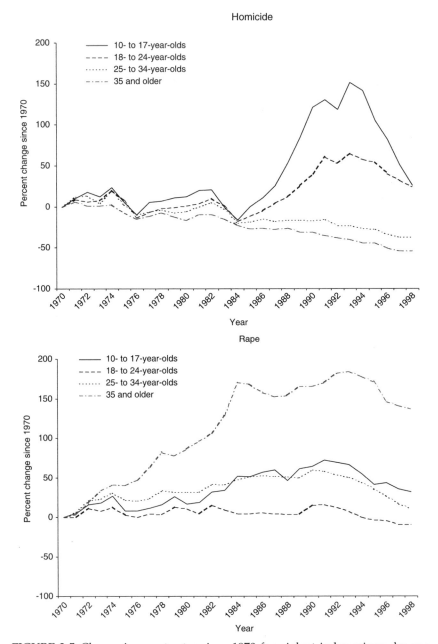

FIGURE 2-5 Change in arrest rates since 1970 for violent index crimes, by age group. Source: Arrest data from Federal Bureau of Investigation (1971-1999); population data from U.S. Census Bureau (1982) and online at http://www.census.gov/population/estimates.

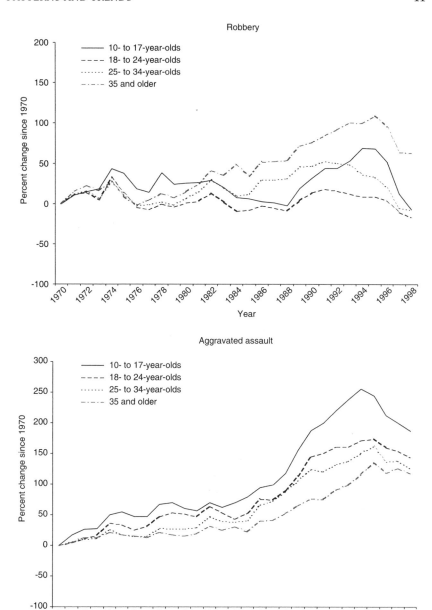

FIGURE 2-5 Continued

include information about the circumstances of the crime, the weapon used, and the information that is known about both the victim and the killer or killers, whether or not an arrest has been made. The FBI receives these data on about 80 to 90 percent of all known homicides. The National Center for Health Statistics (NCHS) also collects information on all deaths, including homicides. Information from medical examiners' reports is compiled each year for all known homicides. Although the NCHS data do not provide information on the perpetrators, the data serve as a useful check on the number of homicides.

Using Supplemental Homicide Reports data, corrected for under-reporting by information from NCHS, Cook and Laub (1998) analyzed homicide commission and victimization rates for 13- to 17-year-olds and 18- to 24-year-olds. They found that victimization and commission rates for both age groups followed similar trends, increasing rapidly in the late 1980s, and beginning to decrease in the early 1990s. The pattern of homicide commission for these younger age groups differed from those over 25, for whom homicide commission rates were declining as the younger groups experienced a sharp increase. Rates for young adults (18- to 24-year-olds) were higher than rates for adolescents (13- to 17-year-olds) or for older groups. Within the adolescent group, homicide commission varied by age. The number and rate of homicide offenders known to the police are consistently higher for older teenagers than for younger ones (Figure 2-6). The peak in homicides in the early 1990s was also greatest for older adolescents.

The increase in homicide victimization and commission was particularly pronounced among young black males. Cook and Laub (1998) note that the increase in the black juvenile homicide rate began about three years earlier than that of white juveniles, and it was greater both proportionally and in absolute count. Homicides by juveniles were also concentrated geographically, with one-quarter of known juvenile offenders in 1995 coming from just five counties—those containing Los Angeles, Chicago, Houston, Detroit, and New York City. The vast majority of counties (84 percent in 1995) reported no known juvenile homicide offenders (Sickmund et al., 1997).

The increase in homicide rates among juveniles from the late 1980s through the early 1990s was entirely due to an increase in homicides committed with firearms by adolescents (see Figure 2-7). Similarly, the declining homicide rate since the mid-1990s seems to involve primarily handgun-related homicides (Blumstein and Rosenfeld, 1998). Some researchers have argued that if the increase in homicides (and other violence) by young people was due to an increased viciousness or amorality among them, then there should have been an increase in homicide rates for all weapons, not just guns, and an increase in all crimes, not just

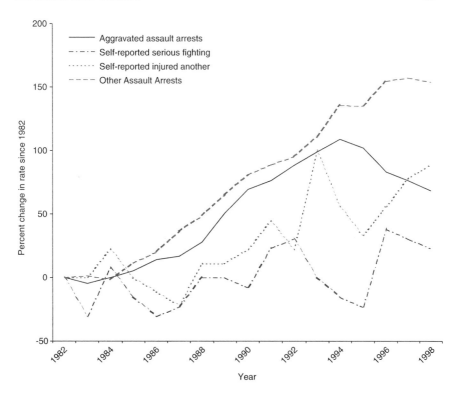

FIGURE 2-6 Rate of known homicide offenders by age. Source: Snyder and Sickmund (1999); population estimates accessed online at http://www.census.gov/population/estimates.

violent crimes (e.g., Blumstein, 1995; Blumstein and Cork, 1996; Cook and Laub, 1998). The fact that the increase in homicides was confined to those committed with guns and that property crimes did not increase in the same way that violent crimes did argues against the explanation of increasingly vicious young people. Blumstein (1995) argues that the homicide increase was a result of the introduction of crack cocaine markets, particularly in inner cities, in the mid-1980s. These drug markets used children and adolescents as sellers. Because of the nature of the drug trade, these sellers were well armed. Other young people in their neighborhoods began carrying guns out of a perceived need for protection. Since guns are more deadly than other weapons, conflicts among young people became more deadly.

Fagan and Wilkinson (1998) argue that Blumstein's explanation relies on indirect measures and provides no direct evidence of a causal link

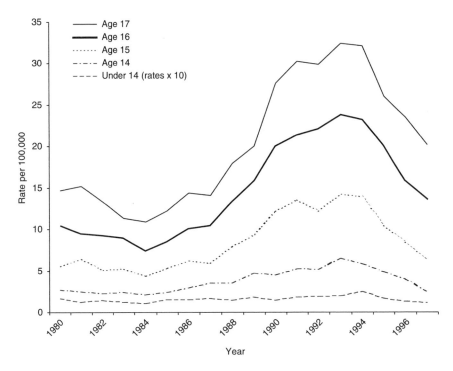

FIGURE 2-7 Juvenile homicide rate by weapon. Source: Snyder and Sickmund (1999); population estimates accessed online at http://www.census.gov/population/estimates.

between adolescents' involvement in drug markets and adolescent homicide commission. The extent to which homicides committed by adolescents are related to drug selling remains unknown. Qualitative studies suggest that adolescent violence in recent years involves material goods or personal slights and may be unrelated or only tangentially related to drugs (Anderson, 1997; Canada, 1995, Wilkinson and Fagan, 1996). Levitt (1998) analyzed relative incarceration rates and violent crime rates for juveniles and adults. The results of his analysis suggest that 60 percent of the larger increase in violence among juveniles compared with adults was accounted for by the relative lenience of juvenile sanctions compared with adult sanctions, which had gotten much harsher during the 1980s.

Whether as a result of drug markets or not, a number of sources point to increased possession of guns by juveniles beginning in the mid- to late 1980s. Arrests for weapons offenses among adolescents doubled between 1985 and 1993 (Greenfeld and Zawitz, 1995). The percentage of adolescent suicides committed by guns also began increasing in the late 1980s (Blumstein and Cork, 1996). Ethnographic reports also indicate that gun possession by young people has increased, but there is little information about how those guns were obtained (Fagan and Wilkinson, 1998).

The decrease in homicides by young people has also been entirely a decrease in homicides committed with handguns. Blumstein and Rosenfeld (1998) suggest several possible explanations for the decrease. First, the crack market began to mature, reducing disputes over territorial control, and the crack epidemic, which spurred the arming of many inner-city juveniles, began to abate in the early 1990s. These changes led to less need for juveniles to carry guns. Second, the economic expansion of the mid- and late 1990s may have played a part in moving young people into legitimate jobs. At the same time, police crackdowns on drug markets may have limited the opportunities for revenue from illegal activities, increasing the likelihood of taking the more available legal jobs. Finally, the high rate of incarceration of drug offenders may have had an impact on homicide rates, although Blumstein and Rosenfeld (1998) point out that it is unlikely to have played a major role for young offenders.

The argument that juveniles' access to guns influenced the homicide rate is buttressed by the similar role that gun availability played in juvenile suicide rates (Kachur et al., 1995). The suicide rate increased from 1980 to 1992 by 121 percent for children ages 10 to 14 and by 27 percent for adolescents ages 15 to 19. As Table 2-2 shows, the increase in suicides among black adolescents ages 15 to 19 almost entirely involved suicides committed with firearms. Males, both black and white, had a higher rate of firearm suicides than females. At approximately the same time that homicide rates began dropping, so did firearm-related suicides. In fact, the decrease in firearm-related suicides accounted for all the suicide decrease in this age group between 1994 and 1996. Just as the proliferation of firearms appears to have played a part in making violence by young people more deadly, so, too, the use of firearms in suicide attempts is much more likely to result in death than the use of other means. In a study of suicides in one state, Hopkins et al. (1995) found that 3.2 percent of all suicide attempts resulted in death, but 78.2 percent of attempts involving firearms resulted in death. Males appear to be more likely to use firearms in suicide attempts than females. This may account for their high rate of completed suicides compared with females, in spite of females' much higher rate of suicide attempts.

Interestingly, the rates of homicides by juveniles in Canada, although much lower than the rate in the United States, followed a similar pattern of rising in the mid- to late 1980s and declining in the early 1990s. In Canada, handgun use did not play a part in the increase or decrease in homicide rates (Hagan and Foster, 2000). Thus a satisfactory explanation

TABLE 2-2 Suicide Rates (per 100,000) for Adolescents, Ages 15-19

	1980	1985	1990	1994	1995	1996	1997
Total	8.51	9.87	11.07	11.06	10.46	9.74	9.45
Firearm	5.37	5.96	7.45	7.82	7.01	6.15	5.95
Nonfirearm	3.15	3.91	3.64	3.22	3.43	3.59	3.50
Males	13.83	15.78	18.05	18.25	17.44	15.55	15.16
Firearm	8.94	9.94	12.55	13.32	12.09	10.31	9.92
Nonfirearm	4.89	5.84	5.54	4.88	5.30	5.24	5.24
Females	3.03	3.71	3.71	3.48	3.11	3.55	3.38
Firearm	1.69	1.81	2.08	2.02	1.66	1.71	1.73
Nonfirearm	1.34	1.90	1.64	1.47	1.45	1.84	1.64
Whites	9.29	10.7	11.85	11.31	11.05	10.26	9.96
Firearm	5.94	6.51	7.99	7.87	7.30	6.38	6.24
Nonfirearm	3.36	4.19	3.89	3.42	3.72	3.88	3.72
Blacks	3.59	4.90	6.74	9.62	8.12	6.72	7.12
Firearm	1.99	3.01	5.05	8.01	6.21	5.17	5.00
Nonfirearm	1.60	1.89	1.70	1.61	1.91	1.55	2.13

Source: Data from Centers for Disease Control and Prevention, available online at http://www.cdc.gov/ncipc/osp/usmort.htm (accessed 6/24/99 and 3/14/00).

cannot depend entirely on handguns or local reactions to crack markets. Current information is insufficient to explain either the causes of the growth in homicide and other violent acts or their decline in the past few years.

Aggravated Assault

Self-report data by young people for some offenses show less change since the early 1980s than arrest data. Figure 2-8 shows the change in UCR-reported arrest for aggravated and other assaults compared with two self-reported items from the Monitoring the Future survey. Young people's self-reports of engaging in serious fighting are relatively flat from 1982 to 1998; self-reports of injuring someone badly enough to need bandages or a doctor rose somewhat beginning in 1989 and in 1998 were 27 percent higher than in 1982. Aggravated assault arrests, in contrast, began rising above 1982 levels in 1986 and reached a peak in 1994 that was 2.1 times the 1982 rate. Arrests for other assaults have been steadily increasing since 1985.

It should be noted that official reports of assault are influenced by police policies and discretion. Aggravated assaults represent a heterogeneous set of acts, from threatening with a weapon with no resulting injury

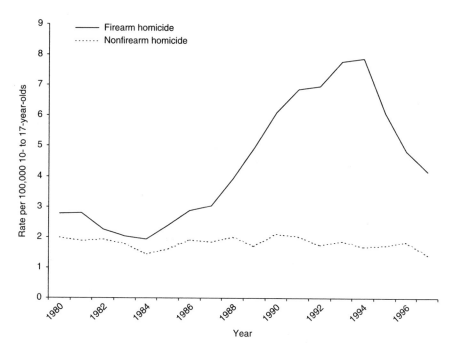

FIGURE 2-8 Change since 1982 in assault arrests versus self-report behavior. Source: Arrest data from Federal Bureau of Investigation (1983-1999); self-report data from Maguire and Pastore (1994-1998).

to the victim to attempted murder. From the official arrest statistics it is impossible to ascertain what percentage of aggravated assaults falls at the less serious end of the offense category, in contrast to the percentage that is very serious. How assaults are counted and classified is essentially a matter of police discretion. There is considerable circumstantial evidence from a number of sources that indicates that a changing police threshold for charging aggravated assault was responsible for the increase in aggravated assault arrests during the 1980s (Zimring, 1998). The patterns of arrests for aggravated assault of 10- to 17-year-olds and 25- to 34-year-olds from 1980 to 1995 are nearly identical, but the two groups' homicide arrest patterns were very different, with the older group's homicide arrest rates declining at the same time the younger groups was growing rapidly.

If the rate of aggravated assaults was really increasing, Zimring argues, the older groups' homicide rates should have also increased. Arrests for simple assaults increased for both age groups over this same time, consistent with increased police willingness to arrest for assault.

Victim reports of assault and self-reports of serious fighting were both much more stable than the arrest rate over this time period. On the basis of this evidence, Zimring (1998) concluded that "the major reason for increasing arrest rates in the younger age bracket for assault was not a change in the behavior of young offenders but a change in the classification of attacks that are close to the line that separates simple from aggravated assaults." It is quite possible that the increase in arrests for aggravated assault is as much a reflection of increased willingness of the police to arrest juveniles in assault cases and for charges of aggravated assault (rather than simple assault) to be brought against them as it is of a change in juvenile behavior. An increased willingness to arrest juveniles may also account for the increase in arrests for other assaults.

Property Crime Trends

Property crimes make up the majority of juvenile offending. In contrast to the trends for violent crimes, index property crime arrest rates have remained fairly constant for juveniles. Victims report a 60 percent decrease in all property crimes between 1973 and 1998. Because there is no victim report information on perpetrators of property crimes, it is impossible to tell whether the decline was attributable to a decrease in offenses by juveniles, by adults, or by both. Self-report trends on property crimes by juveniles vary depending on type of behavior. Figure 2-9 compares several self-reported property offenses to arrest rates for juveniles. Self-reports of taking something worth less than $50 has remained relatively stable since 1982, similar to arrest rates. In contrast to the stability in arrest rates, self-reports of other property crimes by juveniles have increased. Since 1992 the rate of damaging school property has been 10 to 20 percent higher than the 1982 rate. Taking a car without permission has fluctuated a good deal since 1982, but has been consistently higher than the 1982 rate. Taking something worth more than $50 has increased since 1982, peaking in 1997 at 1.9 times the 1982 rate. The two questions from the Monitoring the Future survey that do not reflect inflation—about automobile theft and damage to school property—do not show the magnitude of increase shown for theft of property worth more than $50. Thus, it is possible that the increase in stealing items worth more than $50 is at least partially explained by inflation.

Just as with the index violent crimes, arrest rates for the index property crimes vary from one another (see Figure 2-10). Arrest rates for 10- to 17-year-olds are higher than rates for other age groups for all four index property offenses. Arrest for larceny/theft and burglary dominate index property arrests. Arrest rates for burglary have been dropping since the early 1980s for both 10- to 17-year-olds and 18- to 24-year-olds and by

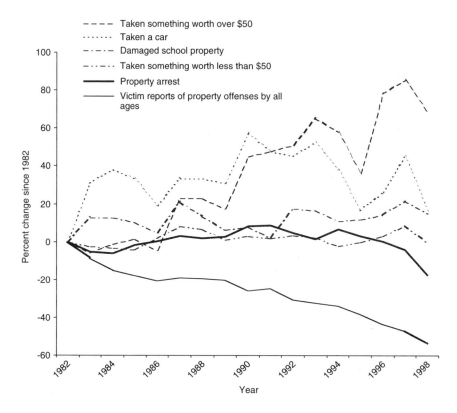

FIGURE 2-9 Change since 1982 in property arrest rates of 10- to 17-year-olds compared to self-reported property offense rates by high school seniors and victim reports of property offenses for all ages. Source: Arrrest rates from Federal Bureau of Investigation (1983-1999); self-report data from Monitoring the Future as reported in Maguire and Pastore (1994-1998); victim reports from the National Crime Victimization Survey, accessed online at http://www.ojp.usdoj.gov/bjs/glance/proptrd.txt.

1998 were 35 and 23 percent lower than 1970 rates, respectively (Figure 2-11). For older groups, the burglary arrest rate began increasing in the early 1980s and remained nearly 60 percent higher than in 1970 for those 35 and older. As can be seen in Figures 2-10 and 2-11, although the property arrest rates are higher for 10- to 17-year-olds and 18- to 24-year-olds, the increase in the arrest rate has been larger among 25- to 34-year-olds and those 35 and older.

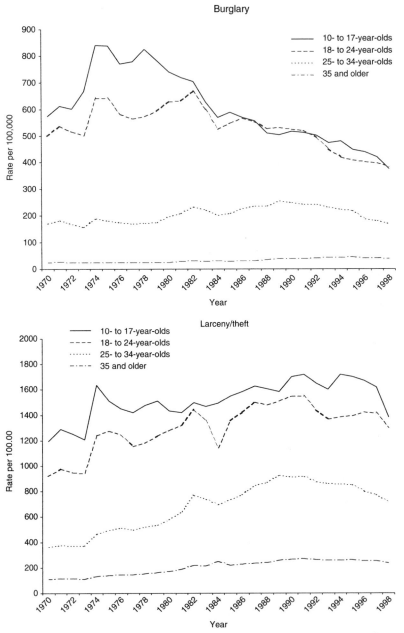

FIGURE 2-10 Arrest rates for index property crimes, by age groups. Source: Arrest data from Federal Bureau of Investigation (1971-1998); population data from Bureau of the Census (1982) and online at http://www.census.gov/population/estimates.

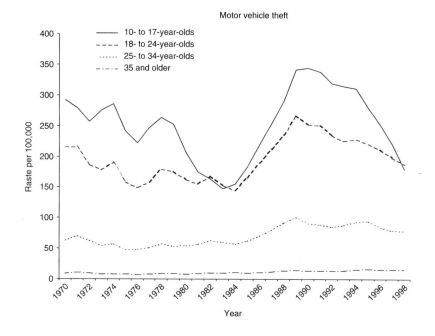

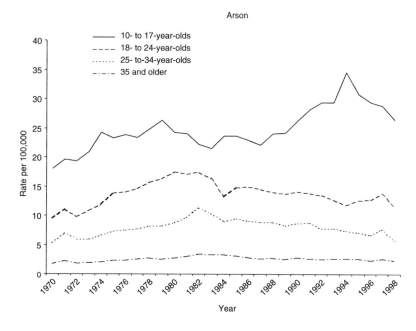

FIGURE 2-10 Continued

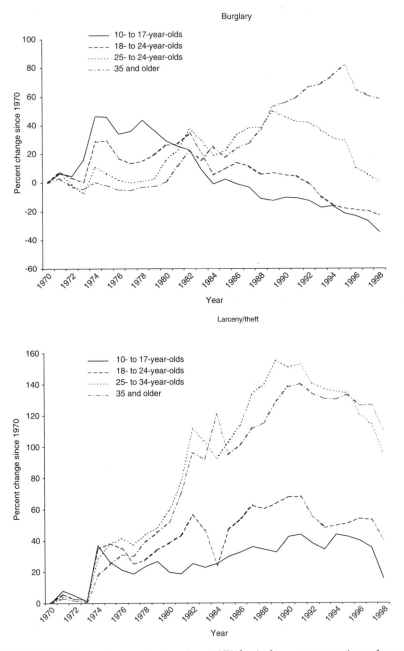

FIGURE 2-11 Change in arrest rates since 1970 for index property crimes, by age group. Source: Arrest data from Federal Bureau of Investigation (1971-1998); population data from Bureau of the Census (1982) and online at http://www.census.gov/population/estimates.

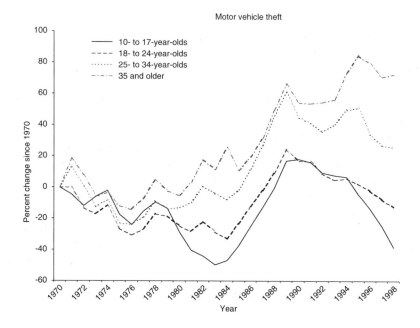

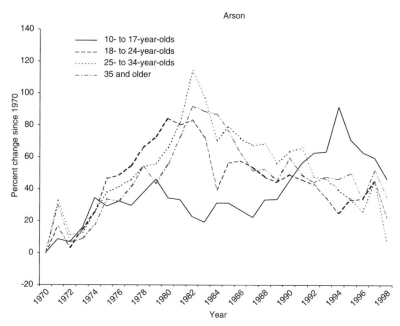

FIGURE 2-11 Continued

Status Offenses

A category of offenses that affects only juveniles is status offenses—acts that are considered unlawful only because of the age of the offender. The status offenses for which arrest data are available include curfew violations, running away, liquor law violations, and weapons possession. Figure 2-12 shows the change in arrest rates relative to 1970 rates for these four status offenses.

Starting with the mid-1970s through 1993, arrest rates for curfew violations and running away were consistently 20 to 40 percent below the 1970 rates. Because one of the provisions of the Juvenile Justice and Delinquency Prevention Act of 1974 was the deinstitutionalization of status offenders, in order to receive federal juvenile justice funding, states could no longer keep status offenders in secure detention facilities. Although the decline in status offense arrests began prior to the passage of the act, it is possible that the act reinforced the trend away from arresting juveniles for status offenses. The public discussions prior to the passage of the act may have also encouraged states to begin changing their policies regarding status offense arrests in anticipation of the federal law.

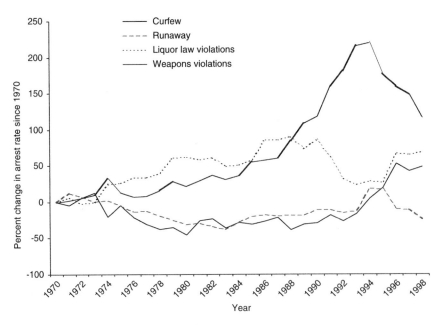

FIGURE 2-12 Change in arrest rates for status offenses. Source: Arrest data from Federal Bureau of Investigation (1971-1998); population data from Bureau of the Census (1982) and online at http://www.census.gov/population/estimates.

In 1993, arrests for curfew violations begin increasing and by 1996 had reached a level 50 percent higher than their 1970 rate. With the increase in concern over juvenile violence in the late 1980s and early 1990s, curfews gained popularity in various locales around the country. The emphasis on curfews as a way to curb juvenile crime could explain the sudden increase in curfew violation arrests beginning around 1993. The increase in curfew arrests began the year following the increase in drug arrests of juveniles (see Figure 2-13) and both peaked in the same year. Police efforts to curb drugs may have emphasized keeping young people off streets through more strict enforcement of curfew laws. More detailed analyses (perhaps using time series), which were beyond the panel's resources, would be necessary to determine the effects of the fed-

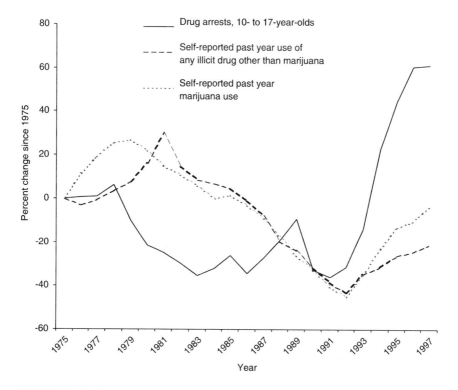

FIGURE 2-13 Change in arrest rates for drug offenses versus change in self-reported drug use. Source: Arrest data from Federal Bureau of Investigation (1976-1998); population data from Bureau of the Census (1982) and online at http://www.census.gov/population/estimates; self-report data from Monitoring the Future (Johnston et al., 1998).

eral, state, and local laws and policies on the various status offense arrest rates.

Girls have consistently had a higher rate of arrest for running away than have boys. For example, in 1997, the rate of runaway arrests for girls ages 10 to 17 was 764 per 100,000 compared with 527 per 100,000 for boys. Studies of runaways, however, have found that boys and girls are about equally likely to run away (Finkelhor et al., 1990; Kaufman and Widom, 1999). This disproportionate arrest of girls for running away has been explained by "a unique and intense preoccupation with girls' sexuality and their obedience to parental authority" (Chesney-Lind and Shelden, 1998:135), but it could also reflect a greater concern for their safety.

Drug Offenses

The availability of data on self-reported drug use provides an interesting comparison to arrest data for drug offenses. National surveys of high school students—in particular, Monitoring the Future—have collected information on self-reported drug use since the mid-1970s. As Figure 2-13 shows, arrest rates for drug offenses rose in the late 1980s at the same time as self-reported illicit drug use for both marijuana and other illicit drugs continued to decline. Use began rising again in 1993, but still remained lower than the rates in the late 1970s. Arrest rates for drug offenses, however, dramatically increased beginning in 1993, to a rate in 1997 that was 67 percent higher than 1975 arrest rates. It should be noted that drug arrests and self-reported drug use may be measuring different activities. Arrests can be for actions other than drug use, such as possession or sales. Drug use and drug sales may be correlated, however (Huizinga and Jakob-Chien, 1998). UCR published data do not specify the type of drug or the type of activity for which the arrest was made and the national self-report surveys, such as Monitoring the Future and the Youth Risk Behavior Survey, do not ask about involvement in drug sales.

Although rates and trends of drug arrests were similar for both blacks and whites prior to 1981, whites were more likely than blacks to be arrested for drug offenses. Since 1981, arrests of blacks for drug offenses have soared. Were one to use arrest data alone, it could be concluded that there has been an explosion of drug use among black juveniles since the late 1980s. This conclusion is not borne out by self-reported drug use data. In fact, black 8th, 10th, and 12th graders consistently report lower use of all illegal drugs than is reported by white students (Johnston et al., 1998).

As with most offenses, boys are more likely to be arrested for drug offenses than are girls. Since the early 1980s, the drug arrest rate for male adolescents has been between 5 and 6 times higher than that for girls. In

1997, the drug offense arrest rate for boys was 1,240 per 100,000, and the arrest rate for girls was 200 per 100,000 (Snyder, 1999b). Although males report higher drug use than females, the differences are much smaller than arrest rates would indicate. For example, in 1997, 40.9 percent of male and 35.5 percent of female high school seniors reported having used marijuana in the past year. Past-year cocaine use was reported by 6.6 and 4.2 percent of 12th grade males and females, respectively (Johnston et al., 1998). Yet boys were arrested more than 6 times as often as girls for drug offenses in 1997. If drug use by boys is more frequent or done in more public places than drug use by girls, boys could be more likely to be arrested.

It is obvious that the arrest rates for drug offenses do not reflect drug use as reported by young people, whether one looks at young people in the aggregate or by race or sex. Drug offenses exemplify the need for caution when using any single data source as an indicator of offense rate.

GIRLS AND DELINQUENCY

The study of delinquency and juvenile crime has historically focused on males in spite of the fact that girls account for about one-quarter of all juvenile arrests (Chesney-Lind, 1997). Of the 2.6 million arrests of those under age 18 in 1998, 26 percent were females. As a proportion of juveniles arrested, the number of girls has increased since 1981, when they accounted for 20 percent of all arrests of those under 18 (Snyder, 1999b). Prior to 1981, the FBI did not record arrests by sex and age, so national data on arrests of adolescent girls before the 1980s are not available. Arrests of girls for both property crimes and violent crimes have increased over the past two decades (see Figure 2-14). For violent crime, the arrest rate of young females increased more than that of young males—120 percent between 1981 and 1994 compared with 60 percent for males. In 1997, the young male violent arrest rate was just under 20 percent higher than in 1981, but the young female rate was about 90 percent above the 1981 rate (Snyder and Sickmund, 1999). Nevertheless, of all reported juvenile arrests in 1997, only 2.7 percent of girls' arrests and 4.9 percent of boys' arrests were for violent offenses.

The types of offenses for which girls are arrested differ from the types for which boys are arrested. Table 2-3 presents the five most frequent offenses for which boys and girls were arrested in 1985, 1994, and 1997. Girls have consistently been most likely to be arrested for larceny/theft, which usually involves shoplifting (Chesney-Lind and Shelden, 1998), and for running away from home. Larceny/theft is also a common cause of arrest for boys, but running away accounts for only 3.9 percent of their arrests compared with 15.4 percent of arrests for girls. In fact, running

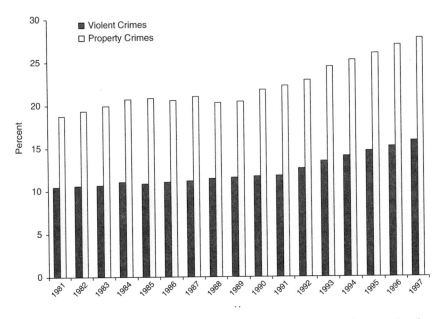

FIGURE 2-14 Female proportion of arrests of those under age 18. Source: Snyder (1999b).

away and curfew violations make up nearly a quarter of the offenses for which girls are arrested.

Boys have consistently higher arrest rates than girls for all crimes except for prostitution and running away. In 1998, boys and girls were arrested for index violent crimes at a rate of 603 per 100,000 and 127 per 100,000, respectively and for index property crimes at a rate of 2,733 per 100,000 and 1,156 per 100,000, respectively.[6] Self-report data show more similarity between boys' and girls' behavior than do arrest data for some offenses (see Table 2-4). For example, in 1998, 21 percent of male high school seniors reported having been in a serious fight within the past 12 months, compared with 11 percent of female high school seniors (Bureau of Justice Statistics, 1999). This 2:1 ratio for self-reports of serious fighting compares to a 3:1 boy to girl ratio for simple assault arrests. For more serious assaults, arrests and self-report data are more similar. The ratio of

---

[6]Arrest rates by sex calculated from UCR data by committee staff with the methodology used by Snyder (1999b).

TABLE 2-3 Rank Order of Adolescent Male and Female Arrests for Specific Offenses

Females

Offense	% of Total 1985	Offense	% of Total 1994	Offense	% of Total 1997
(1) Larceny/theft	26.4	(1) Larceny/theft	25.6	(1) Larceny/theft	22.8
(2) Runaway	20.2	(2) Runaway	17.1	(2) Runaway	15.4
(3) Other offenses	15.4	(3) Other offenses	14.4	(3) Other offenses	15.2
(4) Liquor laws	7.3	(4) Other assaults	8.6	(4) Other assaults	9.5
(5) Other assaults	4.9	(5) Disorderly conduct	6.0	(5) Disorderly conduct	7.6

	1985	1994	1997
Arrests for violent offenses	2.1	3.4	2.7
Arrests for status offenses	24.6	22.9	23.1

Males

Offense	% of Total 1985	Offense	% of Total 1994	Offense	% of Total 1997
(1) Larceny/theft	20.2	(1) Larceny/theft	17.2	(1) Other offenses	16.9
(2) Other offenses	16.8	(2) Other offenses	16.4	(2) Larceny/theft	15.5
(3) Burglary	10.0	(3) Other assaults	7.7	(3) Drug offenses	9.1
(4) Vandalism	6.6	(4) Drug offenses	7.1	(4) Other assaults	8.1
(5) Liquor laws	5.8	(5) Vandalism	6.7	(5) Disorderly conduct	7.6

	1985	1994	1997
Arrests for violent offenses	4.9	6.6	4.9
Arrests for status offenses	8.2	8.6	9.9

Source: Adapted from Chesney-Lind (1997), Snyder (1999a), and Snyder and Sickmund (1999).

TABLE 2-4 Self-Reported Involvement in Delinquent Behavior of High School Seniors by Sex in 1998 (percentage) Compared to Arrests in 1998 (percentage)

	Male	Female	Ratio
Serious fight at school	21	11	2:1
Simple assault arrest	1.2	0.35	3:1
Hurt someone enough to need bandages or doctor	23	6	4:1
Aggravated assault arrest	0.4	0.09	4:1
Used a weapon to take something from someone	7	2	4:1
Robbery arrest	0.19	0.02	9:1
Stole something worth more than $50	17	7	2:1
Stole something worth less than $50	39	25	2:1
Theft arrest	1.8	0.97	2:1
Damaged property at school or work	21	8	3:1
Vandalism arrest	0.67	0.12	5:1

Source: Monitoring the Future data from Pastore and Maguire (1998); arrest data from committee analysis of UCR (Federal Bureau of Investigation, 1999).

boys to girls for aggravated assault arrests is 4:1, the same ratio as self-reports of hurting someone badly enough to need bandages or a doctor.

The differences between male and female self-reports of offending have remained fairly constant since the early 1980s (Bureau of Justice Statistics, 1999). The increase in arrest rates of girls for index crimes, however, was greater than that of boys. This increase may be due as much to a change in police behavior toward girls as to a change in girls' behavior (Chesney-Lind and Shelden, 1998).

FORECASTING TRENDS IN JUVENILE CRIME[7]

How much crime will there be in the United States in the next 5 or 10 years? Will crime rates go up or down or remain about the same? Since juvenile crime is often an indication of crime problems to come, how many juvenile offenses will there be? Will the number of juvenile serious violent offenders or homicide perpetrators increase? What will be the resulting demands on the juvenile and the criminal justice systems? Will trends in juvenile crime influence trends in adult crime? Over the past three decades, criminologists have made a number of attempts to address

---

[7]Appendix B is a more complete and technical discussion of forecasting trends in juvenile crime.

these and related questions. These attempts have usually taken the form of efforts to explain past variations or to project future levels of crime by applying techniques of demographic and statistical analysis. Such analyses may be useful exercises with respect to explanation of past experiences in the ups and downs of observed crime or to the projection of recent trends in order to anticipate resources that will be needed in the near future by the juvenile and the criminal justice systems. Users of such analyses must be aware, however, that all projections are fraught with uncertainty, and the farther into the future the projection is made, the more uncertainty there is.

A review of several existing contributions to the crime forecasting literature suggests that these forecasts are heavily influenced by trends in crime rates in the years just prior to the period for which the forecasts are made. For example, based on crime rates in the early 1980s and anticipated decreases in the population at high risk of committing crimes (i.e., those between 15 and 24), Steffensmeier and Harer (1987) forecast that violent crime rates would fall about 13 percent during the period 1980 to 2000. Using a different methodology, other researchers also predicted falling rates of violent crime during the 1980s (Cohen and Land, 1987; Fox, 1978) with a gradual increase in the 1990s (Fox, 1978) or in the 2000s (Cohen and Land, 1987). None of these predictions was borne out—the juvenile population did not behave as expected in the projections. Similarly, forecasts based on the sudden rise in juvenile violent crime in the mid-1980s to early 1990s also proved incorrect. Shortly before violent crime rates dramatically decreased, Bennett et al. (1996), Fox (1996), and Wilson (1995) all predicted continually rising violent crime trends. To the extent that crime forecasts are meant to represent likely paths that crime rates may take, they should attempt to minimize, or at least be cognizant of, the effects of continuity bias—that is, the assumption that the current patterns will continue—on the forecasts.

Uncertainty can be built into crime forecasts by adapting and applying the high-, medium-, and low-scenarios approach widely employed in demography. By using high-low projection cones (the range of predictions between the low and high scenario), the scary forecasts of a new wave of juvenile homicide offenders in the first decade of the 21st century, made by some researchers in the mid-1990s, are shown to be relatively implausible. Appendix B presents this type of projection with respect to juvenile homicide. The most likely projection suggests that the numbers of juvenile male homicide offenders will continue to decline during the period 1998 to 2002 and then increase slightly thereafter to the year 2007. However, the possibility that juvenile homicide rates will increase dramatically in the near future also exists and is portrayed by the upper bounds of the projections.

There are two additional implications of the uncertainty in forecasts of crime rates and offenders: the periods over which crime forecasts are made should be as short as possible and the forecasts should be updated frequently. Large-scale social systems have elements of complexity or nonlinear dynamics and uncertainty that militate against the accuracy of long-term forecasts. In practical terms, this means that forecasting cones (upper and lower bounds) for enveloping the ranges within which crime is likely to fall with a high probability will grow very rapidly from the base year into the future. To take this into account, the time periods of the forecasts should be relatively short and the forecasts should be revised when new information becomes available. For most police, court, and penal components of the juvenile and the criminal justice systems, this is not particularly problematic, as forecasts typically are necessary only for one- or two-year government budgeting cycles. Only occasionally are projections more than five years into the future required for budgeting or planning purposes.

CONCLUSIONS

Official data to track or monitor crimes committed by juveniles and the justice system responses to juvenile offenders are clearly inadequate. They provide, at best, only a crude measure of perpetrators estimated by victims to be under 18 or of the number of arrests for the various crimes of juveniles under 18. The reporting of crimes known to the police and arrest data is voluntary on the part of local police agencies and states. Therefore, published FBI annual crime figures are based on different agencies' and states' reports each year, depending on which agencies and states submitted their data on time. Official data are insufficient for studies to determine whether changing arrest rates are related to changes in police policies and practices or to changes in juvenile behavior. Comparing victim reports and arrest data to juvenile self-reports of behavior improves the situation somewhat. Many self-report studies, however, are conducted with school-based samples, omitting dropouts and truants who may have higher offending rates than children and adolescents who attend school regularly.

Although the panel acknowledges the weaknesses in available data, we nevertheless had to rely on currently available data to analyze juvenile crime trends. Based on our analysis, the panel drew the following conclusions.

• There was an increase in juvenile homicide beginning in the mid-1980s, peaking in the early 1990s, and decreasing in the late 1990s. This increase was not confined to juveniles, however. For example, homicide rates increased similarly among young adults and were higher among 18- to 24-year-olds than among 10- to 17-year-olds over the same period of time. Although there are theories about the reasons for the increase and subsequent decrease in homicide, current research is inadequate to completely explain the trends. Some of the rise in other violent crime arrest rates between the mid-1980s and early 1990s seems to have been a result of changes in police policies regarding whether to consider specific types of assault as aggravated assaults rather than simple assaults and an increasing willingness to arrest for assault. Much of the rise in juvenile homicides appears to be linked to an increase in the use of firearms. Even at the peak rate of violence in the early 1990s, the vast majority of arrests of those under age 18 were for property crimes, not serious violent crimes.

• Blacks are disproportionately represented among juveniles arrested for crimes committed in the United States. The degree to which this is a consequence of differential behavior or biases in the system remains a continuing debate, one to which the report returns in Chapter 6.

• The increase in homicide rates among juveniles from the late 1980s to the early 1990s was entirely due to an increase in homicides committed with firearms. Similarly, the decline in homicide rates since the mid-1990s seems to involve primarily handgun-related homicides.

• Rising rates of arrests for black youth on drug-related charges are not paralleled by increased reporting of drug use among black youth. Therefore, at least some of the discrepancy between arrest rates for blacks and whites for drug offenses may be related to differential visibility of black and white drug use and criminal justice system practices rather than to the juveniles' behavior.

• Forecasts of juvenile crime based on the spike in homicide rates proved to be misleading and highlight the caution with which predictions of future juvenile crime trends must be made.

RECOMMENDATIONS

Data to track or monitor crime committed by juveniles are inadequate. The UCR data do not lend themselves to analyses of specific crimes in relation to the ages of juveniles who are arrested. Therefore, we do not know, for example whether changes in policies on violent crimes or on drugs and guns have led to changes in the age of juveniles being arrested. Because of the known high level of co-offending among juveniles, neither arrests nor self-reporting of offenses can currently be used to measure the impact of policies on social order.

The voluntary nature of UCR reporting results in unstable, potentially nonrepresentative samples of law enforcement agencies. Reporting both among and within states varies so widely that state-to-state comparisons cannot be made using the UCR, and year-to-year comparisons are likely to be misleading. Although the National Incident Based Reporting System may eventually provide much improved information about juvenile crime, full implementation is years away. In the interim, measures to improve the quality of the data and increase the number of agencies that report are needed. Furthermore, no system is in place to monitor the collection of data submitted to the FBI, yet FBI figures are used for policy making.

Recommendation: Incentives need to be established to encourage all police agencies to report data to the FBI. In addition, a monitoring system should be established to oversee the accuracy and completeness of the information received by the FBI for the Uniform Crime Reports and the National Incident Based Reporting System.

Even with improvements in official arrest data, not all crimes result in arrest. Furthermore, until the full implementation of NIBRS, arrest data provide no information about co-offending, the circumstances of the crime, the use of weapons during commission of the crime, and so forth. There will remain a need for better self-report and victim report data to provide a more complete picture of juvenile offending. Each of the current sources of self-report information have limitations and are the subject of continuing critiques and arguments. There is an urgent need for alternative sources of information to permit better estimates of the extent of juvenile crime and the circumstances under which it occurs.

Recommendation: Congress should appropriate additional funding to the Bureau of Justice Statistics and the Office of Juvenile Justice and Delinquency Prevention to improve the quality of existing information and to develop alternative sources of juvenile crime information. There is a need to test the reliability and validity of reported age, race, and ethnicity estimates by victims in the National Crime Victimization Survey. In addition, self-report surveys of juvenile criminal behavior should collect information regarding co-offending.

Public policy on juvenile crime, particularly the trend toward more punitive sanctions (see Chapter 5), has been greatly influenced by predictions of future crime rates—predictions that have proven notoriously inaccurate. Although short-term forecasts are necessary for allocating resources at the local, state, and federal levels, long-term forecasting is fraught with uncertainty.

Recommendation: Because of the inaccuracies inherent in long-range predictions, public policy should not be based on the

assumption that any specific forecast will be true. To improve future forecasts of crime rates and the number of offenders, the panel recommends the following:

- forecasts should be accompanied by warnings of their inherent inaccuracy and cautions about their appropriate use;
- forecasts should guard against continuity biases or at least explicitly recognize their presence in projections of which the objective is to draw out implications of recent trends;
- forecasts should take into account uncertainty in the predictions by developing upper and lower bounds within which paths of crime rates are expected to lie;
- the forecast time period should be shortened as much as the purpose for which the forecasts are produced will allow; and
- forecasts should be updated frequently.

The incorporation of these characteristics into crime forecasts should result in more realistic uses and assessments of the forecasts. Nevertheless, current capacity to forecast crime rates is very limited. Errors in forecasts over even relatively short time periods of 2 to 3 years, let alone for a decade or more, are very large.

3

The Development of Delinquency

Research over the past few decades on normal child development and on development of delinquent behavior has shown that individual, social, and community conditions as well as their interactions influence behavior. There is general agreement that behavior, including antisocial and delinquent behavior, is the result of a complex interplay of individual biological and genetic factors and environmental factors, starting during fetal development and continuing throughout life (Bock and Goode, 1996). Clearly, genes affect biological development, but there is no biological development without environmental input. Thus, both biology and environment influence behavior.

Many children reach adulthood without involvement in serious delinquent behavior, even in the face of multiple risks. Although risk factors may help identify which children are most in need of preventive interventions, they cannot identify which particular children will become serious or chronic offenders. It has long been known that most adult criminals were involved in delinquent behavior as children and adolescents; most delinquent children and adolescents, however, do not grow up to be adult criminals (Robins, 1978). Similarly, most serious, chronically delinquent children and adolescents experience a number of risk factors at various levels, but most children and adolescents with risk factors do not become serious, chronic delinquents. Furthermore, any individual factor contributes only a small part to the increase in risk. It is, however, widely recognized that the more risk factors a child or adolescent experiences, the higher their risk for delinquent behavior.

A difficulty with the literature on risk factors is the diversity of the outcome behaviors studied. Some studies focus on behavior that meets diagnostic criteria for conduct disorder or other antisocial behavior disorders; others look at aggressive behavior, or lying, or shoplifting; still others rely on juvenile court referral or arrest as the outcome of interest. Furthermore, different risk factors and different outcomes may be more salient at some stages of child and adolescent development than at others.

Much of the literature that has examined risk factors for delinquency is based on longitudinal studies, primarily of white males. Some of the samples were specifically chosen from high-risk environments. Care must be taken in generalizing this literature to girls and minorities and to general populations. Nevertheless, over the past 20 years, much has been learned about risks for antisocial and delinquent behavior.

This chapter is not meant to be a comprehensive overview of all the literature on risk factors. Rather it focuses on factors that are most relevant to prevention efforts. (For reviews of risk factor literature, see, for example, Hawkins et al., 1998; Lipsey and Derzon, 1998; Rutter et al., 1998.) The chapter discusses risk factors for offending, beginning with risks at the individual level, including biological, psychological, behavioral, and cognitive factors. Social-level risk factors are discussed next; these include family and peer relationships. Finally, community-level risk factors, including school and neighborhood attributes, are examined. Although individual, social, and community-level factors interact, each level is discussed separately for clarity.

INDIVIDUAL-LEVEL RISK FACTORS

A large number of individual factors and characteristics has been associated with the development of juvenile delinquency. These individual factors include age, gender, complications during pregnancy and delivery, impulsivity, aggressiveness, and substance use. Some factors operate before birth (prenatal) or close to, during, and shortly after birth (perinatal); some can be identified in early childhood; and other factors may not be evident until late childhood or during adolescence. To fully appreciate the development of these individual characteristics and their relations to delinquency, one needs to study the development of the individual in interaction with the environment. In order to simplify presentation of the research, however, this section deals only with individual factors.

Age

Studies of criminal activity by age consistently find that rates of offending begin to rise in preadolescence or early adolescence, reach a peak in late adolescence, and fall through young adulthood (see, e.g., Farrington, 1986a; National Research Council, 1986). Some lawbreaking experience at some time during adolescence is nearly universal in American children, although much of this behavior is reasonably mild and temporary. Although the exact age of onset, peak, and age of desistance varies by offense, the general pattern has been remarkably consistent over time, in different countries, and for official and self-reported data. For example, Farrington (1983, 1986a), in a longitudinal study of a sample of boys in London (the Cambridge Longitudinal Study), found an eightfold increase in the number of different boys convicted of delinquent behavior from age 10 to age 17, followed by a decrease to a quarter of the maximum level by age 24. The number of self-reported offenses in the same sample also peaked between ages 15 and 18, then dropped sharply by age 24. In a longitudinal study of boys in inner-city Pittsburgh (just over half the sample was black and just under half was white), the percentage of boys who self-reported serious delinquent behavior rose from 5 percent at age 6 to about 18 percent for whites and 27 percent for blacks at age 16 (Loeber et al., 1998). A longitudinal study of a representative sample from high-risk neighborhoods in Denver also found a growth in the self-reported prevalence of serious violence from age 10 through late adolescence (Kelley et al., 1997). Females in the Denver sample exhibited a peak in serious violence in midadolescence, but prevalence continued to increase through age 19 for the boys. The study is continuing to follow these boys to see if their prevalence drops in early adulthood. Laub et al. (1998), using the Gluecks' data on 500 juvenile offenders from the 1940s, found that only 25 percent of them were still offending by age 32.

Much research has concentrated on the onset of delinquency, examining risk factors for onset, and differences between those who begin offending early (prior to adolescence) versus those who begin offending in midadolescence. There have been suggestions that early-onset delinquents are more likely than later-onset delinquents to be more serious and persistent offenders (e.g., Moffitt, 1993). There is evidence, however, that predictors associated with onset do not predict persistence particularly well (Farrington and Hawkins, 1991). There are also important problems with the choice of statistical models to create categories of developmental trajectories (Nagin and Tremblay, 1999).

Research by Nagin and Tremblay (1999) found no evidence of late-onset physical aggression. Physical aggression was highest at age 6 (the earliest age for which data were collected for this study) and declined into adolescence. The available data on very young children indicates that frequency of physical aggression reaches a peak around age 2 and then slowly declines up to adolescence (Restoin et al., 1985; Tremblay et al., 1996a).

Those who persist in offending into adulthood may differ from those who desist in a number of ways, including attachment to school, military service (Elder, 1986; Sampson and Laub, 1996), sex, age of onset of offending, incarceration, and adult social bonds (e.g., marriage, quality of marriage, job stability) (Farrington and West, 1995; Quinton et al., 1993; Quinton and Rutter, 1988; Sampson and Laub, 1990). Sampson and Laub (1993) found that marital attachment and job stability significantly reduced deviant behavior in adulthood. Farrington and West (1995) found that offenders and nonoffenders were equally likely to get married, but those who got married and lived with their spouse decreased their offending more than those who remained single or who did not live with their spouse. They also found that offending increased after separation from a spouse. Similarly, Horney et al. (1995) found that married male offenders decreased their offending when living with their spouses and resumed it when not living with them. Within marriages, only good marriages predicted reduction in crime, and these had an increasing effect over time (Laub et al., 1998). Warr (1998) also found that offending decreased after marriage but attributed the decrease to a reduction in the time spent with peers and a reduction in the number of deviant peers following marriage rather than to increased attachment to conventional society through marriage.

Laub et al. (1998) found no difference between persisters and desisters in most family characteristics during childhood (e.g., poverty, parental alcohol abuse or crime, discipline, supervision) or in most individual differences in childhood (e.g., aggression, tantrums, difficult child, verbal IQ). Brannigan (1997) points out that crime is highest when males have the fewest resources, and it lasts longest in those with the fewest investments in society (job, wife, children). Crime is not an effective strategy for getting resources. There is evidence that chronic offenders gain fewer resources than nonoffenders, after the adolescent period (Moffitt, 1993).

The evidence for desistance in girls is not clear. One review of the literature suggests that 25 to 50 percent of antisocial girls commit crimes as adults (Pajer, 1998). There is also some evidence that women are less likely to be recidivists, and that they end their criminal careers earlier than men (Kelley et al., 1997). However, the sexes appear to become more similar with time in rates of all but violent crimes. There is a suggestion that women who persist in crime past adolescence may be more disturbed than men who persist (Jordan et al., 1996; Pajer, 1998).

Prenatal and Perinatal Factors

Several studies have found an association between prenatal and perinatal complications and later delinquent or criminal behavior (Kandel et al., 1989; Kandel and Mednick, 1991; Raine et al., 1994). Prenatal and perinatal risk factors represent a host of latent and manifest conditions that influence subsequent development.

Many studies use the terms "prenatal or perinatal complications" to describe what is a very heterogeneous set of latent and clinical conditions. Under the heading of prenatal factors, one finds a broad variety of conditions that occurs before birth through the seventh month of gestation (Kopp and Krakow, 1983). Similarly, perinatal factors include conditions as varied as apnea of prematurity (poor breathing) to severe respiratory distress syndrome. The former condition is relatively benign, while the latter is often life-threatening. Although they are risk factors, low birthweight and premature birth do not necessarily presage problems in development.

Prenatal and perinatal risk factors may compromise the nervous system, creating vulnerabilities in the child that can lead to abnormal behavior. Children with prenatal and perinatal complications who live in impoverished, deviant, or abusive environments face added difficulties. According to three major large-scale, long-term studies: (1) developmental risks have additive negative effects on child outcomes, (2) most infants with perinatal complications develop into normally functioning children, and (3) children with long-term negative outcomes who suffered perinatal complications more often than not came from socially disadvantaged backgrounds (Brennan and Mednick, 1997; Broman et al., 1975; Drillien et al., 1980; Werner et al., 1971).

Mednick and colleagues (Brennan and Mednick, 1997; Kandel and Mednick, 1991; Raine et al., 1994) have conducted several investigations in an attempt to elucidate the relationship between criminal behavior and perinatal risk. These and other studies have been unable to identify specific mechanisms to account for the fact that the number of prenatal and perinatal abnormalities tend to correlate with the probability that a child will become a criminal. In addition to the lack of specificity regarding the predictors and the mechanisms of risk, similar measures predict learning disabilities, mental retardation, minimal brain dysfunction, and others (Towbin, 1978). An association between perinatal risk factors and violent offending is particularly strong among offenders whose parents are mentally ill or very poor (Raine et al., 1994, 1997).

Most measures indicate that males are more likely to commit crimes. They are also more vulnerable to prenatal and perinatal stress, as is shown through studies of negative outcomes, including death (Davis and Emory, 1995; Emory et al., 1996).

Hyperactivity, attention problems, and impulsiveness in children have been found to be associated with delinquency. These behaviors can be assessed very early in life and are associated with certain prenatal and perinatal histories (DiPietro et al., 1996; Emory and Noonan, 1984; Lester et al., 1976; Sameroff and Chandler, 1975). For example, exposure to environmental toxins, such as prenatal lead exposure at very low levels, tends to adversely affect neonatal motor and attentional performance (Emory et al., 1999). Hyperactivity and aggression are associated with prenatal alcohol exposure (Brown et al., 1991; Institute of Medicine, 1996). Prenatal exposure to alcohol, cocaine, heroin, and nicotine appear to have similar effects. Each tends to be associated with hyperactivity, attention deficit, and impulsiveness (Karr-Morse and Wiley, 1997).

Individual Capabilities, Competencies, and Characteristics

In recent investigations, observable behaviors, such as duration of attention to a toy and compliance with mother's instructions not to touch an object, that are particularly relevant to later misbehavior are observable in the first year of life (Kochanska et al., 1998). However, the ability to predict behavior at later ages (in adolescence and adulthood) from such traits early in life is not yet known. Aggressive behavior is nevertheless one of the more stable dimensions, and significant stability may be seen from toddlerhood to adulthood (Tremblay, 2000).

The social behaviors that developmentalists study during childhood can be divided into two broad categories: prosocial and antisocial. Prosocial behaviors include helping, sharing, and cooperation, while antisocial behaviors include different forms of oppositional and aggressive behavior. The development of empathy, guilt feelings, social cognition, and moral reasoning are generally considered important emotional and cognitive correlates of social development.

Impulsivity and hyperactivity have both been associated with later antisocial behavior (Rutter et al., 1998). The social behavior characteristics that best predict delinquent behavior, however, are physical aggression and oppositionality (Lahey et al., 1999; Nagin and Tremblay, 1999). Most children start manifesting these behaviors between the end of the first and second years. The peak level in frequency of physical aggression is generally reached between 24 and 36 months, an age at which the consequences of the aggression are generally relatively minor (Goodenough, 1931; Sand, 1966; Tremblay et al., 1996a, 1999a). By entry into kindergarten, the majority of children have learned to use other means than physical aggression to get what they want and to solve conflicts. Those who have not learned, who are oppositional and show few prosocial behaviors toward peers, are at high risk of being rejected by their peers, of failing in school, and eventually of getting involved in serious delinquency (Farrington and Wikstrom, 1994; Huesmann et al., 1984; Miller and Eisenberg, 1988; Nagin and Tremblay, 1999; Tremblay et al., 1992a, 1994; White et al., 1990).

The differentiation of emotions and emotional regulation occurs during the 2-year period, from 12 months to 36 months, when the frequency of physical aggression increases sharply and then decreases almost as sharply (Tremblay, 2000; Tremblay et al., 1996a, 1999a). A number of longitudinal studies have shown that children who are behaviorally inhibited (shy, anxious) are less at risk of juvenile delinquency, while children who tend to be fearless, those who are impulsive, and those who have difficulty delaying gratification are more at risk of delinquent behavior (Blumstein et al., 1984; Ensminger et al., 1983; Kerr et al., 1997; Mischel et al., 1989; Tremblay et al., 1994).

A large number of studies report that delinquents have a lower verbal IQ compared with nondelinquents, as well as lower school achievement (Fergusson and Horwood, 1995; Maguin and Loeber, 1996; Moffitt, 1997). Antisocial youth also tend to show cognitive deficits in the areas of executive functions[1] (Moffitt et al., 1994; Seguin et al., 1995), perception of social cues, and problem-solving processing patterns (Dodge et al., 1997; Huesmann, 1988). The association between cognitive deficits and delinquency remains after controlling for social class and race (Moffitt, 1990; Lynam et al., 1993). Few studies, however, have assessed cognitive functioning during the preschool years or followed the children into adolescence to understand the long-term link between early cognitive deficits and juvenile delinquency. The studies that did look at children's early cognitive development have shown that poor language performance by the second year after birth, poor fine motor skills by the third year, and low IQ by kindergarten were all associated with later antisocial behavior (Kopp and Krakow, 1983; Stattin and Klackenberg-Larsson, 1993; White et al., 1990). Stattin and Klackenberg-Larsson (1993) found that the association between poor early language performance and later criminal behavior remained significant even after controlling for socioeconomic status.

Epidemiological studies have found a correlation between language delay and aggressive behavior (Richman et al., 1982). Language delays may contribute to poor peer relations that, in turn, result in aggression (Campbell, 1990a). The long-term impact of cognitively oriented preschool programs on the reduction of antisocial behavior is a more direct indication that fostering early cognitive development can play an important role in the prevention of juvenile delinquency (Schweinhart et al., 1993; Schweinhart and Weikart, 1997). It is important to note that since poor cognitive abilities and problem behaviors in the preschool years also

---

[1]Executive functions refer to a variety of independent skills that are necessary for purposeful, goal-directed activity. Executive functions require generating and maintaining appropriate mental representations, monitoring the flow of information, and modifying problem-solving strategies in order to keep behavior directed toward the goal.

lead to poor school performance, they probably explain a large part of the association observed during adolescence between school failure and delinquency (Fergusson and Horwood, 1995; Maguin and Loeber, 1996; Tremblay et al., 1992).

Several mental health disorders of childhood have been found to put children at risk for future delinquent behavior. Conduct disorder is often diagnosed when a child is troublesome and breaking rules or norms but not necessarily doing illegal behavior, especially at younger ages. This behavior may include lying, bullying, cruelty to animals, fighting, and truancy. Most adolescents in U.S. society at some time engage in illegal behaviors, whether some kind of theft, aggression, or status offense. Many adolescents, in the period during which they engage in these behaviors, are likely to meet formal criteria for conduct disorder. Behavior characterized by willful disobedience and defiance is considered a different disorder (oppositional defiant disorder), but often occurs in conjunction with conduct disorder and may precede it.

Several prospective longitudinal studies have found that children with attention and hyperactivity problems, such as attention deficit hyperactivity disorder, show high levels of antisocial and aggressive behavior (Campbell, 1990b; Hechtman et al., 1984; Loney et al., 1982; Sanson et al., 1993; Satterfield et al., 1982). Early hyperactivity and attention problems without concurrent aggression, however, appear not to be related to later aggressive behavior (Loeber, 1988; Magnusson and Bergman, 1990; Nagin and Tremblay, 1999), although a few studies do report such relationships (Gittelman et al., 1985; Mannuzza et al., 1993, 1991).

Another disorder that is often associated with antisocial behavior and conduct disorder is major depressive disorder, particularly in girls (Kovacs, 1996; Offord et al., 1986; Renouf and Harter, 1990). It is hypothesized that depression during adolescence may be "a central pathway through which girls' serious antisocial behavior develops" (Obeidallah and Earls, 1999:1). In girls, conduct disorder may be a kind of manifestation of the hopelessness, frustration, and low self-esteem that often characterizes major depression.

For juveniles as well as adults, the use of drugs and alcohol is common among offenders. In 1998, about half of juvenile arrestees in the Arrestee Drug Abuse Monitoring Program tested positive for at least one drug. In these same cities,[2] about two-thirds of adult arrestees tested

---

[2]This program collects information on both juvenile and adult arrestees in Birmingham, Alabama; Cleveland, Ohio; Denver, Colorado; Indianapolis, Indiana; Los Angeles, California; Phoenix, Arizona; Portland, Oregon; St. Louis, Missouri; San Antonio, Texas; San Diego, California; San Jose, California; Tuscon, Arizona; and Washington, DC. Data on adults are collected in 35 cities altogether.

positive for at least one drug (National Institute of Justice, 1999). Of course, drug use is a criminal offense on its own, and for juveniles, alcohol use is also a status delinquent offense. A number of studies have consistently found that as the seriousness of offending goes up, so does the seriousness of drug use as measured both by frequency of use and type of drug (see Huizinga and Jakob-Chien, 1998). In the longitudinal studies of causes and correlates of delinquency in Denver, Pittsburgh, and Rochester (see Thornberry et al., 1995), serious offenders had a higher prevalence of drug and alcohol use than did minor offenders or nonoffenders. In addition, about three-quarters of drug users in each sample were also involved in serious delinquency (Huizinga and Jakob-Chien, 1998). Similarly, in the Denver Youth Survey, serious offenders had the highest prevalence and frequency of use of alcohol and marijuana of all youth in the study. Nevertheless, only about one-third of serious delinquents were problem drug users (Huizinga and Jakob-Chien, 1998).

Although there appears to be a relationship between alcohol and drug use and criminal delinquency, not all delinquents use alcohol or drugs, nor do all alcohol and drug users commit delinquent acts (other than the alcohol or drug use itself). Those who are both serious delinquents and serious drug users may be involved in a great deal of crime, however. Johnson et al. (1991) found that the small group (less than 5 percent of a national sample) who were both serious delinquents and serious drug users accounted for over half of all serious crimes. Neverthless, it would be premature to conclude that serious drug use causes serious crime (McCord, 2001).

Whatever characteristics individuals have, resulting personalities and behavior are influenced by the social environments in which they are raised. Characteristics of individuals always develop in social contexts.

SOCIAL FACTORS

Children's and adolescents' interactions and relationships with family and peers influence the development of antisocial behavior and delinquency. Family interactions are most important during early childhood, but they can have long-lasting effects. In early adolescence, relationships with peers take on greater importance. This section will first consider factors within the family that have been found to be associated with the development of delinquency and then consider peer influences on delinquent behavior. Note that issues concerning poverty and race are dealt with under the community factors section of this chapter. Chapter 7 deals specifically with issues concerning race.

Family Influences

In assigning responsibility for childrearing to parents, most Western cultures place a heavy charge on families. Such cultures assign parents the task of raising children to follow society's rules for acceptable behavior. It should be no surprise, therefore, when families have difficulties with the task laid on them, that the product often is juvenile delinquency (Kazdin, 1997). Family structure (who lives in a household) and family functioning (how the family members treat one another) are two general categories under which family effects on delinquency have been examined.

Family Structure

Before embarking on a review of the effects of family structure, it is important to raise the question of mechanisms (Rutter et al., 1998). It may not be the family structure itself that increases the risk of delinquency, but rather some other factor that explains why that structure is present. Alternatively, a certain family structure may increase the risk of delinquency, but only as one more stressor in a series; it may be the number rather than specific nature of the stressors that is harmful.

Historically, one aspect of family structure that has received a great deal of attention as a risk factor for delinquency is growing up in a family that has experienced separation or divorce.[3] Although many studies have found an association between broken homes and delinquency (Farrington and Loeber, 1999; Rutter and Giller, 1983; Wells and Rankin, 1991; Wilson and Herrnstein, 1985), there is considerable debate about the meaning of the association. For example, longitudinal studies have found an increased level of conduct disorder and behavioral disturbance in children of divorcing parents before the divorce took place (Block et al., 1986; Cherlin et al., 1991). Capaldi and Patterson (1991) showed that disruptive parenting practices and antisocial personality of the parent(s) accounted for apparent effects of divorce and remarriage. Thus, it is likely that the increased risk of delinquency experienced among children of broken homes is related to the family conflict prior to the divorce or separation, rather than to family breakup itself (Rutter et al., 1998). In their longitudinal study of family disruption, Juby and Farrington (2001) found that boys who stayed with their mothers following disruption had delinquency rates that were almost identical to those reared in intact families.

---

[3]Many discussions of family structure treat single-parent households and divorced families as the same. In this section, the literature on single-parents is reported separately from that on separated and divorced families because there may be considerable differences in the experiences of children born to single parents and those whose parents divorce.

Being born and raised in a single-parent family has also been associated with increased risk of delinquency and antisocial behavior. Research that takes into account the socioeconomic conditions of single-parent households and other risks, including disciplinary styles and problems in supervising and monitoring children, show that these other factors account for the differential outcomes in these families. The important role of socioeconomic conditions is shown by the absence of differences in delinquency between children in single-parent and two-parent homes within homogeneous socioeconomic classes (Austin, 1978). Careful analyses of juvenile court cases in the United States shows that economic conditions rather than family composition influenced children's delinquency (Chilton and Markle, 1972). Statistical controls for the mothers' age and poverty have been found to remove effects attributed to single-parent families (Crockett et al., 1993). Furthermore, the significance of being born to a single mother has changed dramatically over the past 30 years. In 1970, 10.7 percent of all births in the United States were to unmarried women (U.S. Census Bureau, 1977). By 1997, births to unmarried women accounted for 32.4 percent of U.S. births (U.S. Census Bureau, 1999). As Rutter and colleagues (1998:185) noted about similar statistics in the United Kingdom: "It cannot be assumed that the risks for antisocial behavior (from being born to a single parent) evident in studies of children born several decades ago will apply to the present generation of births." Recent work seems to bear out this conclusion. Gorman-Smith and colleagues found no association between single parenthood and delinquency in a poor, urban U.S. community (Gorman-Smith et al., 1999).

Nevertheless, children in single-parent families are more likely to be exposed to other criminogenic influences, such as frequent changes in the resident father figure (Johnson, 1987; Stern et al., 1984). Single parents often find it hard to get assistance (Ensminger et al., 1983; Spicer and Hampe, 1975). If they must work to support themselves and their families, they are likely to have difficulty providing supervision for their children. Poor supervision is associated with the development of delinquency (Dornbusch et al., 1985; Glueck and Glueck, 1950; Hirschi, 1969; Jensen, 1972; Maccoby, 1958; McCord, 1979, 1982). Summarizing their work on race, family structure, and delinquency in white and black families, Matsueda and Heimer (1987:836) noted: "Yet in both racial groups nonintact homes influence delinquency through a similar process—by attenuating parental supervision, which in turn increases delinquent companions, prodelinquent definitions, and, ultimately, delinquent behavior." It looks as if the effects of living with a single parent vary with the amount of supervision, as well as the emotional and economic resources that the parent is able to bring to the situation.

A number of studies have found that children born to teenage mothers are more likely to be not only delinquent, but also chronic juvenile offenders (Farrington and Loeber, 1999; Furstenberg et al., 1987; Kolvin et al., 1990; Maynard, 1997; Nagin et al., 1997). An analysis of children born in 1974 and 1975 in Washington state found that being born to a mother under age 18 tripled the risk of being chronic offender. Males born to unmarried mothers under age 18 were 11 times more likely to become chronic juvenile offenders than were males born to married mothers over the age of 20 (Conseur et al., 1997).

What accounts for the increase in risk from having a young mother? Characteristics of women who become teenage parents appear to account for some of the risk. Longitudinal studies in both Britain and the United States have found that girls who exhibit antisocial behavior are at increased risk of teenage motherhood, of having impulsive liaisons with antisocial men, and of having parenting difficulties (Maughan and Lindelow, 1997; Quinton et al., 1993; Quinton and Rutter, 1988). In Grogger's analysis of data from the National Longitudinal Study of youth, both within-family comparisons and multivariate analysis showed that the characteristics and backgrounds of the women who became teenage mothers accounted for a large part of the risk of their offsprings' delinquency (Grogger, 1997), but the age at which the mother gave birth also contributed to the risk. A teenager who becomes pregnant is also more likely than older mothers to be poor, to be on welfare, to have curtailed her education, and to deliver a baby with low birthweight. Separately or together, these correlates of teenage parenthood have been found to increase risk for delinquency (Rutter et al., 1998). Nagin et al. (1997), in an analysis of data from the Cambridge Study in Delinquent Development, found that the risk of criminality was increased for children in large families born to women who began childbearing as a teenager. They concluded that "the onset of early childbearing is not a cause of children's subsequent problem behavior, but rather is a marker for a set of behaviors and social forces that give rise to adverse consequences for the life chances of children" (Nagin et al., 1997:423).

Children raised in families of four or more children have an increased risk of delinquency (Farrington and Loeber, 1999; Rutter and Giller, 1983). It has been suggested that large family size is associated with less adequate discipline and supervision of children, and that it is the parenting difficulties that account for much of the association with delinquency (Farrington and Loeber, 1999). Work by Offord (1982) points to the influence of delinquent siblings rather than to parenting qualities. Rowe and Farrington (1997), in an analysis of a London longitudinal study, found that there was a tendency for antisocial individuals to have large families. The effect of family size on delinquency was reduced when parents' criminality was taken into account.

Family Interaction

Even in intact, two-parent families, children may not receive the supervision, training, and advocacy needed to ensure a positive developmental course. A number of studies have found that poor parental management and disciplinary practices are associated with the development of delinquent behavior. Failure to set clear expectations for children's behavior, inconsistent discipline, excessively severe or aggressive discipline, and poor monitoring and supervision of children predict later delinquency (Capaldi and Patterson, 1996; Farrington, 1989; Hawkins et al., 1995b; McCord, 1979). As Patterson (1976, 1995) indicates through his research, parents who nag or use idle threats are likely to generate coercive systems in which children gain control through misbehaving. Several longitudinal studies investigating the effects of punishment on aggressive behavior have shown that physical punishments are more likely to result in defiance than compliance (McCord, 1997b; Power and Chapieski, 1986; Strassberg et al., 1994). Perhaps the best grounds for believing that family interaction influences delinquency are programs that alter parental management techniques and thereby benefit siblings as well as reduce delinquent behavior by the child whose conduct brought the parents into the program (Arnold et al., 1975; Kazdin, 1997; Klein et al., 1977; Tremblay et al., 1995).

Consistent discipline, supervision, and affection help to create well-socialized adolescents (Austin, 1978; Bender, 1947; Bowlby, 1940; Glueck and Glueck, 1950; Goldfarb, 1945; Hirschi, 1969; Laub and Sampson, 1988; McCord, 1991; Sampson and Laub, 1993). Furthermore, reductions in delinquency between the ages of 15 and 17 years appear to be related to friendly interaction between teenagers and their parents, a situation that seems to promote school attachment and stronger family ties (Liska and Reed, 1985). In contrast, children who have suffered parental neglect have an increased risk of delinquency. Widom (1989) and McCord (1983) both found that children who had been neglected were as likely as those who had been physically abused to commit violent crimes later in life. In their review of many studies investigating relationships between socialization in families and juvenile delinquency, Loeber and Stouthamer-Loeber (1986) concluded that parental neglect had the largest impact.

Child abuse, as well as neglect, has been implicated in the development of delinquent behavior. In three quite different prospective studies from different parts of the country, childhood abuse and neglect have been found to increase a child's risk of delinquency (Maxfield and Widom, 1996; Smith and Thornberry, 1995; Widom, 1989; Zingraff et al., 1993). These studies examined children of different ages, cases of childhood abuse and neglect from different time periods, different definitions of child abuse and neglect, and both official and self-reports of offending, but came to the same conclusions. The findings are true for girls as well as boys, and for black as well as for white children. In addition, abused and neglected children start offending earlier than children who are not abused or neglected, and they are more likely to become chronic offenders (Maxfield and Widom, 1996). Victims of childhood abuse and neglect are also at higher risk than other children of being arrested for a violent crime as a juvenile (Maxfield and Widom, 1996).

There are problems in carrying out scientific investigations of each of these components as predictors of juvenile delinquency. First, these behaviors are not empirically independent of one another. Parents who do not watch their young children consistently are less likely to prevent destructive or other unwanted behaviors and therefore more likely to punish. Parents who are themselves unclear about what they expect of their children are likely to be inconsistent and to be unclear in communications with their children. Parenting that involves few positive shared parent-child activities will often also involve less monitoring and more punishing. Parents who reject their children or who express hostility toward them are more likely to punish them. Parents who punish are more likely to punish too much (abuse).

Another problem is the lack of specificity of effects of problems in childrearing practices. In general, problems in each of these areas are likely to be associated with problems of a variety of types—performance and behavior in school, with peers, with authorities, and eventually with partners and offspring. There are also some children who appear to elicit punishing behavior from parents, and this may predate such parenting. Therefore, it is necessary to take account of children's behavior as a potential confounder of the relationship between early parenting and later child problems, because harsh parenting may be a response to a particular child's behavior (Tremblay, 1995). It is also possible that unnecessarily harsh punishment is more frequently and intensely used by parents who are themselves more aggressive and antisocial. Children of antisocial parents are at heightened risk for aggressive, antisocial, and delinquent behavior (e.g., McCord, 1991; Serbin et al., 1998).

Social Setting

Where a family lives affects the nature of opportunities that will be available to its members. In some communities, public transportation permits easy travel for those who do not own automobiles. Opportunities for employment and entertainment extend beyond the local boundaries. In other communities, street-corner gatherings open possibilities for illegal activities. Lack of socially acceptable opportunities leads to frustration and a search for alternative means to success. Community-based statistics show high correlations among joblessness, household disruption, housing density, infant deaths, poverty, and crime (Sampson, 1987, 1992).

Community variations may account for the fact that some varieties of family life have different effects on delinquency in different communities (Larzelere and Patterson, 1990; Simcha-Fagan and Schwartz, 1986). In general, consistent friendly parental guidance seems to protect children from delinquency regardless of neighborhoods. But poor socialization practices seem to be more potent in disrupted neighborhoods (McCord, 2000).

Neighborhoods influence children's behavior by providing examples of the values that people hold, and these examples influence children's perception of what is acceptable behavior. Communities in which criminal activities are common tend to establish criminal behavior as acceptable. Tolerance for gang activities varies by community (Curry and Spergel, 1988; Horowitz, 1987).

In sum, family life influences delinquency in a variety of ways. Children reared by affectionate, consistent parents are unlikely to commit serious crimes either as juveniles or as adults. Children reared by parents who neglect or reject them are likely to be greatly influenced by their community environments. When communities offer opportunities for and examples of criminal behavior, children reared by neglecting or rejecting parents are more likely to become delinquents. And delinquents are likely to become inadequate parents.

Peer Influences

A very robust finding in the delinquency literature is that antisocial behavior is strongly related to involvement with deviant peers. One longitudinal study reported that involvement with antisocial peers was the only variable that had a direct effect on subsequent delinquency other than prior delinquency (Elliott et al., 1985). Factors such as peer delinquent behavior, peer approval of deviant behavior, attachment or allegiance to peers, time spent with peers, and peer pressure for deviance have all been associated with adolescent antisocial behavior (Hoge et al., 1994; Thornberry et al., 1994). In other words, the effects of deviant peers on delinquency are heightened if adolescents believe that their peers approve of delinquency, if they are attached to those peers, if they spend much time with them, and if they perceive pressure from those peers to engage in delinquent acts.

There is a dramatic increase during adolescence in the amount of time adolescents spend with their friends, and peers become increasingly important during this developmental period. Moreover, peers appear to be most important during late adolescence, with their importance peaking at about age 17 and declining thereafter (Warr, 1993). Thus the decline in delinquency after about age 18 parallels the decline in the importance of peers, including those with deviant influences. Consistent with this view, in the longitudinal research of antisocial British youth by West and Farrington (1977), deviant youth reported that withdrawal from delinquent peer affiliations was an important factor in desistance from offending.

Peer influences appear to have a particularly strong relationship to delinquency in the context of family conflict. For example, adolescents' lack of respect for their parents influenced their antisocial behavior only because it led to increases in antisocial peer affiliations (Simmons et al., 1991). Patterson et al. (1991) showed that association with deviant peers in 6th grade could be predicted from poor parental monitoring and antisocial activity in 4th grade. And 6th grade association with deviant peers, in turn, predicted delinquency in 8th grade. In adolescence, susceptibility to peer influence is inversely related to interaction with parents (Kandel, 1980; Kandel and Andrews, 1987; Steinberg, 1987).

Other research suggests that adolescents usually become involved with delinquent peers before they become delinquent themselves (Elliott, 1994b; Elliott et al., 1985; Simons et al., 1994). In those cases in which an adolescent was delinquent prior to having delinquent friends, the delinquency was exacerbated by association with deviant peers (Elliott, 1994b; Elliott and Menard, 1996; Thornberry et al., 1993).

The influence of peers varies depending on the influence of parents. In general, peer influence is greater among children and adolescents who have little interaction with their parents (Kandel et al., 1978; Steinberg, 1987). Parents seem to have more influence on the use of drugs among working-class than among middle-class families, and among blacks more than whites (Biddle et al., 1980). Parents also appear to be more influential for the initial decision whether to use any drugs than for ongoing decisions about how and when to use them (Kandel and Andrews, 1987). Patterson and his coworkers emphasize both family socialization practices and association with deviant peers as having strong influences on the onset of delinquency. He hypothesized that "the more antisocial the child, the earlier he or she will become a member of a deviant peer group" (Patterson and Yoerger, 1997:152).

Adolescents report an increasing admiration of defiant and antisocial behavior and less admiration of conventional virtues and talents from age 10 to age 18. They also consistently report that their peers are more antisocial and less admiring of conventional virtues than they are. At age 11, boys report peer admiration of antisocial behavior at a level that is equivalent to what peers actually report at age 17 (Cohen and Cohen,

1996). Adolescents may be more influenced by what they think their peers are doing than by what they actually are doing (Radecki and Jaccard, 1995).

Not only may association with delinquent peers influence delinquent behavior, but also committing a crime with others—co-offending—is a common phenomenon among adolescents (Cohen, 1955; Reiss and Farrington, 1991; Reiss, 1988; Sarnecki, 1986). Much of this behavior occurs in relatively unstable pairings or small groups, not in organized gangs (Klein, 1971; Reiss, 1988). The fact that teenagers commit most of their crimes in pairs or groups does not, of course, prove that peers influence delinquency. Such an influence may be inferred, however, from the increase in crime that followed successful organization of gangs in Los Angeles (Klein, 1971). More direct evidence comes from a study by Dishion and his colleagues. Their research points to reinforcement processes as a reason why deviance increases when misbehaving youngsters get together. Delinquent and nondelinquent boys brought a friend to the laboratory. Conversations were videotaped and coded to show positive and neutral responses by the partner. Among the delinquent pairs, misbehavior received approving responses—in contrast with the nondelinquent dyads, who ignored talk about deviance (Dishion et al., 1996). In addition, reinforcement of deviant talk was associated with violent behavior, even after statistically controlling the boys' histories of antisocial behavior and parental use of harsh, inconsistent, and coercive discipline (Dishion et al., 1997).

The powerful influence of peers has probably not been adequately acknowledged in interventions designed to reduce delinquency and antisocial behavior. Regarding school-based interventions, among the least effective, and at times harmful, are those that aggregate deviant youth without adult supervision, such as in peer counseling and peer mediation (Gottfredson et al., 1998). Furthermore, high-risk youth are particularly likely to support and reinforce one another's deviant behavior (e.g., in discussions of rule breaking) when they are grouped together for intervention. Dishion and his colleagues have labeled this process "deviancy training," which was shown to be associated with later increases in substance use, delinquency, and violence (see the review in Dishion et al., 1999). They argued that youth who are reinforced for deviancy through laughter or attention, for example, are more likely to actually engage in deviant behavior. It is evident that intervenors need to give serious attention to the composition of treatment groups, especially in school settings. It may be more fruitful to construct intervention groups so that low- and moderate-risk youth are included with their high-risk counterparts to minimize the possibility of deviancy training and harmful intervention effects.

Studies of gang participants suggest that, compared with offenders who are not gang members, gang offenders tend to be younger when they begin their criminal careers, are more likely to be violent in public places, and are more likely to use guns (Maxson et al., 1985). Several studies have shown that gang membership is associated with high rates of criminal activities (e.g., Battin et al., 1998; Esbensen et al., 1993; Huff, 1998; Thornberry, 1998; Thornberry et al., 1993). These and other studies (e.g., Pfeiffer, 1998) also suggest that gangs facilitate violence. The heightened criminality and violence of gang members seem not to be reducible to selection. That is, gang members do tend to be more active criminals prior to joining a gang than are their nonjoining, even delinquent peers. During periods of gang participation, however, gang members are more criminally active and more frequently violent than they were either before joining or after leaving gangs. Furthermore, some evidence suggests that gang membership had the greatest effects on those who had not previously committed crimes (Zhang et al., 1999). The literature on gang participation, however, does not go much beyond suggesting that there is a process that facilitates antisocial, often violent, behavior. Norms and pressure to conform to deviant values have been suggested as mechanisms. How and why these are effective has received little attention.

COMMUNITY FACTORS

School Policies That Affect Juvenile Delinquency

Delinquency is associated with poor school performance, truancy, and leaving school at a young age (Elliott et al., 1978; Elliott and Voss, 1974; Farrington, 1986b; Hagan and McCarthy, 1997; Hawkins et al., 1998; Huizinga and Jakob-Chien, 1998; Kelly, 1971; Maguin and Loeber, 1996; Polk, 1975; Rhodes and Reiss, 1969; Thornberry and Christenson, 1984). To what extent do school policies contribute to these outcomes for high-risk youngsters? This section outlines what is known about the effects of some of the major school policies that have a particular impact on adolescent delinquents and those at risk for delinquency. The topics covered are grade retention, suspension, and expulsion as disciplinary techniques and academic tracking. These are complex topics about which there is a large literature. This section does not attempt to summarize that literature, but rather to highlight issues that appear to affect juvenile criminality.

Grade Retention

Grade retention refers to the practice of not promoting students to the next grade level upon completion of the current grade at the end of the school year. Low academic achievement is the most frequent reason given by teachers who recommend retention for their students (Jimerson et al., 1997).

There is no precise national estimate of the number of youths who experience grade retention, but the practice was widespread in the 1990s. Contrary to the public perception that few students fail a grade (Westbury, 1994), it is estimated that approximately 15 to 19 percent of students experience grade retention.

Despite the intuitive appeal of retention as a mechanism for improving student performance, the retention literature overwhelmingly concludes that it is not as effective as promotion. Smith and Shepard (1987:130) summarize the effects of grade retention as follows:

> The consistent conclusion of reviews is that children make progress during the year in which they repeat a grade, but not as much progress as similar children who were promoted. In controlled studies of the effect of nonpromotion on both achievement and personal adjustment, children who repeat a grade are worse off than comparable children who are promoted with their age-mates. Contrary to popular belief, the average negative effect of retention on achievement is even greater than the negative effect on emotional adjustment and self-concept.

Aside from the effectiveness issue, there are other negative consequences of retention. Retention increases the cost of educating a pupil (Smith and Shepard, 1987). According to Smith and Shepard (1987), alternatives to retention, such as tutoring and summer school, are both more effective and less costly. Retention has negative effects on the emotional adjustment of retainees. For example, Yamamoto and Byrnes (1984) reported that next to blindness and the death of a parent, children rated the prospect of retention as the most stressful event they could suffer. Retained students have more negative attitudes about school and develop characteristics of "learned helplessness," whereby they blame themselves for their failure and show low levels of persistence. There is a consistent relationship between retention and school dropout (Roderick, 1994; Shepard and Smith, 1990). Dropouts are five times more likely to have repeated a grade than nondropouts, and students who repeat two grades have nearly a 100 percent probability of dropping out. Finally, there are issues of fairness and equity, in that males and ethnic minority children are more likely to be retained (Jimerson et al., 1997).

School Suspension and Expulsion

Unlike grade retention, which is a school policy primarily for young children in the early elementary grades who display academic problems, suspension and expulsion are mainly directed toward older (secondary school) students whose school difficulties manifest themselves as behavioral problems. Both suspension and expulsion are forms of school exclusion, with the latter being presumably reserved for the most serious offenses.

Supporters of suspension argue that, like any other disciplinary action, suspension reduces the likelihood of misbehavior for the period immediately after suspension and that it can serve as a deterrent to other potentially misbehaving students. Opponents of suspension view the consequences of this disciplinary action as far outweighing any potential benefits. Some of the consequences cited include loss of self-respect, increased chances of coming into contact with a delinquent subculture, the vicious cyclical effects of being unable to catch up with schoolwork, and the stigma associated with suspension once the target child returns to school (Williams, 1989). Furthermore, most investigations of school suspensions have found that serious disciplinary problems are quite rarely the cause of suspension (Cottle, 1975; Kaeser, 1979; McFadden et al., 1992). The majority of suspensions in districts with high suspension rates are for behavior that is not threatening or serious.

The probability of being suspended is unequal among students. Urban students have the highest suspension rates, suburban students have the second highest rates, and rural school students have the lowest rates (Wu et al., 1982). Suspension rates also vary according to sex, race, socioeconomic background, and family characteristics. Male students in every kind of school and education level are about three times more likely to be suspended as females. Suspension rates also vary by race. Statistics indicate that minority students are suspended disproportionately compared with their share in the population and their share of misbehavior, and these racial disparities have the greatest impact on black students; their rate of suspension is over twice that of other ethnic groups, including whites, Hispanics, and Asians (Williams, 1989). Furthermore, black students are likely to receive more severe forms of suspension than other students, even for similar behaviors requiring disciplinary action. In one study, for example, white students were more likely to receive in-school suspension than out-of-school suspension, whereas the reverse pattern was true for black students who had violated school rules (McFadden et al., 1992). This inequality in treatment exists even when factors such as poverty, behavior and attitudes, academic performance, parental attention, and school governance are considered. Students at the lower end of the socioeconomic spectrum tend to be more frequently suspended. Many suspended students come from single-parent families in which the parent had less than a 10th grade education.

Suspended students frequently have learning disabilities or inadequate academic skills. Wu et al. (1982) noted a positive relationship between the student suspension rate in a school and the average percentage of students of low ability reported by all teachers in a school. Low-ability students are suspended more than expected, given the number of incidents of misbehavior attributed to them. According to Wu et al. (1982), this phenomenon appears to work in either of two ways. If a student's academic performance is below average, the probability of being suspended increases. And if a school places considerable emphasis on the academic ability of its students, the probability of suspension increases.

Although there is not very much recent empirical research on the effects of school suspension, it appears to be especially detrimental to low-achieving students who may misbehave because they are doing poorly in school. Nor does suspension appear to reduce the behavior it is designed to punish. For example, McFadden et al. (1992) reported that the rate of recidivism remained extremely high across all groups of suspended students in their large study of a Florida school district. Less than 1 percent of disciplined youngsters were one-time offenders, 75 percent were cited for one to five subsequent events during the school year, and 25 percent engaged in more than five serious misbehaviors.

There appear to be clear biases in the use of suspension as a disciplinary action, with black students more likely to be the target of this bias. In the McFadden et al. (1992) study, white students were more likely than their black counterparts to be referred for such misbehaviors as truancy, defiance of authority, and fighting. However, it was the black students who were disproportionately more likely to receive the most severe sanctions, including corporal punishment and out-of-school suspension. As these authors state: "Even though black pupils accounted for only 36.7% of the disciplinary referrals, they received 54.1% of the corporal punishment and 43.9% of the school suspensions, but only 23.1% of the internal suspensions. Additionally, 44.6% of all black pupils referred received corporal punishment, compared to only 21.7% of white pupils and 22.7% of Hispanic pupils" (p. 144).

In sum, the literature reveals that school suspension is academically detrimental, does not contribute to a modification of misbehavior, and is disproportionately experienced by black males, among students who misbehave.

In recent years, expulsion has become a part of the debate on school discipline that has accompanied the rising concern about school violence, particularly that related to weapons possession and increasingly defiant, aggressive behavior by students in school. One result of this debate has been what Morrison et al. (1997) refer to as "zero-tolerance" disciplinary policies. In California, for example, principals and superintendents are legally obligated to recommend expulsion from the school district for any student who commits certain offenses, such as bringing weapons to school, brandishing a knife at another person, or unlawfully selling illegal drugs (California Department of Education, 1996-Education Code Section 48900). Such a policy may be expected to increase expulsion given that school officials are required to recommend it in these cases.

Characteristics of children who are expelled parallel those of children who are suspended from school. Students who are expelled tend to be in grades 8 through 12 (Bain and MacPherson, 1990; Hayden and Ward, 1996). There is a fairly substantial group of younger schoolchildren expelled from school; most of them come from the higher age range of students in elementary school. Expulsion is, however, primarily a secondary school phenomenon. About 80 to 90 percent of expelled students are boys, urban students are expelled at a higher rate that students from suburban and rural areas, and minority students are more likely to be expelled than white students.

Morrison and D'Incau (1997) specified four factors related to school adjustment that predicted behavior resulting in recommendation for expulsion. The first is academic performance; poor grade point average, particularly in English and math, and low achievement scores appear to be related to behavior that leads to expulsion. The second is attendance; many expelled students were habitual truants. The third is discipline; many students who experienced expulsion had records of previous suspension. The last factor is special education history; approximately 25 percent of expelled students were either currently, in the past, or in the process of being determined as eligible for special education services.

When children are suspended or expelled from school, their risk for delinquency increases. Exclusion from school makes it more difficult for a child to keep up with academic subjects. Furthermore, with extra time out of school, children are likely to have more time without supervision, and therefore be in a situation known to encourage crime. Effects of school suspension seem to extend beyond childhood. Even after accounting for juvenile criminality, in a national sample of male high school graduates, those who had been suspended were more likely to be incarcerated by the age of 30 (Arum and Beattie, 1999).

School Tracking

Academic tracking, also known as "ability grouping" or "streaming," describes teaching practices whereby students who seem to be similar in ability are grouped together for instruction. The idea is to reduce the range of individual differences in class groups in order to simplify the task of teaching. Informal tracking is common in elementary schools. For example, teachers may divide children into reading groups based on their reading skills. Some schools divide students into classrooms based on their assumed ability to learn. These groupings typically also set off upper- and middle-class white children from all others. Because of the fluidity of learning, the particular group into which a child is placed reflects the opinions of the person making the placement at least as much as the ability of the child (see Ball et al., 1984).

Unlike retention, which has been employed mostly in elementary school, and suspension and expulsion, which are largely secondary school phenomena, tracking has proliferated at all levels of schooling in American education. According to Slavin (1987), the practice is nearly universal in some form in secondary schools and very common in elementary schools. A good deal of informal evidence shows that when children considered to be slow learners are grouped together, they come to see themselves in an unfavorable light. Such self-denigration contributes to dislike for school, to truancy, and even to delinquency (Berends, 1995; Gold and Mann, 1972; Kaplan and Johnson, 1991).

Reviews of the effects of tracking in secondary school reach four general conclusions, all suggesting that the impact is largely negative for students in low tracks (see Oakes, 1987). Students in the low-track classes show poorer achievement than their nontracked counterparts. Slavin (1990) found no achievement advantage among secondary school students in high- or average-track classes over their peers of comparable ability in nontracked classes. Rosenbaum (1976) studied the effects of tracking on IQ longitudinally and found that test scores of students in low tracks became homogenized, with a lower mean score over time. Furthermore, he found that students in low tracks tend to be less employable and earn lower wages than other high school graduates; they also often suffer diminished self-esteem and lowered aspirations, and they come to hold more negative attitudes about school. These emotional consequences greatly increase the likelihood of dropping out of school and engaging in delinquent behavior (both in and out of school). One of the clearest findings in research on academic tracking in secondary school is that disproportionate numbers of poor and ethnic minority youngsters (particularly black and Hispanic) are placed in low-ability or noncollege prep tracks (Oakes, 1987). Even within the low-ability (e.g., vocational) tracks, minority students are frequently trained for the lowest-level jobs. At the same time, minority youngsters are consistently underrepresented in programs for the talented and gifted. These disparities occur whether placements are based on standardized test scores or on counselor and teacher recommendations. Oakes and other sociologists of education (e.g., Gamoran, 1992; Kilgore, 1991; Rosenbaum, 1976) have argued that academic tracking frequently operates to perpetuate racial inequality and social stratification in American society.

It is quite evident that all of the policies reviewed here are associated with more negative than positive effects on children at risk for delinquency. As policies to deal with low academic achievement or low ability, neither retention nor tracking leads to positive benefits for students who are experiencing academic difficulty and may reinforce ethnic stereotypes among students who do well. As policies to deal with school misbehavior, neither suspension nor expulsion appears to reduce undesired behavior, and both place excluded children at greater risk for delinquency. Furthermore, every policy covered in this overview has been found to impact ethnic minority youngsters disproportionately.

Neighborhood

Growing up in an adverse environment increases the likelihood that a young person will become involved in serious criminal activity during adolescence. Existing research points strongly to the relationship between certain kinds of residential neighborhoods and high levels of crime among young people. Research also points to a number of mechanisms that may account for this association between neighborhood and youth crime. While more research is needed to improve understanding of the mechanisms involved, the link between neighborhood environment and serious youth crime is sufficiently clear to indicate a need for close attention to neighborhood factors in the design of prevention and control efforts.

Two different kinds of research point to the importance of social environment in the generation of antisocial behavior and crime. First, research on the characteristics of communities reveals the extremely unequal geographic distribution of criminal activity. Second, research on human development points consistently to the importance of environment in the emergence of antisocial and criminal behavior. While researchers differ on their interpretation of the exact ways in which personal factors and environment interact in the process of human development, most agree on the continuous interaction of person and environment over time as a fundamental characteristic of developmental processes. Although certain persons and families may be strongly at risk for criminal behavior in any environment, living in a neighborhood where there are high levels of poverty and crime increases the risk of involvement in serious crime for all children growing up there.

This section reviews various strands of research on neighborhoods and crime and on the effects of environment on human development for the purpose of evaluating the contributions of neighborhood environment to patterns of youth crime and prospects for its prevention and control.

Neighborhood Concentrations of Serious Youth Crime

Crime and delinquency are very unequally distributed in space. The geographic concentration of crime occurs at various levels of aggregation, in certain cities and counties and also in certain neighborhoods within a given city or county. For example, cities with higher levels of poverty, larger and more densely settled populations, and higher proportions of unmarried men consistently experience higher homicide rates than those that do not share these characteristics (Land et al., 1990). Serious youth crime in recent years has also been concentrated in certain urban areas. At the peak of the recent epidemic of juvenile homicide, a quarter of all apprehended offenders in the entire United States were arrested in just five counties, containing the cities of Los Angeles, Chicago, Houston, Detroit, and New York. In contrast, during that same year, 84 percent of counties in the United States reported no juvenile homicides (Sickmund et al., 1997).

The concentration of serious crime, especially juvenile crime, in certain neighborhoods within a given city is just as pronounced as the concentration in certain cities. A great deal of research over a period of many decades employing a wide range of methods has documented the geographic concentration of high rates of crime in poor, urban neighborhoods. Classic studies established the concentration of arrests (Shaw and McKay, 1942) and youth gang activity (Thrasher, 1927) in poor neighborhoods located in inner cities. This relationship has been confirmed in replication studies over the years (Bordua, 1958; Chilton, 1964; Lander, 1954; Sampson and Groves, 1989).

In addition to this correlation of neighborhood poverty levels and high crime rates at any given time, research has also found that change in neighborhood poverty levels for the worse is associated with increasing rates of crime and delinquency (Schuerman and Kobrin, 1986; Shannon, 1986). The causal relationship between increases in neighborhood poverty and increases in crime can move in either direction. In the earlier stages of the process of neighborhood deterioration, increases in poverty may cause increases in crime, while, in later stages, crime reaches such a level that those who can afford to move out do so, thereby increasing the poverty rate even further.

Other social characteristics of poor urban neighborhoods change over time and between nations. In the early part of the 20th century in the United States, poor urban neighborhoods tended to be quite mixed in ethnicity (e.g., Italian, Irish, Polish, Jewish), reflecting an era of immigration, and were often located in the older, central parts of cities that were expanding rapidly in outward, concentric waves (Shaw and McKay, 1942). Since the 1950s, poor, urban neighborhoods in the United States have been much more likely to be dominated by a single cultural group. Blacks and Hispanics, in particular, have experienced an extraordinary degree of residential segregation and concentration in the poorest areas of large cities as a result of racial discrimination in labor and housing markets (Massey and Denton, 1993). In their reanalysis of the Chicago data collected by Shaw and McKay (1942), Bursik and Webb (1982) found that after 1950, changing rates of community racial composition provided a better predictor of juvenile delinquency rates than did the ecological variables.

Poverty and residential segregation are not always urban phenomena. American Indians also experience a great degree of residential segregation and poverty, but rather than in cities, they are segregated on poor, rural reservations. Elsewhere in the developed world, residential concentrations of poor people occur on the periphery of large urban areas, rather than in the center. The construction of large public housing estates in England following World War II produced this kind of urban configuration (Bottoms and Wiles, 1986), in contrast to the concentration on inner-city public housing projects in the United States.

Two important qualifications must be noted with respect to the well-documented patterns of local concentrations of crime and delinquency. First, these patterns do not hold true for minor forms of delinquency. Since a large majority of all adolescent males break the law at some point, such factors as neighborhood, race, and social class do not differentiate very well between those who do or do not commit occasional minor offenses (Elliott and Ageton, 1980).

Second, although some areas have particularly high rates of deviance, in no area do all or most children commit seroius crimes (Elliott et al., 1996; Furstenburg et al., 1999). Still, the concentration of serious juvenile crime in a relatively few residential neighborhoods is well documented and a legitimate cause for concern, both to those living in these high-risk neighborhoods and to the wider society.

Neighborhoods as Mediators of Race and Social Class Disparities in Offending

While studies using differing methods and sources of data are not in agreement on the magnitude of differences in rates of involvement in youth crime across racial, ethnic, and social class categories, most research shows that race, poverty, and residential segregation interact to predict delinquency rates. For example, the three most common approaches to measurement—self-report surveys, victimization surveys, and official arrest and conviction statistics—all indicate high rates of serious offending among young black Americans. There is substantial reason to believe that these disparate offending rates are directly related to the community conditions under which black children grow up. There is no other racial or ethnic group in the United States of comparable size whose members are nearly as likely to grow up in neighborhoods of concentrated urban poverty (Wilson, 1987). Summarizing this situation, Sampson (1987:353-354) wrote: "the worst urban contexts in which whites reside with respect to poverty and family disruption are considerably better off than the *mean* levels for black communities." Although there are more poor white than black families in absolute number, poor white families are far less likely to live in areas where most of their neighbors are also poor. Studies that show stronger effects of race than of class on delinquency must be interpreted in light of the additional stresses suffered by poor blacks as a result of residential segregation.

In comprehensive reviews, scholars have found that adding controls for concentrated neighborhood poverty can entirely eliminate neighborhood-level associations between the proportion of blacks and crime rates. Without controls for concentrated poverty, this relationship is quite strong (Sampson, 1997; Short, 1997). Such research strongly indicates that the unique combination of poverty and residential segregation suffered by black Americans is associated with high rates of crime through the mediating pathway of neighborhood effects on families and children.

These deleterious neighborhood effects have been studied mostly with respect to blacks, but, as the United States has experienced renewed immigration, evidence has also begun to point to similar problems among newer groups of immigrants from Asia, Europe, and Latin America. Much of the evidence at this point is contained in ethnographic studies of youthful gang members and drug dealers (Bourgois, 1995; Chin, 1996; Moore, 1978, 1991; Padilla, 1992; Pinderhughes, 1997; Sullivan, 1989; Vigil, 1988; Vigil and Yun, 1990).

Neighborhood-Level Characteristics Associated with High Rates of Crime and Delinquency

Although the relationship between neighborhood poverty and crime is robust over time and space, a number of other social characteristics of neighborhoods are also associated with elevated levels of crime and delinquency. Factors such as concentrations of multifamily and public housing, unemployed and underemployed men, younger people, and single-parent households tend to be linked to higher crime rates (Sampson, 1987; Wilson, 1985). These social characteristics frequently go along with overall high levels of poverty, but they also vary among both poor and nonpoor neighborhoods and help to explain why neighborhoods with similar average income levels can have different rates of crime.

Recent research has also begun to examine the social atmosphere of neighborhoods and has found significant relationships with crime rates. Neighborhoods in which people tell interviewers that they have a greater sense of collective efficacy—the sense that they can solve problems in cooperation with their neighbors if they have to—have lower crime rates, even when controlling for poverty levels and other neighborhood characteristics (Sampson et al., 1997).

The number and type of local institutions have often been thought to have an effect on neighborhood safety, and some research seems to confirm this. High concentrations of barrooms are clearly associated with crime (Roncek and Maier, 1991). One recent study has also found a crime-averting effect of youth recreation facilities when comparing neighborhoods with otherwise very high rates of crime and criminogenic characteristics to one another (Peterson et al., 2000). Since assessing the number, characteristics, and quality of neighborhood institutions is quite difficult, this remains an understudied area of great importance, given its considerable theoretical and practical interest.

One type of pernicious neighborhood institution, the youth gang, has been studied extensively and is clearly associated with, though by no means synonymous with, delinquency and crime. Although it is true that an adolescent's involvement with youth gangs is associated with a greatly increased risk of criminal behavior, that risk also accompanies association with delinquent peer groups more generally. A very high proportion of youth crime, much higher than for adults, is committed by groups of co-offenders (Elliott and Menard, 1996; Miller, 1982). Most of these delinquent peer groups do not fit the popular stereotypes of youth gangs, with the attendant ritual trappings of distinctive group names, costumes, hand signs, and initiation ceremonies (Sullivan, 1983, 1996). The broader category of delinquent peer groups, most of which are not ritualized youth gangs, drives up neighborhood delinquency rates.

Comparative neighborhood studies, examining the presence of delinquent and unsupervised adolescent peer groups, have found that these groups are more likely to be found in poor neighborhoods. The strength of this finding is such that the presence of these groups appears to be one of the major factors connecting neighborhood poverty and delinquency (Elliott and Menard, 1996; Sampson and Groves, 1989).

Although most adolescent co-offending is committed in the context of delinquent peer groups that are not ritualized youth gangs, the emergence of ritualized gangs in a neighborhood appears to be associated with even higher levels of offending than occur when ritualized gangs are not present (Spergel, 1995; Thornberry, 1998). For this reason, the recent spread of youth gangs across the United States is cause for serious concern. In the decade from the mid-1980s through the mid-1990s, youth gangs emerged in a growing number of cities in the United States, not only in large cities, but also in smaller cities and towns (Klein, 1995; National Youth Gang Center, 1997).

Despite widespread rumors and mass media allegations, this spread of youth gangs does not appear to be the result of systematic outreach, recruitment, and organization from one city to another. The fact that groups calling themselves by similar names, such as Bloods and Crips, have been spreading from city to city may have very little to do with conscious efforts by members of those groups in Los Angeles to build criminal organizations in other cities. Movies and popular music, rather than direct connections between cities, seem to be at least partly responsible for this copying of gang terminology between cities (Decker and Van Winkle, 1996).

Ethnographic Perspectives on Neighborhoods and Development

A second stream of research that examines adolescent development from the perspective of neighborhood environment consists of ethnographic field studies of delinquent individuals and groups growing up in high-crime neighborhoods. These studies range from classic studies conducted in the 1920s and 1930s (Shaw, 1930; Whyte, 1943), through a second wave in the 1960s (Short and Strodtbeck, 1965; Suttles, 1968) and a more recent wave since the late 1980s (Bourgois, 1995; Chin, 1996; Moore, 1978, 1991; Padilla, 1992; Pinderhughes, 1997; Sullivan, 1989; Vigil, 1988; Vigil and Yun, 1990).

Drawing conclusions from these studies about neighborhood effects on child and adolescent development must be approached carefully, because these studies were primarily designed to describe systems of activity and interaction rather than processes of personal development. As a result, there are many limitations on using this body of research for the purpose of examining neighborhood effects on development, chief among them the predominant focus on single, high-crime areas and the focus within those areas on those engaged in delinquent and criminal activity. Because of this double selection on the dependent variables of both area and individual criminal behavior, these studies generally do not allow systematic comparison between high-crime and low-crime areas or between nondelinquent and delinquent youth within areas.

Despite these limitations, the authors of the studies virtually always end up attributing the ongoing nature of delinquent activity in the areas studied to the influences of the local area on development, particularly among males. In other words, studies not designed primarily to examine development appeal to neighborhood-level influences on development in order to explain their findings. These conclusions about neighborhood influence on development generally emerge from a much closer scrutiny of the social contexts of development made possible by the in-depth approach of case study and qualitative methods (Sullivan, 1998; Yin, 1989).

One exception to the general lack of comparisons across neighborhoods in the ethnographic studies of development is Sullivan's systematic comparison of three groups of criminally active youths in different neighborhoods of New York City. Using this comparative approach, he demonstrated close links between the array of legitimate and illegitimate opportunities in each place and the developmental trajectories of boys who became involved in delinquency and crime. Even though the early stages of involvement were similar in all three areas, youths from the white, working-class area aged out of crime much faster than their black and Hispanic peers living in neighborhoods characterized by racial and ethnic segregation, concentrated poverty, adult joblessness, and single-parent households. The youths from the more disadvantaged areas had less access to employment and more freedom to experiment with illegal activity as a result of lower levels of informal social control in their immediate neighborhoods (Sullivan, 1989).

Neighborhood-Level Concentrations of Developmental Risk Factors

If neighborhood effects are defined as the influence of neighborhood environment on individual development net of personal and family characteristics, then the amount of variation left over to be attributed to neighborhood in a given study can vary a great deal according to the data and methods used. As many researchers note, neighborhood effects may be mediated by personal and family factors (see, e.g., Farrington and Loeber, 1999); however, it is also necessary to examine whether personal and family characteristics are themselves affected by neighborhood environment. To the extent that this is the case, then neighborhoods affect individual development through their effects on such things as the formation of enduring personal characteristics during early childhood and the family environments in which children grow up. From this perspective, efforts such as those described earlier to measure neighborhood effects net of personal and family characteristics may substantially underestimate neighborhood effects as a result of artificially separating personal and family characteristics from those neighborhood environments. Similarly, if the subsets are not separately analyzed, neighborhood effects will be artificially minimized if some, but not all, types of family constellations increase the impact of neighborhood conditions (McCord, 2000).

A number of studies demonstrate neighborhood concentrations of risk factors for impaired physical and mental health and for the development of antisocial behavior patterns. To date, little research has been able to trace direct pathways from these neighborhood risk factors through child and adolescent development, although some of the larger ongoing studies, such as the Project on Human Development in Chicago Neighborhoods, are collecting the kind of comprehensive data on biological and social aspects of individual development as well as on the characteristics of a large number of ecological areas that could make this kind of analysis possible (Tonry et al., 1991). Nonetheless, existing research does indicate a number of ways in which deleterious conditions for individual development are concentrated at the neighborhood level. Furthermore, the neighborhoods in which they are concentrated are the same ones that have concentrations of serious youth crime. The risks involved begin for individuals in these areas before birth and continue into adulthood. They include child health problems, parental stress, child abuse, and exposure to community violence.

Neighborhoods with high rates of poverty and crime are often also neighborhoods with concentrations of health problems among children. In New York City, for example, there is a high degree of correlation at the neighborhood level of low birthweight and infant mortality with rates of violent death (Wallace and Wallace, 1990). Moffitt (1997) has pointed to a number of conditions prevalent in inner-city neighborhoods that are capable of inflicting neuropsychological damage, including fetal exposure to toxic chemicals, which are disproportionately stored in such areas, and child malnutrition. Thus, even to the extent that some neighborhoods have larger proportions of persons with clinically identifiable physical and psychological problems, these problems may themselves be due to neighborhood conditions. Thus it can be difficult to disentangle individual developmental risk factors from neighborhood risk factors.

Similarly, some parenting practices that contribute to the development of antisocial and criminal behavior are themselves concentrated in certain areas. McLloyd (1990) has reviewed a wide range of studies documenting the high levels of parental stress experienced by low-income black mothers who, as we have already seen, experience an extremely high degree of residential segregation (Massey and Denton, 1993). This parental stress may in turn lead, in some cases, to child abuse, which contributes to subsequent delinquent and criminal behavior (Widom, 1989). Child abuse is also disproportionately concentrated in certain neighborhoods. Korbin and Coulton's studies of the distribution of child maltreatment in Cleveland neighborhoods have shown both higher rates in poorer neighborhoods and a moderating effect of age structure. Using a combination of qualitative and quantitative methods, they showed that neighborhoods with a younger age structure experienced higher rates of child maltreatment, as measured by reported child abuse cases and interviews in a subset of the neighborhoods, than other neighborhoods with similar average family income levels (Korbin and Coulton, 1997).

Recent research has begun to demonstrate high levels of exposure to community violence across a wide range of American communities (Singer et al., 1995), but the degree of exposure also varies by community and reaches extraordinary levels in some neighborhoods. Studies in inner-city neighborhoods have found that one-quarter or more of young people have directly witnessed confrontations involving serious, life-threatening acts of violence, while even larger proportions have witnessed attacks with weapons (Bell and Jenkins, 1993; Osofsky et al., 1993; Richters and Martinez, 1993; Selner-O'Hagan et al., 1998). Various outcomes of this kind of exposure to community violence have been identified. The most commonly cited of these include depressive disorders and posttraumatic stress syndrome, but some links have also been found to increases in aggressive and antisocial behavior (Farrell and Bruce, 1997). Experimental research has shown a pathway from exposure to violence to states of mind conducive to and associated with aggressive behavior, particularly a pattern of social cognition characterized as hostile attribution bias, in which people erroneously perceive others' behavior as threatening (Dodge et al., 1990).

Taken together, these studies point to a multitude of physical, psychological, and social stressors concentrated in the same, relatively few, highly disadvantaged neighborhood environments. Besides affecting people individually, these stressors may combine with and amplify one another, as highly stressed individuals encounter each other in crowded streets, apartment buildings, and public facilities, leading to an exponential increase in triggers for violence (Bernard, 1990). Agnew (1999), having demonstrated the effects of general psychological strain on criminal behavior in previous research, has recently reviewed a wide range of studies that point to just such an amplification effect at the community level.

Environmental and Situational Influences

Other aspects of the environment that have been examined as factors that may influence the risk of offending include drug markets, availability of guns, and the impact of violence in the media.

The presence of illegal drug markets increases the likelihood for violence at the points where drugs are exchanged for money (Haller, 1989). The rise in violent juvenile crime during the 1980s has been attributed to the increase in drug markets, particularly open-air markets for crack cocaine (Blumstein, 1995; National Research Council, 1993). Blumstein (1995) points out the coincidence in timing of the rise in drug arrests of nonwhite juveniles, particularly blacks, beginning in 1985, and the rise in juvenile, gun-related homicide rates, particularly among blacks. As mentioned earlier, Blumstein argues that the introduction of open-air crack cocaine markets in about 1985 may explain both trends. The low price of crack brought many low-income people, who could afford to buy only one hit at a time, into the cocaine market. These factors led to an increase in the number of drug transactions and a need for more sellers. Juveniles provided a ready labor force and were recruited into crack markets. Blumstein (1995:30) explains how this led to an increase in handgun carrying by juveniles:

> These juveniles, like many other participants in the illicit-drug industry, are likely to carry guns for self-protection, largely because that industry uses guns as an important instrument for dispute resolution. Also, the participants in the industry are likely to be carrying a considerable amount of valuable product—drugs or money derived from selling drugs—and are not likely to be able to call on the police if someone tries to rob them. Thus, they are forced to provide for their own defense; a gun is a natural instrument.
>
> Since the drug markets are pervasive in many inner-city neighborhoods, and the young people recruited into them are fairly tightly networked with other young people in their neighborhoods, it became easy for the guns to be diffused to other teenagers who go to the same school or who walk the same streets. These other young people are also likely to arm themselves, primarily for their own protection, but also because possession of a weapon may become a means of status-seeking in the community. This initiates an escalating process: as more guns appear in the community, the incentive for any single individual to arm himself increases.

Other researchers concur that juveniles responded to the increased threat of violence in their neighborhoods by arming themselves or joining gangs for self-protection and adopting a more aggressive interpersonal style (Anderson, 1990, 1994; Fagan and Wilkinson, 1998; Hemenway et al., 1996; Wilkinson and Fagan, 1996). The number of juveniles who report carrying guns has increased. In 1990, approximately 6 percent of teenage boys reported carrying a firearm in the 30 days preceding the survey (Centers for Disease Control and Prevention, 1991). By 1993, 13.7 percent reported carrying guns (Centers for Disease Control and Prevention, 1995). Hemenway et al. (1996) surveyed a sample of 7th and 10th graders in schools in high-risk neighborhoods in a Northeastern and a Midwestern city. Of these, 29 percent of 10th grade males and 23 percent of 7th grade males reported having carried a concealed gun, as did 12 percent of 10th grade females and 8 percent of 7th grade females. The overwhelming majority gave self-defense or protection as their primary reason for carrying weapons. Moreover, juveniles who reported living in a neighborhood with a lot of shootings or having a family member who had been shot were significantly more likely to carry a gun than other students. Additional student surveys also have found that protection is the most common reason given for carrying a gun (e.g., Centers for Disease Control and Prevention, 1993; Sheley and Wright, 1998).

By studying trends in homicide rates, several researchers have concluded that the increase in juvenile homicides during the late 1980s and early 1990s resulted from the increase in the availability of guns, in particular handguns, rather than from an increase in violent propensities of youth (Blumstein and Cork, 1996; Cook and Laub, 1998; Zimring, 1996). Certainly, assaults in which guns are involved are more likely to turn deadly than when other weapons or just fists are involved. The increase in gun use occurred for all types of youth homicides (e.g., family killings, gang-related killings, brawls and arguments). Furthermore, the rates of nonhandgun homicides remained stable; only handgun-related homicides increased.

Public concern about the role of media in producing misbehavior is as old as concern regarding the socialization of children. Although few believe that the media operate in isolation to influence crime, scientific studies show that children may imitate behavior, whether it is shown in pictures of real people or in cartoons or merely described in stories (Bandura, 1962, 1965, 1986; Maccoby, 1964, 1980). Prosocial as well as aggressive antisocial behavior has been inspired through the use of examples (Anderson, 1998; Eisenberg and Mussen, 1989; Eron and Huesmann, 1986; Huston and Wright, 1998; Staub, 1979). Thus media models can be seen as potentially influencing either risk or protectiveness of environments.

In addition to modeling behavior, exposure to media violence has been shown to increase fear of victimization and to desensitize witnesses to effects of violence (Slaby, 1997; Wilson et al., 1998). Children seem particularly susceptible to such effects, although not all children are equally susceptible. Violent video games, movies, and music lyrics have also been criticized as inciting violence among young people. Cooper and Mackie (1986) found that after playing a violent video game, 4th and 5th graders exhibited more aggression in play than did their classmates who had been randomly assigned to play with a nonviolent video game or to no video game. Anderson and Dill (2000) randomly assigned college students to play either a violent or a nonviolent video game that had been matched for interest, frustration, and difficulty. Students played the same game three times, for a total of 45 minutes, after which they played a competitive game that involved using unpleasant sound blasts against the rival player. After the second time, measures of the accessibility of aggressive concepts showed a cognitive effect of playing violent video games. After the third time, those who had played the violent video game gave longer blasts of the unpleasant sound, a result mediated by accessibility of aggression as a cognitive factor. The authors concluded that violent video games have adverse behavioral effects and that these occur through increasing the aggressive outlooks of participants.

None of these studies, however, finds direct connections between media exposure to violence and subsequent serious violent behavior. Steinberg (2000:37) summarized the literature on media and juvenile violence by noting: "exposure to violence in the media plays a significant, but very small, role in adolescents' actual involvement in violent activity. The images young people are exposed to may provide the material for violent fantasies and may, under rare circumstances, give young people concrete ideas about how to act out these impulses. But the violent impulses themselves, and the motivation to follow through on them, rarely come from watching violent films or violent television or from listening to violent music . . . . I know of no research that links the sort of serious violence this working group is concerned about with exposure to violent entertainment."

THE DEVELOPMENT OF DELINQUENCY IN GIRLS

Research on the development of conduct disorder, aggression, and delinquency has often been confined to studies of boys. Many of the individual factors found to be related to delinquency have not been well studied in girls. For example, impulsivity, which has been linked to the development of conduct problems in boys (Caspi et al., 1994; White et al., 1994), has scarcely been studied in girls (Keenan et al., in press).

Behavioral differences between boys and girls have been documented from infancy. Weinberg and Tronick (1997) report that infant girls exhibit better emotional regulation than infant boys, and that infant boys are more likely to show anger than infant girls. This may have implications for the development of conduct problems and delinquency. Although peer-directed aggressive behavior appears to be similar in both girls and boys during toddlerhood (Loeber and Hay, 1997), between the ages of 3 and 6, boys begin to display higher rates of physical aggression than do girls (Coie and Dodge, 1998). Girls tend to use verbal and indirect aggression, such as peer exclusion, ostracism, and character defamation (Bjorkqvist et al., 1992; Crick and Grotpeter, 1995), rather than physical aggression. Research by Pepler and Craig (1995), however, found that girls do use physical aggression against peers, but tend to hide it from adults. Through remote audiovisual recordings of children on a playground, they found the rates of bullying by girls and boys to be the same, although girls were less likely than boys to admit to the behavior in interviews.

Internalizing disorders, such as anxiety and depression, are more frequent in girls and may well overlap with their conduct problems (Loeber and Keenan, 1994; McCord and Ensminger, 1997). Theoreticians have suggested that adolescent females may direct rage and hurt inward as a reaction to abuse and maltreatment. These inward-directed feelings may manifest themselves in conduct problems, such as drug abuse, prostitution, and other self-destructive behaviors (Belknap, 1996).

Whether or not the rate of conduct problems and conduct disorder in girls is lower than that in boys remains to be definitively proven. Girls who do exhibit aggressive behavior or conduct disorder exhibit as much stability in that behavior and are as much at risk for later problems as are boys. Tremblay et al. (1992) found equally high correlations between aggression in early elementary school and later delinquency in boys and girls. Boys and girls with conduct disorder are also equally likely to qualify for later antisocial personality disorder (Zoccolillo et al., 1992).

Delinquency in girls, as well as boys, is often preceded by some form of childhood victimization (Maxfield and Widom, 1996; Smith and Thornberry, 1995; Widom, 1989). Some have speculated that one of the first steps in female delinquency is status offending (truancy, running away from home, being incorrigible), frequently in response to abusive situations in the home (Chesney-Lind and Shelden, 1998). Indeed, Chesney-Lind (1997) has written that status offenses, including running away, may play an important role in female delinquency. In what she refers to as the "criminalization of girls' survival strategies," Chesney-Lind (1989:11) suggests that young females run away from the violence and abuse in their homes and become vulnerable to further involvement in crime as a means of survival. In one community-based longitudinal study, however, a larger proportion of boys than of girls had left home prior to their sixteenth birthday (McCord and Ensminger, 1997). In a long-term follow-up of a sample of documented cases of childhood abuse and neglect, Kaufman and Widom (1999) reported preliminary results indicating that males and females are equally likely to run away from home, and that childhood sexual abuse was not more often associated with running away than other forms of abuse or neglect. However, the motivation for running away may differ for males and females. For example, females may be running away to escape physical or sexual abuse or neglect in their homes. For boys, running away may be an indirect consequence of childhood victimization or may be part of a larger constellation of antisocial and problem behaviors (Luntz and Widom, 1994).

From the small amount of research that has been done on girls, it appears that they share many risk factors for delinquency with boys. These risk factors include early drug use (Covington, 1998), association with delinquent peers (Acoca and Dedel, 1998), and problems in school (Bergsmann, 1994). McCord and Ensminger (1997) found, however, that, on average, girls were exposed to fewer risk factors (e.g., aggressiveness, frequent spanking, low I.Q., first-grade truancy, early leaving home, and racial discrimination) than were boys.

Delinquent girls report experiencing serious mental health problems, including depression and anxiety, and suicidal thoughts. In a study of delinquent girls conducted by Bergsmann (1994), fully half said that they had considered suicide, and some 64 percent of these had thought about it more than once.

In a survey of mental disorders in juvenile justice facilities, Timmons-Mitchell and colleagues (1997) compared the prevalence of disorders among a sample of males and females and found that the estimated prevalence of mental disorders among females was over three times that among males (84 versus 27 percent). The females in the sample scored significantly higher than males on scales of the Milton Adolescent Clinical Inventory, which measure suicidal tendency, substance abuse proneness, impulsivity, family dysfunction, childhood abuse, and delinquent predisposition. Timmons-Mitchell et al. (1997) concluded from these data that incarcerated female juveniles had significantly more mental health problems and treatment needs than their male counterparts.

Teen motherhood and pregnancy are also concerns among female juvenile offenders. Female delinquents become sexually active at an earlier age than females who are not delinquent (Greene, Peters and Associates, 1998). Sexual activity at an early age sets girls up for a host of problems, including disease and teenage pregnancy, that have far-reaching impacts on their lives and health. Teen mothers face nearly insurmountable challenges that undermine their ability to take adequate care of themselves and their families. Dropping out of school, welfare dependence, and living in poor communities are only a few of the consequences of teen motherhood. And the effects are not limited to one generation. Teen mothers are more likely than women who have children in their early 20s to have children who are incarcerated as adults (Grogger, 1997; Nagin et al., 1997; Robin Hood Foundation, 1996).

CONCLUSIONS

Although a large proportion of adolescents gets arrested and an even larger proportion commits illegal acts, only a small proportion commits serious crimes. Furthermore, most of those who engage in illegal behavior as adolescents do not become adult criminals.

Risk factors at the individual, social, and community level most likely interact in complex ways to promote antisocial and delinquent behavior in juveniles. Although there is some research evidence that different risk factors are more salient at different stages of child and adolescent development, it remains unclear which particular risk factors alone, or in combination, are most important to delinquency. It appears, however, that the more risk factors that are present, the higher the likelihood of delinquency. Particular risk factors considered by the panel are poor parenting practices, school practices that may contribute to school failure, and community-wide settings.

Poor parenting practices are important risk factors for delinquency. Several aspects of parenting have been found to be related to delinquency:

- neglect or the absence of supervision throughout childhood and adolescence;
- the presence of overt conflict or abuse;
- discipline that is inconsistent or inappropriate to the behavior; and
- a lack of emotional warmth in the family.

School failure is related to delinquency, and some widely used school practices are associated with school failure in high-risk children. These practices include tracking and grade retention, as well as suspension and expulsion. Minorities are disproportionately affected by these educational and social practices in schools.

Both serious crime and developmental risk factors for children and adolescents are highly concentrated in some communities. These communities are characterized by concentrated poverty. Residents of these communities often do not have access to the level of public resources available in the wider society, including good schools, supervised activities, and health services. Individual-level risk factors are also concentrated in these communities, including health problems, parental stress, and exposure to family and community violence. The combination of concentrated poverty and residential segregation suffered by ethnic minorities in some places contributes to high rates of crime.

Although risk factors can identify groups of adolescents whose probabilities for committing serious crimes are greater than average, they are not capable of identifying the particular individuals who will become criminals.

RECOMMENDATIONS

Delinquency is associated with poor school performance, truancy, and leaving school at a young age. Some pedagogical practices may exacerbate these problems. The available research on grade retention and tracking and the disciplinary practices of suspension and expulsion reveal that such policies have more negative than positive effects. For students already experiencing academic difficulty, tracking and grade retention have been found to further impair their academic performance. Furthermore, tracking does not appear to improve the academic performance of students in high tracks compared with similar students in schools that do not use tracking. Suspension and expulsion deny education in the name of discipline, yet these practices have not been shown to be effective in reducing school misbehavior. Little is known about the effects of these policies on other students in the school. Given the fact that the policies disproportionately affect minorities, such policies may unintentionally reinforce negative stereotypes.

Recommendation: Federal programs should be developed to promote alternatives to grade retention and tracking in schools.

Given that school failure has been found to be a precursor to delinquency, not enough research to date has specifically examined school policies, such as tracking, grade retention, suspension, and expulsion in terms of their effects on delinquent behavior in general. It is important that evaluations of school practices and policies consider their effects on aggressive and antisocial behavior, incuding delinquency. This type of research is particularly salient given the concern over school violence. Research on tracking should examine the effects on children and adolescents in all tracks, not only on those in low tracks.

Recommendation: A thorough review of the effects of school policies and pedagogical practices, such as grade retention, tracking, suspension, and expulsion, should be undertaken. This review should include the effects of such policies on delinquency, as well as the effects on educational attainment and school atmosphere and environment.

Prenatal exposure to alcohol, cocaine, heroin, and nicotine is associated with hyperactivity, attention deficit, and impulsiveness, which are risk factors for later antisocial behavior and delinquency. Biological insults suffered during the prenatal period may have some devastating effects on development. Consequently, preventive efforts during the prenatal period, such as preventing fetal exposure to alcohol and drugs, may have great benefits. Reducing alcohol and drug abuse among expectant parents may also improve their ability to parent, thus reducing family-related risk factors for delinquency.

Recommendation: Federal, state, and local governments should act to provide treatment for drug abuse (including alcohol and tobacco use) among pregnant women, particularly, adolescents.

Most longitudinal studies of delinquent behavior have begun after children enter school. Yet earlier development appears to contribute to problems that become apparent during the early school years. Much remains to be known about the extent to which potential problems can be identified at an early age.

Recommendation: Prospective longitudinal studies should be used to increase the understanding of the role of factors in prenatal, peri-natal, and early infant development on mechanisms that increase the likelihood of healthy development, as well as the development of antisocial behavior.

Research has shown that the greater the number of risk factors that are present, the higher the likelihood of delinquency. It is not clear, however, whether some risk factors or combinations of risk factors are more important than other risk factors or combinations in the development of delinquency. Furthermore, the timing, severity, and duration of risk factors, in interaction with the age, gender, and the environment in which the individual lives undoubtedly affect the behavioral outcomes. A better understanding of how risk factors interact is important for the development of prevention efforts, especially efforts in communities in which risk factors are concentrated.

Recommendation: Research on risk factors for delinquency needs to focus on effects of interactions among various risk factors. In particular, research on effects of differences in neighborhoods and their interactions with individual and family conditions should be expanded.

The panel recommends the following areas as needing particular research attention to increase understanding of the development of delinquency:

• Research on the development of language skills and the impact of delayed or poor language skills on the development of aggressive and antisocial behavior, including delinquency;

- Research on children's and adolescents' access to guns, in particular handguns, and whether that access influences attitudes toward or fear of crime;
- Research on ways to increase children's and adolescents' protective factors; and
- Research on the development of physical aggression regulation in early childhood.

Research on delinquency has traditionally focused on boys. Although boys are more likely to be arrested than girls, the rate of increase in arrest and incarceration has been much larger in recent years for girls than boys, and the seriousness of the crimes committed by girls has increased.

Recommendation: The Department of Justice should develop and fund a systematic research program on female juvenile offending. At a minimum, this program should include:

- Research on etiology, life course, and societal consequences of female juvenile offending;
- Research on the role of childhood experiences, neighborhoods and communities, and family and individual characteristics that lead young females into crime; and
- Research on the role of psychiatric disorders in the etiology of female juvenile crime, as well as its role as a consequence of crime or the justice system's response.

4

Preventing Juvenile Crime

Efforts to prevent juvenile delinquency have a long history, but generally they have not been subjected to scientific evaluation of their effects. The following sections discuss programs aimed at families, programs aimed at children and adolescents in schools, and community-based programs. This discussion is not intended as a catalog of all programs available around the country. A comprehensive review of the entire body of prevention program research was beyond the resource capacity of the panel. The literature analyzed for this report was culled largely from a number of published reviews (Barnett, 1995; Brewer et al., 1995; Catalano et al., 1998; Gottfredson, 1997; Gottfredson et al., 1998; Hawkins et al., 1995b; Hope, 1995; Karoly et al., 1998; Lipsey and Wilson, 1998; Sherman, 1997a, 1997b; Tolan and Guerra, 1998; Tremblay and Craig, 1995; Wasserman and Miller, 1998; Yoshikawa, 1995). The panel confined its discussions to prevention programs that have been subjected to experimental or quasi-experimental evaluation research.[1] In selecting evaluations to include, the panel chose to look at programs that measured effects on risk factors for delinquency as well as on delinquent behavior itself. Few programs for families and young children have follow-ups that are long enough to test for delinquent behavior. Programs delivered to delinquent youth or that invoke juvenile justice sanctions are covered in Chapter 5.

---

[1]For an excellent discussion of the stages of evaluation research and the criteria for quasi-experimental and experimental designs, see National Research Council (1998, Chapter 3).

PREVENTION OF JUVENILE DELINQUENCY THROUGH FAMILY INTERVENTIONS

How parents interact with their children and, in particular, their disciplinary styles, can increase or decrease the likelihood of later antisocial and delinquent behavior by their offspring. As Patterson and his colleagues (Patterson, 1976, 1995; Patterson et al., 1984) indicate through their research, parents who nag or use idle threats are likely to generate coercive systems in which children gain control through misbehaving. So important does the family appear to be in terms of the development of youth crime that programs have been designed to help parents cope with their offspring. Kazdin (1997:1351) summarized this line of research by noting that parent management training "has led to marked improvements in child behavior on parent and teacher reports of deviant behavior, direct observation of behavior at home and school, and institutional records (e.g., school truancy, police contacts, arrest rates, institutionalization)." The following section discusses evaluations of programs that were wholly or in part focused on assisting and training parents. These programs are summarized in Table 4-1.

Interventions with Parents and Young Children

A strong case for interventions with expectant parents can be made because of the nature of human growth. Brain development during the fetal period has lifelong consequences (Carnegie Task Force on Meeting the Needs of Our Youngest Children, 1994) and can be altered by chemical agents (such as alcohol, nicotine, and drugs), by mothers' behavior and health, and by environmental effects on the mother (Coe, 1999; Wakschlag et al., 1997).

Parents with a history of social adjustment problems are most likely to maintain risky behaviors during pregnancy. From this perspective, a number of preventive interventions have targeted pregnant adolescents. These experiments can often be considered interventions with disruptive adolescents in an effort to prevent the intergenerational continuity of antisocial behavior. Unfortunately, participants in these intervention studies generally have not been followed long enough to document the program's impact on the development of disruptive behavior for either the mother or the child.

The Elmira Home Visitation study (Olds et al., 1997b, 1998) is an exception. Participants in this targeted prevention experiment were pregnant women with no prior live births and were either unmarried, adolescent, or poor. Other pregnant women were included in the study to prevent stigmatization. Three experimental groups were created by random allocation. Women in the first group were visited weekly by a nurse for the first month after enrollment in the study, twice a month until birth, weekly for the first six weeks after birth, twice a month until the baby reached 21 months, and monthly until the child reached the end of the second year. Women in the second group received home visits only during pregnancy, while women in the third group had a screening interview after birth and free transport to the health clinic between the child's birth and the end of the second year. Mothers and children have been followed up to the child's 15th birthday. Fewer mothers in the first group were identified as perpetrators of child abuse and neglect. In addition, significant differences between the first group and controls have been observed when the comparison is limited to those women who were unmarried and had low incomes at initial enrollment. The unmarried, low-income mothers in the first group had fewer subsequent births, longer intervals between the birth of the first and second child, fewer substance abuse impairments, fewer self-reported and officially recorded arrests, and were less often on Aid to Families with Dependent Children (AFDC) than similar mothers in the control groups (Olds et al., 1997a). When the children reached 15 years of age, their delinquency involvement was assessed. Results showed that the adolescent children of the unmarried, low-income mothers who were visited by nurses during pregnancy and the first two years after birth, compared with the comparison groups, reported fewer instances of running away, fewer arrests, fewer convictions and violations of probation, fewer lifetime sex partners, fewer cigarettes smoked per day, and fewer days having consumed alcohol in the last six months (Olds et al., 1998).

Olds et al. (1998) reported that the program cost was between $2,800 and $3,200 per family per year. They also estimated that the reduction of the number of pregnancies for low-income mothers and the related reduction in welfare costs were such that the costs of the intervention program were recovered four years after the birth of these women's first child. The Rand Corporation estimated that when the children reached 15 years of age, savings had reached four times the cost of the program (Karoly et al., 1998).

The Elmira nurse home-visiting model has been replicated in Memphis. The goal of the Memphis replication was to see the effects of the model when delivered through the existing health department with minimal input from the researchers (Olds, 1998). Low-income women experiencing their first pregnancy were recruited at the Memphis Regional Medical Center and were randomly assigned to one of four conditions: (1) free transportation to prenatal care appointments; (2) free transportation to prenatal care appointments plus developmental screening and referral services for the child at 6, 12, and 24 months; (3) free transportation,

TABLE 4-1 Family Interventions for Prevention of Juvenile Delinquency

Intervention	Evaluation Type	Number of subjects at follow-up	Program components
Adolescent Transitions Program (Dishion and Andrews, 1995; Dishion et al., 1996)	Random assignment to one of three treatments; quasi-experimental control group	N(parent only) = 21 N(teen only) = 29 N(parent & teen) = 29 N(self-directed, control) = 26 N(control) = 36	Parent group education; teen group; family consultation; self-study materials
Elmira Nurse Home Visitation Program (Olds et al., 1997a, b, 1998)	Experimental (Randomized controlled trial)	N(exp) = 97 N(control) = 148	Nurse home visiting
Memphis Nurse Home Visiting (Kitzman et al., 1997)	Experimental (Randomized controlled trial)	N(exp) = 223 N(control) = 515	Nurse home visiting
High/Scope Perry Preschool (Schweinhart et al., 1993)	Experimental (Randomized controlled trial)	N(exp) = 58 N(control) = 65	Preschool and home visiting
Houston Parent-Child Development Center (Johnson and Walker, 1987)	Experimental (Randomized controlled trial)	N(exp) = 51 N(control) = 88	Home visiting, center-based parent training, and day care

Age at treatment	Length of treatment	Length of follow-up	Delinquency and antisocial behavior outcomes	Other outcomes
10 to 14 years	12 weeks	1 year	Teen-focus group had more teacher identified behavior problems at follow-up than those in other groups	Parent-focus and teen-focus groups had improved family functioning; teen-focus group had significantly more tobacco use at follow-up than parent-focus or controls
Prenatal to age 2	2 years	15 years	Fewer arrests, convictions, and probation violations among treatment group; fewer incidents of running away from home among treatment group	Less cigarette and tobacco use and fewer sexual partners among treatment group; lower rate of child abuse and neglect by treatment group parents
Prenatal to age 2	2 years	0 years		Fewer injuries and hospitalizations of program children; fewer subsequent pregnancies and less time on welfare for program mothers
Age 3-4	1 to 2 years	24 years	Significantly fewer arrests by age 27 among treatment group	Treatment group had significantly higher high school graduation rates, significantly higher incomes, were significantly more likely to be home owners, and were less likely to receive social services
Ages 1 to 3 years	2 years	5 to 8 years	Program children had fewer acting out, aggressive behavior problems	

continued

TABLE 4-1 Continued

Intervention	Evaluation Type	Number of subjects at follow-up	Program components
Mailman Center for Child Development (Field et al., 1982)	Experimental (Randomized controlled trial)	N(exp) = 64 N(control) = 30	Home visiting and day care
Mailman Center for Child Development (Stone et al., 1988)	Experimental (Randomized controlled trial)	N(exp) = 31 N(control) = 30	Home visiting and day care
Montreal Longitudinal Experimental Study (Tremblay et al., 1995)	Experimental (Randomized controlled trial)	N(exp) = 46 N(attention-control) = 84 N(no-contact control) = 42	Parent training and school-based social skills training
Newcastle-upon-Tyne (Kolvin et al., 1981)	Experimental		Group therapy, parent counseling and teacher consultation, and behavior modification (older children) or nurturing work (younger children)
PARTNERS program with Head Start families (Webster-Stratton, 1998)	Experimental (Random assignment of Head Start centers to treatment or control conditions)	N(exp) = 189 N(control) = 107	Parent and teacher training

Age at treatment	Length of treatment	Length of follow-up	Delinquency and antisocial behavior outcomes	Other outcomes
Birth to age 1	1 year	1 year		Better growth and development among treatment group; treatment mothers had greater rate of return to work or school and fewer repeat pregnancies
Birth to age 1	1 year	5 to 8 years		No differences on academic, behavioral, or social-emotional skills
Age 7	2 years	10 years	Significantly less delinquent behavior among intervention group	
7- to 8-year-olds, 11- to 12-year-olds	Parent counseling- up to 10 visits; group therapy- 10 sessions; behavior modification-2 school terms; nurturing work- 5 school terms	3 years after baseline assessments	Less antisocial behavior among play group therapy treatment group; no difference between treatment and control groups for other treatment conditions	
Age 4	8 to 9 weeks	12 to 18 months	Intervention children significantly decreased their misbehavior compared to no change in control group	Intervention children significantly increased their positive affect compared to no change in control group.

continued

TABLE 4-1 Continued

Intervention	Evaluation Type	Number of subjects at follow-up	Program components
Seattle Social Development Project (Hawkins et al., 1999)	Non-controlled Randomized trial	N = 598	Teacher training, parent education, social competence training for children
Syracuse University Family Development Research Program (Lally et al., 1988)	Quasi-experimental (Matched Pair control group)	N(program) = 65 N(control) = 54	Home visiting and day care

developmental screening, and intensive nurse home visitation during pregnancy with one postpartum visit in the hospital and one postpartum visit at home; and (4) free transportation, developmental screening, and nurse home visitation during pregnancy continuing to child's second birthday. When the children were age 2, the group that received the full home visitation program (the experimental group) was compared with the group that had free transportation and developmental screening and referral services (the control). Mothers in the experimental group had fewer subsequent pregnancies and less time on welfare than mothers in the control group. Children in the experimental group had fewer injuries and ingestions and fewer hospitalizations for injuries and ingestions than the control children (Kitzman et al., 1997). Continuing follow-ups are planned.

The Syracuse University Family Development Research Program (Honig, 1977; Honig and Lally, 1982; Lally and Honig, 1977) began providing services to low-income mothers during their last trimester of pregnancy and continuing for the first five years of the childrens' lives. The program consisted of weekly home visits by paraprofessionals to assist the family with issues of childrearing, family relations, employment, and community functioning. The program also provided day care services for

Age at treatment	Length of treatment	Length of follow-up	Delinquency and antisocial behavior outcomes	Other outcomes
1st to 6th grade	6 years	6 year (age 18)	Significantly less violent delinquent behavior among experimental group	Less heavy drinking, sexual intercourse, multiple sex partners, and pregnancy among experimental group; higher academic achievement among experimental group
Prenatal to age 5	5 years	10 years	Treatment group less likely to have juvenile justice system involvement	

the children for 50 weeks a year. Children from 6 to 15 months of age were provided with half-day care for 5 days a week. Full-day care was provided 5 days a week for children from 15 to 60 months of age.

When the program children were 36 months old, a matched-pair control group was established. The control group children were matched in pairs with program children with respect to age, ethnicity, birth ordinality, sex, family income, family marital status, maternal age, and maternal educational status at the time of the child's birth. Lally et al. (1988) conducted a follow-up study of both control and program groups 10 years after program completion. Data on delinquency were collected from probation and court records. Children in the program group were less likely to have been involved in the juvenile justice system than were the control group children. Only 6 percent of program children, compared with 22 percent of the control children, had been processed as probation cases for delinquent behavior. Furthermore, the program children had committed less severe offenses than the control children.

Although beginning parent training prenatally may be preferable to beginning postnatally, one would expect interventions with parents of infants to have a significant impact on their parenting skills, and thus on the socialization of their children.

The Mailman Center program (Field et al., 1982) study randomly allocated low-income, adolescent mothers to a program that offered home visitation over the first year of life, to a second program that added work as teacher's aides in their infants' nursery program, or to a control group that received no specific treatment. At age 2, children from the second intervention group had higher developmental scores, and their mothers had a higher rate of return to work or school and fewer pregnancies compared with the first intervention group and to the no-intervention control group (Field et al., 1982). However, at a later follow-up, when the children were between 5 and 8 years of age, no significant differences were observed between children in both intervention groups and those in the control group on academic, behavioral, and socioemotional assessments (Stone et al., 1988). Although the investigators assessed only half the families, no significant differences were found between the original sample and those followed up. The authors concluded that the low socioeconomic status of the mothers may have overridden the early positive effects of the interventions. Results of the Elmira and Syracuse studies that also targeted low-income adolescent mothers suggest that the lack of long-term effects of the Mailman Center program could be due to failure to include a prenatal component and to the short duration of the intervention.

Programs for parents of infants seem to save money in the long run. Most of the reported savings in the Elmira program was due to increased employment and reduced welfare dependence among the mothers in the program. Karoly and colleagues (1998) noted that even more savings may be realized when information is available about employment of the children in the program. Furthermore, their study did not attempt to assign monetary value to other benefits of the program, such as increased IQ or less child abuse. Savings were not evident for the low-risk families who received services in the Elmira program. The authors point out that, at least from the perspective of government savings, this finding "underscores the need for matching the program to the population that needs its services" (Karoly et al., 1998:90-91).

More recently, Webster-Stratton (1998) administered a parent training program that targeted risk factors for disruptive behavior in Head Start centers. Nine Head Start centers (64 classes) were randomly assigned to experimental (345 children) and control conditions (167 children). The 8 to 9 week program focused on teaching effective parenting skills, positive discipline strategies, and ways to strengthen children's social skills and prosocial behaviors to parents of the 4-year-olds attending the Head Start centers. Groups of parents (8-16) met weekly for two hours with a trained family service worker and a professional to view videotapes of modeled parenting skills and discuss parent-child interaction. Posttest and one year follow-up assessments of parental competencies (mother reports and home observations) showed significant differences between the experimental and control condition parents. Teachers reported more parental involvement in the children's education and fewer behavior problems among the children whose parents had received the training.

Experiments have tested the impact of quality day care centers on the development of high-risk children. The impact of day care without any other form of intervention, however, is not known because experiments generally include other forms of intervention, such as parent training and medical services. To the extent that cognitive development, emotional regulation, and peer interaction underlie the development of behavior problems, one would expect that quality day care programs would be an essential component of preventive efforts with at-risk infants and toddlers.

The High/Scope Perry Preschool program (Schweinhart et al., 1986; Weikart and others, 1970), which targeted poor minority families, was successful in preventing crime through the age of 27, when those in the preschool program and in the comparison group were last traced (Schweinhart et al., 1993). The intervention included a high-quality pre-school program for 3- and 4-year-olds and home visits by preschool teachers, during which the mothers were taught how to help their children with their preschool activities. Families were randomly assigned to the preschool or to a control group. At age 27, program participants were significantly less likely to have been arrested than were controls. Program participants also showed other positive outcomes. They were significantly more likely to have completed high school, earned significantly more money per year, and were significantly more likely to be home owners than members of the control group.

The Houston Parent-Child Development Center Project (Johnson and Walker, 1987) randomly assigned low-income Mexican-American families with healthy 1-year-olds to a treatment or a control group. The treatment group received home visits by a paraprofessional for the first year of their involvement in the program. During the second year of program involvement, mother and child attended a center-based program four mornings per week. Mothers received classes in child management, child cognitive development, family communication skills, and other family life topics while children spent time in a nursery school. Teacher assessments of externalizing problems 5 to 8 years after the end of the program, when children were ages 8 to 11, showed a substantial positive impact. Children in the program were less likely than those in the control group to exhibit acting-out, aggressive problem behaviors.

On the whole, there is good evidence for a positive impact of quality day care in preventing behavior problems for high-risk children, thus contributing to the long-term prevention of delinquency. The prevention of delinquency by high-quality day care programs contributes to their cost-effectiveness. Karoly et al. (1998) performed a cost-savings analysis on the Perry Preschool program (the only one of the evaluated preschool programs that had measured outcomes appropriate to a cost analysis). The analysis found that the Perry Preschool program paid for itself through savings in future government expenditures. And 40 percent of those savings came from reductions in criminal justice system costs because the children in the program (followed up to age 27) had less juvenile justice and criminal justice system involvement than did controls. The remaining savings resulted from reduction in need for special education services, increased employment, or reduced welfare use among children who had been in the program (Schweinhart et al., 1993). It is important to note that the savings occurred years after the expenditures.

Interventions with Parents and Elementary Schoolchildren

Three experiments with elementary schoolchildren included programs for parents to prevent antisocial behavior. The Newcastle-upon-Tyne project (Kolvin et al., 1981) included a parent counseling/teacher consultation program for a cohort of 7- to 8-year-olds and a cohort of 11- to 12-year-olds. A total of 574 children, who had been identified through screening as at-risk for social or psychiatric disturbance or learning difficulties, were randomly assigned to various treatment or control conditions. The treatments offered to the younger children were a nurturing work program, a play group therapy program, or a parent counseling and teacher consultation program. The older children's treatments included a behavior modification program, a group therapy program, or a parent counseling and teacher consultation program. In the parent counseling/teacher consultation program, social workers were given the task of consulting with teachers to assist in planning individualized curricula, discussing the home environment of the child, and promoting links between home and school. They also visited parents to help them understand how family factors influenced the child's school performance. Families were visited up to 10 times, most receiving 4 to 6 visits. Assessments two years after the intervention indicated no significant effects of the parent program for either age cohort. Of all the treatments, only the play group therapy with the younger children resulted in a significant decrease in antisocial behavior compared with the control group.

The Seattle Social Development Project (Hawkins et al., 1998a) is a longitudinal field experiment following a group of multiethnic urban students who entered first grade in eight Seattle public schools in 1981. The intervention involved teacher training, social competence training for students,[2] and two parent training components offered on a voluntary basis. The first parent program was a seven-session curriculum on monitoring, teaching expectations for behavior, and positive reinforcement, which was offered to parents when their children were in 1st and 2nd grade. The second was a four-session curriculum on how to help children succeed in school, offered to parents during the spring of the 2nd grade and during the 3rd grade. Unfortunately, only 43 percent of the parents attended at least one of the parenting classes. Attendance is an important and frequent problem with parent training for children at risk of delinquency. Many of the parents have a history of problem behaviors themselves and will not easily and regularly come to group meetings at school. In most cases, individual attention is needed, preferably by visits in their homes. A follow-up study when children were age 18 found significantly higher academic achievement and lower rates of self-reported lifetime violent delinquent behavior among children exposed to the full intervention compared with those in the control group (Hawkins et al., 1999). The contributions of the different components (parent, teacher, student) were not examined separately.

The Montréal Longitudinal-Experimental Study (McCord et al., 1994; Tremblay et al., 1995), a preventive intervention, offered a parent training program to the parents of a random sample of boys who had been rated as disruptive during their kindergarten year in schools in low-income areas. The parent training component was based on one developed by the Oregon Social Learning Center (Patterson et al., 1975). However, instead of asking the parents to come to the school or to a clinic, professionals went to their homes approximately once every three weeks over a two-year period. The average number of visits was 17.4, including families that dropped out during the course of the experiment. Because a social skills program was also offered to the children at school, this study could not assess the specific effects of the parent training program. However, the combined programs showed significant positive effects on self-reported delinquent behavior up to seven years after the end of the intervention, when the boys were 15 years old.

Interventions with Parents and Adolescents

Fewer interventions with adolescents than with younger children focus on parents or families. The Adolescent Transition Program (Dishion and Andrews, 1995; Dishion et al., 1996) compared a control (noninter-

---

[2]The teacher and student components of this program are discussed under school-based interventions.

vention) group with the effects of a parent-focused group intervention, an adolescent-focused group intervention, and a combination of the two on adolescents at high risk of developing delinquent behavior. Families who qualified as at risk were randomly assigned to one of the three treatment conditions or to a self-directed study group; a quasi-experimental control group was also recruited. Both parent and teen groups resulted in less family conflict. One year after the intervention, adolescents whose parents were in the parent group showed fewer teacher-reported externalizing behaviors compared with the control group (because no differences were found between the self-directed study group and the no-intervention control group, they were both considered together as the control group). Both one and three years after the intervention, however, adolescents in the teen group exhibited higher levels of externalizing behaviors and of tobacco use than did the controls (Dishion et al., 1996, 1999). The negative impact of the adolescent-focused group appeared to outweigh the positive impact of the parent-focused group for those assigned to the combined treatment.

Interventions with Future Parents

Preventive interventions with parents of at-risk children should most likely start before they actually become parents. Because parents of children with behavior problems often have, themselves, a history of disruptive and antisocial behavior (Huesmann et al., 1984; Rowe and Farrington, 1997), one would expect that, if successful, interventions with disruptive and antisocial children in one generation would be a preventive intervention for the children of the next generation. While classrooms and neighborhoods are disrupted more by the deviant behavior of males than of females, the health of females affects their fetuses and the behavior of females influences crime through the adequacy of their childrearing techniques (Cohen, 1998; Perry et al., 1996; Serbin et al., 1998).

There appears to be no experimental or quasi-experimental study that has assessed the disruptive or antisocial behavior of the children of boys and girls who were in an intervention experiment as children or adolescents themselves. Most interventions that have shown long-term effects could do these assessments. The experiments that included both males and females would be especially useful in comparing the long-term benefits of interventions with males compared with females.

SCHOOL-BASED PREVENTIVE INTERVENTIONS

Using Schools to Prevent Delinquency

There are many reasons why schools play an important role in the prevention, treatment, and control of juvenile crime. First, longitudinal studies have demonstrated that low measured intelligence, poor academic achievement, small vocabulary, and poor verbal reasoning are predictors of chronic delinquency (Farrington, 1985, 1987; Hawkins et al., 1998b; Maguin and Loeber, 1996; Stattin and Klackenberg-Larsson, 1993). Poor executive functions, including the ability to plan and sequence behavior, have also been associated with stable aggressive behavior in early-adolescent boys (Seguin et al., 1995). Low cognitive ability is thought to precede the development of delinquent behavior; however, it is possible that early aggressive behavior may lead to lower IQ, or that third variables (e.g., parental psychopathology) may account for the cognitive deficit-delinquency association (see, e.g., Fergusson and Horwood, 1995; Fergusson and Lynskey, 1997). At present there is not enough evidence to clearly specify a direction of causality (Yoshikawa, 1994). A causal link between low cognitive ability and delinquency might be mediated by academic success and bonding to the school environment. Low bonding to school, truancy, and school dropout have been related to later violent delinquency (Hawkins et al., 1998b). Low cognitive ability leading to academic failure and reduced bonding to the school may lead to skipping school and dropping out, increasing the time available for becoming involved in delinquent behavior. School interventions designed to improve cognitive functioning could contribute to a reduction in delinquency and provide confirmation of a causal link between reduced cognitive ability and later delinquency.

Second, behavior problems exhibited in school are important targets for intervention in and of themselves. Disruptive behavior in the classroom consumes a teacher's time and energy and interferes with the learning processes of disruptive and nondisruptive students, which may lead to a classwide reduction in academic achievement. Moreover, classroom behavior problems may represent early expressions of disruptiveness that may later develop into delinquent behavior. Childhood aggressive behavior, as well as hyperactivity, attention difficulties, impulsivity, and oppositional behavior, are related to delinquent behavior in adolescence (Farrington, 1991; Huesmann et al., 1984; Pulkkinen and Tremblay, 1992; Tremblay et al., 1994; White et al., 1990). More specifically, teacher-rated aggressive behavior in school is related to later delinquency, particularly in males (Hawkins et al., 1998b; McCord and Ensminger, in press; Stattin and Magnusson, 1989).

Third, school processes and climate are related to levels of achievement and delinquency (Figueira-McDonough, 1986; Rutter, 1983). A number of early studies (summarized in Rutter, 1983) have demonstrated a wide variability in delinquency rates across schools. A school environment characterized by competitive academic achievement, a formalized process for handling all discipline problems, and lax supervision is associated with higher rates of minor delinquency than a school environment characterized by an emphasis on stimulating interest in learning, handling nonserious disciplinary problems informally, and strict supervision (Figueira-McDonough, 1986).

Another advantage of intervening in the schools to prevent and reduce delinquency is that, with few exceptions, most children attend school, and most also attend kindergarten. This facilitates the early identification of children who exhibit behavior problems, academic difficulties, or both, which are known predictors of later delinquent behavior (Stattin and Klackenberg-Larsson, 1993; Tremblay et al., 1994; White et al., 1990). Following identification, a school intervention can be implemented for individuals or groups with greater ease than if implemented in the home or a clinic. The following section discusses evaluations of school-based preventive interventions. These studies are summarized in Table 4-2.

Have School-Based Interventions Been Successful in Preventing Delinquency?

Wide variability exists among school-based studies in the types of interventions implemented, the characteristics of the study participants (age, background, personality), the length of the interventions, the length of follow-up periods, and the types of outcome measures. Some interventions are aimed at changing the school or classroom environment, while others are focused on changing student behavior, skills, or attitudes. Few evaluations of school-based interventions directly measure delinquency as an outcome, particularly for interventions in elementary school. Alcohol use and drug use, however, are often examined. In addition, few evaluations include long-term follow-up, making it impossible to know whether reductions in risk factors result in reduced delinquency or whether delinquent behaviors shortly following an intervention are maintained over time. These factors make difficult the task of drawing conclusions concerning which school interventions, or components thereof, are most effective in reducing delinquency.

Programs aimed at building the capacity of schools to initiate and sustain innovation have reduced delinquent behavior, drug use, and suspensions (Gottfredson, 1986, 1987; Kenney and Watson, 1996). Part of these programs involved clarifying school rules and consistently enforcing them. Interventions that have focused primarily on rule clarification and setting norms for behavior in school have also been found to reduce vandalism and disruption (Mayer et al., 1983), bullying (Olweus, 1991, 1992; Olweus and Alsaker, 1991), and drug and alcohol use (Hansen and Graham, 1991).

The application of behavioral techniques in the classroom appears to hold promise for the prevention of delinquency. Kellam and colleagues (1998, 1994) instituted a behavior management program (The Good Behavior Game) in randomly selected 1st grade classrooms. Several schools in each of five areas in eastern Baltimore were matched and randomly assigned to an intervention or control condition. In the intervention schools, teachers were randomly assigned to classrooms and intervention conditions. Children in intervention schools were assigned sequentially to control classrooms or to intervention classrooms, with reassignment if necessary to achieve balance. The five areas from which the schools were drawn were diverse and included a white ethnic low- to middle-income area with well-maintained row houses, a predominantly black, very low-income area with the population living predominantly in housing projects, a black middle-income area with families living in well-maintained row houses, an integrated middle-income area with families living in detached frame houses, and a predominantly white moderate-income area with families living in detached and semidetached houses. The program was designed to have teachers clearly define unacceptable behaviors and to socialize children to regulate their own and their teammates' behavior through team contingent reinforcement. Children were kept in treatment or control classes for the two years of the intervention. When assessed in 6th grade, boys in the treatment group showed a reduction in aggressive, disruptive behavior. This was particularly so for those from 1st grade classrooms with high levels of aggression. Kellam et al. (1998) point out that the findings had a number of limitations.

The study by Hawkins et al. (1998a) of the Seattle Social Development Project demonstrated that teacher training in classroom management, interactive teaching, and cooperative learning, particularly in the context of a multimodal intervention package, can lead to long-term reductions in delinquent behavior and other negative outcomes. The Seattle project is a longitudinal nonrandomized controlled trial study that has followed a group of multiethnic urban students who entered 1st grade in 1981 (Hawkins et al., 1992). Two schools were assigned as full control schools, two schools were full experimental schools, and in six schools entering students were randomly assigned to a control or experimental classroom. The intervention included skills training components for students and parents, as well as the teacher training component. In 1985, all fifth graders in 10 more schools were added to the study. Students in the

TABLE 4-2 School-Based Delinquency Prevention Programs

Intervention	Evaluation Type	Number of subjects at follow-up	Program components
Behavioral contracts with adolescents (Stuart et al., 1976)	Experimental (random assignment of school referred pre-delinquent youth)	N(exp) = 30 N(control) = 25	Behavioral contracts, family treatment sessions
Behavior modification (Bry, 1982)	Experimental (random assignment of at-risk youth)	N(exp) = 30 N(control) = 30	Teacher consultations, group meetings with students, periodic parent contact
Behavior modification (Brooks, 1975)	Experimental (random assignment of persistenty truant students)		Awards for attendance
Fast Track (Conduct Problems Prevention Research Group, 1999a, b)	Random assignment by school	N(exp) = 198 classrooms N(control) = 180 classrooms	Social and emotional competency training— all students; parent training, home visits, tutoring, and small-group social skills work—at-risk students
Good Behavior Game (Kellam et al., 1998)	Quasi-experimental	N(exp) = 238 N(control) = 680	Classroom mangement
Moral Reasoning (Arbuthnot and Gordon, 1986)	Matched and randomly assigned aggressive and disruptive students	Post Intervention N(exp) = 24 N(control) = 24 Follow up N(exp) = 13 N(control) = 9	Guided moral dilemma discussions

Age at treatment	Length of treatment	Length of follow-up	Delinquency and antisocial behavior outcomes	Other outcomes
12- to 17-years-old	4 months	0	More court contacts among control group, but differences not statistically significant	School and home behavior more likely to improve among experimental group
7th-8th graders	2 years	5 years	Significantly fewer court contacts among program group	
High School	8 weeks	0	Increased school attendance rates for experimental group	
1st grade	1 year	1 month	Intervention schools had lower rates of peer- and teacher-rated aggression and lower rates of teacher rated conduct problems	Intervention schools had more positive classroom atmospheres as rated by independent observers
1st and 2nd grades	2 years	6 years	For program boys, reduction in aggressive behavior	
13- to 17-year-olds	16 to 20 weeks	Post inter-vention and 1 year	Fewer police and court contacts among intervention group immediately post intervention, but no difference at 1 year follow-up	Fewer referrals to principal's office, less absenteeism, and better grades in humanities and social sciences among intervention group at post-intervention and 1 year

continued

TABLE 4-2 Continued

Intervention	Evaluation Type	Number of subjects at follow-up	Program components
Promoting Alternative Thinking Strategies—Regular Education Students (Greenberg and Kusché, 1996, 1998)	Random, by school (2 control schools, 2 experimental schools)	N(exp) = 87 N(control) = 113	Social and emotional competency training
Promoting Alternative Thinking Strategies—Special Education Students (Greenberg and Kusché, 1996, 1998)	Random by classroom (7 control classes, 7 experimental classes)	N(exp) = 49 N(control) = 59	Social and emotional competency training
Resolving Conflict Creatively Program (Aber et al., 1996)	Quasi-experimental	N=289 classrooms	Teacher training, classroom instruction, peer mediation
School Safety Program (Kenney and Watson, 1996)	Quasi-experimental	N(program) = 1 school, 259 students, 91 teachers N(control) = 1 school, 192 students, 90 teachers	Problem solving lessons in class; joint problem solving of school problems with students, teachers, police
Seattle Social Development Project (Hawkins et al., 1999)	Non-randomized controlled trial	N=598	Teacher training, parent education, social competence training for children

Age at treatment	Length of treatment	Length of follow-up	Delinquency and antisocial behavior outcomes	Other outcomes
2nd or 3rd grade	1 year	2 years	Significantly lower externalizing behavior problems among experimental group (measured by CBCL)	
1st to 3rd grade	1 year	2 years	Significantly lower externalizing and internalizing behavior problems among experimental group (measured by CBCL)	
2nd to 6th grades	1 year	0	Classrooms in which teachers gave a high number of RCCP lessons exhibited a slowed rate of growth in aggressive behaviors and maintenance of prosocial behaviors	
11th grade	1 year	0	Program school had reduction in student fights, student-teacher conflicts, and incidents resulting in student suspension	Students and teachers in program both reported increased feelings of safety
1st to 6th grade	6 years	6 years (age 18)	Significantly less violent delinquent behavior among experimental group	Less heavy drinking, sexual intercourse, multiple sex partners, and pregnancy among experimental group; higher academic achievement among experimental group

continued

TABLE 4-2 Continued

Intervention	Evaluation Type	Number of subjects at follow-up	Program components
Student Training Through Urban Strategies (Gottfredson and Gottfredson, 1992)	Random assignment attempted, but incomplete; statistical controls applied to correct for nonequivalence between groups	N(treatment) = 120 N(control) = 127	Alternative class focusing on the role of rules, law, government, the justice system, and responsibilities of individuals
Teacher and Staff Development (Mayer et al., 1983)	Random assignment of volunteer schools to treatment or delayed treatment	N(treatment) = 5 schools N(delayed treatment) = 6 schools	Teacher and staff training; on-going consulting with teachers and staff

intervention group received training in communication, decision making, negotiation, and conflict resolution. Parents were offered training in child management and helping children succeed in school. At age 18, children in the intervention had significantly higher academic achievement and lower rates of lifetime violent delinquent behavior than children in the control group (Hawkins et al., 1999).

The Promoting Alternative Thinking Strategies (PATHS) curriculum is designed to promote social and emotional competence and prevent or reduce behavior and emotional problems in elementary school children (Greenberg and Kusché, 1998). Evaluations using randomized control and experimental groups have been conducted, one with regular education students in 2nd and 3rd grades and one with special education students in 1st to 3rd grades. Both evaluations found reductions in aggressive and disruptive behavior among the experimental groups at a two-year follow-up (as measured by teacher reports using the Child Behavior Check List). The PATHS curriculum has been integrated into a comprehensive program that involves child, school, family, and community and that has components for all students and additional services for high-risk students. Referred to as Fast Track, this model has been implemented in

Age at treatment	Length of treatment	Length of follow-up	Delinquency and antisocial behavior outcomes	Other outcomes
Junior and senior high school	1 school year	0	Treatment students reported less serious delinquency (significant only in senior high group) and significantly less drug use	Treatment group had better grades than controls
Elementary and junior high school	3 years (treatment group), 2 years (delayed treatment group)	End of first year of intervention	Significant reductions in vandalism in treatment school	Increase in positive teacher-student interactions in treatment schools; decrease in 'off-task' behaviors among students in treatment schools

four locations (Seattle, Washington; Nashville, Tennessee; Durham, North Carolina; and rural Pennsylvania). In each location, approximately 14 schools were randomized equally to intervention or control conditions. The intervention was delivered to first graders in each of three successive years. There were 198 intervention classrooms and 180 matched comparison classrooms across the three years. The classroom was the unit of analysis for the evaluation (Greenberg and Kusché, 1998).

In intervention schools, the PATHS curriculum was followed in first grade classes for all first graders. A screening process identified the 10 percent of children with the greatest degree of early conduct problems. These children received additional interventions that included weekly parenting support classes, small-group social-skills interventions, academic tutoring, and home visiting. Initial evaluations at the end of the first grade indicated that in schools with the Fast Track program there were lower rates of peer-rated aggression and hyperactivity, lower rates of teacher-rated aggression and conduct problems, and more positive classroom atmosphere as rated by independent observers (Conduct Problems Prevention Research Group, 1999a, 1999b).

Two studies utilizing behavioral contracts for the completion of academic and behavioral goals, with clear rewards for successful completion and costs for breaches, demonstrated short-term (Stuart et al., 1976) behavioral improvements and long-term (Bry, 1982) reductions in delinquency. Stuart et al. (1976) randomly assigned school-referred students with disciplinary problems either to an experimental family and school intervention or to a group treatment placebo control condition. The experimental group used behavioral contracts that specified privileges that could be earned by meeting specific responsibilities and sanctions for noncompliance. Therapists met with families in the experimental group to refine and revise the behavioral contracts. Teachers completed class evaluation cards to let parents know how students in the experimental group were performing at school. The control group families met periodically with a member of the research team. At these sessions, games and other recreational activities selected by the youth were undertaken. Pre- and postprogram assessments by parents and teachers were collected. Information was also gathered from school records and court records. At the end of the intervention, the experimental group showed more improvement on all outcome measures than controls, although improvements on only 4 of 13 measures were statistically significant: school behavior as rated by teachers and school counselors, mother's rating of the parent-child relationship, and mother's rating of marital adjustment. The control group had more juvenile court contacts at posttest than the experimental group, but the differences were not statistically significant.

Seventh graders from a low-income urban school system and a middle-class suburban school system were selected based on low academic achievement, a disregard for rules, and a feeling of distance from their families. Selected students were randomly assigned to intervention and control groups. Researchers monitored attendance and discipline records and met weekly with teachers of intervention students to fill out a weekly report card. Researchers met with the intervention students in small groups to distribute and discuss the report cards. Students accumulated points based on teacher ratings, school attendance, lack of disciplinary referrals, and behavior in small groups. Points were used for an extra school trip of the students' choosing. Parents were contacted often by letter, telephone, and home visits to discuss their child's progress. The intervention lasted two years, while subjects were in 7th and 8th grades. Five years after program completion, county court and probation department records were checked for program and control subjects. Significantly fewer of the intervention subjects had county court files than the control group (Bry, 1982).

Shorter behavioral modification programs have also been found to have positive effects, at least in the short term. An eight-week program aimed at increasing attendance of truant high school students was evaluated by Brooks (1975). Students were randomly assigned to a treatment or a no-treatment control group. Students in the treatment condition signed a contract agreeing to not have unexcused absences and to have their teachers sign daily attendance sheets, which were turned in each school day to the school counselor. A ticket was earned for each teacher's signature and each positive written comment from a teacher. The tickets were used in raffles with prizes of money, movie tickets, record albums, and gift certificates. The raffles were held halfway through the intervention and at the end of the program. Students with better attendance earned more tickets, giving them a better chance of winning in the raffle. Compared with the control group, students in the experimental group increased their attendance significantly over baseline observations.

Research on intrinsic versus extrinsic motivation of students suggests that programs based on contingent reinforcement must be carefully designed. Children who resist engaging in a behavior in the face of strong punishment or who engage in a behavior because of a highly sought-after reward are less likely to internalize the behavioral rules and to behave accordingly when not under supervision or when the reward is removed (e.g., Lepper, 1983).

School interventions emphasizing moral reasoning skills have also demonstrated some efficacy in reducing delinquent behavior. Arbuthnot and Gordon (1986) asked teachers in four rural schools to nominate students with histories of unruliness, aggressiveness, impulsivity, disruptiveness, or specific behavior problems for their study. A total of 48 students were nominated and rated on a behavior rating scale (School Adjustment Index). The students were rank ordered on the basis of their scores on the scale and sequentially paired. By coin toss, one of each pair was assigned to the intervention and one to the no-treatment control group. The intervention consisted of guided moral dilemma discussion groups that were held weekly for one class period over a 16 to 20 week period. At the end of the intervention, teacher ratings of the students showed no difference between intervention and control groups. Students in the intervention group, however, were significantly less likely to be sent to the principal's office for behavior problems and had significantly better grade point averages in humanities and social sciences than controls. The intervention group was also much less likely to have a recorded police or court contact than the controls. Only two of the four schools granted permission for the one-year follow-up, so the sample size was quite small for that evaluation. At the one-year follow-up, students in the intervention group continued to have fewer referrals to the principal's office, lower rates of absenteeism, and better grades in humanities and social sciences than controls. Neither group had contact with the police by the time of follow-up.

The Student Training Through Urban Strategies (STATUS) project emphasized personal responsibility and the importance of order and rules (Gottfredson and Gottfredson, 1992). Students in one junior and one senior high school who were nominated by teachers or who volunteered were randomly assigned to the intervention or a no-treatment control group. Difficulties with class scheduling prevented full implementation of the random assignment, yielding nonequivalent treatment and control groups. Students in the intervention group attended an alternative class that covered the function of rules and laws, codes of conduct, the role of the family, individual responsibility, social contracts, and criminal justice issues. The class lasted for the entire school year. Both junior and senior high school students in the treatment group reported significantly less drug use than controls. Treatment students also reported less serious delinquent behavior than controls, although the difference was significant only for senior high school students. Treatment students had fewer contacts with the justice system than controls, but the differences were not significant.

Peer counseling, in which an adult guides group discussion of behavior, values, and attitudes, was found to increase antisocial attitudes and delinquent behavior (Gottfredson, 1987). Lipsey's meta-analysis of programs (Lipsey, 1992) also found individual counseling to be ineffective in reducing delinquency.

Peer mediation and conflict resolution programs have become quite popular in schools. Most studies of peer mediation have been too methodologically weak to justify drawing conclusions about them, and the few that have sufficient methodological rigor found no significant effects on student behavior of peer mediation (Brewer et al., 1995).

One of the few conflict resolution programs to be evaluated is the Resolving Conflict Creatively Program (RCCP) in New York City. The evaluation included 15 elementary schools, in which there were 289 teachers and 5,053 students. The schools were in various stages of program implementation, with some having not begun the program during the first year of the evaluation, and others having fully implemented all program components. Classroom teachers voluntarily received training and support in presenting the RCCP lessons, teachers chose how many lessons to give in the classroom, and children in the classroom could be trained as peer mediators in the program (Aber et al., 1996). The researchers chose a quasi-experimental evaluation design because it did not interfere with a defining characteristic of the program, which was to begin in a school by recruiting and training a few highly motivated teachers and to slowly recruit and train more teachers and add more program components over a period of several years. This means that teachers self-select into the program, but children do not. Data were collected for all students in a school (unless their parents refused permission) in the fall and spring.

Through the use of statistical procedures (agglomerative hierarchical clustering procedure followed by a k-means iterative clustering), three profiles of exposure to the program emerged. The first cluster included 51 teachers and was characterized by a high number of RCCP lessons, a moderate amount of teacher training, and few peer mediators. The second cluster, which included 186 teachers, was characterized by no lessons or teacher training and an average number of peer mediators. The third cluster of 52 teachers had the most teacher training, a low number of lessons given, and a high number of peer mediators.

After the first year of the evaluation, children in cluster one classes, in which their teachers taught the most lessons (up to 30 are available), showed the slowest growth of antisocial behaviors and the greatest retention of prosocial behaviors of all children. (Note that it is a common pattern during elementary school for children in urban schools to increase aggressive interpersonal strategies and decrease prosocial or competent interpersonal strategies over time [Dryfoos, 1990; Farrell and Meyer, 1997; Grossman et al., 1997].) Those in cluster two classrooms, in which no lessons were given, and in cluster three classes, in which teachers received training but presented few lessons, exhibited more hostile attributions, more aggressive interpersonal negotiation strategies, and fewer competent interpersonal negotiation strategies than those in the classrooms with high numbers of lessons (Aber et al., 1998). The researchers speculated that teachers who gave high numbers of lessons may have been more motivated, or that low lesson teachers may have been less skilled at giving the lessons and less committed to the program.

It is important to understand which programs do not work, so that investments of time and money are not wasted. Strategies that have been found to be ineffective, and sometimes even harmful, include instructional programs that focus on information dissemination and fear arousal; counseling students, particularly in peer groups; and providing alternative activities without any prevention programming (Gottfredson et al., 1998:5-35). One such program, which has been extensively evaluated, is the drug prevention program D.A.R.E. None of the methodologically rigorous evaluations have found any reduction in drug use among students who have been through the D.A.R.E. program (Clayton et al., 1996; Ennett et al., 1997; Rosenbaum et al., 1994; Sigler and Talley, 1995). In fact, a six-year follow-up evaluation found that students in suburban schools who had been through the D.A.R.E. program had a slight increase in drug use over those who had not been through the program (Rosenbaum and Hanson, 1998). Gottfredson (Gottfredson et al., 1998:5-35) summarized the research on D.A.R.E. as follows:

D.A.R.E. does not work to reduce substance use. The program's content, teaching methods, and use of uniformed police officers rather than teachers might each explain its weak evaluations. No scientific evidence suggests that D.A.R.E. core curriculum, as originally designed or revised in 1993, will reduce substance use in the absence of continued instruction more focused on social competency development.

A school-based gang prevention program based on D.A.R.E.—Gang Resistance Education and Training (G.R.E.A.T.) began to be implemented in 1991 and was incorporated into the curriculum in 47 states by 1996. A national evaluation was begun in 1994. A one-year follow-up has been completed to date and found significantly more prosocial behaviors and attitudes among 8th graders who attended G.R.E.A.T. than among those who did not (Esbensen and Osgood, 1999). It remains to be seen whether these prosocial attitudes will translate into gang avoidance as these youngsters grow older.

Programs that focus on a range of social competency skills, such as developing self-control, stress management, responsible decision making, social problem solving, and communication skills, reduce disruptive and antisocial behavior if they use cognitive-behavioral training methods (e.g., role playing, rehearsal of skills, and behavioral modeling) and are delivered over a long period of time so that skills are continually reinforced (Gottfredson et al., 1998; Rotherman, 1982). More generally, interventions that incorporate school components along with other components, such as home visits (Schweinhart et al., 1993; Schweinhart and Weikart, 1997), parent training (Hawkins et al., 1998a; McCord et al., 1994; Vitaro et al., in press), and child social skills training (Hawkins et al., 1998a) appear to be more effective than those with only one component. Intuitively, it makes sense that changing relationships and environments in multiple areas (e.g., school, family, peers) would lead to greater behavioral change than altering one area only. A home visit or parent component may allow for the generalization of classroom learning to the home environment, perhaps facilitating continued learning after the completion of the intervention. Similarly, changing the classroom or school environment may complement interventions targeted at small groups of students, allowing carryover of skills into more than one setting.

Intervening at younger ages, before the development of delinquent behavior, may be a profitable course of action. Also, the length of the intervention may be important. Studies with larger effects on delinquency tended to be those with intervention periods greater than one year (e.g., Bry, 1982; Gottfredson and Gottfredson, 1992; Hawkins, 1997; Schweinhart et al., 1993; Schweinhart and Weikart, 1997; Tremblay et al., 1995; Vitaro et al., in press), with some notable exceptions (Ahlstrom and Havighurst, 1982; Gottfredson, 1986).

Although a variety of school-based strategies appear to have the potential for reducing antisocial and delinquent behavior, how best to replicate such programs while maintaining their quality and intensity remains an unanswered question. Gottfredson (1997:5-61) points out that when studies report effects separately for groups that differed on the strength and fidelity of the program implementation, "the evidence always suggests that more delinquency is prevented when strategies are implemented with greater fidelity over prolonged periods and that these conditions are met more easily in some schools than in others." Programs that rely on classroom teachers and classroom time compete with other requirements of the school day and other school system priorities. In addition, not all schools have the capacity to incorporate programs well.

PEER GROUP-BASED INTERVENTIONS

Peers play increasingly important roles as children reach adolescence. Both because of a clear relationship between peer activities and delinquency and because of apparent cost-effectiveness, many intervention programs are provided in group settings. Nevertheless, there are good grounds for believing that in some circumstances such settings may exacerbate problem behaviors among young adolescents (Dishion et al., 1999). Evaluations of peer group based interventions are summarized in Table 4-3.

For example, one study randomly assigned juveniles on probation to special services including group counseling, individual counseling, and tutoring given by volunteers. Those who received special services increased the number of crimes they reported and their records showed increases in the number of their police contacts. In contrast, those who received ordinary services of the juvenile court reduced their criminality (Berger et al., 1975). Another study used random selection to include students in public elementary and high schools in either the treatment or the control group of a Guided Group Interaction program. Overall, the results for elementary schoolchildren showed no effects. For the high school students, however, the Guided Group Interaction program tended to increase misbehavior and delinquency (G.D. Gottfredson, 1987). Other research used a random-allocation design to evaluate the impact of teaching techniques of family management (parent groups and family consultations) and of focusing on peer relations and interactions (adolescent groups). Youths were assigned to one, both, or neither type of intervention. The group assigned to family management improved, but the groups assigned to interventions with a teen focus increased their smoking and aggressive

TABLE 4-3 Peer Group-Based Intervention Programs

Intervention	Evaluation Type	Number of subjects at follow-up	Program components
Adolescent Transitions Program (Dishion and Andrews, 1995; Dishion et al., 1996, 1999)	Random assignment to one of four intervention conditions; quasi-experimental control group recruited	N(parent only) = 21 N(teen only) = 29 N(parent and teen) = 29 N(self-directed) = 26 N(control) = 37	Parent education; teen structured discussion group; both of above; Self-directed group provided materials only
Cambridge-Somerville Youth Study (McCord, 1978, 1981; 1992)	Matched pairs, one randomly assigned to treatment, one to control	N(exp) = 248 N(control) = 246	Counseling for child and parents; tutoring; summer camp; group recreational activities
Guided Group Interaction: Peer Culture Development (PCD) (G.D. Gottfredson, 1987)	Random assignment	N(exp) = 184 N(control) = 176	Daily group school-based meetings intended to alter peer interaction; Participants screened for leadership characteristics, attitudes, and conduct prior to selection
The St. Louis Experiment (Feldman, 1992; Feldman et al., 1983)	Random assignment of antisocial youth to mixed or all antisocial groups; random assignment of groups to one of three treatment modalities	N = 701 boys of whom 263 were antisocial	Three group modalities: traditional social work, behavior modification, unstructured; Two leadership modalities: experienced and inexperienced

Age at treatment	Length of treatment	Length of follow-up	Delinquency and antisocial behavior outcomes	Other outcomes
10- to 14-year olds	3 to 4 months	1 year	Teens in teen only group showed increase in behavior problems; teens in parent only group showed decrease in behavior problems	
under 12 (at start of treatment)	5.5 years	Age 47	Treatment group more likely to have been convicted of a crime, diagnosed as alcoholic, schizophrenic or manic-depressive, or died prior to age 35	
15.42 (exp avg.); 15.46 (control avg.)	15 week period over one semester	Not reported	Increased waywardness, increased tardiness, decreased attachment to parents, and more self-reported delinquent behavior among high school students in treatment group	
7- to 15-year-olds	1 year	1 year	Antisocial behavior of antisocial boys in groups with prosocial boys declined and their prosocial behavior increased compared to no decrease in antisocial behavior in groups of all antisocial boys	

types of behavior more than did the control group (Dishion and Andrews, 1995). These negative effects were found at both one- and three-year follow-ups (Dishion et al., 1999).

The negative influence of grouping deviant or high-risk peers appears to be stronger during early adolescence. Grouping younger children in interventions has been found to be successful for reducing aggressive behaviors (Hudley and Graham, 1993; McCord et al., 1994). For older adolescents, the research is mixed, with some group interventions resulting in negative outcomes (Catterall, 1987; Dishion et al., 1999) and others finding positive results (Eggert et al., 1994). Positive outcomes from grouping young children but negative outcomes from grouping adolescents makes sense developmentally. Peer influence becomes highly salient during early adolescence and misbehaving youngsters may be more sensitive to peer approval than to that of adults.

The composition of the group may also affect the outcomes. Feldman (1992) found that putting one or two at-risk juveniles in groups of prosocial juveniles reduced antisocial behaviors and increased prosocial behaviors, whereas groups of at-risk juveniles receiving the same interventions increased their misbehavior.

Putting antisocial or at-risk juveniles together may provide them the opportunity to actively reinforce deviant behavior through laughter and social attention while talking about such behavior (Dishion et al., 1995, 1997). In addition, high-risk adolescents may adjust their values as a result of associating with peers who approve of misbehavior and, as a consequence, be more likely to misbehave themselves (McCord, 1997c, 1999).

COMMUNITY-BASED INTERVENTIONS

Although what constitutes the community is often not well defined, community-oriented interventions have been at the forefront of policy and program innovation in a wide range of areas relevant to the understanding, prevention, and control of juvenile crime. These include education, economic development, social services, policing, corrections, and crime prevention. The possibilities and limits of interventions and treatments that take the individual as the unit of treatment have become known and are often disappointing. Furthermore, much evidence suggests that the effects of individually oriented treatments (including sanctions) can be eroded by community characteristics. This has led to increasing efforts to make communities themselves amenable to intervention. Some of the most promising comprehensive prevention programs have been adapted from models that include community-based foci (Hawkins et al., 1997; Institute of Medicine, 1994; Moore, 1995).

Despite growing interest in community-oriented interventions, evaluation of them is still in its infancy and problems of conception, design, and implementation are substantial. Pointing to generally acknowledged successes is difficult because, in contrast to well-established standards for evaluating interventions directed toward individuals, methods for evaluating community interventions are still being devised (see, e.g., Connell et al., 1995). One of the most difficult aspects of evaluating community interventions is devising an appropriate control group (Hollister and Hill, 1995). It is much more difficult to use random assignment with neighborhoods or communities than with individuals. All the other methods of establishing comparison groups are problematic. The few studies that have compared randomly assigned groups to comparison groups established through other methods have found the comparison groups to be much different from the randomly assigned control group. One such study by Friedlander and Robins (1994) found that not only was the magnitude of the effect estimated from the constructed comparison groups different from that of the randomly assigned group, but the direction of the effect was different as well. That is, in the random assignment case, the intervention was shown to be successful in improving the status of the experimental group, but when the experimental group was compared with constructed comparison groups, the program appeared to have detrimental effects on those who received it. (See Hollister and Hill, 1995, for a complete discussion of the difficulties of constructing comparison groups for communities.)

Another difficulty in evaluating effects of interventions at the community level is small sample size. The number of communities or institutions involved in evaluations is so small that statistical inferences, which generally rely on large sample sizes, cannot reliably be made (Hollister and Hill, 1995).

Because there are few evaluations of community-level interventions that use experimental designs with the community as the unit of analysis, the studies reported on in this section that use a community or institution as the unit of analysis relied primarily on quasi-experimental designs. The results of such studies must be considered tentative. Table 4-4 summarizes the studies discussed in this section.

The results of an experimental study, Moving to Opportunity, underscores the importance of the community on juveniles. The Department of Housing and Urban Development funded an experimental housing mobility program that explicitly uses random assignment in five cities. Families are eligible for the program if they have children and reside in public housing or Section 8 assisted housing in a census tract with a 1990 poverty rate of 40 percent or more. Eligible families who completed an application and a survey were randomly assigned to one of three condi-

TABLE 4-4 Community-Based Intervention Programs

Intervention	Evaluation Type	Number of subjects at follow-up	Program components
Big Brothers/ Big Sisters (Tierney et al., 1995)	Experimental (random assignment to program or wait list)	N(exp) = 487 N(control) = 472	Mentoring
Job Corps (Schochet et al., 2000)	Experimental	N(exp) = 7,311 N(control) = 4,476	Academic education, vocational training, residential living, health care and health education, counseling, and job placement assistance
Midwestern Prevention Project— Indianapolis (Chou et al., 1998)	Experimental (random assignment of schools to program or control)	N(exp) = 32 schools, 557 high-risk students N(control) = 25 schools, 516 high-risk students	Mass media, school-based educational program, parent education, community organization
Midwestern Prevention Project— Kansas City (Johnson et al., 1990; Pentz et al., 1989a, b, c)	Quasi-experimental	N(exp) = 24 schools, 3011 students N(control) = 18 schools, 2054 students	Mass media, school-based educational program, parent education, community organization
Minnesota Heart Health Program (Perry et al., 1994)	Quasi-experimental (matched community control)	N = 1,443 students	Behavioral health educational program, teacher and peer leader training, community-wide activities
Moving to Opportunity (Katz et al., 2000)	Experimental	N(exp) = 236 families N(comparison) = 113 families N(control) = 176 families	Rental subsidy vouchers plus assistance in moving to low poverty neighborhood

Age at treatment	Length of treatment	Length of follow-up	Delinquency and antisocial behavior outcomes	Other outcomes
10- to 16-year-olds	12 months average	18 months after random assignment	Treatment group less likely to initiate alcohol or drug use and less likely to hit someone	Less truancy, improved grades for treatment group
16- to 24-year-olds	Up to 2 years (8 months average)	2.5 years after random assignment	Reductions in arrests, convictions, and incarcerations among 16- to 17-year-olds in treatment group	Higher earnings, higher rate of completion of high school or GED among 16- to 17-year-olds in treatment group
6th and 7th grade	2 years	3.5 years from baseline		Significant reductions in tobacco use at 6 months and alcohol use at 1.5 years in treatment schools
6th and 7th grade	2 years	1 year		Less tobacco, alcohol, and marijuana use among experimental group
6th through 10th grade	5 years	2 years	Less heavy drinking among 9th graders in treatment community	Lower smoking rates, more exercise, and better food choices in treatment community
Families with minor children		1 to 3.5 years after random assignment	Fewer behavioral problems among boys in treatment groups	Better health and less victimization among treatment groups

continued

TABLE 4-4 Community-Based Intervention Programs

Intervention	Evaluation Type	Number of subjects at follow-up	Program components
PALS (Jones and Offord, 1989)	Quasi-experimental (nonequivalent comparison group)	N(exp) = 1 housing project, 417 youngsters N(comparison) = 1 housing project, 488 youngsters	Skill development
Project Northland (Perry et al., 1996)	Experimental	N(exp) = 10 school districts N(control) = 10 school districts	Parent involvement and education, behavioral curricula for students, peer leadership training, community task force
Urban Crime Prevention Program (Rosenbaum et al., 1986)	Quasi-experimental	N = selected target areas from 5 neighborhoods	Door to door contacts, block meetings, neighborhood meetings, and the distribution of educational materials; focusing on establishing and maintaining block watches and/or youth-focused activities

tions. The experimental group received vouchers for rent subsidy that could be used only in an area with a poverty rate under 10 percent. This group also received assistance in searching for an apartment and adjusting to their new neighborhood. The Section 8 comparison group received vouchers that could be used anywhere, but received no assistance in locating new housing. The control group remained on a waiting list. Katz et

Age at treatment	Length of treatment	Length of follow-up	Delinquency and antisocial behavior outcomes	Other outcomes
5- to 15-year-olds	32 months	16 months	Fewer police charges against experimental juveniles during treatment and at follow-up	
6th, 7th, and 8th grades	3 years	0	Less onset and prevalence of alcohol use in treatment school districts	
Not reported	1 year		Patterns of significant changes apparent by neighborhood: Increased awareness of and participation in crime prevention meetings, reduced proportion of residents known by name, increased victimization levels, increased youth disorder, increased fear of crime and perceptions of local crime rates, decreased optimism about changes in the neighborhood	

al. (2000) report on the status of Moving to Opportunity families in Boston. One to three and a half years after random assignment, 48 percent of the experimental group and 62 percent of the Section 8 comparison group had moved. Families in both the experimental group and comparison group were more likely to be residing in neighborhoods with low poverty rates and high education levels than were families in the control group.

Experimental group families who moved were more likely to be living in suburban areas than were comparison families who moved, but a higher percentage of experimental families did not move and remained in high poverty areas. Experimental and comparison group families who moved experienced improvements in multiple measures of well-being compared to the control group, including increased safety, improved health, and fewer behavior problems among boys. Katz et al. (2000:34) concluded that the short-term effects of providing vouchers to families who want to move out of high-poverty neighborhoods improves their well-being. In addition, "the MTO-Boston results strongly imply that neighborhoods have large impacts on the health and behaviors of children and adults from low-income families."

Policing Approaches and Community Mobilization Strategies

Community-oriented policing has been embraced by national and local government throughout the United States. The enthusiasm for this approach, however, has been such that the term now encompasses a variety of meanings. In the mid-1980s, community policing seemed to mean getting police officers out of patrol cars and back in touch with ordinary citizens on a day-to-day to basis, rather than just when crises arose. The term *problem-solving policing* has also become popular, pointing to a process in which police, other public agencies, and local citizens in high-crime areas try to resolve recurrent problems in particular hot spots. Other recent trends in policing include zero-tolerance policies based on the broken windows theory of Wilson and Kelling (1982). The idea is that minor crimes that disturb the quality of life lead to more serious crime; therefore, cracking down on minor crimes can lead to decreases in all crime. All of these policing strategies involve working with the affected communities. Scientifically credible evaluations have not demonstrated the usefulness of these approaches.

Efforts that may or may not involve working with police rely on organizing grassroots efforts to address community problems, including crime. Community organization, which was particularly popular during the 1980s, seemed more successful in affluent than in impoverished neighborhoods. Hope (1995) reports that in high-crime neighborhoods, people are wary of their neighbors and are therefore less likely to join community anti-crime efforts than are those in neighborhoods with less crime. The few credible evaluations of such activities as block watches have failed to show reductions in crime rates (Hope, 1995). Using a quasi-experimental design, Rosenbaum et al. (1986) tested a block watch program in middle- and lower-class neighborhoods in Chicago. Five experimental neighborhoods were selected. These neighborhoods had well-established volunteer community organizations, were interested in a block watch program, and had the resources to carry out the program. One set of comparison neighborhoods was selected on the basis of having well-established volunteer community organizations. Another set was selected randomly from among neighborhoods with demographic characteristics similar to the experimental neighborhoods. After a year of the intervention, no changes in victimization or in residents' crime prevention activities were found in the experimental areas. Compared with control neighborhoods, those in the experimental areas showed significant increases in fear of crime and decreases in attachment to their neighborhood.

Another popular strategy is the imposition of curfews for juveniles. Curfew laws tend to be enforced primarily in high-crime areas in cities. Evaluation of curfew laws has found no consistent effect on crime reduction (Sherman, 1997a). In a statistical analysis of the effect of curfew enforcement in California, Macallair and Males (1998) found no correlation between strict curfew enforcement and juvenile arrests for crimes, with a few exceptions in areas where curfew enforcement was associated with an increase in juvenile arrests for offenses other than curfew violations.

Community Economic Development and Situational Prevention

Community economic development has grown enormously as a field, based primarily on the production and management of affordable low-income housing. As community groups have become substantial landlords and developers, they have been confronted with issues of public safety and have developed a number of ways of trying to make their housing developments and neighborhoods safer. These include hiring their own private security, working directly with local police, organizing their own tenants and other community residents, and redevelopment of blighted buildings and public areas (Keyes, 1992; Sullivan, 1998). Although not evaluated specifically for their effect on juvenile crime, some of these measures have been found to reduce crime, particularly property crimes— offenses in which juveniles are likely to be involved. Unfortunately, these evaluations seldom use experimental or even quasi-experimental designs.

Closing of streets in high-crime areas has been another tactic aimed particularly at reducing prostitution and drive-by shootings. The one study with particular relevance to juvenile offenses took place in Los Angeles. In 1990, the Los Angeles Police Department installed 14 traffic barriers in a neighborhood with a high level of drug activity, shootings, and homicides, much of the crime gang-related. The traffic barriers were designed to make drive-up drug sales and drive-by shootings more difficult. The barriers were in place for a two-year period. Lasley (1996) compared violent crimes in the area for a year prior to the installation of barriers and for the four years after their removal. In addition, crime rates in four adjacent areas were compared with the crime rate in the experimental area. Homicides declined 65 percent while the barriers were in place, then rose 800 percent in the follow-up period. Other violent crimes also fell during the period the barriers were in place, then rose when they were removed. The adjacent areas had steady crime rates during these same periods. Although the findings suggest that the barriers were helpful in reducing crime, the design of the study makes it impossible to rule out alternative explanations for the differences.

Community Interventions

Comprehensive community initiatives for children and families are a relatively new form of providing social services that emphasize not just individual programs, but also the coordination of different programs in particular local areas and the involvement of local residents in the process. The goals of coordinated community interventions are those of healthy development of children and adolescents, including prevention of delinquency and substance abuses (Catalano et al., 1998; Connell et al., 1995). As noted above, methods for evaluating comprehensive community interventions are still being devised.

Although there have been no evaluations of the effects on juvenile crime of comprehensive community interventions, some more narrow community-based programs aimed at reducing drug, alcohol, and tobacco use among youngsters have found effects on substance use. Pentz et al. (1989a, 1989b, 1989c) reported on the Midwestern Prevention Project, which included mass media, school-based educational curricula, parent education and organization, community organization, and health policy. About one-third of the 6th and 7th grade students from all of the middle schools and junior high schools in Kansas City Standard Metropolitan Sampling Area (as designated in the U.S. census in 1980) were included in the baseline sample. All 6th and 7th grade classes in 16 schools and a random sample of classrooms in the remaining 34 schools were included. By the time the intervention was to be put in place, 6 of the 50 schools had closed and 2 could not schedule the baseline data collection. Of the remaining 42 schools, 8 were randomly assigned to either program or control conditions, 20 schools had the flexibility to institute the intervention programming and were assigned to the program condition, and 14 did not have such flexibility and were assigned to the control condition. Analyses were done using the school as the unit of analysis. In addition, 30 percent of the individual students were tracked, and analyses for them were also completed. Pentz and colleagues found significantly lower cigarette and drug use in intervention schools than in comparison schools and among intervention students compared with control students. Since all students in the area were potentially exposed to the mass media, the researchers concluded that the other components of the program were more effective than the mass media alone (Johnson et al., 1990). A replication of the program using an experimental design in Indianapolis also found reduced cigarette and alcohol use among students who had already initiated use at baseline in the experimental schools (Chou et al., 1998).

Perry et al. (1994) found significantly reduced tobacco use among students in communities in which a seven-year Minnesota Heart Health Program was implemented. The program combined a school-based component with community-wide activities, mass media, and adult education. The study employed a quasi-experimental design, in which a comparison community was matched to the experimental community on population size, socioeconomic makeup, and distance to a large metropolitan area. A similar program, Project Northland, for reduction of alcohol use among adolescents was also tested by Perry et al. (1996). The school districts in six primarily rural counties were blocked by size and randomly assigned to an intervention or control condition. The intervention included parent involvement and education, behavioral curricula for 6th, 7th, and 8th graders, peer leadership training, and community task forces. After three years, students in experimental areas were significantly less likely to use alcohol, tobacco, and marijuana than students in control areas. The researchers noted that the experimental and control communities had some differences at baseline, with more white students in the control communities and greater alcohol use in the experimental communities.

Mentoring

Evaluations of mentoring programs have consistently found that non-contingent, supportive mentoring relationships do not have the desired effects on academic achievement, school attendance, dropout, child behavior, or employment (Dicken et al., 1977; Goodman, 1972; McPartland and Nettles, 1991; Poorjak and Bockelman, 1973; Rowland, 1992; Slicker and Palmer, 1993). When mentors used behavior management techniques, Fo and O'Donnell (1974) found improvement in school attendance. Truancy was reduced when the mentor relationship included reinforcement contingent on appropriate behavior, but not when mentoring did not include contingent reinforcement. This evaluation suffered from a small sample size and short program length. Given the promotion of mentoring in recent years, the techniques used by mentors need more attention and evaluation, especially because there are some indications that some mentoring programs may increase delinquency (O'Donnell et al., 1979).

In the Cambridge-Somerville Youth Study, negative effects of treatment were evident. One boy from each matched pairs of boys, all of whom were under the age of 12 and living in poor neighborhoods, was randomly assigned to a treatment group. Those in the treatment group were assigned a counselor who visited them in their homes, at school, and on the streets approximately twice a month for more than five yeas. Boys in the treatment group also received a variety of services, including tutoring, medical and psychiatric care, and recreational activities. McCord (1978, 1981, 1992) found that those who had been in treatment were more likely to have a number of adverse outcomes by middle age, including more convictions for serious crimes.

A more recent evaluation of mentoring reported positive effects on delaying the initiation of drug and alcohol use, on reducing the use of hitting, on improving academic performance, and improving relationships with family. Tierney et al. (1995) randomly assigned youngsters ages 10 to 16 accepted into the Big Brothers/Big Sisters program to be assigned a big brother or big sister or to an 18-month waiting list. Both program and control groups were assessed at time of random assignment and 18 months later through surveys administered to the youth, through surveys administered to the parent or guardian of the youth, and through data collected by the case managers. At 18 months, youngsters in the program group were 46 percent less likely than controls to have initiated drug use and 27 percent less likely to have initiated alcohol use. Program youth were 32 percent less likely than controls to have hit someone in the previous year. Program youth also had better school attendance and grades and better relationships with parent and peers than controls.

Tierney et al. (1995) stressed the importance of the Big Brothers/Big Sisters infrastructure to the pairing of mentors and young people and the development and maintenance of their relationship. Volunteer mentors are carefully screened before being accepted. Training on program requirements, youth development, communication and limit-setting skills, and relationship-building skills are provided for the mentors. Youth and mentors are matched by gender, race (when possible), and interests. Case managers establish regular contact with mentors, parents, and youth. This infrastructure facilitates regular and sustained contact between mentor and young person. A earlier study of Big Brothers/Big Sisters found that 96 percent of mentor-youth matches had at least one meeting in the previous four weeks during the first year of their relationship and averaged 3.1 meetings per 4-week period (Furano et al., 1993). By comparison, studies of less structured mentoring programs found much lower rates of meeting—57 percent meeting on a somewhat regular basis among six campus-based mentoring programs (Tierney and Branch, 1992) and 40 percent of scheduled meetings occurring between mentors and youth in a juvenile justice setting (Mecartney et al., 1994).

Mentors are not the only ones carefully selected for Big Brothers/Big Sisters. In order to participate, a youngster must also be found eligible for the program. The screening process includes a written application, interviews with both parent and youngster, and a home assessment. In addition, both youngster and parent must agree to follow agency rules. Participating youngsters have a high level of motivation to enter the program. Although this evaluation accounts for that level of motivation by its random assignment of qualified youngsters to either program or waiting list conditions, it is possible that a mentoring program such as Big Brothers/ Big Sisters may be less successful for young people who are not as motivated.

After-School and Nonschool-Hours Programs

Increasing attention in recent years has been given to providing children and adolescents with supervised activities during nonschool hours. Although relatively few evaluations of such programs have focused on their effects on delinquency, it seems plausible that providing prosocial activities during the nonschool hours could deter delinquent behavior. Violent offenses by juveniles peak in the after-school hours (Snyder and Sickmund, 1999). Furthermore, parental monitoring and supervision, the lack of which is associated with delinquent behavior, may be missing during after-school hours. By 1997, 78 percent of mothers with children between the ages of 6 and 13 were in the labor market (Bureau of Labor Statistics, 1998), making many of them unavailable for child supervision after school. Several studies have found that children's and adolescents' involvement in unsupervised self-care in the company of peers was associated with behavior problems, particularly for juveniles in high-risk environments (Pettit et al., 1999; Vandell and Posner, 1999).

One quasi-experimental study in Ottawa (Jones and Offord, 1989) showed that an after-school and weekend program in which special efforts were made to attract nonparticipants in one housing unit resulted in reduced security arrests, whereas the matched comparison housing unit with some recreational programs that made no attempts to attract nonparticipants had increasing security problems during the 32 months of program activity. Adult arrests were comparable in both areas. And 16 months after the program ended, the positive changes in the experimental area had diminished significantly. The program actively recruited all children in the housing complex to participate in structured courses for improving skills in sports, music, dance, scouting, and other nonsports activities. The program also encouraged participation in ongoing leagues and other competitive activities in community. Despite cost-effectiveness in terms of reduced vandalism and other minor crimes, the program was not adopted into an ongoing funding stream, a problem that has typified even successful programs.

As discussed in the section on peer group interventions above, grouping high-risk young adolescents, even with adult supervision, has the potential of exacerbating antisocial behavior (Dishion et al., 1999). Vandell and Posner (1999) studied the effects of participating in a formal after-school program among low-income 3rd to 5th graders. Although participating in the program was associated with positive behavioral outcomes for 3rd graders, for 5th graders program participation was associated with increased school and behavioral problems. Upon further analysis, it appeared that the 5th grade participants had been more troubled prior to the program than were the 3rd graders. The increasing salience of peers as children age, coupled with the association with a more troubled group of peers, may have been a factor in the negative outcomes for 5th graders.

Feldman and colleagues (Feldman, 1992; Feldman et al., 1983) examined the group makeup of programs on their outcomes for antisocial boys. They placed antisocial boys who had been referred by juvenile courts, special schools, mental health facilities, and residential treatment centers into programs at a suburban community center. Boys who regularly participated in programs at the community center (nonreferred) were also included in the study. Boys were randomly assigned to a group composed of all referred boys, of all nonreferred boys, or in mixed groups composed of one or two referred boys in a group of nonreferred boys. Groups met once per week during the school year and participated in a wide range of recreational and leisure activities. Referred boys in the mixed groups significantly reduced their antisocial behaviors and increased their prosocial behaviors over the course of the year, but referred boys in the nonmixed group did not show decreases in antisocial behavior. Furthermore, the nonreferred boys in the mixed group were not negatively affected by their association with the referred boys; there was no significant difference between them and the nonreferred boys in the nonmixed group. This study showed the potential for improving the behaviors among at-risk boys by grouping a small number of them with a group of predominantly prosocial boys.

Job Training

Job training programs have long been a part of efforts to improve the conditions of the poor. Since lack of opportunities to earn money in legitimate jobs is a risk factor for participation in crime, improving the chances for legitimate employment may reduce crime rates among young people. A recent evaluation of Job Corps (Schochet et al., 2000) found positive short-term effects of participation among 16- and 17-year-olds, including reduced rates of arrest, incarceration, and conviction. Job Corps is a comprehensive, residential program[3] that provides academic and vocational training, health care and education, counseling, and job placement assistance. The program is available to economically disadvantaged youth, ages 16 to 24, who are high school dropouts or in need of additional education or training; are not on probation or parole; are free of serious medical or behavioral problems; and who come from disruptive environments. Participants may be enrolled in Job Corps for up to two years.

A random sample of all first-time Job Corps eligible applicants between November 1994 and December 1995 were randomly assigned to the research treatment group or a control group. The control group members were not allowed to enroll in Job Corps for three years, but could participate in any other available programs. Both groups were interviewed 12 months and 30 months after random assignment. At the 30 month follow-up, the treatment group had increased their education and earnings more than the control group, and had significantly reduced their involvement in the criminal justice system. Results for 16- and 17-year-olds were particularly encouraging: their arrest rates dropped by 14 percent and incarceration rates by 26 percent (Schochet et al., 2000). A four year follow-up is planned to investigate longer term impacts.

CONCLUSIONS

Our review of attempts at intervention has turned up very few successful programs that have credible evaluations. Work with pregnant women, with preschool children and their mothers, with teachers and their parents in high-risk neighborhoods have been shown, using scientifically appropriate evaluations, to have clear benefits in terms of reducing delinquency. But several widely used intervention strategies have been found to increase delinquency. Many such programs rest on drawing young misbehaving adolescents together. The panel concluded that innovative approaches to delivering interventions, which avoid the danger of grouping misbehaving adolescents, should be encouraged.

The most effective crime prevention programs, the panel concluded, addressed a range of difficulties. Thus, rather than targeting crime alone, successful preschool approaches helped young mothers teach their chil-

---

[3]About 90 percent of the participants live in supervised dormitory housing; the remainder participate on a nonresidential basis.

dren, improved the health of pregnant women and their infants, and encouraged education in the classrooms.

Based on its review of the literature on preventing delinquency, the panel drew the following conclusions:

• Programs that facilitate healthy births, infancy, and childhood appear to be effective crime prevention interventions.

• Programs that include multiple components for parents, youngsters, and environment (school or community) and that target multiple behaviors appear more beneficial than narrowly focused programs.

Public concern about juvenile crime should be used to encourage adequate, scientifically credible evaluations of the programs instituted to address that concern.

RECOMMENDATIONS

A variety of interventions with infants, preschoolers, and elementary school children have been found to successfully reduce risk factors for delinquency. It is frequently assumed that reducing known risk factors associated with delinquency will result in reduced delinquency. Few of the studies, however, have long enough follow-up periods to assess whether criminal delinquency is actually reduced. Although reducing various risk factors may be a positive outcome in and of itself, it is important to know which preventive interventions have long-term effects on delinquency and crime. Mounting follow-up studies of participants from programs that were shown to be effective in reducing risk factors for delinquency is also a relatively inexpensive research strategy.

Recommendation: Federal agencies concerned with the development of youth, in particular the Office of Juvenile Justice and Delinquency Prevention, the National Institute of Justice, the National Institute for Mental Health, and the National Institute on Child Health and Human Development, should encourage and fund studies of long-term outcomes for well-designed interventions that have shown short-term promise for reducing risk factors for delinquency.

Although evaluation research has resulted in some information about what types of programs may be effective in preventing delinquency, much remains to be known. Is it best for a program to begin prenatally? Is there an ideal length of program delivery? Are some programs more effective for certain types of children or families or at certain ages? Which programs are counter productive? Some relatively well-evaluated programs, such as D.A.R.E. and shock incarceration programs (see Chapter 5) have been shown to have little impact on the targeted behavior and even counter productive impacts among some populations. Until aspects of programs are systematically varied and well evaluated, these questions will remain.

Recommendation: All publicly supported intervention programs should be evaluated for both safety and efficacy using scientifically credible methods for doing so. Adequate funding for such evaluations should be included in the public support of intervention programs. Funding for programs whose effectiveness is shown to be limited should be discontinued.

Placing one or two antisocial juveniles in a group of primarily prosocial young people can decrease their antisocial behavior and increase their prosocial behavior without negatively influencing the prosocial youngsters. Some well-designed evaluations of treatments for at-risk juveniles found, however, that placing such youngsters in groups, even under careful adult supervision, had the undesired outcome of increasing their antisocial behavior.

Recommendation: Federal and state funds should be used to develop treatments for misbehaving youngsters that do not aggregate aggressive or antisocial youth.

5

The Juvenile Justice System

A separate juvenile justice system was established in the United States about 100 years ago with the goal of diverting youthful offenders from the destructive punishments of criminal courts and encouraging rehabilitation based on the individual juvenile's needs. This system was to differ from adult or criminal court in a number of ways. It was to focus on the child or adolescent as a person in need of assistance, not on the act that brought him or her before the court. The proceedings were informal, with much discretion left to the juvenile court judge. Because the judge was to act in the best interests of the child, procedural safeguards available to adults, such as the right to an attorney, the right to know the charges brought against one, the right to trial by jury, and the right to confront one's accuser, were thought unnecessary. Juvenile court proceedings were closed to the public and juvenile records were to remain confidential so as not to interfere with the child's or adolescent's ability to be rehabilitated and reintegrated into society. The very language used in juvenile court underscored these differences. Juveniles are not charged with crimes, but rather with delinquencies; they are not found guilty, but rather are adjudicated delinquent; they are not sent to prison, but to training school or reformatory.

In practice, there was always a tension between social welfare and social control—that is, focusing on the best interests of the individual child versus focusing on punishment, incapacitation, and protecting society from certain offenses. This tension has shifted over time and has varied significantly from jurisdiction to jurisdiction, and it remains today.

In response to the increase in violent crime in the 1980s, state legal reforms in juvenile justice, particularly those that deal with serious offenses, have stressed punitiveness, accountability, and a concern for public safety, rejecting traditional concerns for diversion and rehabilitation in favor of a get-tough approach to juvenile crime and punishment. This change in emphasis from a focus on rehabilitating the individual to punishing the act is exemplified by the 17 states that redefined the purpose clause of their juvenile courts to emphasize public safety, certainty of sanctions, and offender accountability (Torbet and Szymanski, 1998). Inherent in this change in focus is the belief that the juvenile justice system is too soft on delinquents, who are thought to be potentially as much a threat to public safety as their adult criminal counterparts.

It is important to remember that the United States has at least 51 different juvenile justice systems, not one. Each state and the District of Columbia has its own laws that govern its juvenile justice system. How juvenile courts operate may vary from county to county and municipality to municipality within a state. The federal government has jurisdiction over a small number of juveniles, such as those who commit crimes on Indian reservations or in national parks, and it has its own laws to govern juveniles within its system. States that receive money under the federal Juvenile Justice and Delinquency Prevention Act must meet certain requirements, such as not housing juveniles with adults in detention or incarceration facilities, but it is state law that governs the structure of juvenile courts and juvenile corrections facilities. When this report refers to the juvenile justice system, it is referring to a generic framework that is more or less representative of what happens in any given state.

Legal reforms and policy changes that have taken place under the get-tough rubric include more aggressive policing of juveniles, making it easier (or in some cases mandatory) to treat a juvenile who has committed certain offenses as an adult, moving decision making about where to try a juvenile from the judge to the prosecutor or the state legislature, changing sentencing options, and opening juvenile proceedings and records.

Changes in laws do not necessarily translate into changes in practice. In addition to the belief that at least some juvenile offenders are amenable to treatment and rehabilitation, other factors limit overreliance on get-tough measures: (1) the expense of incarceration, (2) overcrowding that results from sentencing offenders more harshly, and (3) research evidence that finds few gains, in terms of reduced rates of recidivism, from simply incapacitating youth without any attention to treatment or rehabilitation (Beck and Shipley, 1987; Byrne and Kelly, 1989; Hagan, 1991; National Research Council, 1993a; National Research Council, 1993b; Shannon et al., 1988). Practice may also move in ways not envisioned when laws are passed. For example, many jurisdictions have been experimenting with alternative models of juvenile justice, such as the restorative justice model. Whereas the traditional juvenile justice model focuses attention on offender rehabilitation and the current get-tough changes focus on offense punishment, the restorative model focuses on balancing the needs of victims, offenders, and communities (Bazemore and Umbreit, 1995).

Tracking changes in practice is difficult, not only because of the differences in structure of the juvenile justice system among the states, but also because the information collected about case processing and about incarcerated juveniles differs from state to state, and because there are few national data. Some states collect and publish a large amount of data on various aspects of the juvenile justice system, but for most states the data are not readily available. Although data are collected nationally on juvenile court case processing,[1] the courts are not required to submit data, so that national juvenile court statistics are derived from courts that cover only about two-thirds of the entire juvenile population (Stahl et al., 1999). Furthermore, there are no published national data on the number of juveniles convicted by offense, the number incarcerated by offense, sentence length, time served in confinement, or time served on parole (Langan and Farrington, 1998).[2] Such national information is available on adults incarcerated in prisons and jails.

The center of the juvenile justice system is the juvenile or family court (Moore and Wakeling, 1997). In fact, the term *juvenile justice* is often used synonymously with the juvenile court, but it also may refer to other affiliated institutions in addition to the court, including the police, prosecuting and defense attorneys, probation, juvenile detention centers, and juvenile correctional facilities (Rosenheim, 1983). In this chapter, juvenile justice is used in the latter, larger sense.

After providing a brief historical background of the juvenile court and a description of stages in the juvenile justice system, we examine the various legal and policy changes that have taken place in recent years, the impact those changes have had on practice, and the result of the laws, policy, and practice on juveniles caught up in the juvenile justice system.

Throughout the chapter, differences by race and by gender in involvement in the juvenile justice system are noted. Chapter 6 examines in more detail the overrepresentation of minorities in the juvenile justice system.

---

[1]The National Center for Juvenile Justice, under contract with the Office of Juvenile Justice and Delinquency Prevention, U.S. Department of Justice, has collected and analyzed juvenile court statistics since 1975.

[2]Data on the first two categories are already collected but not published. Data on the latter three categories are not now collected nationally.

HISTORY OF THE JUVENILE JUSTICE SYSTEM

Until the early 19th century in the United States, children as young as 7 years old could be tried in criminal court and, if convicted, sentenced to prison or even to death. Children under the age of 7 were presumed to be unable to form criminal intent and were therefore exempt from punishment. The establishment of special courts and incarceration facilities for juveniles was part of Progressive Era reforms, along with kindergarten, child labor laws, mandatory education, school lunches, and vocational education, that were aimed at enhancing optimal child development in the industrial city (Schlossman, 1983). Reformers believed that treating children and adolescents as adult criminals was unnecessarily harsh and resulted in their corruption. In the words of one reformer, the main reason for the establishment of the juvenile court was "to prevent children from being treated as criminals" (Van Waters, 1927:217). Based on the premise that children and young adolescents are developmentally different from adults and are therefore more amenable to rehabilitation, and that they are not criminally responsible for their actions, children and adolescents brought before the court were assumed to require the court's intervention and guidance, rather than solely punishment. They were not to be accused of specific crimes. The reason a juvenile came before the court—be it for committing an offense or because of abuse or neglect by his or her parents or for being uncontrollable—was less important than understanding the child's life situation and finding appropriate, individualized rehabilitative services (Coalition for Juvenile Justice, 1998; Schlossman, 1983). Historians have noted that the establishment of the juvenile court not only diverted youngsters from the criminal court, but also expanded the net of social control over juveniles through the incorporation of status jurisdiction into states' juvenile codes (e.g., Platt, 1977; Schlossman, 1977).

The first juvenile court in the United States, authorized by the Illinois Juvenile Court Act of 1899, was founded in 1899 in Chicago. The act gave the court jurisdiction over neglected, dependent, and delinquent children under age 16. The focus of the court was rehabilitation rather than punishment. Records of the court were to be confidential to minimize stigma. The act required separation of juveniles from adults when incarcerated and barred the detention of children under age 12 in jails. The act also provided for informality in procedures within the court. The idea of the juvenile court spread rapidly. By 1925, a functioning juvenile court existed in every state except Maine and Wyoming (Schlossman, 1983).

How well the juvenile courts around the country lived up to the founders' aspirations is difficult to ascertain. They succeeded in diverting most children and adolescents from the criminal system, but they may have been less successful with their rehabilitative goals. Schlossman (1983:965) noted that the following broad generalizations could be made of early 20th century juvenile courts:

> First, the clientele was overwhelmingly from the lower class and of immigrant parents. Second, boys and girls appeared in court for different reasons, and the courts disposed of their cases differently. The majority of girls, as compared to a very small proportion of boys, were charged under the loose heading of "immorality;" however, higher percentages of girls than boys were sent to reformatories, whereas lower percentages were placed on probation. Third, referral to court by agents other than the police, especially parents, relatives, and neighbors, was a far more common practice than it is today. Fourth, juvenile courts, particularly the probation staffs, often dealt with nearly as many cases "unofficially" (without court appearance) as officially. This placed added burdens on already large case loads and widened the net of the court to embrace every conceivable form of nonconventional behavior.

A case study of the Milwaukee juvenile court in the early 20th century (Schlossman, 1977) found that probation officers had over 200 cases, far too many for the individualized services envisioned by the Progressive Era reformers. The detention center lacked any serious diagnostic function and was sometimes used punitively. The court hearings, rather than relying on "empathy, trust, and a spirit of rapprochement" (Schlossman, 1983:966) as called for by Denver's Judge Ben Lindsey, resorted to "fear, threats, and short-term detention to render children malleable" (Schlossman, 1983:966).

As early as the 1910s, criticisms of the juvenile court's fairness and effectiveness began to be heard. One set of critics called into question the court's informality, charging that it resulted in discrimination and lack of attention to due process. Furthermore, the court treated children who had committed no crime the same as those who had committed a criminal act. Unlike adults, juveniles could be detained and incarcerated without a trial, a lawyer, or even being made aware of the charges against them. Another set of critics charged the court with being too lenient on young offenders. These same criticisms continue today (Dawson, 1990; Feld, 1997).

Three Supreme Court decisions in the second half of the 20th century resulted in more procedural formality in the juvenile court, but other decisions maintained differences between juvenile and criminal courts. In 1966, in *Kent v. the United States*, the Court concluded that Morris Kent was denied due process rights when his case was transferred to criminal court without a hearing and without giving his attorney access to the social information on which the juvenile court judge based his decision.

The Court held that juveniles had the right to a hearing on the issue of transfer to adult court, that there must be the right to meaningful counsel, that counsel must be given access to the social records considered by the juvenile court, and that the juvenile court must provide a statement of its reasons for transfer with any waiver order. Justice Abe Fortas also called into question the fundamental fairness of the juvenile court:

> While there can be no doubt of the original laudable purpose of juvenile courts, studies and critiques in recent years raise serious questions as to whether actual performance measures well enough against theoretical purpose to make tolerable the immunity of the process from the reach of constitutional guaranties applicable to adults. . . . There is evidence, in fact, that there may be grounds for concern that the child receives the worst of both worlds: that he gets neither the protections accorded to adults nor the solicitous care and regenerative treatment postulated for children (*Kent v. United States*, 383 U.S. 541, 555-556).

A year later, the decision of *in re Gault* (387 U.S. 1, 1967) extended the procedural safeguards required in juvenile court even further, giving juveniles many rights similar to those of adults charged with a crime. Fifteen-year-old Gerald Gault was sentenced to a state reformatory for an indeterminate period that could last until his 21st birthday for making an obscene phone call. The maximum sentence for an adult would have been a $50 fine or 2 months in jail. The case embodied nearly every procedural irregularity distinctive of juvenile courts: Gault was detained by the police and held overnight without his parents being notified; he was required to appear at a juvenile court hearing the following day; a probation officer filed a pro forma petition alleging Gault was a delinquent minor in need of care and custody of the court; no witnesses were called; there was no sworn testimony or written record of the court proceedings; and Gault was not advised of his right to remain silent or to have an attorney. The *Gault* decision entitled juveniles to receive notice of charges against them, to have legal counsel, to confront and cross-examine witnesses, to be protected against self-incrimination, to receive a transcript of the court hearing, and to appeal the judge's decision.

In 1970, the Supreme Court raised the standard of proof necessary in juvenile court to that required in adult criminal court. In *in re Winship* (397 U.S. 358), the Court required that juveniles charged with criminal acts be proved "beyond a reasonable doubt" to have committed them. Prior to this ruling, there was no constitutional decision that required more than the less stringent civil court standard of a "preponderance of the evidence."

Protection from double jeopardy was extended to juveniles by the Supreme Court in 1975. In *Breed v. Jones* (421 U.S. 519), the Court held that the double jeopardy clause of the Fifth Amendment prohibits states from trying a person as a juvenile and later as an adult for the same crime. In so doing, the Court recognized juvenile court proceedings as criminal proceedings, not social welfare ones (Feld, 1999). Nevertheless, the Court did not grant full criminal procedural entitlements to juveniles. In *McKeiver v. Pennsylvania* (403 U.S. 528 [1971]), the Court held that juveniles were not entitled to a trial by jury, arguing that the juvenile court proceeding was not the fully adversarial process found in criminal courts. Some critics of the juvenile court argue that, given the punitive changes in juvenile justice legislation since the 1971 decision, the only remaining procedural differences between juvenile and adult criminal courts are access to juries and access to counsel (Feld, 1993). The lack of access to juries may have consequences for the outcome of a trial because judges and juries may decide cases differently. There is some evidence that juvenile court judges may be more likely than juries to convict. For example, a study by Greenwood et al. (1983) of juvenile justice administration in California compared the conviction rates of similar types of cases in juvenile and adult courts, concluding that it "is easier to win a conviction in the juvenile court than in the criminal court, with comparable types of cases" (Greenwood et al., 1983:30-31 cited in Feld, 1999). Furthermore, judges try hundreds of cases every year and consequently may evaluate facts more casually and less meticulously than jurors who focus on only one case. Judges may have preconceptions of the credibility of police and probation officers and of the juvenile in question. In contrast, jurors hear only a few cases and undergo careful procedures to test bias for each case. Also, judges are not required to discuss the law and evidence pertinent to a case with a group before making a decision, and they are often exposed to evidence that would be considered inadmissible in a jury trial (Feld, 1993, 1999).

From their inception, juvenile courts had authority not only over children and adolescents who committed illegal acts, but also over those who defied parental authority or social conventions by such acts as running away from home, skipping school, drinking alcohol in public, or engaging in sexual behavior. These children and adolescents were deemed to be out of control and in need of guidance. Criticism of treating these status offenders (whose acts were considered problematic only because of their status as children) the same as children and adolescents who had committed criminal acts grew during the 1960s. The juvenile courts also had jurisdiction over abused and neglected children who had committed no offense. In the 1960s, many states revised their delinquency laws to move status offenders and nonoffenders into new nondelinquent categories, such as Persons, Children, or Minors in Need of Supervision (referred to as PINS, CHINS, and MINS). In 1974, in response to reported abuses in the nation's training and reform schools and the high numbers of juveniles being held in adult facilities, Congress passed the Juvenile Justice and Delinquency Prevention Act (42 U.S.C. §§5601-5640), creating a federal Office of Juvenile Justice and Delinquency Prevention within the Department of Justice. The Act provided federal leadership in the reform of the treatment of status offenses and nonoffenders. It required states that received federal formula grants to remove noncriminal status offenders and nonoffenders (e.g., abused and neglected children) from secure detention and correctional facilities. The provisions for the deinstitutionalization of status offenders led to a decrease in the numbers of status offenders held in detention facilities and institutions by the early 1980s (Krisberg and Schwartz, 1983; National Research Council, 1982; Schneider, 1984a). Schneider (1984b), however, found that some children and adolescents who, prior to the move to deinstitutionalize status offenders, would have been charged with a status offense, were subsequently being charged with minor delinquent offenses (e.g., theft rather than running away). Therefore, Schneider asserted, they were still coming to the court at the same rate, but as delinquents rather than status cases. Amendments to the 1974 act in 1980 weakened the deinstitutionalization mandate somewhat by allowing detention and incarceration of noncriminal juveniles for violating a valid court order. Status offenders who did not comply with treatment ordered by the court could become criminal delinquents by virtue of being charged with criminal contempt of court.

Young people who might formerly have been processed through the juvenile justice system for status offenses may now be institutionalized in other facilities, such as private mental health and drug and alcohol treatment facilities. Very little is known about the number of youngsters confined to such institutions, the length of their institutionalization, or the conditions of their confinement.

Concern over housing juveniles with adult criminals led to other requirements under the Juvenile Justice and Delinquency Prevention Act. Sight and sound separation of juveniles and adults in detention and correctional facilities and removal of juveniles from adult jails and lockups were mandated. In 1988, the act was amended to require states to address disproportionate confinement of minority juveniles.

At the same time the federal agenda and the voices of reformers were calling for deinstitutionalization procedures and more prevention, the states seemed to be moving in the opposite direction (Schwartz, 1989). Between 1978 and 1981, lawmakers in nearly half the states enacted some form of tougher legislation with regard to handling serious and chronic juvenile offenders. In a handful of states, provisions included making it easier to prosecute juveniles in adult court by lowering the age of judicial waiver (three states); excluding certain offenses from juvenile court jurisdiction (four states); and enacting mandatory minimums or sentencing guidelines for juveniles (three states). The impact of these reforms was an increase in the detention rate on any given day by more than 50 percent between 1977 and 1985.

In response to public concern over crime, in particular violent crime, committed by children and adolescents, almost all states now have made these kinds of changes to the laws governing their juvenile justice systems since the early 1990s. These changes are described following a description of the current juvenile justice system processes.

THE JUVENILE JUSTICE SYSTEM IN THE 1990s

Juvenile justice systems vary greatly by jurisdiction. The organization of courts, case processing procedures, and juvenile corrections facilities are determined by state law. Most juvenile courts have jurisdiction over criminal delinquency, abuse and neglect, and status offense delinquency cases. Criminal delinquency cases are those in which a child has committed an act that would be a crime if committed by an adult. Status offense delinquency cases are acts that would be legal for an adult, but are not allowed for juveniles, such as truancy, running away, incorrigibility (i.e., habitually disobeying reasonable and lawful commands of a parent, guardian, or custodian; also referred to in various statutes as unruly, uncontrollable, or ungovernable), or curfew violations. Some courts also have responsibility for other types of cases involving children, such as dependency, termination of parental rights, juvenile traffic cases, adoption, child support, emancipation, and consent cases (e.g., consent for a minor to marry, have an abortion, enlist in the armed services, or be employed).

Before any court processes come into play, a juvenile must be referred to the court. Referrals may be made by the police, parents, schools, social service agencies, probation officers, and victims. Law enforcement agencies account for the vast majority—86 percent in 1996—of delinquency referrals (Stahl et al., 1999).[3] The police are the principal gatekeepers of the justice system and play a central role in the processing of youths in both the criminal and juvenile justice systems. They have a great deal of contact with youthful offenders and at-risk youth, perhaps more than any other officials do in the justice system. Most of these contacts are undocumented and of low visibility (Goldstein, 1960); only a fraction reach the attention of juvenile court judges or youth detention authorities.

---

[3]An analysis by panel member Steven Schlossman of Los Angeles juvenile court from 1920 to 1950 found that 63 percent of referrals were from police.

There is scant empirical data on police encounters with juveniles (Black and Reiss, 1970; Lundman et al., 1978; Wordes and Bynum, 1995). A study by Sealock and Simpson (1998), based on an analysis of Philadelphia birth cohort data in which police contacts with juveniles from 1968 through 1975 were recorded, is one of the few that deals with juveniles' encounters with police. To further understand the nature of police interactions with juveniles, the panel commissioned an analysis by Worden and Myers (1999) of the data involving juveniles from the Project on Policing Neighborhoods, a multimethod study of police patrols in two cities (Indianapolis, Indiana, and St. Petersburg, Florida). The study involved systematic social observations of patrol officers in the field by trained observers who accompanied officers during their entire work shifts. Observations were based on spatial and temporal sampling, with shifts representing all times of the day and all days of the week. Data were gathered during summer 1996 in Indianapolis and summer 1997 in St. Petersburg. Observers recorded more than 7,000 encounters involving approximately 12,000 citizens. Of these encounters, 421 involved one or more citizens (a total of 626) who appeared to be under 18 years of age and who were treated by the police as suspected offenders. An encounter was defined as "any event in which there is face-to-face communication between a police officer and a member of the public" (Worden and Myers, 1999:13).

Consistent with past research, most of the encounters involved incidents of relatively low seriousness; 55 percent were for public disorder (e.g., disorderly behavior and loitering), nonviolent crimes (e.g., shoplifting and other theft), and traffic offenses. Less than one-tenth of the encounters concerned violent crimes. It appears that police may be initiating more of the encounters than in the past. Worden and Myers (1999) reported that previous research (primarily conducted in the 1960s and 1970s) found that the majority of police encounters with juveniles resulted from a request from a victim or complainant, and only one-quarter to one-third of encounters were initiated by the police themselves. In the study, half of the encounters with juveniles were initiated by the police. This finding may indicate an increase in proactive policing, although direct comparisons with past research are hindered by differences in measurement and sampling. The existence of a juvenile curfew in Indianapolis gave police in that city authority to stop juveniles after hours and contributed to a high percentage (61 compared with 37 percent in St. Petersburg) of their encounters with juveniles being police-initiated.

Worden and Myers (1999) found that only 13 percent of the encounters ended with the arrest of the juvenile(s). Table 5-1 shows the frequency with which each disposition in these encounters was the most authoritative that the police took. The categories are listed from least

TABLE 5-1 Disposition of Police Encounters with Juveniles and Adults

Disposition	Juveniles (%)	Adults (%)
Release	18.5	22.5
Advise	10.4	9.4
Search/interrogate	25.1	26.5
Command/threaten	33.2	27.5
Arrest	13.1	14.2

restrictive (release) to most restrictive (arrest). Over half (56 percent) of the encounters involve interrogation and/or searching of the suspects. As the table shows, dispositions were similarly distributed in police encounters with adults.

Worden and Myers (1999) analyzed factors that affected the likelihood of arrest in juvenile encounters with police. Arrests were significantly more likely when there was strong evidence against a suspect and when the offense was a serious one. The likelihood of arrest more than doubled when a juvenile showed disrespect for the police officer. Possession of a weapon also increased the likelihood of arrest. Female juveniles were significantly less likely to be arrested, independent of other factors, including seriousness of offense.[4] Worden and Myers concluded that "the situational factors on which research on police behavior has dwelt do not suffice to account for arrest decisions, however, and they are of even less value in explaining officers' choices among nonarrest alternatives" (1999:31).

Once a juvenile is taken into custody, it appears as if police are less likely now to deal informally with him or her than in the past. About 22 percent of juveniles taken into custody by police were handled informally within the department and released in 1998, compared with 45 percent in 1970 (Federal Bureau of Investigation, 1999); 69 percent of juveniles taken into police custody in 1998 ended up in juvenile court and 7 percent in criminal (adult) court.

Although there are many differences among juvenile courts in case processing, there are stages that they all must go through: intake, petitioning, adjudication, and disposition. Figure 5-1 provides a simplified view of case flow through the juvenile justice system. Cases that are referred to the court are screened through an intake process, in which charges are delineated. In some systems, this process is done within the

---

[4]Information on the Worden and Myers analysis of differences by race appears in Chapter 6.

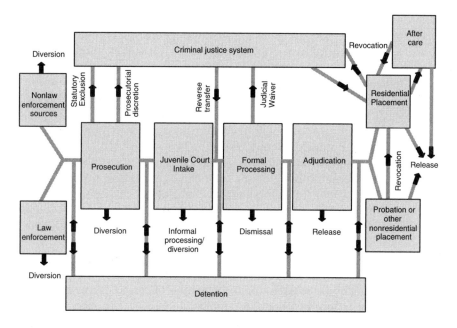

FIGURE 5-1 Simplified view of case flow through the juvenile justice system. Source: Adapted from Snyder and Sickmund (1999).

court system; in others, it occurs outside the court system, for example, in a probation department, a state juvenile justice department, or the prosecutor's office. The intake screening determines whether a case should not be filed because of insufficient evidence, resolved by diversion to a program or specified set of conditions, or should proceed to formal processing in the juvenile court (i.e., petitioning, which is similar to indictment in criminal court). Depending on state law, a decision to waive a case to criminal court may also be made at intake processing.

If a case proceeds to formal handling, a petition is filed and the case is scheduled for an adjudicatory hearing in the juvenile court, or the case may be waived to criminal court. At the adjudicatory hearing, which establishes the facts of the case (similar to a trial in criminal court), the juvenile may be judged to be delinquent (similar to a finding of guilty in criminal court) and scheduled for a disposition hearing; the juvenile may be found not guilty, and the case may be dismissed; or the case may be continued in contemplation of dismissal. In the latter event, the juvenile may be asked to take some action prior to the final decision being made, such as paying restitution or receiving treatment. If a juvenile has been adjudicated delinquent (i.e., found guilty), a disposition hearing (similar to sentencing in criminal court) is held to determine the appropriate sanction. Dispositions include commitment to an institution, placement in a group or foster home or other residential facility, probation, referral to an outside agency or treatment program, imposition of a fine, community service, or restitution. At any point during the process, some juveniles may be held in a secure detention facility. In 1996, juveniles were detained in 18 percent of criminal delinquency cases processed by the juvenile courts (Snyder and Sickmund, 1999).

Juvenile courts also vary by the extent of services for which they are responsible. Some courts oversee only the adjudication process, while others provide a full array of preadjudication and postdisposition services. In over half the states, juvenile courts administer their own probation services, and many are responsible for detention and intake as well (Torbet, 1990).

Some researchers have expressed concerns regarding certain juvenile justice procedures. As mentioned previously, the lack of a right to a jury trial may have consequences for the outcome of a trial. Also at issue is legal representation for juveniles. As in adult court, juveniles have the right to be represented by an attorney. The majority of states, however, allow juveniles to decide independently to waive their rights to an attorney without having had legal counsel prior to the decision (U.S. General Accounting Office, 1995b). This practice is inconsistent with the assumption that children are different from and should be treated differently than adults, in that it implies that juveniles can make the decision "voluntarily and intelligently," although studies suggest that juveniles are not as competent as adults to waive their rights in a "knowing and intelligent" manner (Feld, 1993:31).

Studies from 1980 to 1990 found that the majority of juveniles were not represented by an attorney, including the majority of youths who received out-of-home placement (Feld, 1993). Rates of representation varied between urban and rural jurisdictions, and among states and within states (U.S. General Accounting Office, 1995b).

Also of possible concern are the quality and impact of attorney representation. Some studies suggest that there are grounds for concern about the effectiveness of defense counsel in juvenile trials, possibly because of inexperience and large caseloads (Feld, 1993). Studies also indicate that presence of counsel in juvenile courts is related to differences in pretrial detention, sentencing, and case-processing practices (Feld, 1993). One study (U.S. General Accounting Office, 1995b) found that, in general, while unrepresented juveniles were as likely as represented juveniles to be adjudicated as delinquents, they were less likely to receive out-of-home placement for certain crimes than juveniles with attorneys. The study also found that other factors, including the type of counsel, were more strongly associated with placement outcomes than the mere fact of being represented by counsel.

Juvenile courts processed nearly 1.8 million criminal delinquency cases[5] and 162,000 status offense delinquency cases in 1996 (Stahl et al., 1999). Figures 5-2 and 5-3 show how criminal and status delinquency cases, respectively, were handled by the courts in 1996, the most recent year for which data are available. A total of 56 percent of the criminal delinquency cases that were referred to juvenile courts in 1996 were formally handled by the court (petitioned); that is, these cases appeared on the official court calendar in response to the filing of a petition, complaint, or other legal instrument. Over the past 10 years, there has been an increase in the percentage of cases (from 47 percent in 1986 to 56 percent in 1996) handled formally for all juveniles, regardless of age, race, or gender. Criminal delinquency cases involving older juveniles, males, and blacks, however, are more likely to be petitioned than those involving younger juveniles, females, and whites or other races, respectively (Stahl et al., 1999). Arguably, formal handling of cases can be considered more punitive than release or diversion to other systems. Therefore, the increase in formal handling of juveniles who come into contact with the police or who are referred to juvenile court may be interpreted as a system that is becoming more punitive.

Diversion

Diversion covers a wide range of interventions that are alternatives to initial or continued formal processing in the system (Kammer et al., 1997). The idea behind diversion is that processing through the juvenile justice system may do more harm than good for some offenders (Lundman, 1993). First offenders or minor offenders may be diverted to an intervention at intake processing or prior to formal adjudication. Juveniles may be diverted from detention while awaiting adjudication and disposition. After adjudication, minors may be diverted from incarceration by being placed on probation or given some other sanction or intervention.

One concern that is often raised about diversion programs is that they may result in net widening which is "a phenomenon whereby a program is set up to divert youth away from an institutional placement or some other type of juvenile court disposition, but, instead, merely brings more youth into the juvenile justice system who previously would never have

---

[5]"A case represents a youth processed by a juvenile court on a new referral regardless of the number of violations contained in the referral" (Sickmund et al., 1998:1).

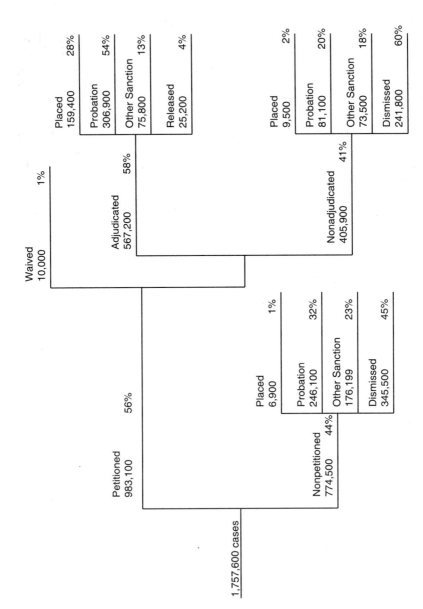

FIGURE 5-2 Juvenile court processing of criminal delinquency cases, 1996. Source: Stahl et al. (1999:Figure 2).

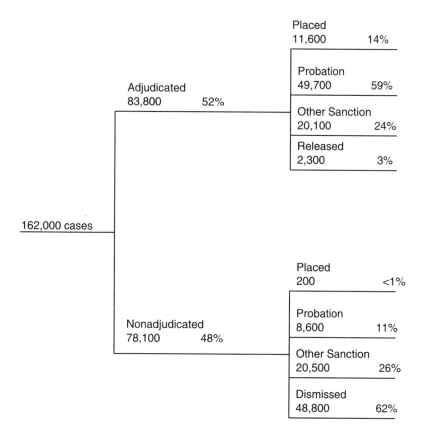

FIGURE 5-3 Juvenile court processing of petitioned status delinquency cases, 1996. Source: Stahl et al. (1999:Figure 16).

entered" (Shelden, 1999:4). A true diversion program takes only juveniles who would ordinarily be involved in the juvenile justice system and places them in an alternative program.

The array of interventions covered under the term *diversion* makes it difficult to generalize about them or their effects. Some researchers have found significantly lower recidivism rates among diverted juveniles than among controls who received normal juvenile justice system processing (e.g., Henggeler et al., 1993; Pogrebin et al., 1984). (For an overview of studies discussed in this section, see Table 5-2.) Other research has found no difference in recidivism rates between juveniles diverted from the juvenile justice system and those who remained in it (Rausch, 1983; Rojek and Erickson, 1982) or more recidivism among diverted juveniles (Brown

TABLE 5-2 Interventions in the Juvenile Justice System:
Evaluations of Diversion Programs

Intervention	Evaluation Type	Number of subjects at follow-up	Program components
Adams County Juvenile Diversion Program (Pogrebin et al., 1984)	Random assignment	N = 560 cases	Individual, parent, and family counseling, referrals to other services as needed
Diversion of Status Offenders Project (Rojek and Erickson, 1982)	Quasi-experimental	N(diverted) = 766 N(comparison1) = 508 N(comparison2) = 375	Diversion without treatment; diversion with referral to community agency (various treatments)
Connecticut's Deinstitutional-ization of Status Offenders Project (Rausch, 1983)	Quasi-experimental	N(community, minimum) = 18 N(court, minimum) = 94 N(community, maximum) = 47 N(comparison) = 201	Minimum intervention = short term crisis counseling by either community agency or probation officers; Maximum intervention = full assessments and referral to appropriate community agencies
Mediation (Umbreit and Coates, 1993)	Quasi-experimental	N(mediation, victims) = 280 N(mediation, offenders) = 252 N(comparison 1, victims) = 103 N(comparison 1, offenders) = 95 N(comparison 2, victims) = 107 N(comparison 2, offenders) = 111	Victim-Offender Mediation

Age at treatment	Length of treatment	Length of follow-up	Delinquency and antisocial behavior outcomes	Other outcomes
not reported	Up to six months	18 months	Lower recidivism (measured by arrest) among treatment group	
not reported	Average of 2 days (diverted not treatment); average of 88 days (diverted with referral)	not reported	No differences in arrests of self-reported delinquency between diverted with or without referral; no differences in arrests among diverted groups and comparison groups of samples drawn of arrested status offenders before diversion program was implemented	
up to age 16	Minimum = up to 5 sessions; Maximum = up to 6 months	6 months	No difference in subsequent court referrals among any of the groups	
7- to 18-year-olds (avg. age 15)	4 to 8 hours	1 year	Mediation group had lower recidivism and less serious subsequent offenses than comparison, although not statistically significant.	Mediation victims more satisfied than comparisons with process; no difference in satisfaction of offenders with justice system treatment. Mediation offenders more likely to complete their restitution than comparisons.

continued

TABLE 5-2 Continued

Intervention	Evaluation Type	Number of subjects at follow-up	Program components
Multisystemic therapy (Henggeler et al., 1992, 1993)	Randomized clinical trial	N(exp) = 43 N(control) = 41	Family therapy; problem-focused interventions within family, peer, school, and neighborhood; other strategies as relevant (e.g., cognitive behavioral therapy)
Multisystemic therapy (Borduin et al., 1995)	Pretest-posttest control group design with random assignment to conditions	N(exp) = 70 N(control) = 56	Family therapy; problem-focused interventions within family, peer, school, and neighborhood; other strategies as relevant (e.g., cognitive behavioral therapy) Control group received individual therapy
Multidimensional treatment foster care (Chamberlain and Reid, 1998)	Random assignment of referred boys to one of two treatment conditions	N(group care) = 42 N(treatment foster care) = 37	Foster care parents trained in behavioral techniques
Restitution (Schneider, 1986)	Random assignment to restitution or traditional disposition	Boise, ID: N(exp) = 86 N(control) = 95 Washington, DC: N(exp) = 143 N(control) = 137 Clayton Co., GA: N(exp) = 73 (control) = 55 Oklahoma Co., OK: N(exp) = 104 N(control) = 78	Adjudicated youths required to pay fine or perform community service

Age at treatment	Length of treatment	Length of follow-up	Delinquency and antisocial behavior outcomes	Other outcomes
15.2 years (mean age)	13 weeks (average)	2.4 years	Treatment group less likely to be rearrested and, if rearrested, had longer time to rearrest	Improved family relations; improved peer relations
12- to 17-year-olds (mean age 14.8)	Average: 24 hours of treatment for multi-systemic therapy group; 28 hours for individual therapy controls	4 years	Treatment group less likely to be rearrested and, if rearrested, had longer time to rearrest and less serious offenses	Improved family relations; decreased psychiatric symptomatology
12- to 17-year-olds (mean age 14.9)	up to a year	1 year	Fewer arrests and days incarcerated among juveniles in treatment foster care than in group care	Treatment foster care group more likely to finish treatment
15 to 15.5 (avg.)	Not reported	22 to 36 months	Reduced recidivism among offenders assigned to restitution	

et al., 1989; Lincoln, 1976). The variety in findings may be due to the types of juveniles involved and the types of treatment and services provided.

For a diversion program to be successful, it may have to provide intensive and comprehensive services (Dryfoos, 1990); services that include the juveniles' families and take into account community, school, and peer interactions (Henggeler et al., 1993); and use experienced caseworkers (Feldman et al., 1983). Elliott and colleagues (1978) found that whether intervention occurred in the juvenile justice system or in another program, juveniles experienced increases in their perception of being labeled as delinquent and increases in self-reported delinquency. It is even possible that some diversion programs are more intrusive than traditional juvenile justice processing. Frazier and Cochran (1986b) found that juveniles in the diversion program they studied were actually in the system longer and had at least as much, if not more, official intervention in their lives than those not diverted.

One well-studied intervention for both juveniles diverted from incarceration as well as for juveniles at various stages of processing in the juvenile justice system is multisystemic therapy. Multisystemic therapy is a family- and community-based treatment derived from theories and research that trace the development of antisocial behavior to a combination of individual, family, peer, school, and community factors and their interactions. The intervention is not limited to the adolescent or the family but includes work on the intersections between various systems, such as family-school and family-peer interactions. Treatment is individualized to meet the needs of the adolescent and his or her family using empirically based treatment models, such as cognitive behavioral therapies, behavioral parent training, and structural family therapy (Henggeler, 1999). In addition, attention is paid to treatment fidelity through supervision of and support for treatment providers. A study that randomly assigned serious, violent juveniles either to multisystemic therapy or to the usual juvenile justice system processing (Henggeler et al., 1993) found that multisystemic therapy reduced recidivism at 2.4 years after referral to half of that for those who received the usual juvenile justice services. Borduin and colleagues (1995) found that juvenile offenders randomly assigned to multisystemic therapy, at four years after treatment, had better family relations and fewer psychiatric symptoms and were significantly less likely to be rearrested than those randomly assigned to individual therapy. A meta-analysis of family-based treatments of drug abuse found that multisystemic therapy had one of the largest effect sizes of all treatments reviewed (Stanton and Shadish, 1997).

A promising approach for youngsters for whom home-based programs have failed is multidimensional treatment foster care (see, e.g., Chamberlain, 1998; Chamberlain and Mihalic, 1998; Chamberlain and

Reid, 1998). This approach recruits, trains, and supports foster care families to implement a structured, individualized program for each youngster. Juveniles are placed in the foster care family for six to nine months, during which time their appropriate behavior is reinforced, they are closely supervised, and their peer associations are carefully monitored. Foster care families have daily contact with program staff to work out difficulties and review program plans. Juveniles also receive individual skill-focused treatment. Other components of the program include frequent visits with and weekly family therapy for biological parents (or guardians) to prepare them for after care and coordination with school and other needed service systems after their children return to their homes. Chamberlain and Reid (1998) compared chronic delinquent boys (with an average of 13 prior arrests and 4.6 prior felonies) who were randomly assigned to treatment foster care or to group homes in lieu of incarceration. Boys in treatment foster care were more likely to complete treatment and less likely to be rearrested or to spend time incarcerated than boys assigned to the group home.

Victim-offender mediation is one increasingly popular form of diversion. A national survey discovered 94 victim-offender programs dealing with juveniles in 1996, 46 of which were dedicated exclusively to them (Umbreit and Greenwood, 1998). The programs ranged from having 1 to 900 case referrals, with a mean of 136 cases. Referrals to victim-offender mediation are typically for vandalism, minor assaults, theft, and burglary (Umbreit and Greenwood, 1998). The vast majority of mediation cases are first-time offenders. Typically, mediation occurs prior to adjudication. Some pressure appears to be mounting to include more serious cases in mediation programs (Umbreit and Greenwood, 1998). Whether more serious or complicated cases can be handled through mediation remains to be seen.

Studies have consistently shown that victims tend to be more satisfied with the process of mediation than with court processes (Coates and Gehm, 1989; Marshall and Merry, 1990; Umbreit, 1990; Umbreit and Coates, 1992, 1993). This may be because victims are included in the mediation process only if they volunteer to do so. In their quasi-experimental study of four sites in the United States, Umbreit and Coates (1992:12) concluded that for offenders, "participation in mediation appears to not have significantly increased their satisfaction with how the juvenile justice system handled their case." The study included interviews with victims and offenders who completed the mediation process. Two comparison groups were devised—the first of victims and offenders who had been referred to the mediation process but did not participate and the second victims and offenders who had not been referred to mediation in the same jurisdiction as the mediation sample, and matched on age, race, sex, and offense.

Over 90 percent of mediations resulted in a restitution plan agreed to by both victims and offenders (Neimeyer and Shichor, 1996; Umbreit and Coates, 1992) and significantly more juvenile offenders completed the agreed-on restitution than did those whose restitution was ordered by the court (Umbreit and Coates, 1993).

Findings on recidivism for juveniles who have been part of mediation programs are mixed. Schneider (1986) reported a significant reduction in recidivism among offenders in a mediation program. Other studies have found small but statistically nonsignificant reductions in recidivism among mediation program participants (Marshall and Merry, 1990; Umbreit and Coates, 1993).

Victim-offender mediation programs are one part of a larger diversion movement in juvenile justice that has been gaining attention worldwide—the restorative justice model. Under a restorative justice model, victims are given the opportunity to come face to face with the offender to negotiate restitution. In addition, restorative justice programs keep youth in the community and maintain community safety by community-based surveillance practices designed to limit the opportunities for juveniles to reoffend and strengthen rather than sever their connections with the community. These practices include monitored school attendance, monitored employment attendance, monitored program attendance, supervised community work service, supervised recreation, adult mentors and supervisors, training offenders' families to provide appropriate monitoring and disciplinary practices, day reporting centers, electronic monitoring, house arrest, and random drug testing. Placement in a secure facility is reserved for those juveniles who continue to offend or who pose a high risk to others. (For a more complete discussion of restorative justice, see Bazemore and Umbreit, 1995; Office of Juvenile Justice and Delinquency Prevention, 1998.) The restorative justice model is currently being evaluated in Australia.

On balance, the research on diversion and intensive probation (discussed in below) suggests that some community-based interventions can serve the needs of many juvenile offenders without added danger to the community. There also may be advantages to keeping juveniles in a less restrictive setting. Well-structured and well-run programs with appropriate services have the potential for improving the lives of diverted juveniles and their families and maintaining community safety.

Detention

Figures 5-2 and 5-3, which illustrate juvenile court processing of criminal delinquency and petitioned status delinquency cases, respectively, do not include the percentages of detained juveniles, because reported detention figures do not differentiate between preadjudication detention and postadjudication detention. Juveniles may be detained at any stage during the court process if it is believed that they pose a threat to the community, will be at risk if returned to the community, or may fail to appear at an upcoming hearing. Children and adolescents may also be detained for evaluation purposes. Juveniles who have been adjudicated delinquent and sentenced to incarceration may also be kept in secure detention until a placement in a long-term facility can be made. In 1996, 18 percent (320,900 cases)[6] of the 1.8 million criminal delinquency cases referred to the court resulted in detention, as did 6 percent (12,700) of the 162,000 status delinquency cases (Sickmund et al., 1998; Stahl et al., 1999). The percentage of criminal delinquency cases that result in detention has remained fairly stable over the past 10 years, and the percentage of status delinquency cases that result in detention has dropped. However, because the overall number of criminal delinquency cases coming to the court has increased, the number of cases that result in secure detention has increased, even though the percentage of cases detained has remained steady. Research consistently shows that juveniles who have been in detention are more likely to be formally processed and receive more punitive sanctions at disposition than those not placed in detention, after controlling for demographic and legal factors, such as current offense and history of past offenses (Frazier and Bishop, 1985; Frazier and Cochran, 1986a; McCarthy and Smith, 1986). Researchers have been unable to determine the variables that affect the initial decision to detain a juvenile, however. For example, Frazier and Bishop (1985), in an analysis of initial detention decisions, could explain less than 10 percent of variance in the decisions. Therefore, there may be unidentified factors related to the initial decision to detain that affect the impact of detention on eventual court dispositions.

It is important to remember that the court statistics do not refer to the number of juveniles detained, but only to the number of cases (in the course of a year, one juvenile may be detained in several cases). Based on one-day censuses of detention centers, it appears that the rate of detention of juveniles increased by 68 percent from the mid-1980s to the mid-1990s (Wordes and Jones, 1998). The average length of detention in the mid-1990s was 15 days (Wordes and Jones, 1998).

Of all juvenile cases resulting in detention in 1996, 26 percent were for person offenses, 38 percent were for property offenses, 21 percent were for public order offenses, 12 percent for drug law violations, and 3 percent

---

[6]For comparison purposes, about 37 percent of the adult felony cases in the 75 most populous counties in the United States result in pretrial detention (Hart and Reaves, 1999). Misdemeanor cases do not usually result in detention.

for status delinquency cases (Snyder and Sickmund, 1999). Males are detained at a rate six times higher than females, and blacks are detained at eight times the rate of whites (Wordes and Jones, 1998).

The two generally accepted uses of preadjudication detention are to ensure that a juvenile will show up for his or her hearing and to prevent reoffending prior to adjudication. However, detention is also used as punishment, protection, and as a place to keep juveniles when more appropriate placements are unavailable (Office of Juvenile Justice and Delinquency Prevention, 1997). Intake workers and juvenile judges have a great deal of discretion in deciding whether to place a juvenile in detention. Several studies found evidence that detention rates varied in direct proportion to the availability of detention facilities (Kramer and Steffensmeier, 1978; Lerman, 1977; Pawlak, 1977). Anecdotal evidence suggests that whether a juvenile in crisis is kept in detention or sent to a mental health facility may depend on whether the juvenile's family has health insurance to cover private psychological or psychiatric treatment. The result of the use of detention for such diverse reasons is that a juvenile who has run away from an abusive home may be placed in detention alongside a juvenile awaiting trial for violent crimes.

Detention can be quite disruptive to children's and adolescents' lives. It separates them from their families, friends, and support systems, and it interrupts their schooling. Although some detention centers have many services in place to assess and treat physical and mental health problems and behavioral problems and to provide educational services, the scope and quality of services varies greatly from jurisdiction to jurisdiction. In addition, many detention centers have become overcrowded, jeopardizing their ability to provide services. Nearly 70 percent of children in public detention centers are in facilities operating above their designed capacity (Smith, 1998). Overcrowded conditions have been found to be associated with increased altercations between juveniles and staff and increased injuries to juveniles (Wordes and Jones, 1998). Even under the best of circumstances, providing services to an ever-changing, heterogeneous group of young people can be difficult. The average length of stay in juvenile detention centers is 15 days, but many youngsters may be there for only a few days, while some are there for much longer periods (Parent et al., 1994). For marginal students, even a few days of school missed because of detention may increase their educational difficulties.

The negative effects of being in detention and the overcrowded conditions in many detention centers have led to investigations of alternatives to detention. Table 5-3 summarizes the evaluations of alternatives to detention programs discussed in this section. A study in North Carolina (Land et al., 1998) examined 19 alternatives to detention programs around the state. The programs varied from site to site, but all were characterized by the following factors: careful screening and interviews for case admission of secure custody-eligible juveniles; intensive monitoring and supervision; small caseloads with individualized attention; strict rules for compliance and curfew; contacts at nights and weekends; verification of compliance at home and school; inclusion of supportive community resources; and rapid placement into secure confinement if needed. Land and colleagues (1998) found the programs to provide less restrictive options to secure detention in a cost-effective manner without compromising public safety. Over three-quarters of the cases served by the alternative programs successfully avoided secure detention. The vast majority (80 to 90 percent) of the cases that failed in the alternative program and were sent to secure detention were for technical program violations, not for new offenses. Less than 5 percent of all alternative placement admissions committed new offenses while in the program.

The Annie E. Casey Foundation began a Juvenile Detention Alternatives Initiative in 1992 (Rust, 1999). Five urban jurisdictions—Cook County, Illinois (Chicago); Milwaukee County, Wisconsin; Multnomah County, Oregon (Portland); New York City; and Sacramento County, California—were awarded grants to establish programs to eliminate the inappropriate or unnecessary use of detention, reduce the number of delinquents who fail to appear for court or who commit a new offense, develop alternatives to secure detention rather than adding new detention beds, and to improve conditions and alleviate overcrowding in secure detention facilities. The final evaluation of the programs in Chicago, Portland, and Sacramento, by the National Council on Crime and Delinquency, was due in 2000. Preliminary indications from the evaluation are that the programs achieved significant reductions in admissions to detention and alleviated overcrowding without increasing failure-to-appear rates or pretrial crime rates (Rust, 1999).

After adjudicatory hearings, cases in juvenile court are scheduled for disposition hearings, in which the sanction is determined. Juveniles may be put on probation, placed in a correctional institution or other out-of-home placement, sent to treatment or other programs, or given some other sanction, such as paying restitution or performing community service. The most common disposition is probation; over half of the cases adjudicated delinquent were placed on probation in 1996; 28 percent of those adjudicated delinquent in 1996 were sent to out-of-home placement. Males were more likely than females to be placed (29 and 22 percent of adjudicated delinquency cases involving males and females, respectively) and females were more likely to be put on probation (53 and 59 percent for males and females, respectively). A higher proportion of cases involving blacks and other races results in out-of-home placement than do cases

TABLE 5-3 Interventions in the Juvenile Justice System:
Evaluations of Alternatives to Detention

Intervention	Evaluation Type	Number of subjects at follow-up	Program components
Alternatives to Detention (ATD) programs (Land et al., 1998)		N = 3,183	Alternative to secure detention to allow juveniles to remain at home, with relatives, or other approved placement
Intensive supervision: Intensive Probation Unit (IPU), Michigan Human Services (MHS), and the Comprehensive Youth Training and Community Involvement Program (CYTCIP) (Barton and Butts, 1991)	Random assignment to IPU, MHS, CYTCIP, or state training school (control)	N(exp) = 326 N(control) = 185	IPU: Counseling, monitoring of school attendance, general behavioral supervision; MHS: Youth and family counseling; CYTCIP: Job training and preparedness
North Carolina Court Counselors' Intensive Protective Supervision Randomized Experimental Project (Land et al., 1990, 1992)	Random assignment to intensive protective supervision or regular probation	N(exp) = 90 N(control) = 84	Extensive and proactive contact between counselor, youth, and youth's family; professional analytic or therapeutic services available

Age at treatment	Length of treatment	Length of follow-up	Delinquency and antisocial behavior outcomes	Other outcomes
Not reported	Not reported	6 months	ATD programs successful in avoiding secure detention; Rate of post-program recidivism for successful ATD program completers ranged from 26.4% to 33.8%	
Not reported	Not reported	2 years	No difference in official or self-reported recidivism	
11- to 16-year-olds	Up to a year	1 year	In first 1-1/2 years of program implementation, youths with no prior delinquent offenses less likely to be referred to juvenile court for a delinquent act during period of supervision, but no difference in second 1-1/2 years of program	In first 1-1/2 years of program implementation, youths with no prior delinquent offenses more likely to successfully complete protective supervision program, but no difference in second 1-1/2 years of program

continued

TABLE 5-3 Continued

Intervention	Evaluation Type	Number of subjects at follow-up	Program components
Serious 602 Offender Project (Fagan and Reinarman, 1991)	Random assignment	N(exp) = 267 N(control) = 102	Intensive probation supervision for youths charged with serious offenses: individual and family counseling, school follow-up, group activities, and substance abuse services

involving white juveniles (32 percent for blacks and other races, 26 percent for whites in 1996) (Stahl et al., 1999).

Probation

Over half of juveniles adjudicated delinquent in juvenile court are put on probation, as are one-fifth of those nonadjudicated (found not guilty). One-third of the cases that do not receive formal juvenile court processing are also placed on probation at intake (Stahl et al., 1999). In 1996, 634,100 criminal delinquent cases and 58,300 status offense delinquent cases resulted in probation. These figures do not include juveniles who were under the supervision of probation departments after serving time in a residential facility. National figures for the latter group are not collected.

Probation is essentially surveillance designed to prevent reoffending, with the threat of punishment and to detect reoffending if it should occur. Surveillance alone may be insufficient to prevent reoffending. Research with adults has found that the most successful probation programs combine both treatment and surveillance (Petersilia, 1997).

The early founders of juvenile courts saw probation as one of the most significant components of the juvenile court system (Schlossman, 1983). Probation provided the opportunity to rehabilitate juveniles in their homes rather than incarcerating them. Probation officers could get

Age at treatment	Length of treatment	Length of follow-up	Delinquency and antisocial behavior outcomes	Other outcomes
Up to 17.5 years; 15.02 (avg.)	Not reported	36 months	No difference in recidivism between experimental group in Contra Costa County or control group; Experimental group in Richmond had more youths arrested for violent offenses but a lower number of youths rearrested for any offenses in general	

to know the individual juveniles and their families and therefore provide individualized guidance. As with other ideals of the juvenile court, the reality of probation did not always live up to its expectations, either at the beginning of the juvenile courts 100 years ago or today. Nevertheless, probation has remained the overwhelming dispositional choice for adjudicated offenders of juvenile courts since statistics were first kept in 1927 (Torbet, 1996).

There is a great deal of variety in the responsibilities and structure of probation departments from state to state and even within states. In general, juvenile probation departments have three basic functions: intake screening of cases referred to juvenile court, presentence investigations, and court-ordered supervision of juveniles. This section deals only with court-ordered supervision of juveniles who were given probation as their primary disposition. The use of probation officers to supervise juveniles following incarceration is covered in the section on after care; it is not always easy to separate the two conditions, however. The same parole officers may oversee juveniles whose primary sanction was probation (probationers) and juveniles who have been released from incarceration (parolees). Conditions of probation may be similar for both groups of juveniles. Both probationers and parolees may attend the same treatment programs while serving their probation.

There has been little evaluation of traditional probation practices, with more research emphasis being focused on such alternatives as intensive supervision (Clear and Braga, 1995). Intensive supervision, as its name implies, involves more intense scrutiny and monitoring than traditional probation. Interest in intensive supervision probation has waxed and waned since the 1960s. Spurred by both increasing overcrowding in correctional facilities and the get-tough approach, intensive supervision programs grew in popularity in the late 1980s (Armstrong, 1991). Studies of intensive supervision for adult offenders have not found increased monitoring alone to reduce recidivism. In fact, increased monitoring may detect more cases of technical probation violations than regular probation (MacKenzie, 1997), leading to higher rates of measured reoffending if technical violations are included in recidivism measures.

A study by Land and colleagues (1990, 1992) examined an intensive supervision program for status delinquency cases. Status offenders were randomly assigned to regular probation or to intensive supervision. In addition to frequent visits with the juvenile and his or her family from the counselor (as often as daily at first, then at least weekly thereafter, compared with visits once every 90 days for regular probation), juveniles and their families in intensive supervision were directed to community programs to assist them. Based on individualized assessments and program plans, juveniles in the intensive supervision program were given behavioral objectives to be met and were regularly assessed on their progress. A year after treatment end, juveniles in intensive supervision had significantly fewer criminal delinquency referrals than did those in regular probation. There was no difference between the groups in status offense referrals. As the program matured and became routinized, it appeared to become less effective. Status offenders who entered the program after it had been in existence for 1.5 years were as likely to be referred for criminal delinquency as were those in regular probation. Land et al. (1992) noted that there were fewer referrals to services made in the mature program than occurred when it was new, and that staff received less attention and support after the program was well established. Intensive supervision coupled with treatment and well-supported staff appears to have the potential to keep status offenders who have not already been involved in criminal delinquency from committing criminal delinquent acts.

Most of the intensive supervision probation programs instituted beginning in the late 1980s and throughout the 1990s have been targeted not at status offenders, but at high-risk juveniles for whom community safety demands more intense supervision than can be provided under routine probation (Armstrong, 1991). These intensive supervision programs vary greatly from jurisdiction to jurisdiction. Some include short-term residential placements with intensive community-based services; others rely on frequent contact between the probation officer and the juvenile. The definition of *frequent* also varies from daily to weekly, but it is always more frequent than traditional probation.

Several studies have evaluated intensive supervision of probationers.[7] A study in which juveniles were randomly assigned to one of three in-home programs in Detroit, Michigan, or to the state training school (the control group), found no significant differences in recidivism (measured by court appearances for new offenses) or self-reported criminal delinquency among all four groups during the two-year follow-up (Barton and Butts, 1991). The in-home programs cost only one-third the expense of incarceration in training schools. The evaluators concluded that intensive in-home programs were cost-effective and posed no increased danger to the community.

A three-year follow-up of juvenile offenders randomly assigned to regular probation or intensive probation in Contra Costa County, California, found little difference in recidivism (measured by rearrest, court appearances, incarceration, and self-reported offending) between the two groups (Fagan and Reinarman, 1991). Although the intensive program was designed to include more therapeutic programs than regular probation, in practice, the major difference was the number of contacts between probation officers and juveniles—weekly for intensive supervision and monthly for regular probation. The program was originally intended for serious and violent offenders, but many nonviolent, less serious offenders ended up in the program. The authors concluded that regular probation suffices for most juvenile offenders and that intensive supervision should be reserved for serious and violent offenders who have failed under regular probation conditions.

A number of researchers (e.g., Altschuler and Armstrong, 1991; Baird, 1991; Clear, 1991) argue that intensive supervision is warranted only for juveniles at high risk of serious reoffending. Defining which juveniles are high risk and therefore warrant intensive supervision, however, is a complicated and difficult task. Relying solely on the seriousness of the current offense is inadequate, as that alone is a poor predictor of future offending (see, for example, Wolfgang et al., 1972). Judicial judgments of dangerousness have been shown to be quite poor at accurately predicting which offenders are dangerous (Fagan and Guggenheim, 1996). Demonstrating the success or failure of intensive supervision programs may ride on their ability to identify the appropriate group of juveniles to serve.

---

[7]Studies that evaluate intensive supervision programs for parolees or for a combination of probationers and parolees are discussed in the section below on after care.

Incarceration

Deprivation of liberty through incarceration is usually thought to be the most severe sanction that can be meted out by the justice system.[8] Of all juvenile criminal delinquency cases disposed in 1996, 18 percent (320,900 cases) resulted in detention. The type of offenses for which juveniles are detained include not only violent offenses but also property and drug offenses.

The Census of Juveniles in Residential Placement (CJRP), conducted on October 29, 1997, found that nearly 93,000 youngsters under age 18 were held in public or private detention, correctional, and shelter facilities (Gallagher, 1999). The CJRP, which collects individual data on each person under age 21 held in residential facilities, replaced the Children in Custody census, which collected aggregate data on persons under age 21 in each facility biennially from 1971 through 1995. Differences in methodology between the two censuses make direct comparisons of the numbers of juveniles in custody over time problematic. It appears that the numbers of juveniles in custody has grown steadily since 1975 (see Figure 5-4). It is impossible to determine, however, how much of the increase from 1995 to 1997 is real and how much is an artifact of the change in method of data collection. Nevertheless, the United States has a high rate of juveniles in custody—368 per 100,000 juveniles (Snyder and Sickmund, 1999)—a rate that is higher than the adult incarceration rate in most other countries (Mauer, 1997).

It is easy to forget that most children who are incarcerated will be out on the streets in a few years or months. What they learn through the juvenile justice system is likely to influence their behavior later. Their access to appropriate education and vocational training and to mental health services may make all the difference between successful reintegration into society and reoffending.

Conditions in juvenile facilities vary greatly, from those in which appropriate educational and other services are provided and staff are well trained to those in which many juveniles spend much of their time in cells with nothing to do, and where facilities are unsafe and unsanitary, services are lacking, and staff are poorly trained and may even be abusive. In 1995, Human Rights Watch (1995) documented physical abuse of juveniles in Louisiana's Tallulah Correctional Center for Youth. The *New York Times* (1998) documented continuing physical abuse and other problems in this facility in 1998, which "houses 620 boys and young men, age

---

[8]Research has found that some adult offenders prefer incarceration to intensive supervision probation, indicating that at least some offenders find intensive supervision more punitive (Crouch, 1993; Petersilia and Deschenes, 1994).

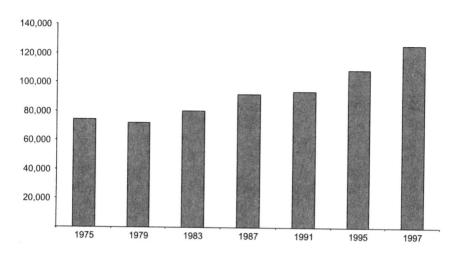

FIGURE 5-4 Total number of youth under 21 in custody. Source: Data for 1975 to 1991 from Smith (1998); data for 1995 and 1997 from Snyder and Sickmund (1999).

11 to 20, in stifling corrugated-iron barracks jammed with bunks. . . . Meals are so meager that many boys lose weight. Clothing is so scarce that boys fight over shirts and shoes. Almost all of the teachers are uncertified, instruction amounts to as little as an hour a day, and until recently there were no books." In late 1999, three boot camps in Maryland were closed and top juvenile justice officials lost their jobs after physical abuse of juveniles by staff was found to be widespread (*The Washington Post*, 1999). The *Arkansas Democrat-Gazette* reported in June 1998 that boys in the Central Arkansas Observation and Assessment Center seldom saw daylight, were given clean clothing only every other week, and were subjected to the unsanitary condition of raw sewage backing up into shower drains whenever toilets were flushed (Coalition for Juvenile Justice, 1999).

In contrast, some facilities provide a wide range of programs in well-kept settings. The Giddings State Training School in Texas has modern educational facilities that are wired for the Internet and offers high school equivalency classes and vocational training. The facility has intensive treatment for drug abusers, sexual offenders, and capital offenders. The facilities are tended by the residents and are clean and well kept (Coalition for Juvenile Justice, 1999).[9] Ferris School in Delaware, after years of fighting lawsuits, was rebuilt and restructured in the mid-1990s. Education is now stressed over punishment there. In fact, Ferris is the only education program in a juvenile secure care facility in the Mid-Atlantic region to receive accreditation (Coalition for Juvenile Justice, 1999).

Even in well-kept settings, however, some misbehaving youth are punished through isolation or deprivation of privileges. The panel could find no studies of the impact of these punishments on the behavior of juveniles either during incarceration or upon release.

The only national study of conditions of confinement in juvenile correctional facilities (Parent et al., 1994) found substantial and widespread problems concerning amount of living space, health care, security, and control of suicidal behavior. Crowded conditions are widespread in juvenile training and reform schools. In 1995, 68 percent of juveniles in public facilities and 15 percent in private facilities were in facilities that housed more juveniles than they had been designed to house (Smith, 1998). Overcrowded conditions are not only unpleasant, but also may be dangerous—both staff and juveniles have higher rates of injury in overcrowded facilities (Parent et al., 1994). Injury rates were also higher for both juveniles and staff in facilities in which living units were locked 24 hours a day, regardless of the percentage of youth incarcerated for violent crimes, than in less secure facilities. The study found that large dormitory sleeping arrangements were accompanied by high rates of juvenile-on-juvenile injuries. Single sleeping rooms were related to suicidal behavior, with the rate of suicide attempts increasing as the percentage of juveniles in single rooms increased (Parent et al., 1994). Apparently, rooms housing two or three juveniles are preferable to either single rooms or large dormitories.

Parent and colleagues (1994) also found serious deficiencies in health care for incarcerated juveniles. Health care screenings, which national standards say should occur within one hour of admissions, and appraisals, which should occur within seven days of admission, are often not completed in a timely manner. Timely screenings are important to identify injuries and acute health problems that may require immediate attention. Timely health appraisals are important to identify health care needs that require treatment during confinement and to prevent the spread of infectious diseases. In addition, the Parent et al. study found that health care screenings may be performed by staff with no health training. This was a particular problem in detention centers, where one-third of juveniles were screened by untrained staff.

---

[9]Members of the study panel visited the Giddings School and can corroborate the praise of the facility by the Coalition for Juvenile Justice. How to handle very disruptive and violent youth, who end up in isolated lock-up, however, remains a problem for this facility.

Parent et al. (1994) also examined education, recreation, and mental health programming in juvenile facilities. They found that, in the early 1990s, 65 percent of juveniles in public facilities were in institutions with current court orders or consent decrees related to programming deficiencies. They could not determine which areas of programming were specified in the orders and decrees, however. Nevertheless, this finding points to widespread inadequacies in services available to juveniles held in residential facilities.

Educational Needs and Services

Many children and adolescents involved in the juvenile justice system have fared poorly in school and have significant educational needs. Although not as well studied as the mental health needs of these youngsters (discussed in the next section), many have not attended school recently and many perform below grade level. In addition, for most incarcerated juveniles, correctional education services are their last exposure to formal education (Dedel, 1997). In site visits made during their study, Parent et al. (1994) received estimates from language teachers in juvenile facilities that 32 percent of their students read at or below 4th-grade level, 27 percent at 5th- or 6th-grade level, 20 percent at 7th- or 8th-grade level, and 21 percent at or above 9th-grade level. A Massachusetts state court decision (*Green v. Johnson*, 513F. Supp. 965, 968 D. Mass., 1981) estimated that 50 to 80 percent of children in juvenile facilities were handicapped under the definitions in the federal Education for All Handicapped Children Act.

The Parent et al. (1994) study found that nearly all juveniles are held in facilities that provide some kind of educational programming: 95 percent of juveniles in detention centers had access to educational programming, as did 97 percent in training schools, and 96 percent in ranches, camps, or farms.[10] The quality of the educational programming, however, appeared to vary greatly from site to site. The American Correctional Association standards recommend that educational programs in juvenile facilities use state-certified teachers, have a maximum student-to-teacher ratio of 15:1, and assess the educational status of juveniles to develop individualized educational plans. Only 55 percent of training school residents and 29 percent of ranch, camp, or farm residents are in facilities that meet all the recommended educational standards. The

---

[10]Adjudicated delinquents who do not require strict confinement in a training school may be sent to a ranch, camp, or farm run by the state or local government or by private organizations for long-term residential placement.

Parent et al. (1994) study did not have access to information on educational outcomes to assess the effects of the educational programming on residents. Dedel (1997) reports that 75 percent of students in custody advanced less than a full grade level per year while in custody.

Mental Health Needs

A number of studies of incarcerated juveniles have found the prevalence of psychiatric disorders, diagnosed from structured interviews or clinical assessments, to be three to five times higher than in the general population of young people (Chiles et al., 1980; Davis et al., 1991; Eppright et al., 1993; Hollander and Turner, 1985; Lewis et al., 1987; McManus et al., 1984a; McManus et al., 1984b; Miller et al., 1982; Shelton, 1998; Steiner et al., 1997; Timmons-Mitchell et al., 1997). Conduct disorder was present in over 80 percent of incarcerated youth (Davis et al., 1991; Eppright et al., 1993; Hollander and Turner, 1985; Timmons-Mitchell et al., 1997). This finding is not surprising because the criteria for a diagnosis of conduct disorder includes delinquent and criminal behavior, such as truancy, arson, theft, breaking and entering, and assault. Other psychiatric disorders found among detained and incarcerated young people included depressive disorders, attention deficit hyperactivity disorder (ADHD), and psychotic disorders. Studies also report many times more personality disorders, especially borderline personality disorder, among incarcerated youth than among the general population of young people. At least half of juvenile detainees also report substance abuse (Davis et al., 1991; Timmons-Mitchell et al., 1997).

A study of randomly selected incarcerated boys and girls in Ohio found that girls displayed significantly more mental health problems (other than conduct disorder) than boys—84 percent of girls had a mental health disorder compared with 27 percent of boys. Studies of adult incarcerated women suggest that psychiatric disorders are also much more prevalent in adult incarcerated women than in either adult incarcerated men or the general population (Jordan et al., 1996; Teplin et al., 1996).

Juvenile offenders have been found to have a high rate of drug and alcohol use. In 1998, the Arrestee Drug Abuse Monitoring Program found illegal substances in the urine of 40 to over 60 percent (depending on the city) of male juvenile arrestees (National Institute of Justice, 1999). An analysis of the National Youth Survey found a strong correlation between serious substance use and serious delinquent behavior (Johnson et al., 1993): 23 percent of juveniles who reported involvement in multiple serious crimes were current cocaine users, compared with 3 percent of nondelinquents. Drug and alcohol use often coexist with other mental health problems (McBride et al., 1999).

Young people with substance abuse or mental health disorders in juvenile correctional facilities have little chance of receiving either an adequate assessment or appropriate treatment. Furthermore, treatment is very rarely coordinated with services after youth are released. Longitudinal evidence suggests that delinquents with serious psychiatric disorders are less likely than others to desist from delinquency in their late teens or twenties (Hare et al., 1988; Robins, 1974). The lack of adequate mental health treatment in the juvenile correctional facilities represents a lost opportunity for these juveniles.

Evaluations of Treatments in the Juvenile Justice System

Although no treatment program works 100 percent of the time for 100 percent of the participants, there are treatment programs that have been found to reduce the rate of future offending, whereas some get-tough sanctions have been found to increase recidivism. The panel did not have the resources to examine all the literature relevant to treatment of juveniles under the control of the juvenile justice system (Lipsey and Wilson, 1998, alone found 200 experimental or quasiexperimental studies for their meta-analysis). Rather, we relied on published reviews (Krisberg and Howell, 1998; MacKenzie, 1997; Petrosino et al., 2000) and several meta-analyses (Gottschalk et al., 1987; Lipsey, 1995; Lipsey and Wilson, 1998; Mayer et al., 1986).

Lipsey and colleagues have performed several meta-analytic studies of treatments for juvenile offenders (Lipsey, 1995; Lipsey and Wilson, 1998). Meta-analysis allows the quantitative findings of many studies to be combined and statistically analyzed. Differences in study methods and procedures can be controlled for statistically, allowing a pattern of treatment effects across studies to be revealed. Effect size is the usual measure employed in meta-analyses. It should be noted that effect size is influenced as much by the nature of the comparison group as by the treatment programs being evaluated. Meta-analyses can be an extremely important aid to identifying good treatment programs, but their use cannot overcome problems of poor research design. In fact, when meta-analyses are not based on rigorous criteria for inclusion, the results can be misleading.

In a meta-analysis of 400 research studies of programs for delinquency reduction, Lipsey (1995) found that the average effect across all the programs studied was a 10 percent reduction in delinquency among participants in the program compared with a control group. However, there was wide variety from program to program, with some studies finding increased delinquency among participants in certain programs and studies of other types of programs finding a 30 percent improvement in the program participants over the control group. Overall, Lipsey (1995) found that programs that targeted behavioral change in a relatively structured and concrete manner had a greater effect on reducing delinquency than programs that targeted psychological change through traditional counseling or casework approaches. Other meta-analyses have similarly found that cognitive-behavioral, skill-oriented, and multimodal programs have the best effects (Gottschalk et al., 1987; Mayer et al., 1986). This pattern held for programs conducted under the auspices of the juvenile justice system and for those run by other institutions.

Of particular concern are programs that increased delinquency. Lipsey (1995:74) says about them:

> Most notable are the deterrence approaches such as shock incarceration. Despite their popularity, the available studies indicate that they actually result in delinquency increases rather than decreases. Unfortunately, there are distressingly few studies in this category, making any conclusions provisional. The studies we do have, however, raise grave doubts about the effectiveness of these forms of treatment.

A systematic review of evaluations of deterrence programs, such as Scared Straight, that involve exposing youngsters who have come in contact with the juvenile justice system to prison life and adult inmates was undertaken by Petrosino and colleagues (2000). None of the nine evaluations that involved random assignment of youngsters to the treatment or control groups found any positive effect on future delinquency. Seven of the studies found that the effects of the program were harmful, that is, youngsters in treatment were more likely to commit additional delinquent acts than were those in the control group who received no treatment.

Lipsey (1995) also found that the length of the program and how well it was planned and delivered affected how well the program reduced delinquency. Programs that were monitored to ensure that they were delivered as planned had larger effects than programs that were not monitored. More of an otherwise effective program appears to be better than less. In general, Lipsey (1995) recommended that programs should have 100 hours or more of total contact with the juvenile, delivered at two or more contacts per week, over a period of 26 weeks or longer. Because the average length of stay for juveniles in residential placement is less than four months (Smith, 1998)—significantly shorter than 26 weeks—it may be difficult to provide programs over a sufficient length of time to make a difference for many youth in residential placement. Continuity of programming after release may be a way to increase effectiveness. It should be noted, however, that Lipsey and Wilson (1998) found that characteristics of effective programming both inside and outside institutions differed.

Lipsey and Wilson (1998) performed a separate meta-analysis on 200 studies of all the experimental or quasi-experimental studies of the effects of interventions with serious juvenile offenders. They summarize their results as follows (Lipsey and Wilson, 1998:229-230): "The average intervention effect for these studies was positive, statistically significant, and equivalent to a recidivism reduction of about 6 percentage points, for example, from 50 percent to 44 percent (mean effect size = 0.12). The variation around this overall mean, however, was considerable."

Lipsey and Wilson (1998:330) note that the primary lesson of their study is "that sufficient research has not yet been conducted on the effects of intervention with serious juvenile offenders." They found that the dimensions that characterized good programs for incarcerated offenders differed from those for nonincarcerated offenders. Therefore, they searched separately for effective programs in these two settings. Programs that provided interpersonal skills and insight into their own behavior and programs that placed offenders into community-based teaching family homes were most consistently effective for incarcerated offenders. Individual counseling, teaching of interpersonal skills and insight into their own behavior, and behavioral programming were most successful for the nonincarcerated offenders.

Of course, no program is effective for all offenders. A variety of attempts have been made to match offenders to programs on the basis of assessed needs. Whether such matching can be the basis for improved results has been the subject of some debate (see, e.g., Andrews et al., 1990b; Lab and Whitehead, 1990). Because effective programming can be costly, benefits should be carefully determined and reported (MacKenzie, 1997).

Although studies have focused on recidivism rates for treatment programs, there seem to be few credible studies of effects of policies in residential facilities, such as television viewing, recreational privileges, or the use of isolation or of lockups that occur in training or reform schools designed for juveniles. Many juvenile correction systems employ a behavior modification strategy tying rewards (e.g., to purchase special food, watch TV, use the library, play athletic games) to compliance. These systems also typically link punishments to misbehavior. Although designed to teach inmates better behavior, empirical evidence has demonstrated that the strategy may backfire with some populations (Deci, 1971; Kruglanski et al., 1971; Lepper et al., 1997). Because the punishments used in reformatories involve physical force, lockups, isolation, and a variety of forms of deprivation, some juveniles may be learning that force is appropriate to obtain compliance. Studies are needed to learn about effects of lockups and of behavior modification strategies in order to ensure that the juvenile justice system is not creating or exacerbating problems it is designed to alleviate.

After Care and Reintegration

Following incarceration, most juvenile offenders will return to the communities from which they came. As with the adult system, juvenile corrections officials have a poor record of controlling juvenile parolees released from secure detention into the community. As in the adult system, concerns have been raised that heavy caseloads and poor quality and delivery of services affect offender rehabilitation and public safety. This situation has led to the testing of models of intensive parole supervision and after care (Altschuler and Armstrong, 1994a). Knowing how difficult it is for all individuals to make major changes in complex behavior patterns, it should not be surprising that juvenile offenders may need assistance if they are to avoid reoffending. Even for those who received appropriate treatment programs while incarcerated, change may be difficult to maintain when they return to their old environment. For juveniles to succeed in reintegrating into the community, more emphasis may have to be placed on continued treatment rather than merely on surveillance and monitoring.

Intensive after-care programs have evolved over the past 10 years out of the adult supervision probation movement and juvenile intensive supervision probation programs (Altschuler and Armstrong, 1994a). The intensive after-care model, as designed by Altschuler and Armstrong (1994b), represents a reintegrative alternative to confinement and release into the community under traditional parole supervision. From initial confinement to transition into the community, the goals of intensive after-care programs are to prepare the offender for prosocial adjustment to life in the community and in social networks (e.g., family, peers, school, and employment). The after-care component combines surveillance and control of offenders in the community with the provision of treatment and services based on the offender's needs and an assessment of factors that might increase his or her chances of reoffending. The combination of treatment and surveillance is critical to the intensive after-care model. Reviews of the research suggest that community corrections programs that emphasize surveillance and control only may not be enough (Byrne and Brewster, 1993; Petersilia, 1997; Petersilia and Turner, 1993). Community-based corrections programs that balance the provision of treatment and rehabilitation services (i.e., individual and family counseling, drug treatment, and vocational or employment training and assistance) with offender surveillance and monitoring (i.e., drug testing, curfew, and electronic monitoring) should be carefully evaluated to learn what mix is effective.

Very few studies have been conducted that evaluate the effectiveness of juvenile corrections programs; even less is known about how juveniles adjust to the community when they are released from secure confinement. Although there is evidence that rehabilitation programs, in general, can work (Andrews and Bonta, 1994; Andrews et al., 1990a, 1990b; Gendreau and Ross, 1979; Palmer, 1975), more information is needed on what programs work best for whom.

There is evidence that elements of the confinement experience increase the probability of failure upon release (Byrne and Kelly,1989; Hagan, 1991; National Research Council, 1993; Shannon, 1988). Moreover, researchers have found that the provision of services to offenders may be more effective when administered in the community rather than in secure facilities (Lipsey, 1992). Some research has also shown that length of confinement has no effect on rearrest rates of juvenile parolees (Beck and Shipley, 1987; Cohen and Canela-Cacho, 1994; National Research Council, 1993).

The most promising programs and strategies for use in juvenile after-care programs include those that address the needs and risk factors for reoffending of high-risk juveniles leaving secure confinement. Lipsey and Wilson's (1998) meta-analysis suggests that programs that provide interpersonal skill training (i.e., social skills training), behavioral contracting, and cognitive-behavioral individualized counseling are best at reducing recidivism rates for noninstitutionalized youth. These are the types of treatment and rehabilitation programs offered in many intensive after-care programs.

There have been very few scientifically rigorous evaluations of juvenile after-care programs. In addition, intensive supervision programs often mix probationers and parolees, making it difficult to separate possible different effects on juveniles diverted from incarceration and on those released from incarceration. Generally, these studies have failed to find consistent evidence of the effectiveness of juvenile intensive supervision programs and after care in reducing reoffending (Altschuler et al., 1999). As noted in the discussion of probation, intensive supervision may simply bring more technical violations of parole conditions or other delinquent acts to the attention of authorities than would be the case under routine parole or probation. Outcomes in addition to rearrest or reincarceration should be considered in evaluating program success. Intensive supervision after-care programs often include goals similar to those found in the restorative justice model, such as restitution and reintegration. How successful programs are in having juveniles pay fines, complete victim restitution conditions, attend school, or find a job are some of the other areas that could be considered in addition to recidivism measures. Evaluations of after-care programs are summarized in Table 5-4.

TABLE 5-4 Interventions in the Juvenile Justice System:
Evaluations of After Care Programs

Intervention	Evaluation Type	Number of subjects at follow-up	Program components
Philadelphia Intensive Probation Aftercare Program (Sontheimer and Goodstein, 1993)	Random assignment to intensive aftercare probation or traditional probation	N(exp) = 44 N(control) = 46	Frequent contact by probation officer with youth and youth's family; aftercare plan including education, job placement, and counseling
Maryland Drug Treatment Program (Sealock et al., 1997)	Quasi-experimental	N(aftercare) = 120 N(comparison) - 132	Intense supervision, youth support group meetings, family support group meetings, counseling
Skillman Aftercare Experiment (Greenwood et al., 1993)	Random assignment	N(exp) = 57 N(control) = 67	Intense supervision and assistance by well-trained aftercare workers; family counseling and referral for assistance
Minnesota diversion and after care (Deschenes et al., 1996)	Quasi-experimental	N(program) = 97 N(comparison) = 95	Wilderness activities, skills training followed by community surveillance and treatment including family services

Age at treatment	Length of treatment	Length of follow-up	Delinquency and antisocial behavior outcomes	Other outcomes
17.1 years (avg.)	3 to 16 months (11 months average)		Fewer arrests among intensive probation group; lower rate of subsequent conviction and incarceration among experimental group	
not reported	44 weeks (average)	18 months (from entry into study)	No difference between groups on proportion arrested, but aftercare group had fewer arrests for crimes against persons	
17 (avg.)	6 months	1 year	No difference between groups on proportion arrested, self-reported offending, or drug use	
14 and older	3 months residential followed by 9 months intensive community supervision	2 years	No difference in felony arrest rate between intervention and comparison groups	

continued

TABLE 5-4 Continued

Intervention	Evaluation Type	Number of subjects at follow-up	Program components
Multifaceted intensive supervision (Minor and Elrod, 1990)	Random assignment (2 x 2 factorial between-groups design)	N(exp, intensive) = 7 N(exp, moderate) = 15 N(control, intensive) = 8 N(control, moderate) = 15	Job preparation, outdoor experience, family skill building
Intensive supervision (Barton and Butts, 1990)	Random assignment	N(exp) = 326 N(control) = 185	Intensive probation (in lieu of incarceration — not aftercare move to chapter 5?)

Some evaluations of intensive after care have indicated moderate benefits. For example, an evaluation of the Philadelphia Intensive Probation Aftercare Program, in which serious juvenile offenders in one institution were randomly assigned to intensive after care or typical probation, found that, although the same proportions of youths in after care as without after care had been arrested, those in after care had fewer arrests (Sontheimer and Goodstein, 1993). The Philadelphia youth in the intensive probation group who were arrested were significantly less likely to be convicted or reincarcerated than those assigned to typical probation. Youth participating in juvenile after care as part of the Maryland Drug Treatment Program performed no better in terms of alleged or adjudicated offenses than those in a control group; however, after-care participants did have significantly fewer new crimes against persons than controls (Sealock et al., 1995, 1997).

In an evaluation conducted by Greenwood and colleagues (1993) of two intensive after-care programs implemented in Detroit and Pittsburgh,

Age at treatment	Length of treatment	Length of follow-up	Delinquency and antisocial behavior outcomes	Other outcomes
12- to 17-year olds (avg. age of 15)	3 months	18 months	No differences in self-reported or officially recorded delinquency except for experimental subjects with extensive offending histories, who had significantly fewer offenses during follow-up than controls with similar backgrounds.	
15.4 (avg. age)	1 year	2 years	No difference in criminal charges brought against the two groups; no difference in self-reported offending	

youth randomly assigned to either intensive after care or traditional supervision performed equally well when compared on the proportion of arrests, self-reported offending, and drug use during a 12-month follow-up period. Deschenes et al. (1996) conducted a quasi-experimental evaluation of youth participating in a program that combined an alternative to traditional residential confinement (three months of participation in a wilderness camp) with placement in intensive after-care supervision (treatment and surveillance) upon release. When compared with youth placed in a traditional residential facility (the control group), program participants did no better on measures of arrest and self-reported drug use. Program participants did, however, report less involvement in drug selling than the control group.

Other studies show less positive findings. Minor and Elrod (1990) found no significant differences in self-reported or officially recorded delinquency overall, although juveniles in intensive supervision with extensive offending histories had significantly fewer offenses during an

18-month follow-up than controls with similar backgrounds. In an experimental study conducted by Barton and Butts (1990), juveniles randomly assigned to intensive supervision had more delinquency charges than those randomly assigned to the control group, but these charges were less severe. When only criminal charges were considered, the two groups had similar levels of charges. Both groups also had similar levels of self-reported reoffending.

This research is far from conclusive. It seems clear that delinquent juveniles require more than intensive surveillance and control to affect rates of future offending. Determining the appropriate amount and type of treatment and services is clearly an issue in need of further research and clarification. Change among delinquents may involve some backsliding. Relapse is known to be part of other forms of habit change (e.g., smoking, drinking, and drug use) and relapse prevention has become a standard part of drug and alcohol treatment programs (Institute of Medicine, 1990, 1997).

No clear evidence shows whether services or treatment are better received in the community or in secure confinement. As for program content, more research is needed that untangles effects attributable to intensive supervision from those of treatment and rehabilitation provided along with the supervision. It is also unclear from existing intensive supervision evaluations which specific rehabilitation and treatment programs are effective and for whom (Altschuler et al., 1999). Several intensive after-care programs are currently being evaluated through grants from the Office of Juvenile Justice and Delinquency Prevention.

JUSTICE SYSTEM INVOLVEMENT AND EMPLOYMENT

Being caught by the police and caught up in the juvenile or criminal justice systems are especially hazardous for youth from disadvantaged backgrounds, because becoming involved in crime can produce not only future criminality, but also later problems in finding employment. These problems can be further conceptualized in terms of a process of "criminal embeddedness" (Hagan, 1993; Hagan and McCarthy, 1997).

For most individuals, the key to a successful transition from adolescence to adulthood is finding a job, and this involves social embeddedness. The personal contacts of individuals, friends, and families and the network of relations that flow from these contacts are important sources of social capital used in finding jobs and making job changes (Coleman, 1990; Granovetter, 1974). Youth from advantaged class backgrounds are more likely than others to have the social capital that derives from being socially embedded in job networks. This embeddedness facilitates finding and changing jobs.

However, just as early employment contacts can enhance the prospects of getting a job and subsequent occupational mobility, contacts with crime and the justice system seem likely, in a converse way, to increase the probability of unemployment. For example, criminal involvements of family and friends are more likely to integrate young people into the criminal underworld than into referral networks of legal employment. And youthful delinquent acts and justice system supervision are likely to further distance juveniles from the job contacts that initiate and sustain legitimate occupational careers. Criminal embeddedness is a liability in terms of prospects for stable adult employment. This embeddedness is compounded by the effects of becoming officially labeled and known as a criminal offender, especially in distressed community settings in which few jobs are available in any case.

These risks are reflected in a recent analysis of juveniles tracked from childhood through adulthood in a London working-class neighborhood (Hagan, 1993). This study reveals that intergenerational patterns of criminal conviction make youth especially prone to subsequent delinquency and adult unemployment (Hagan, 1993; Hagan and Palloni, 1990; Ward and Tittle, 1993). Other studies similarly show that working-class males with conviction records are uniquely disadvantaged in finding and maintaining employment (Laub and Sampson, 1995; Schwartz and Skolnick, 1964), and that a criminal arrest record can have negative effects on employment as much as eight years later (Freeman, 1992; Grogger, 1995; Thornberry and Christenson, 1984). Conviction and imprisonment have also been shown to have a permanent impact on legal earnings (Freeman, 1992; Hunt et al., 1993; Needels, 1996; Sampson and Laub, 1993). For example, Freeman's (1992) analysis of the Boston Youth Survey indicated that youths who were incarcerated had exceptionally low chances of employment; similarly, his analysis of the National Longitudinal Survey of Youth revealed that men who had been in jail or on probation experienced "massive long-term effects on employment" (Freeman, 1992:217). Sampson and Laub (1993) found that unstable employment and a higher likelihood of welfare dependence characterized the lives of the delinquent boys in a prospective sample of 500 delinquents and 500 nondelinquents. Moreover, juvenile incarceration was found to have an indirect effect on the incidence of future crime, because "incarceration appears to cut off opportunities and prospects for stable employment [and] job stability in turn has importance in explaining later crime" (Laub and Sampson, 1995:256). Other data indicate that while more than half of state prisoners are employed before going to jail, only about a fifth of those on parole are employed following imprisonment (Irwin and Austin, 1994).

It is therefore important to emphasize the role of the police, courts, and prisons in the development of these youthful criminal careers. Sullivan (1989) found in the more stable white neighborhood he studied that parents, using their well-developed social networks and resulting social capital, "sought to manipulate the system—and were often successful in doing so—by means of money and personal connections" (p. 196). In contrast, in both of the minority neighborhoods Sullivan studied, youth began to move further away from home to commit violent economic crimes and encountered more serious sanctions when they did so. These crimes produced short-term gains, but they also separated minority youths from the legitimate labor market, stigmatizing and further damaging their social and cultural capital in terms of later job prospects. Of the minority youth, Sullivan writes that "their participation in regular acts of income-producing crime and the resulting involvement with the criminal justice system in turn kept them out of school and forced them to abandon their earlier occupational goals" (p. 64). Court appearances and resulting confinements removed these youth from whatever possibility for inclusion in job referral networks school might provide and placed them in prison and community-based crime networks that further isolated them from legitimate employment.

It is not surprising, therefore, that Sullivan's work and other recent ethnographies of poverty and crime make the point that the material gains associated with embeddedness in the drug economy usually prove to be transitory. For example, in *Getting Paid*, Sullivan (1989) argues that although participation in the underground economy may yield temporary material gains, over time it becomes a limitation, and those involved "age out of youth crime and accept . . . low wage, unstable jobs" (Sullivan, 1989:250). Joan Moore, in *Going Down to the Barrio*, suggests a similar conclusion when she observes that "the very culture of defiance at best dooms the boys to jobs just like their fathers hold," serving in the end "to keep working-class kids in the working class" (Moore, 1991:42). Felix Padilla echoes this theme in his ethnography of *The Gang as an American Enterprise*, noting that "instead of functioning as a progressive and liberating agent capable of transforming and correcting the youngsters' economic plight, the gang assisted in reinforcing it" (Padilla, 1992:163). In each of these ethnographies and in the related studies noted earlier, it is embeddedness in crime networks, including the juvenile and the criminal justice systems, that seals the economic fate of these young people.

Thus a number of studies now confirm that as time spent in prison increases, net of other background factors and involvements, the subsequent likelihood of disengagement from the legal economy increases. This is not surprising, given that even those in disadvantaged neighborhoods who do not have criminal records have difficulty finding employment. Hagan (1991), using data from a 13-year panel study, and Grogger (1995), analyzing arrest data from the California Justice Department's Adult Criminal Justice Statistical System and earnings records from the California Employment Development Department, have demonstrated that even being charged and arrested are detrimental in the near term for occupational outcomes and earnings.

GIRLS IN THE JUVENILE JUSTICE SYSTEM

As discussed in Chapter 2, arrests of girls, although smaller in number than those of boys, have increased at a faster rate. The police are not the only justice system agency to see an increase in the number of female juvenile offenders; increases also extend to juvenile courts. Between 1987 and 1996, the number of cases involving female juveniles that were petitioned to juvenile court increased 76 percent, while the number involving male juveniles increased 42 percent. Girls, however, still only made up a little over 20 percent of juvenile court criminal delinquency cases and about 40 percent of status delinquency cases in 1996 (Stahl et al., 1999).

The nature of the offenses for which girls are seen in juvenile court has changed over time. Girls are increasingly referred to juvenile court for violent crimes. The rate for violent female juvenile court cases increased 127 percent from 1987 to 1996. During the same period, the rate for male juveniles increased 68 percent. Property offense case rates also increased from 1987 to 1996 by 37 percent for girls and 4 percent for boys. Drug case rates, in contrast, increased faster for boys (123 percent) than for girls (100 percent) (Stahl et al., 1999).

The handling of girls in the juvenile justice system also appears to have changed somewhat over the past 30 years. Studies done during the 1970s found that girls were considerably more likely than boys to be referred to juvenile court for status delinquency offenses (e.g., running away from home, incorrigibility, truancy). Girls were also more likely than boys to be formally processed, detained, and sentenced to incarceration for status delinquency offenses (see, e.g., Andrews and Cohn, 1974; Chesney-Lind, 1973; Conway and Bogdan, 1977; Datesman and Scarpitti, 1977; Gibbons and Griswold, 1957; Pawlak, 1977). However, girls were less likely to be arrested for criminal delinquency offenses, to be formally charged if arrested, or to be incarcerated (Chesney-Lind, 1973; Cohen and Kluegel, 1979; Datesman and Scarpitti, 1977). More recent studies have equivocal findings, with some showing differences in treatment of males and females (Pope and Feyerherm, 1982; Tittle and Curran, 1988) and some showing no differences (Clarke and Koch, 1980; Teilmann and Landry, 1981; U.S. General Accounting Office, 1995c) with regard to dispositions of status delinquency cases.

Criminal delinquency cases involving females, however, are less likely than cases involving males to be disposed of by detention or long-term confinement in secure facilities, after controlling for severity of offense and previous offenses (Bishop and Frazier, 1992). When contempt status (i.e., when the delinquency charge is for violation of a previously ordered condition of supervision) was introduced as a variable and interaction effects examined, however, Bishop and Frazier (1992) found that girls' risk of incarceration was substantially elevated in cases of contempt, whereas contempt had only a small impact on boys' risk of incarceration. In many cases, for girls, the original charge for which they were held in contempt was a status offense. In essence, for girls, the contempt charge means they are essentially treated as a criminal delinquent for a status offense, receiving harsher punishment for the contempt charge than for other criminal delinquency charges. Bishop and Frazier (1992:1183) reported that "the typical male offender who is not in contempt has a 3.9 percent probability of incarceration. The risk is increased only slightly, to 4.4 percent, when he is found in contempt. In sharp contrast, the typical female offender not in contempt has a 1.8 percent probability of incarceration, which increases markedly to 63.2 percent if she is held in contempt."

In a study conducted on a geographically diverse, longitudinal (nine years of data) sample of approximately 36,000 court referrals, Johnson and Scheuble (1991) found that, after controlling for the nature of the offense, past offending, and other background variables, girls were more likely than boys to have their cases dismissed and boys were more likely than girls to be put on probation or to be locked up.

Very few programs address the unique needs and problems of female juvenile offenders. In a meta-analysis of juvenile prevention and intervention programs, the author reported that only 8 percent of the programs primarily served girls (Lipsey, 1992). When females get involved in the juvenile justice system, there are fewer options for them than for boys. Although delinquent girls share some problems with delinquent boys, they also have unique problems, including higher rates of childhood sexual victimization and depression (see Chapter 3) and greater, more central parenting roles. Yet programs are rarely tailored specifically for the needs of girls and their experiences.

RECENT LEGISLATIVE CHANGES AFFECTING THE JUVENILE COURT

In response to the rise in violent crime by juveniles during the late 1980s and early 1990s, states around the country made changes to their juvenile justice laws. These changes mainly involved making it easier to transfer juveniles to adult court, changing sentencing structures, and modifying or removing traditional confidentiality provisions. Between

1992 and 1997, 47 states and the District of Columbia changed their laws in at least one of these ways. State laws have also been changed in two other areas: regarding the rights of victims of juvenile crimes and in correctional programming. Table 5-5 indicates the type of changes made in each state between 1992 and 1997.

Ease of Transfer to Criminal Court

Determining which children belong in juvenile court has been an issue since the court's beginnings (Tanenhaus, 2000). There are a number

TABLE 5-5 How States Have Stiffened Laws Relating to Juvenile Justice in 1992-1997, by Type of Change

State	Type of Changes in Law					State	Type of Changes in Law				
Alabama	T		C	V		Montana	T	S	C	V	CP
Alaska	T		C	V		Nebraska					
Arizona	T	S	C	V	CP	Nevada	T		C	V	CP
Arkansas	T	S	C		CP	New Hampshire	T	S	C	V	
California	T		C	V	CP	New Jersey		S	C		CP
Colorado	T	S	C		CP	New Mexico	T	S	C	V	CP
Connecticut	T	S	C	V	CP	New York					
Delaware	T	S	C			North Carolina	T		C		CP
D.C.	T	S				North Dakota	T		C	V	CP
Florida	T	S	C	V	CP	Ohio	T	S	C	V	CP
Georgia	T	S	C	V	CP	Oklahoma	T	S	C	V	CP
Hawaii	T		C		CP	Oregon	T	S	C	V	CP
Idaho	T	S	C	V	CP	Pennsylvania	T		C	V	
Illinois	T	S	C	V		Rhode Island	T	S	C		CP
Indiana	T	S	C	V		South Carolina	T		C	V	CP
Iowa	T	S	C	V		South Dakota	T			V	CP
Kansas	T	S	C		CP	Tennessee	T	S	C		CP
Kentucky	T	S	C	V	CP	Texas	T	S	C	V	CP
Louisiana	T	S	C	V	CP	Utah	T		C	V	CP
Maine			C	V	CP	Vermont				V	CP
Maryland	T		C	V	CP	Virginia	T	S	C		
Massachusetts	T	S	C	V		Washington	T		C		CP
Michigan	T	S	C		CP	West Virginia	T		C		
Minnesota	T	S	C	V	CP	Wisconsin	T	S	C		CP
Mississippi	T		C		CP	Wyoming			C	V	CP
Missouri	T	S	C		CP						

T = transfer provisions; S = sentencing authority; C = confidentiality; V = victims' rights; CP = correctional programming.

Source: Adapted from Snyder and Sickmund (1999) and Torbet et al. (1996).

of ways in which courts have excluded certain juveniles from juvenile court jurisdiction. These include setting an age above which the juvenile court no longer has jurisdiction and various mechanisms for transferring juveniles under that age to criminal court.

Maximum and Minimum Ages of Jurisdiction

State laws set a maximum age for adolescents for which the juvenile court has original jurisdiction. This age varies by state and sometimes by offense. In Connecticut, New York, and North Carolina, the highest age of juvenile court jurisdiction in criminal delinquency cases is 15; that is, anyone age 16 and older is handled in the criminal (adult) court. In Georgia, Illinois, Louisiana, Massachusetts, Michigan, Missouri, New Hampshire, South Carolina, Texas, and Wisconsin, juvenile court jurisdiction applies through age 16. In the remaining states and the District of Columbia, the highest age of jurisdiction is 17 (Griffin et al., 1998). Assuming that children under a certain age cannot be responsible for their behavior, 15 states specify the lowest age for juvenile court jurisdiction. In North Carolina, the lowest minimum age is 6 years; it is 7 in Maryland, Massachusetts, and New York; 8 in Arizona; and 10 in Arkansas, Colorado, Kansas, Louisiana, Minnesota, Mississippi, Pennsylvania, South Dakota, Texas, Vermont, and Wisconsin (Snyder and Sickmund, 1999). In practice, very few children under the age of 10 appear before the juvenile court for delinquency charges.

Lowering the maximum age of juvenile court jurisdiction is one of the most drastic steps a state can take, because it moves an entire age group of adolescents into the adult system. In recent years, only three states have changed their laws to lower the maximum age of juvenile court jurisdiction. In 1993, Wyoming dropped its maximum age from 18 to 17. In 1995, New Hampshire and Wisconsin lowered their maximum ages from 17 to 16 (Torbet et al., 1996). Although it is difficult to determine exactly how many juveniles these changes affected, 17-year-olds accounted for 24 percent of the arrests of all those under 18 in 1998. Therefore, moving 17-year-olds to the criminal justice system could reduce the case flow in the juvenile system by as much as one-fourth. The fact that so few states have chosen this option suggests that legislative concern has been focused on serious and violent crime rather than all juvenile crime (Dawson, 2000).

Transfer Mechanisms

From the inception of the juvenile court, juvenile court judges have had the discretion to waive jurisdiction to the criminal court. These waivers generally fit one of three case types: serious offense, extensive juvenile record, or juvenile near the age limit. In the first case, the offense with which the juvenile is charged is so serious that the sanctions available to the juvenile court are felt to be insufficient. These cases usually involve violent crimes, most often murder. The second type of case involve juveniles with extensive histories of arrests and juvenile court sanctions who are deemed unable to benefit from juvenile court. In the third type of case, the juvenile is very close to the age limit of the juvenile court's jurisdiction. These cases are waived because the juvenile court would not have jurisdiction over the particular youth for a long enough period of time or because the juvenile is thought to be appropriate for adult court (Zimring, 1998).

All states have some mechanism for treating juveniles, under certain conditions, as adults (Torbet and Szymanski, 1998). How the decision to transfer is made is governed by state law and therefore varies from state to state. The state laws, including the District of Columbia, use one or more of the following methods to place a child in the adult criminal court: judicial waiver, prosecutorial direct file, and statutory exclusion. Judicial waiver, in which the transfer decision is left to the discretion of the juvenile court judge, is the traditional method that juvenile courts have used for transfer. Statutory changes in recent years have removed some of the judicial discretion and given it to either the prosecutor, through direct file, or to the state legislature, through statutory exclusions.

During the 1990s, most states made it easier to transfer juveniles to adult court (Torbet and Szymanski, 1998). The most common ways in which state laws were changed were by adding offenses that allow or mandate transfer to criminal court and lowering the age at which certain juveniles could be tried in criminal court.

Judicial Waiver. Most states and the District of Columbia have laws that permit juvenile court judges to waive jurisdiction from the juvenile court to the criminal court under certain conditions. The transfer decision is up to the juvenile court judge. There are three types of waiver proceedings: discretionary waiver, mandatory waiver, and presumptive waiver. There is also a provision known as reverse waiver, as well as a special transfer category described as "once an adult, always an adult."

In all, 46 states give juvenile court judges the discretion to decide whether a matter will be tried in the juvenile court or the criminal court (Griffin et al., 1998). Some states require that the prosecutor initiate the process by filing a motion. Other states allow any party or the court to initiate the action.

The discretionary statutes in most states specify criteria similar to those set forth in *Kent v. United States* (383 U.S. 541, 566-67 [1966]) that should be considered by the juvenile court in deciding whether to transfer jurisdiction to the criminal court. Generally, the states require the court to consider the following factors in the exercise of its discretion: whether a waiver of jurisdiction would serve the interests of the juvenile and the public; whether public safety requires it; whether there are further services available for the juvenile through the juvenile court system; and whether the child is amenable to rehabilitation (Griffin et al., 1998).

The statutes in 14 states provide for mandatory waivers in cases in which the age and offense criteria are met. Mandatory waiver proceedings are initiated in the juvenile court; however, the involvement of the juvenile court in a mandatory waiver case is minimal. Generally there is a preliminary hearing to determine if the case is one to which the mandatory statute applies. If the threshold criterion is met, the court has the authority only to appoint counsel and to issue interim detention and transfer orders (Griffin et al., 1998); the juvenile court judge may not opt to keep the case in juvenile court. Mandatory waivers leave no room for judicial discretion.

In 15 states, the statutes designate cases in which waiver to the adult criminal court is presumed to be appropriate (presumptive waiver). In these cases, the burden in the waiver hearing is on the child rather than the state. If a child who meets the age, offense, or other criteria specified in the statute fails to show that he or she is amenable to treatment or that his or her retention in the juvenile court does not jeopardize public safety, the case must be transferred to the criminal court.

The statutory criteria that activate presumptive waiver cases fall into three broad categories (Griffin et al., 1998). The first category focuses primarily on the current offense. In the second category, the statutes presumptively require a waiver for an older child, even if the offense for which the child was accused would not otherwise raise the presumption. The third category emphasizes the child's previous juvenile offense history over all other factors.

There are laws in 23 states that provide some mechanism for a child who is being tried in the criminal court to petition to have the case transferred to the juvenile court (Griffin et al., 1998). These provisions are sometimes referred to as reverse waiver. In some states, the statutes authorize the transfer from criminal court to juvenile court even if the case arrived in criminal court by direct file, statutory exclusion, or waiver. Some statutory provisions permit the criminal court to transfer a case to the juvenile court for disposition. Generally when the offense the criminal court is considering is one that was excluded from juvenile court by statute or one in which the prosecutor exercised the discretion to file the case directly in the criminal court, the criminal court's decision is governed by the same considerations and best interests standards as those that the juvenile court must take into account when deciding whether to waive jurisdiction.

A total of 31 states and the District of Columbia have created a special transfer category which is referred to as "once an adult, always an adult" (Griffin et al., 1998). Most states with such statutes provide that once a child has been convicted in the criminal court, all subsequent offenses require criminal prosecution. In Mississippi, even if a child was not convicted on the first adult-prosecuted offense, he or she will be prosecuted in the criminal court for any subsequent offenses. The California statutes limit the application of the "once an adult, always an adult" provision to children who are at least 16 years of age and require that any subsequent offenses must be those for which waiver to the adult court would be appropriate.

Prosecutorial Direct File. The statutes in 15 states designate a category of cases that may be tried in either the juvenile court or the criminal court (i.e., the juvenile and criminal courts have joint or concurrent jurisdiction) (Griffin et al., 1998). In those states, the prosecutor has the authority to decide in which court to file the case; the juvenile court judge has no part in the decision. The state laws vary widely regarding the category of the offenses, the age of the child, the seriousness of the offense, and the extent of the child's juvenile offense history that are to be considered in deciding where to file.

Statutory Exclusion. Certain offenses are excluded by statute from juvenile court jurisdiction in 28 states. The laws provide that a child who has reached a certain age and is accused of a designated offense will be tried as an adult in the criminal court. All proceedings against the juvenile occur in the criminal court in the same manner as if the offense had been committed by an adult. These laws focus on the nature of the offense, rather than on the background or needs of the offender. Some states exclude only the most serious offenses, while others exclude offenses based on age. For example, in New Mexico a child who is at least 15 years of age and is accused of first-degree murder is excluded from juvenile court jurisdiction. Mississippi excludes all felonies committed by juveniles who are 17 years of age. Among the offenses excluded by Indiana is the misdemeanor offense of carrying a handgun without a license. The focus in some states is not so much on the nature of the offense and the age of the juvenile as the previous juvenile offense history. Arizona excludes any felony committed by a juvenile who is at least 15 years of age if the juvenile has been previously adjudicated for two or more offenses that would have been felonies if committed by an adult (Griffin et al., 1998).

Sentencing Structure

Traditionally, sanctions imposed by juvenile courts were to be based on the needs of the offender, with an emphasis on the future welfare of the juvenile (Torbet et al., 1996). Juvenile court judges had a great deal of discretion in the disposition they selected for an individual. Sanctions could be indeterminate in length; that is, juveniles could stay under the oversight of the court until they were too old to be under juvenile court jurisdiction. The traditional goal of sanctions was rehabilitative. State legislative changes in recent years have moved the court away from its rehabilitative goals and toward punishment and accountability. Laws have made some dispositions offense-based rather than offender-based. Offense-based sanctions are to be proportional to the offense and have retribution or deterrence as their goal. Strategies for imposing offense-based sentences in juvenile court include blended sentences, mandatory minimum sentences, and extended jurisdiction (Torbet and Szymanski, 1998). All these sentencing options allow for longer sentences than might have been available under traditional juvenile courts.

Blended Sentences

Blended sentences allow the imposition of a combination of juvenile and adult correctional sanctions.[11] The form of the blended sentences varies from state to state. In some states, a juvenile or criminal court may impose a sanction in either the juvenile or the criminal system. In some states, the juvenile or the criminal court may sentence a youth to the juvenile corrections system to be followed by a sentence in the adult corrections system, which may be suspended if the juvenile successfully completes his juvenile sanctions. In a few states (Colorado, Massachusetts, Rhode Island, and Texas), the juvenile court may impose a sentence that goes beyond the age of its jurisdiction, at which point the case is transferred to adult corrections. In Texas, for example, juveniles as young as 10 can be sentenced to as many as 40 years for certain crimes and can be transferred to the adult corrections system any time after they turn 16 if approved by the sentencing court at a transfer hearing, and automatically

---

[11]In some states, legislatures have called their blended sentence laws *determinate sentencing* because rather than committing a juvenile to supervision by the juvenile court for an indeterminate period of time up to limit of the court's jurisdiction, the sentence is given for a set number of years. In Texas, the "determinate sentencing" law does not necessarily result in the given sentence being served (a true determinate sentence), but rather in a hearing after the juvenile turns 16 to determine if he or she should be released, retained in juvenile corrections, or transferred to adult corrections.

at age 21 if the sentence has not been completed. Because these blended sentences are often longer and more severe than those that traditional juvenile courts could impose, the laws frequently provide for more procedural safeguards for the juveniles subject to these penalties (Torbet et al., 1996).

Proponents of blended sentences see them as a less severe option than outright transfer of juveniles to criminal court. Systems that give juveniles a suspended criminal sentence that only becomes operational if they violate the terms of their juvenile disposition, as well as ones that require a reevaluation of the juvenile after a period in the juvenile correctional system, are intended to give juveniles who commit serious offenses a final opportunity to avoid serious criminal sanctions (Dawson, 2000). Some critics of blended sentencing plans note, however, that the juvenile courts do not provide all the same safeguards of the accused's rights as do the criminal courts, even though blended sentencing can result in adult sanctions. Other critics say that blended sentences represent a procedural and substantive convergence between juvenile and criminal courts and erode the rationale for a separate juvenile justice system (e.g., Feld, 1997).

Mandatory Minimum Sentences

Since 1992, a number of states have modified their laws to allow for mandatory minimum sentences for certain serious crimes. In Massachusetts, for example, a juvenile age 14 or older convicted of murder must receive a sentence of at least 15 years for first-degree murder and at least 10 years for second-degree murder (Torbet et al., 1996). Some states have instituted progressive or graduated sanctions that legislatively tie type of disposition to both current offense and past offense history.

Capital Punishment

The United States is among a handful of countries to have legitimized the use of capital punishment for juveniles. In 23 states, capital punishment is an option for offenders who were under the age of 18 at the time of their offense. The Supreme Court upheld the constitutionality of capital punishment for those over age 16 in a decision made in 1989. Only Georgia, Louisiana, Missouri, Oklahoma, South Carolina, Texas, and Virginia have actually executed juveniles. The practice has been condemned by the United Nations Convention on the Rights of the Child, the American Bar Association, the Children's Defense Fund, and the International Convention on Civil and Political Rights.

Extended Jurisdiction

In response to criticisms that the length of commitment to the juvenile system is too short, some states have increased the maximum age of the juvenile court's jurisdiction over offenders. Many states allow a judge to commit a juvenile to be held in the state's juvenile corrections system up to age 21 (even though the court's jurisdiction for hearing and disposing of cases ends when a juvenile is 16 or 17). In California, Oregon, and Wisconsin, the extended age is 25 and in Colorado, Connecticut, Hawaii, and New Mexico, the juvenile jurisdiction extends for the full term of commitment, regardless of age.

Confidentiality

Traditionally, the rehabilitative philosophy of the juvenile court led to protocols to protect the identity of and information about juveniles who came before it. Proceedings were closed to the public. The identity of juveniles was not disclosed. There was limited access to court records and the records could be sealed or expunged after a certain length of time. These measures were aimed at minimizing the stigma attached to court involvement and promoting the goal of rehabilitation. As state legislatures began stressing punishment and retribution over rehabilitation, many states changed their laws concerning confidentiality in the juvenile court.

As of the end of 1997, 30 states permitted or required open juvenile court hearings in cases involving juveniles charged with violent or serious offenses or repeat offenders (Torbet and Szymanski, 1998). And 22 of those states either created or modified their open hearing statutes between 1992 and 1997. For example, in 1997, Idaho added language to its statute requiring open hearings for all juveniles 14 or older charged with an offense that would be a felony if committed by an adult. States have also changed laws regarding the release of the name of a juvenile to the general public or the media. As of the end of 1997, 42 states allowed the release of a minor's name or picture under certain conditions, such as being found guilty of a serious or violent offense (Torbet and Szymanski, 1998).

Another area of legislative change involves access to juvenile court records. Although court records traditionally have been available by court order to any party who can show a legitimate interest, a number of states now allow access to a wide variety of people or agencies, including law enforcement, social service agencies, the schools, victims, and the general public. A number of states mandate notification of a juvenile's school when the child or adolescent is found guilty of particular offenses.

For example, in North Dakota, if a child or adolescent is found guilty of a sexual assault, the court must notify the child's school superintendent or principal. Juvenile records, fingerprints, and photographs are increasingly being integrated into centralized repositories. In some states, juvenile records are kept in a separate centralized system, but in others they are merged with the centralized criminal system, including sex offender registries (Torbet et al., 1996; Torbet and Szymanski, 1998).

Traditionally, juvenile records could be sealed or expunged after a specified amount of time without offending. These provisions allowed young people who had been successfully rehabilitated to clear their records so that, in effect, the proceedings would be treated as if they had never occurred (Hurst, 1985). Recent changes in state laws have lengthened the amount of time before records can be sealed or have prohibited the sealing of records for some crimes. As of the end of 1997, 25 states had made such changes (Torbet and Szymanski, 1998).

Victims' Rights Legislation

The traditional juvenile court model did not include consideration of the victims of juvenile offenders. During the past 10 years, concerns about violence by juveniles, the victims' rights movement, and interest in a restorative justice approach led to changes in state law that provided for consideration of the victims of juvenile crime. Such legislation includes measures to allow victims to be informed of hearings and dispositions, to attend hearings, to make statements before disposition or sentencing, and to be notified if an offender is released. Between 1992 and 1997, 32 states passed laws dealing with the rights of victims of juvenile crime (Torbet et al., 1996; Torbet and Szymanski, 1998).

Correctional Programming

In a number of states, changes in transfer and sentencing laws have led to changes in laws and administrative rules concerning corrections. These changes included allowing juveniles convicted as adults to be housed in separate facilities or in juvenile facilities until a certain age, creating special programs for juveniles convicted as adults, and enhancing programs in the juvenile correctional system. Between 1992 and 1995, these laws focused on the need for secure detention of violent juvenile offenders; more recently, they have focused on authorizing and funding community-based interventions and supervision of offenders (Torbet and Szymanski, 1998).

IMPACT OF LEGISLATIVE CHANGES

Most of these legislative changes are too recent for research to provide much information about their impact either on practices regarding juvenile offenders or on the young people themselves. In addition, the many inadequacies in the data available on juveniles at various stages of the system make it difficult to examine their effect on changes in practice.

The number of juveniles who are sent to criminal (adult) court nationally is not known (U.S. General Accounting Office, 1995a). In 1994, about 21,000 persons under the age of 18 were convicted of a felony in a state criminal court (Brown and Langan, 1998). And 40 percent of them were convicted of a violent offense, compared with only 18 percent of all felony convictions of those over 18. An estimated 12,000 of the 21,000 were juveniles who had been transferred through judicial waiver, prosecutorial direct file, or statutory exclusion. The remainder were in states whose maximum age for juvenile court jurisdiction is 15 or 16 (i.e., states in which 16- or 17-year-olds are defined as adults). Bishop and Frazier (2000) suggest that the above figures may be a substantial undercount. Prosecutors alone reported filing 27,000 juvenile cases in adult court in 1996 (DeFrances and Steadman, 1998), and 10,000 cases were judicially waived in 1996 (Stahl et al., 1999).

Transfer to Criminal Court

Judicial waivers have been tracked for a number of years, but data on cases transferred by prosecutorial direct file or statutory exclusion are not systematically counted. Waivers by juvenile judges have remained fairly constant over the period 1986 to 1996, representing between 1.0 and 1.6 percent of all petitioned cases (Sickmund et al., 1998). There is some evidence that a similar percentage of cases was transferred in the early years of the juvenile court. About 1 percent of cases were waived by the Milwaukee Juvenile Court in the early 20th century (Schlossman, 1977). In a study of the Chicago juvenile court, Jeter (1922) reported that the percentage of boys transferred to adult court per year was usually less than 1 percent.

Despite some stability in the overall proportion of cases transferred through judicial waiver, there is variety by type of offense. Between 1986 and 1996, cases involving person offenses (i.e., homicide, rape, robbery, aggravated assault, simple assault, other violent sex offenses, and other offenses against persons) were the most likely to be sent to criminal court by juvenile court judges; about 2 percent of person offense cases resulted in judicial waiver (Sickmund et al., 1998; Stahl et al., 1999). In the late 1980s, there was a dramatic increase in waivers for drug offense cases, which increased from 1.2 percent in 1986 to 4.1 percent in 1991. By 1996, the percentage of drug offenses waived dropped back down to 1.2 percent. It seems unlikely that changes such as those seen in waived drug cases were due to changes in legislation. The peak occurred during the height of the war on drugs and the rise in youth violence, which was often associated with drug dealing. Waiver decisions may have been influenced by the general antidrug tenor of the period. Alternatively, the drug cases seen in juvenile court during the early 1990s may have been much more serious offenses than in the years before and after. Research, including data collection, to explain such trends remains to be done.

National data on the number of cases transferred through direct file or statutory exclusion are not available. A study by the U.S. General Accounting Office (1995a), based on data from five states, the District of Columbia, and counties in five additional states, found that the percentage of cases sent to criminal court by prosecutorial direct file ranged from less than 1 percent (in Utah) to 10 percent in Florida and 13 percent in Arkansas. At least in some states, the change to prosecutorial direct file appears to have resulted in more juveniles being processed in adult criminal court.

Recent changes in statutory exclusion laws have generally increased the population of juveniles potentially subject to transfer to the criminal courts, but no national data are currently available to determine the actual number of juveniles affected by exclusion laws, the characteristics of such juveniles, or the offenses for which they are transferred. A 1985 study of 12 jurisdictions (Gragg, 1986) reported that juveniles transferred by legislative exclusion tended to be younger and to have fewer prior arrests and placements than juveniles transferred by other means.

Research has examined the impact of various aspects of transferring juveniles to criminal courts, including studies on the types of cases most likely to be transferred, comparisons of sentences in juvenile and criminal courts, and comparisons of recidivism between transferred and non-transferred juveniles.

Types of Cases

In an analysis of judicial transfer decisions in Boston, Detroit, Newark, and Phoenix from 1981 to 1984, Fagan et al. (1987a) found that age at the time the offense was committed, age of delinquency onset, and seriousness of offense were the factors that most influenced juvenile judges' decisions to transfer a case to criminal court. The cases most likely to be waived involved older juveniles charged with serious, violent offenses, predominantly homicide. Poulos and Orchowsky (1994) examined the factors influencing judicial transfer between 1988 and 1990 in the state of

Virginia. Using multivariate logistic regression, they found that the factors most important to juvenile judges' decisions to transfer a case included current offense, prior record, and age. Most likely to be transferred were juveniles who were charged with homicide, rape, or drug sales; older juveniles; juveniles who used a gun in committing the offense; and those with prior felony person or drug adjudications or prior commitment to a residential juvenile corrections facility (learning center). Judges in metropolitan courts in Virginia were less likely to transfer cases than were those in rural counties. A small study of judicially transferred cases in New Mexico found similar results (Houghtalin and Mays, 1991). Podkopacz and Feld (1996) analyzed transfer motions filed between 1986 and 1992 in Hennepin County, Minnesota, and determined that in addition to age, present offense, and weapon use, the recommendations of probation officers and clinical evaluators significantly affected the eventual judicial waiver decision. They also found prior correctional interventions to be significant: youths with no prior program placements and those with only a few (1 to 3) were less likely to be certified to adult court than youths with four or more placements.

In contrast to the findings on judicial transfers, Bishop and Frazier (1991) found that juveniles transferred through prosecutorial waiver (direct file) in Florida from 1979 to 1981 were less often violent or chronic offenders: 55 percent of those waived were felony property offenses and only 29 percent were felony person offenses. Clarke (1996), in a study of automatic transfer (offenses legislatively excluded from the juvenile court) in Cook County, Illinois, from 1992 to 1994, found that 39 percent of the transfers were for drug or weapon offenses, 25 percent were for murder, and 22 percent were for armed robbery. The proportion of transfer cases for murder had dropped from nearly half of those transferred by judicial waiver from 1975 to 1981 to a quarter under automatic transfer. Clarke (1996) concluded that Illinois's automatic transfer provisions failed to identify and therefore protect the public against serious violent juvenile offenders. Instead, they prosecuted and stigmatized many juveniles who did not represent a threat to public safety and who could benefit from the more rehabilitative programs of the juvenile court.

A high proportion of the juveniles transferred to adult court are minorities. For example, blacks and Hispanics made up 94.7 percent of those transferred in the Cook County, Illinois, study (Clarke, 1996). Hispanics and American Indians made up 67 percent of judicially transferred cases in the New Mexico study (Houghtalin and Mays, 1991). The preponderance of minorities among transferred juveniles may be explained in part by the fact that minorities are disproportionately arrested for serious crimes. In the Fagan et al. (1987a) analysis, the effects of race on the judicial transfer decision were found to be indirect.

Sentencing

One reason given for transferring juveniles to criminal court is that the juvenile court cannot provide adequate sanctions for some offenses. Research on the likelihood and length of sentence in criminal versus juvenile court has mixed results. Brown and Langan (1998), in a national sample, found that a higher percentage of juveniles transferred to adult court were sentenced to incarceration than were those who remained in juvenile court: 63 percent of juveniles transferred to criminal court were sentenced to prison terms and 16 percent to jail terms. Prison sentences averaged 9.25 years. Only 21 percent were given probation. In comparison, only 31 percent of juveniles found guilty of person offenses in juvenile court were sentenced to out-of-home placement, and 53 percent were put on probation (Stahl et al., 1999).

A comparison of robbery and burglary cases in New Jersey and New York suggested that processing juveniles in the criminal court resulted in higher rates of incarceration, but not lengthier sentences than processing in the juvenile court (Fagan, 1995). Fagan also found higher rates of rearrest and reincarceration among young people processed for robbery in the criminal courts than in the juvenile courts; no such differences were found for burglary cases. A comparison of cases transferred to adult court with those adjudicated in juvenile court in St. Louis found that transferred youth did not receive greater punishment than they would have received in juvenile court (Kinder et al., 1995). The U.S. General Accounting Office (1995a) study of transferred juveniles found great variability in incarceration rates by state. In Vermont, for example, one-third of juveniles convicted of violent, property, or drug crimes in criminal court were incarcerated, while Minnesota incarcerated over 90 percent of the transferred juveniles convicted of those three types of crime. Pennsylvania incarcerated 90 percent of transferred juveniles in violent and drug offense cases, but only 10 percent in property cases.

There is some evidence that length of sentence varies in the juvenile and adult systems according to type of offense. For example, Podkopacz and Feld (1996) found in their Hennepin County, Minnesota study that for youths adjudicated of property offenses, the juvenile courts imposed longer sentences than did the criminal courts, while youths convicted of violent offenses in criminal courts received substantially longer sentences than their juvenile counterparts. Length of sentence and actual length of stay in a facility may differ, however. The length of stay in a juvenile facility appears, on average, to be much shorter than that in adult prison. Although national data on length of sentences given in juvenile court are not available, national average length of stay in long-term juvenile facilities was about 8 months in 1990 (Parent et al., 1994) and was down to about 4 months in 1995 (Smith, 1998).

There appears to be variation by state in length of stay, however, with some states well above the national average. For example, in California, the average length of stay in Youth Authority institutions was 25.7 months in fiscal year 1997-1998 (California Youth Authority, 1997-1998); in Texas, the average length of stay in Texas Youth Commission facilities was 23 months for violent offenders (Criminal Justice Policy Council, 1999) and 16.5 months for all offenders in fiscal year 1999 (special data analysis done by the Criminal Justice Policy Council for this report). The California and Texas figures are similar to lengths of stay in reform schools in the late 19th and early 20th centuries.

An analysis was prepared by panel member Steven Schlossman of length of stay in Michigan's Lansing Industrial School for boys and in the New York House of Refuge. In the Michigan reform school, average length of stay was 29 months in the 1870s, dropping to 21 months in the 1890s. In the New York House of Refuge, the average length of stay in 1925 was 20 months. Because there are no national historical figures, it is impossible to tell if the national average length of stay is similar to or has actually dropped considerably over the course of the past century.

Recidivism

Studies have found higher recidivism rates among juveniles who had been transferred to adult court than among those who remained in the juvenile system, even when severity of offense was controlled (Podkopacz and Feld, 1996); the researchers concluded that transfer to adult court may be more likely to increase recidivism than to lessen it (Bishop et al., 1996; Fagan, 1995; Winner et al., 1997). These studies have noted that the higher recidivism rates may be attributable to a number of possible factors: the juvenile system may have correctly identified and consequently transferred youths likely to recidivate; law enforcement may be more vigilant of youths who had been through the adult court; treatment in the juvenile system may have been effective in preventing repeat offending; or adult incarceration may have encouraged further criminality. More research is needed to replicate these studies and to determine the effects on subsequent recidivism of processing in the juvenile versus the adult systems. Studies in New York (Singer and McDowall, 1988) and Idaho (Jensen and Metsger, 1994) on the general deterrent effects of legislative waiver statutes indicate that waiver laws in those two states did not have a deterrent effect on rates of juvenile violent crime.

Levitt (1998) examined the relationship between the relative punitiveness of the juvenile and adult systems and arrest rates. Using state-level panel data from the censuses of public and private juvenile facilities and censuses of adult prisons collected by the Department of Justice for the period 1978-1993, he found that in states in which the adult system was more punitive[12] than the juvenile system, violent crime rates decreased significantly at the age of majority. In states in which the adult system was more lenient than the juvenile system, violent crime rates increased at the age of majority. This suggests that it is the relative punitiveness of the system, not whether it is the juvenile or adult system per se, that may deter crime among young people in the short term. Levitt did not find any long-term relationship between the punitiveness of the sanctions imposed on juveniles and their adult criminal behavior.

Blended Sentences

The number of juveniles affected by blended sentencing is not known on a national level. There is some information at the state level, suggesting that blended sentencing may result in relatively lengthy sentences. For example, in 1996 in Texas, the average blended sentence imposed for all offenses was 10.5 years, ranging from an average of 5 years for burglary to 31 years for capital murder (Texas law permits blended sentences up to 40 years). The percentage of commitments to the Texas Youth Commission that were blended sentences increased from about 2 percent in 1990 to nearly 8 percent in 1996. The addition of 16 offenses eligible for blended sentencing in 1996 led to an increase from 4.7 percent of commitments in 1995 to 7.6 percent in 1996. The majority of juveniles receiving blended sentences in 1996 in Texas were Hispanic (42 percent) and black (32 percent). Nearly one-third of those receiving blended sentences in 1996 were 14 years old or younger (Criminal Justice Policy Council, 1997). The impact of these laws on ultimate sanctions for juveniles sentenced under them will not be known for some years to come; this is an area that is ripe for research to begin.

The effect of these legislative changes, overall, appears to be an increase in the number of juveniles held in adult state prisons. That is not to say that all juveniles who are tried as adults and found guilty end up in adult prison. States have adopted a variety of means to deal with sanctioning these juveniles, including blended sentences that allow juveniles to begin serving time in a juvenile facility and finish their sentence in an adult facility. Some states (e.g., Texas, New York) have created special secure facilities under the auspices of the juvenile or adult corrections

---

[12]Levitt defined punitiveness as the number of juveniles (adults) in custody per reported violent crime by juveniles (adults).

department to house youth found guilty in criminal court. Nevertheless, some of the juveniles sentenced as adults are incarcerated in adult prisons, where the emphasis is on punishment and few services are available.

Youth in Adult Prisons

Between 1985 and 1997, the number of offenders under 18 admitted to state prisons more than doubled, from 3,400 in 1985 to 7,400 in 1997 (Strom, 2000). And 61 percent of those under 18 sent to state prison in 1997 had been convicted of a violent offense. Juveniles arrested for violent offenses are more likely to end up in state prison now than in 1985. In 1997, 33 of every 1,000 juveniles arrested for a violent crime were sentenced to prison, compared with 18 per 1,000 in 1985. Nearly two-fifths of the juveniles sent to state prison in 1997, however, were not there for violent offenses—22 percent had been convicted of a property offense, 11 percent of a drug offense, and 5 percent of a public order offense (Strom, 2000).

Juveniles remain a very small percentage of the total state prison population. Those under 18 make up less than 1 percent of the inmates in state prisons, a figure that has remained steady since the mid-1980s. Since 1985, juveniles have consistently made up about 2 percent of new admissions to state prisons (Strom, 2000).

Minority juveniles are disproportionately represented among juveniles sent to adult prison. In 1997, minorities made up three-quarters of juveniles admitted to adult state prisons,[13] with blacks accounting for 58 percent, Hispanics 15 percent, and Asians and American Indians 2 percent (Strom, 2000). Males accounted for 92 percent of the juveniles admitted to state prisons in 1997.

Based on current sentencing and release policies, prison officials estimate that 78 percent of those who were admitted to prison prior to their 18th birthday would be released by age 21 and 93 percent would be released by age 28 (Strom, 2000). The fact that 90 percent of juveniles admitted to prison had not completed high school, coupled with the paucity of services available to them in adult prison, does not bode well for their reentry into society.

Historical Perspective

To provide some historical perspective on juveniles in state prison, panel member Steven Schlossman analyzed a detailed sample of prison-

---

[13]In 1997, minorities accounted of two-thirds of juveniles committed to public juvenile residential facilities (Snyder and Sickmund, 1999).

ers at San Quentin and Folsom prisons in the late 19th and early 20th centuries.[14] Between the 1870s and the 1930s, mid-teens were committed to San Quentin and Folsom prisons, but in very small numbers and percentages. The largest shares were in the 1870s to 1890s, when 3.7 percent of the inmates were between ages 14 and 17. With the creation of California's juvenile court in 1903 and reform schools for juvenile offenders (see, Schlossman, 1989, for historical details), juveniles under age 18 were eliminated entirely from Folsom by the 1910s. Juveniles under age 16 were eliminated from San Quentin and those ages 16 and 17 declined to less than 1 percent of the inmate population in the 1910s and afterward. This is similar to the percentage of juveniles in adult prisons nationally today (Strom, 2000).

Racial and ethnic minority groups (black, Hispanic, Chinese, Hawaiian, American Indian, Japanese) were represented among the mid-teens committed to San Quentin and Folsom prisons, but only in two decades was there notable overrepresentation of any group: the Chinese in the 1870s, at the height of anti-Chinese period in California; and Hispanics in the 1930s, a period of severe deprivation and outmigration of Mexicans from California following large-scale immigration in the 1920s. Overall, race does not appear to have been a significant factor in influencing commitment patterns to state prison. Whites, not minorities, constituted the overwhelming majority of both mid-teen and adult offenders sent to San Quentin and Folsom prisons between the 1870s and the 1930s (see Table 5-6).

Just as today, a substantial percentage of juveniles in San Quentin and Folsom prisons were sentenced for property offenses (burglary and theft) rather than violent offenses against persons (murder, robbery, assault, rape). Over two-thirds of 14- and 15-year-olds in these two state prisons in the late 19th century were sentenced for property crimes. In the early 20th century—when the share of juveniles in adult prison declined considerably—a new pattern of commitment began to emerge. Their offense profile became significantly more violent; it became as common for juveniles sent to San Quentin or Folsom to have committed a person offense as a property offense. Nonetheless, half of the juveniles who were sent to these state prisons had been committed for property rather than person offenses.

The average length of sentence for juveniles committed to San Quentin and Folsom prisons in the 19th century was 3.5 years (compared to under 2 years for reform schools), much shorter than the 6.8 year national average for juveniles in state prisons in 1997 (Strom, 2000). By the 1920s to

---

[14]The panel thanks Gary Gates, Carnegie Mellon University, for assisting member Steven Schlossman with the analysis of these data.

TABLE 5-6 Race Distribution (Weighted Percentages) by Decade for Those Under 18 and Those Age 18 and Older in San Quentin and Folsom Prisons

Race	1870s	1880s	1890s	1900s	1910s	1920s	1930s	All Decades
Under age 18								
White	57.0	74.8	93.2	73.2	100.0	73.6	57.4	70.7
Black	0.0	7.6	3.4	11.1	0.0	9.9	0.0	5.1
Hispanic	15.5	7.1	3.4	6.5	0.0	16.5	42.6[a]	14.4
Chinese	24.4	8.1	0.0	0.0	0.0	0.0	0.0	7.2
Other Asian	0.0	2.4	0.0	4.6	0.0	0.0	0.0	1.0
Other	3.1	0.0	0.0	4.6	0.0	0.0	0.0	1.6
Total	45	39	28	16	2	7	5	142
18 and older								
White	71.3	77.2	83.2	84.0	78.3	78.3	75.1	77.7
Black	1.5	2.5	3.9	4.9	5.2	7.6	8.9	6.1
Hispanic	8.8	8.4	7.0	7.6	13.6	10.6	11.1[a]	10.5
Chinese	16.1	10.3	4.7	1.5	0.5	1.1	1.2	3.2
Other Asian	0.2	0.1	0.3	0.8	1.2	1.5	3.4	1.5
Other	2.1	1.5	0.9	1.3	1.3	0.9	0.4	1.0
Total	950	949	960	968	985	979	974	6765

[a]Apart from the small number of observations in the sample of those under age 18, we cannot readily explain the disparity between Hispanic commitments under age 18 and 18 and older in the 1930s.

Source: Analysis by panel member Steven Schlossman.

1930s, the average sentence length for juveniles more than doubled to 8 years, more comparable to today's average.

CONCLUSIONS

The origin of the juvenile court reflects an abiding tension between safeguarding children and protecting society. This tension has been present historically and continues to be present today in the policy debates dealing with the juvenile justice system. The balance between rehabilitative goals and concerns about the best interests of the child, on one hand, and punishment, incapacitation, and protecting public safety, on the other, has shifted over time and differed significantly from jurisdiction to jurisdiction. Given the local nature of juvenile justice in the United States, there has never been a single dominant vision of how to deal with delinquent children in law or in practice. The delinquency jurisdiction of the juvenile courts today, as in the past, continues to include both children who break criminal laws and children who commit status delinquency offenses.

Policies of the last decade have become more punitive toward delinquent juveniles, but especially toward juveniles who commit violent crimes. Punitive policies include easier waivers to adult court, excluding certain offenses from juvenile court jurisdiction, blended juvenile and adult sentences, increased authority to prosecutors to decide to file cases in adult court, and more frequent custodial placement of adjudicated delinquents. The great majority of recent changes in juvenile justice law and practice have not been evaluated. Research to date shows that juveniles transferred to adult court may be more likely to recidivate than those who remain under juvenile court jurisdiction. Furthermore, there are negative effects of detention and incarceration of juveniles on behavior and future developmental trajectories. Detained and incarcerated juveniles have higher rates of physical injury, mental health problems, and suicide attempts and have poorer educational outcomes than do their counterparts who are treated in the community. Detention and incarceration also cause severe and long-term problems with future employment, leaving ex-offenders with few economic alternatives to crime. Recent research also demonstrates that many serious as well as nonserious offenders can be treated in the community without endangering public safety.

At the same time that laws have become more punitive, innovative approaches to providing services within the juvenile justice system have been introduced. In addition, a fair amount of evaluation research on some programs has been undertaken. Contrary to those who claim that rehabilitative efforts are a waste of time because nothing works, efforts at diverting children and adolescents from detention or incarceration and providing services for them in the community show some promise. Research on treatment programs in correctional institutions suggests that cognitive-behavioral, skill-oriented, and multimodal programs have the best results in terms of recidivism reduction. Research on intensive after-care programs is less conclusive, but it seems clear that delinquent juveniles require more than just intensive surveillance and control to affect rates of future offending and help them successfully reintegrate into society. Experiments with the restorative justice model point to ways in which juvenile offenders can be held responsible for their offenses, make restitution to victims, and receive services aimed at reintegrating them into society.

Information about the number of juveniles in custody—in detention or juvenile correctional facilities—is very poor. Data on the conditions under which juveniles are incarcerated and the types of services available to them are minimal. From the available data, it appears that the rate of juveniles placed in custodial institutions has increased substantially in the past two decades, leading to widespread overcrowding in detention and correctional facilities. The average length of stay, nationally, in public custodial institutions appears to have decreased. There is a great deal of variety by state, however, in average length of stay in long-term public facilities, with some states reporting average stays that are well above the national norm. The trend toward privatization of juvenile correctional facilities may further complicate understanding of juveniles in custody.

RECOMMENDATIONS

Being placed in secure detention disrupts a young person's life and increases the juvenile's likelihood of receiving formal processing and punitive sanctions. Secure detention and correctional facilities have become increasingly crowded, impairing their ability to provide adequate services to their heterogeneous populations. Overcrowded conditions also increase the risk of injury to both staff and juveniles. Research on alternatives to secure detention and confinement have found them to pose no greater risks to the public than secure detention or confinement. In addition, alternatives to detention or confinement tend to be less costly.

Recommendation: The federal government should assist the states through federal funding and incentives to reduce the use of secure detention and secure confinement, by developing community-based alternatives. The effectiveness of such programs both for the protection of the community and the benefit of the youth in their charge should be monitored.

Research has shown that treating most juvenile offenders within the community does not compromise public safety and may even improve it through reduced recidivism. Considering the negative effects of detention and incarceration, community-based treatment should be expanded. Evaluation components should be built into program delivery with the goal of improving services, expanding the use of programs that work, and ending support for programs that are shown to be ineffective. Replication of programs that have been found successful, such as treatment foster care or multisystemic therapy, is particularly important to advancing knowledge about what works and for whom.

Recommendation: Federal and state funding should be provided to replicate successful research-based community-based treatment programs for all types of offenders with continuing evaluations to ensure their safety and efficacy under the specific circumstances of their application.

OJJDP sponsors a biennial Census of Juveniles in Residential Placement that provides minimum information. This instrument identifies juveniles in custody on the specific date of the survey and therefore over samples juveniles in long-term confinement. Furthermore, neither this instrument nor the newly designed Juvenile Residential Facility Census (begun in October 2000), which collects basic data on size, structure, security arrangements, and ownership of facilities designed to house juveniles, as well as information about the provision of health care, education, substance abuse treatment, and mental health treatment in those facilities, yields information about children or youth housed in jails, adult institutions, or mental hospital facilities. OJJDP is planning a Survey of Youth in Residential Placement that will help to inform the public about conditions of confinement. It should be a matter of public accountability for facilities that hold juveniles in secure confinement to report on a regular basis on the conditions under which those juveniles are kept and the types of services provided.

Recommendation: The Congress should provide adequate funds to OJJDP and the Bureau of Justice Statistics in order to assure proper data collection on conditions of confinement as well as new funds to develop national data collection systems to measure the number and characteristics of children and adolescents outside the juvenile jurisdictions, those transferred to criminal court, and those held in adult prisons or jails.

Despite the large amount of descriptive literature about the juvenile justice system, little research has identified how different laws regarding juvenile crime or different practices in confinement affect juveniles in the juvenile justice system. For example, do behavioral modification programs used in secure facilities have an influence on behavior of juveniles after release? Are there long-term effects of isolation used as punishment for disobedient juveniles in confinement? Are there special benefits for particular educational programs carried out in juvenile institutions? Studies of a variety of policies and practices should be undertaken, with evaluations of psychological, educational, and physical effects on the juveniles, as well as measures of recidivism.

Recommendation: The federal government should assist the states in evaluating the effects of correctional policies and practices such as the use of behavior modification programs, physical restraints, and isolation on incarcerated juveniles, as well as determining the effectiveness of educational and psychological programming in correctional facilities.

The American Correctional Association has set minimum standards that facilities for juveniles should meet, but there is little information on the extent to which these standards are met, nor have the standards been evaluated to determine their impact on incarcerated juveniles. An evaluation of these standards in conjunction with on-going work by the Office of Juvenile Justice and Delinquency Prevention on performance-based standards in juvenile corrections would lead to the development of standards that improve outcomes for juveniles who are incarcerated.

> **Recommendation: Congress should provide funds for an independent evaluation of the adequacy of the American Correctional Association standards for juvenile detention and correctional facilities to ensure that the needs of juveniles in these facilities are met. The evaluation should include both short- and long-term effects on juveniles. States should be encouraged to adopt those parts of the standards that prove to be effective.**

Knowledge about the operations of the juvenile justice system and the effects of a juvenile's involvement with the system is completely inadequate. Much remains to be learned at all stages of processing in the system, from the interaction of juveniles and the police, to the factors considered by various juvenile justice system personnel in decision making, to the effects of juvenile justice system involvement on juveniles' development and future life course. Many areas of juvenile justice system policy currently must rely on anecdotal evidence and best guesses.

> **Recommendation: Congress should provide funding for the Office of Juvenile Justice and Delinquency Prevention, in collaboration with other relevant federal agencies (such as National Institute for Mental Health, National Institute on Child Health and Human Development), to develop a research agenda with the goal of expanding knowledge needed for policy making in the following areas:**

- How police decisions and current police practices affect the number, type, and outcomes of juveniles in the system;
- The nature of decisions made in juvenile court by various professionals, including probation officers, judges, prosecutors, and other key actors;
- The extent, systemic effects, costs, and cost-effectiveness of the various possible dispositions of juvenile cases;
- Long-term effects of transferring juveniles to adult court and incarcerating them in adult facilities;

- The effect of using informal sanctions for juveniles committing first offenses if they are not serious crimes.
- The benefits and disadvantages of secure confinement versus providing services in the community; and
- Identifying appropriate treatments for female juveniles.

6

Race, Crime, and Juvenile Justice: The Issue of Racial Disparity

INTRODUCTION

The panel has noted major disparities in the extent of involvement of minority youth, particularly black youth, compared with white youth in the juvenile justice system. The existence of disproportionate racial representation in the juvenile justice system raises questions about fundamental fairness and equality of treatment of these youth by the police, courts, and other personnel connected with the juvenile justice system. Furthermore, what happens to youth in their dealings (or lack of dealings) with the juvenile justice system may have substantial consequences for subsequent development and prospects for the future.

Disproportional confinement of minorities has been recognized as a problem by the federal government. In 1988, Congress amended the Juvenile Justice and Delinquency Prevention Act of 1974 (P.L. 93-415, 42 U.S.C. 5601 et seq.) to require that states participating in the act's formula grants program address disproportionate confinement of minority juveniles in secure facilities. States were required to assess the level of confinement of minority juveniles and to implement strategies to reduce disproportionate minority representation where it was found to exist. In 1991, the Office of Juvenile Justice and Delinquency Prevention created the Disproportionate Minority Confinement initiative to help states comply with the mandate by testing various approaches for addressing the problem. Pilot projects funded by the initiative suggested that attention should focus on all aspects of the juvenile justice system rather than only on confinement (Devine et al., 1998).

Research and social policy on race, crime, and the administration of justice in the United States are currently marked by a seeming conceptual and methodological impasse. This situation stems from efforts by researchers to explain the persistent overrepresentation of groups of racial and ethnic minorities in the juvenile and adult justice systems. Some researchers and commentators have tended to focus on racially disproportionate offending behavior patterns as the primary cause of such a disparity, whereas others have highlighted the persistence of biases among decision makers in the justice system. The most problematic feature of this "behavior versus justice system" debate has been the suggestion that these can be viewed as alternatives, rather than as processes that feed into one another. Furthermore, much of the debate has been carried out with an exceedingly narrow focus that fails to take account of the role that social injustice has played in the production of crime (Clarke, 1998; Lane, 1986; McCord and Ensminger, in press).

Both selective inattention (ignoring the other point of view) and the either-or approach (mutually exclusive points of view), which have characterized academic and public discourse on race, crime and justice, are problematic in several respects. These explanations not only pose a false dichotomy, but they also oversimplify what is a very complex set of social phenomena. These approaches also detract from increasingly promising efforts by scholars and others to develop and examine more inclusive and complex models that may more fully account for the multiple factors that contribute to racial and ethnic disproportionality in the nation's justice system.

Key Terms

There is considerable confusion and variation in the meaning of terms used to examine and describe the racial disparity in the juvenile justice system. This confusion has contributed to divergent findings regarding the presence or absence of racial bias in the justice system and the tendency to attribute all racial differences in system outcomes to prejudice and bigotry (Walker et al., 1996). Therefore, it is important at the outset of this discussion to define the terms we will use. In this report, we use the terms *disparity* and *disproportionality* to refer to situations in which minority group members are either under- or overrepresented relative to their proportion in the general population. There is no judgment about the cause of the observed disparity; it may stem from differences in actual behavior, or from decision making within the system, including legitimate and extralegal factors, or both.

"Race" has been defined as phenotypic differences in skin color, hair, texture, and other physical attributes that have historically been perceived by some as the surface manifestations or markers of deeper, underlying differences in intelligence, temperament, physical prowess, sexuality, and propensity toward crime and violence. However, biologists, geneticists, and physical anthropologists, among others, have reached the conclusion that race is a biologically meaningless category, and not a scientific concept based on discernible biological differences among the various groupings commonly referred to as races today. In addition, cultural and social anthropologists, sociologists, and behavioral scientists have noted that the attributes often associated with specific racial categories are based frequently on stereotype rather than on evidence of actual differences across groups. Moreover, scientific research often reports as much behavioral and cultural difference within races as between them. Yet there continues to be popular acceptance of race as a social construct, and an important organizing principle of individual identity, collective consciousness, and institutional life (Bobo, in press).

The term *racial disparity*, rather than ethnic disparity, is used in this chapter since most of the evidence available does not permit an examination of disproportionality by various ethnic groups, nor does the literature appropriately distinguish ethnicity within the racially designated groups. Using the term *racial disparity* in this chapter is largely a reflection of the kind of data available. Most official arrest data, as well as victimization and self-report surveys, do not permit an examination of disproportionality by the numerous ethnic groups found in the United States today. Classification as Hispanic permits some comparisons between the various Hispanic ethnic groups and those who are not Hispanic. Thus, whether juvenile offending differs among the various ethnic and nationality subgroups found among European, Asian, and African Americans cannot be determined given the data available. Crime and delinquency data on the race of juvenile offenders focuses primarily on blacks and whites. Official arrest statistics for Hispanic, Asian, and American Indian youth are often unavailable or suffer from problems in assignment of youth to these ethnic and racial groups using vague or ambiguous criteria. For these reasons, this chapter focuses on the one racial minority group for whom we have reasonably reliable data—blacks. The chapter examines the extent to which black youth are disproportionately involved in the juvenile justice system compared with white youth. Whenever possible, attention is called to the situation for minority youth of other racial and ethnic backgrounds.

Because the research reviewed in this chapter is largely focused on potential sources of bias in the juvenile justice system (as opposed to other institutions in American society), we use the term *discrimination* to refer to those situations in which evidence suggests that extralegal or illegitimate factors are the cause of disparate justice system outcomes.

Chapter Organization

Detailed information on patterns and trends in offending has been described earlier in this volume. This chapter is designed to bring together divergent streams of research and scholarly discourse in an attempt to highlight some key issues and to move the field ahead by suggesting useful and potentially useful ways of thinking about race, ethnicity, juvenile crime, and the juvenile justice system in the future. The chapter is divided into three major parts. The first part of this chapter briefly reviews the extent of the racial disparity in the juvenile justice system. The chapter then considers the evidence for racial disparity in the delinquent behavior of youth as well as evidence of bias in the juvenile justice system. The second part of the chapter introduces the concept of compound risk and illustrates how small differences in the treatment of juveniles at one point in the process may have enduring and powerful effects later on, as the youth progresses or does not progress through the juvenile justice system. The third part of the chapter describes promising directions for future research that may prove useful and productive to the field. In the last part of the chapter are the panel's specific recommendations for research and policy.

RACIAL DISPARITY IN THE JUVENILE JUSTICE SYSTEM

Although black youth represented approximately 15 percent of the U.S. population ages 10-17 in 1997, they represented 26 percent of all juvenile arrests, 30 percent of delinquency referrals to juvenile court, 45 percent of preadjudication decisions, 33 percent of petitioned delinquency cases, 46 percent of cases judicially waived to adult criminal court, and 40 percent of juveniles in public long-term institutions (see Figure 6-1). Thus, the proportion of blacks under the supervision of the juvenile or adult criminal justice systems is more than double their proportion in the general population.

In a report produced for the Office of Juvenile Justice and Delinquency Prevention, Hamparian, Leiber, and colleagues (1997) described the extent of disproportionate minority confinement of juveniles in state facilities. The report focused on six decision points (arrest, secure detention, confinement in secure juvenile correctional facilities, in adult jails, and in adult lockups, and transfer to criminal court), using state data from the late 1980s and early 1990s. Table 6-1 presents findings on the over-

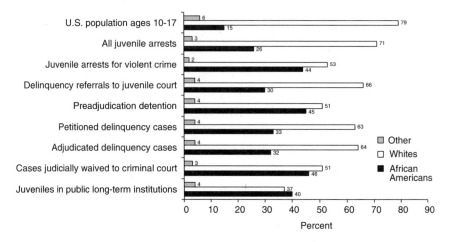

FIGURE 6-1 Involvement of juveniles at various stages of the juvenile justice system, by race, 1996/1997. Note: *Delinquency* = acts committed by a juvenile that if committed by an adult could result in criminal prosecution. *Delinquency referrals* = includes not only arrests, but also all other sources of referral to juvenile court, such as social service agencies, schools, and parents. *Petitioned* = cases sent for formal processing in juvenile court; formal processing includes adjudicatory hearings and waiver hearings. Source: Snyder and Sickmund (1999); Stahl et al. (1999).

representation of minority youth, based on data from the Hamparian et al. (1997) report.[1]

Hamparian et al. (1997) created an index score, which represents the ratio of the number of youth involved at that decision point divided by the state's total juvenile population ages 10-17.[2] An index number of 1.00 means that minorities are represented in the juvenile or criminal justice system in the same proportion as they are represented in the population. An index number larger than 1.0 indicates that minority youth are over-represented; for example, an index number of 2.0 means that minority youth are represented at two times their representation in the juvenile population. The greater the index number, the larger the extent of over-representation.

---

[1]The panel expresses appreciation to Amie Schuck and Jorge Chavez of The University at Albany for their assistance with these analyses.

[2]It should be noted that for some states, information was not available for the entire state. In these cases, the at-risk population was calculated for the designated area.

TABLE 6-1 Overrepresentation of Minorities

	Percent Minority Population	Arrest	Secure Detention	Secure Corrections	Adult Jail	Adult Lockup	Transfer Criminal Court	Probation
All minority youth[a]								
Mean index score[b]	23.2	1.7	2.9	2.8	2.0	2.2	2.4	1.8
Median index score	17.2	1.7	2.6	2.4	1.7	1.3	1.9	1.8
N	46	37	44	40	22	10	22	5
Black youth								
Mean index score	15.4	2.2	3.2	3.3	1.8	2.6	3.1	2.8
Median index score	9.2	2.2	3.2	3.2	1.9	1.8	1.9	2.4
N	40	30	32	33	16	11	15	8

Note: Some of the numbers in this table differ slightly from those reported in Hamparian and Leiber (1997) for unknown reasons.
[a]Minority youth include black, Hispanic, American Indian, and Asian or Pacific Islander.
[b]Index score = ratio of number of youth involved at that decision point divided by the at-risk population.

Source: Based on information from Hamparian et al. (1997)

Table 6-1 clearly reveals that minority youth are overrepresented at all stages of the juvenile justice system included in this analysis. This table also shows that the disparity for black youth is higher, in all cases except one, than for all minorities. This suggests that it is the disparity for blacks that is driving the disproportionate minority representation. This also suggest that some other minorities are underrepresented in the juvenile justice system. Using these data, the smallest index number is 1.6 for arrests of all minority juveniles across the 37 states reporting data on arrests. For black youth, the index for arrests across the 30 states that reported separately for blacks is 2.2. The small number of states that reported data separately for Hispanics, American Indian, and Asian/ Pacific Islanders made it impossible to compare their indices to those for blacks. However, the data suggest that Hispanic and American Indian juveniles experience overrepresentation in the juvenile and adult justice systems, whereas Asian and Pacific Islander juveniles tend to be under-represented.

The above information is presented in an attempt to make concrete the extent of disproportionate representation of racial minorities; however, there are several limitations to these findings that need to be acknowledged. One of the difficulties involved in trying to ascertain the extent of disproportionality in the juvenile justice system is that laws and practices vary by state, and this makes state-by-state comparisons problematic. Thus, there are no standard reporting mechanisms that are comparable across states, and analyses that aggregate across jurisdictions may mask important information. The data used in the analysis by Hamparian and colleagues vary for the time period in which they were collected. Information from some of the states is incomplete. Problems with assigning race or ethnicity are reflected in these statistics as well.

This brief review, along with evidence cited in other chapters of this volume, strongly suggests that there is racial disparity at various points in the juvenile justice system and in various jurisdictions across the nation. The focus of the rest of this chapter is not to further document disparity, since the evidence appears fairly clear, despite the limitations of existing data. Some of the nation's minority juveniles, most notably blacks, experience higher rates of arrest and further justice system involvement than do whites. The remainder of this chapter examines the research findings that may prove helpful for efforts to better interpret and understand these disparities and identify areas in which research or action is most urgently needed. Earlier in the chapter, contrasting explanations of disproportionality were raised. The first—attributing the disparity to the behavior of the youth—suggests that the disparity is an accurate or reasonable reflection of the extent of involvement in delinquent and criminal behavior by these youth. The second perspective—attributing the disparity to the justice system—emphasizes the persistent effect of bias among decision makers in the juvenile justice system. We first consider the evidence for race differences in delinquent behavior and then consider evidence of bias in the juvenile justice system.

Behavior-Based Explanations

To explore the possibility that the racial disparity observed in rates of justice system involvement arises as a result of racial differences in criminal conduct, the possibility of error in crime data must first be entertained. Errors could lead to the appearance of racial disparity that, on closer examination, can be shown not to exist. Then, to the extent that racial disparity can be shown to exist, its causes must be explored. In the field of juvenile and criminal justice research, there are several measures that have been used to determine the extent of criminal behavior. In Chapter 2, the issues of measuring delinquency and crime were discussed and it was pointed out that none of the measures is without problems. There is fairly good agreement that the best approach to measuring crime is to use multiple sources of information (Farrington, 1998; Loeber et al., 1998b; National Research Council, 1993). The use of multiple sources of information may be especially rewarding for efforts to understand the sources and causes of racial and ethnic disparity.

The three most common approaches to measuring delinquency and crime—self-report surveys, victimization surveys, and official arrest and conviction statistics—all indicate high rates of serious offending among young blacks. While studies using differing methods and sources of data are not in agreement on the magnitude of differences in rates of involvement in youth crime across racial, ethnic, and social class categories, most research does show important differences, particularly with regard to race.

Figure 6-1 reveals the substantial overrepresentation of minority youth in official arrest data, showing major discrepancies between black and white youth. These differences are on the order of magnitude of 1.8:1. The racial disparity in offending behavior is lower when the measure used as an index of offending is based on self-reports. For example, using data from the National Youth Survey, Elliott (1994b) found that, at age 17, 36 percent of black males, 25 percent of white males, 18 percent of black females, and 10 percent of white females reported committing a serious violent offense (robbery, rape, or aggravated assault involving injury or a weapon) in the previous year. Thus, self-report data from this large nationally representative sample reveals differences in criminal behavior between black and white juveniles. It should be noted, however, that the discrepancies were not nearly as large as the differential revealed by official arrest data (1.5:1 for self-report compared to 4:1 for arrest—Elliott, 1999).

Greenfeld (1999) presented results to the panel from an analysis of data from the National Crime Victimization Survey (NCVS), the third source of criminal behavior information, for the years 1993 to 1997 (annual average) for robbery and aggravated assault for juvenile offenders. The NCVS, conducted annually by the Bureau of Justice Statistics since 1973, asks victims about their victimization experiences and about characteristics of the offender(s) who victimized them, including race. Information from the NCVS is helpful for crimes involving a personal confrontation like robbery, assault, or rape, but it is not very useful for property crimes for which there was no direct confrontation. Juvenile offenders are defined as those whom victims indicated they believed to have been less than 18 years old.

Table 6-2 shows the race distribution of juvenile offenses for robbery and aggravated assault as reported by victims (NCVS) and in arrests from the Uniform Crime Reports (UCR) of the Federal Bureau of Investigation. Several points are worth noting. First, in both sources of information, black juveniles are overrepresented for these two crime types, compared with their proportion in the general population. Second, in both data sources, a higher proportion of white youth are reported for aggravated

TABLE 6-2 Race Distribution of Juvenile Offenses for Robbery and Aggravated Assault as Reported by Victims (NCVS) and in Arrests (UCR), Annual Average 1993-1997

	Total	Robbery	Aggravated Assault
As reported by victims (NCVS)[a]			
Annual average number	949,992	362,498	587,494
% white	42	27	51
% black	41	58	31
% other	14	12	15
Juvenile arrestees (UCR)			
Annual average number	129,997	49,858	80,139
% white	50	38	57
% black	48	60	41
% other	2	2	2

Note: NCVS = National Crime Victimization Survey. UCR = Uniform Crime Reports
[a]Juvenile offenders are those for whom victims indicated that they believed the offender to have been less than 18 years old.

assault (51 percent for NCVS and 57 percent for UCR), whereas a higher proportion of black youth are reported for robbery offenses (58 percent for NCVS and 60 percent for UCR). Third, one observes an important difference in the two sources of information in the proportion of youth in the "other" race category. In the NCVS, the proportion in the other race (e.g., American Indian, Asian) category ranges from 12 to 15 percent. In contrast, in the UCR, this percentage is only 2 percent. This may reflect the tendency of the police to categorize persons as black or white, because of their record-keeping system. Thus, it is possible that some of the respondents categorized as other in the NCVS data are classified as black in the UCR, inflating the rates for black juveniles.

Comparing the findings from these two important and different data sources does not answer the question about whether police arrest black youth inappropriately or excessively. This comparison does, however, reveal the complexity of trying to disentangle juvenile crime data by race and the urgent need for more focused examination of these issues.

In a further analysis, Greenfeld (1999) presented the results of calculations of juvenile court data based on rates in 17 states[3] in 1994. From that analysis, Greenfeld concluded that black and white juveniles who commit robbery have nearly the same likelihood of being arrested, convicted, and punished with confinement. In contrast, Greenfeld found that for aggravated assault, black juveniles have a one-third higher likelihood of the offense being reported to the police (the rate was 52 per 100 offenders for black youth compared with 39 per 100 for white youth), a 50 percent higher rate of being referred to juvenile courts (rates for black youth were 22 per 100 compared with 15 per 100 for white youth), and a 60 percent higher rate of getting petitioned (rate of 16 per 100 for black youth compared with 10 per 100 for white youth), and a 50 percent greater likelihood of receiving institutional placement (3 per 100 for black youth compared with 2 per 100 for white youth).

This brief summary of crime rates indicates that black juveniles are overrepresented in some types of crimes. The question is *why* should black juveniles be more likely to engage in criminal behavior than whites? Such overrepresentation may be at least partially explained by considering how exposure to risk factors affects the probability of engaging in criminal behavior. The argument has been made that more minority children, and black children in particular, are subject to risk factors associated with crime and that these factors explain the disparity. For example,

---

[3]Alabama, Arizona, California, Florida, Hawaii, Maryland, Mississippi, Montana, New Jersey, North Dakota, Ohio, Pennsylvania, South Dakota, Tennessee, Utah, Virginia, West Virginia. Aggravated data are for 15 states; North Dakota and Tennessee did not report aggravated assault data.

there is ample evidence that poverty is a risk factor for delinquency. Given that many minority children are poor, then the disparity would be expected because of the poverty, not the minority status of the youth. To what extent does this explanation of the racial disparity in delinquent behavior receive support?

Growing Up in a Context of Risk

Throughout the history of the nation's juvenile justice system, substandard living conditions have been associated with an elevated risk of involvement by youth in antisocial conduct. Differential rates of poverty and the social conditions associated with it may be one of the major contributors to the levels of racial disparity seen in the juvenile justice system.

Minority children and adolescents are more likely than whites to be poor and to live in unfavorable environments. Figure 6-2 shows the extent to which black, Hispanic, and white children are likely to grow up in a context of risk. These data reflect the status of children in 1990 and reveal very clearly that black children are at substantially higher risk for factors associated with delinquency (see Chapter 3) and factors less likely to lead to healthy development. For example, in 1990, 40 percent of blacks under age 18 lived below poverty levels, compared with 12 percent of white children. As Figure 6-2 indicates, black children are also more likely to live in poor and very poor neighborhoods. Black children have higher rates of infant mortality, low birthweight, and exposure to lead than white or Hispanic children, and they are less likely to have had mothers who received early prenatal care. Compared with white children, black children are less likely to grow up in households in which one resident parent is fully employed.

In sum, from the early days of childhood, black juveniles have more experiences with poor health care and health conditions and with poor economic conditions, and they are more likely to live in segregated, isolated neighborhoods with concentrated poverty than are white juveniles. Concentrated disadvantages in poor neighborhoods, with low mobility and little racial heterogeneity, have been found to be strongly correlated with assault and burglary rates as measured through calls to police (Warner and Pierce, 1993). They have been found to related to high rates of juvenile delinquency and crime as measured by police reports from the 1950s to the 1970s in Racine, Wisconsin (Shannon, 1986). They have been found across the nation in studies of victimization as well (Sampson, 1986).

Data on Hispanic children indicate that they, too, grow up in environments different from and less advantaged than white children. While the

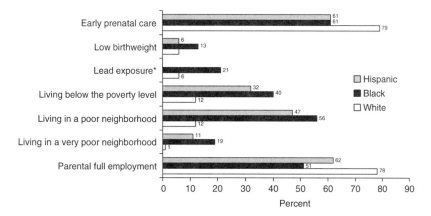

FIGURE 6-2 Child risk indicators by race. Notes: *Early prenatal care* = 1990 percentage of women in the United States receiving prenatal care in the first trimester; *Low birthweight* = 1990 percentage of all low-birthweight infants born in the United States by mother's race; *Lead exposure* = 1988-1991 percentage of children 1-5 years old in the United States with blood lead levels greater than or equal to 10 micrograms per deciliter (*data unavailable for Hispanic population); *Living below the poverty level* = 1989 percentage of children in the United States under age 18 living below the poverty level; *Living in a poor neighborhood* = 1990 percentage of children in the United States living in neighborhoods where 20 percent or more of the persons live in families below the poverty level; *Living in very poor neighborhoods* = 1990 percentage of children in the United States living in neighborhoods where 40 percent or more of the persons live in families below the poverty level; *Parental full employment* = 1989 percentage of children in the United States with at least one fully employed (full time, full year) resident parent. Source: U.S. Department of Health and Human Services (1998).

same proportion of black and Hispanic women receive prenatal health care (61 percent) (see Figure 6-2), the percentage of low-birthweight babies born to Hispanic women is half that of black women (6 and 13 percent respectively) and the same as white women. Economic risk indicators also reflect differences between whites, Hispanics and blacks. A total of 32 percent of Hispanic children live below the poverty level, compared with 40 percent of black children and 12 percent of white children. Hispanic children are also more likely to live in poor (47 percent) and very poor neighborhoods (11 percent) than whites (12 percent and 1 percent, respectively). Differences also exist in the proportion of families with at least one parent employed on a full-time basis; 78 percent of white children live in such households, as do 62 percent of Hispanic children and 51 percent of black children.

Black and Hispanic children remain at greater risk than white children in many ways. Data from 1960 to 1996 on the percentage of children living below the poverty level show very little change in the proportion of white, Hispanic, and black children living in poverty conditions. In 1960, 20 percent of white children lived below the poverty level, 4 percent more than in 1996, with only slight variations in the intervening years (low of 11 percent in 1970 and a high of 17 percent in 1992 and 1993). The proportion of black children living below the poverty level, although much higher than the proportion of white children, was similarly stable. In 1970, 42 percent of black children lived below the poverty level; in 1996 the percentage was 40 percent. Over the 26-year period for which data are available for blacks, the percentage of children living below the poverty level never dropped below 40 percent, varying 2 to 6 percentage points up or down during these years. Poverty figures showed greater variation among Hispanic children. Between 1980 and 1996, the percentage of Hispanic children living below the poverty level has ranged from 33 percent in 1980 to 41 percent in 1994. These figures reinforce the argument that minority and majority families live and grow up in different social contexts and experience different levels of risk.

There is increasing evidence that community-level factors are important in understanding the etiology of juvenile offending and violence. Community-based crime statistics reveal high correlations with joblessness, household disruption, housing density, infant deaths, and poverty (Sampson, 1987, 1992). Where a family lives affects the nature of opportunities available for its children and adults. In some communities, public transportation permits easy travel for those who do not own automobiles, allowing residents to take advantage of opportunities for employment and entertainment outside the neighborhood. In communities that lack these opportunities and resources, street corner gatherings offer possibilities for illegal activities. Neighborhoods can also influence children's behavior by providing examples of socially acceptable behaviors and actions. For example, gang activities vary by community (Curry and Spergel, 1988; Horowitz, 1987).

There is no other racial or ethnic group in the United States of comparable size whose members are nearly as likely to grow up in neighborhoods of concentrated urban poverty as are blacks (Sampson, 1987; Wilson, 1987). While there are more poor white than black families in absolute number, poor white families are less likely to live in areas where most of their neighbors are also poor (Chin, 1996; Moore, 1978, 1991; Padilla, 1992; Pinderhughes, 1997; Sullivan, 1989; Vigil, 1988; Vigil and Yun, 1990).

In an examination of long-term trends in the segregation of blacks and recent trends in the segregation of blacks, Hispanics, and Asians,

Massey has suggested that blacks are unique among groups in showing very high levels of segregation and isolation (Massey, 2000:1):

> As of 1990, the degree of segregation was so severe, and occurred on so many dimensions simultaneously, that it was called "hypersegregation." This pattern of extreme segregation is unique to African Americans and is unrelated to their economic status and unexplained by their housing preferences. ... High levels of African American segregation have interacted with recent shifts in the income distribution and class segregation to produce unusually high concentrations of poverty among African Americans. The spatial isolation of poor African Americans has, in turn, elevated the risks of educational failure, joblessness, unwed parenthood, crime, and mortality.

Effects of deleterious neighborhoods have been studied in relation to both immigrants and blacks (e.g., Shaw and McKay, 1969). Recent research has focused on ethnographic studies of youthful gang members and drug dealers (Bourgois, 1995), although the link between drug use and minority status has a long history in the United States (e.g., Helmer, 1975).

Spatial isolation has been a consequence, in part, of social policies. Taxes promoted an exodus of jobs from the cities, where impoverished blacks lived in public housing that was restricted by ordinances to locations removed from job opportunities. Racial discrimination in housing, enforced by restrictive covenants and threats of violence, set a pattern that left blacks more clearly segregated than other minorities (Jackson, 1985; McCord, 1997c; Robinson, 1993; Sampson and Lauritsen, 1997; Wade, 1972). The resulting disparities may explain at least part of the differential exposure to risks by black youth. The next section examines attempts to consider the influence of exposure to risk factors on rates of violence.

Examining Risk Factors to Account For Racial Disparity

There is scant research that examines the extent to which risk factors explain racial disparity. In one very recent investigation, Farrington and colleagues (in press) used data from the Pittsburgh Youth Study, a prospective longitudinal survey of the development of offending and antisocial behavior in three samples, totaling about 1,500 Pittsburgh boys (for description of Pittsburgh Youth Study, see Loeber et al., 1998a). This analysis is based on the middle sample of boys, who were about age 10 when they were first assessed and screened for inclusion in the study. The first follow-up was six months later, and during this assessment information concerning a large number of explanatory variables was collected. They were then followed up in court records for 5.8 years up to a median of age 16.4. Farrington et al. (in press) used combined reports of violence from mothers, boys, and teachers (rather than self-reports alone), defining violence as whether the boy had (a) attacked someone with the intention of seriously hurting or killing them (labeled aggravated assault), (b) used force to get money or possessions from someone (labeled robbery), or (c) hurt or forced someone to have sex (labeled forcible rape). They also collected information regarding petitions to the juvenile court for index violence up to 1994, when the boys were about 16 years of age.

Strong predictors of a record of violence included poverty and one-parent families, young maternal age, physical punishment, a bad neighborhood, and poor school achievement. The strongest predictor of having a court record was black race. The risk indicators did not completely account for the racial disparity. "After controlling for important risk factors, the relationship between race and reported violence was reduced but not eliminated, showing that [the relationship] could not be completely explained by factors measured in the Pittsburgh Youth Study" (Farrington et al., in press). The risks explained most of the self-, mother-, and teacher-reported racial disparity in violence, but not the 21:1 ratio of court petitions.

A compelling explanation for these differences remains elusive. Future research will need to consider several alternative explanations. For example, it is possible that the risk factors may be more serious or severe for black boys (bad neighborhoods may be worse, physical punishment may be more severe, or poverty may be more desperate) compared with white boys. The risk factors may have different meanings for different races. Risk factors may have longer duration for black boys, or these risk factors may have interactive (or multiplicative) effects. These results may be the effect of enduring chronic poverty and stigma experienced by these youth. Yet another possibility is that protective factors may be less common among black boys. Furthermore, there are many alternative ways in which the juvenile justice system probably influences the crime rate differences (e.g., where police concentrate their efforts). For example, in their models of black and white juvenile arrests for homicide, Messner and colleagues (2000) found that rising and falling rates of juvenile homicide arrests corresponded with rates of child poverty. Living in urban areas increases the likelihood of formal juvenile justice system processing (Feld, 1999). Proportionately more black juveniles reside in urban areas and therefore are exposed to a greater likelihood of formal processing.

Clearly, blacks have been exposed to a wider array of risk factors than have whites. We now consider possible bias in the juvenile justice system.

BIAS IN THE JUVENILE JUSTICE SYSTEM

This section highlights a few points in the juvenile justice system about which there is an empirical literature addressing the issue of racial disparity or bias. We consider three major points in the juvenile justice system process—the police, the courts, and probation officers—and the evidence of bias at each.

Policing

Any examination of the processing of youth through the juvenile justice system needs to consider the role of the police—the primary gatekeepers of the system. Police have contact with a large volume of youth who are offenders and those who are at risk. Many of the contacts are not documented, and many of those documented never result in a court case. As noted earlier (see Chapter 5), cases that reach the juvenile courts represent only a fraction of the contacts that juveniles have with the police. Most of the interactions of police with juveniles are therefore below the surface and relatively out of sight.

Police encounters with juveniles typically involve uniformed patrol officers who are dispatched in response to calls for police service and who also initiate encounters with youth on their own as they conduct patrol. There are also specialized juvenile officers whose encounters with juveniles may be in the context of referrals from parents, school officials, or patrol officers.

As noted in Chapter 5, there is scant empirical evidence on police encounters with juveniles (Black and Reiss, 1970; Lundman et al., 1978; Wordes and Bynum, 1995). A study by Sealock and Simpson (1998), based on an analysis of Philadelphia birth cohort data in which police contacts with juveniles from 1968 through 1975 were recorded, is one of the few that deals with juveniles' encounters with police.

Nonetheless, one of the most researched issues in race and crime research is the role of extralegal factors in police decision making. Empirical findings confirm that police behavior is influenced by legal considerations, but officers' choices are not determined by legal factors, which leaves ample room for bias. This is particularly a concern when police decisions must be made based on few informational cues. Under such circumstances, readily observable characteristics, like race, sex, and juveniles' demeanor, have a substantial influence on the ways in which police officers behave. In one of the few studies of black citizens' perceptions of police behavior, with data from interviews, focus groups, and observations, Conley (1994) found that citizens consider police behavior to be among the most important sources of racial disparity. Police often accuse black youth of theft when they have purchased clothing. They often seem to seek to frighten youth, thereby generating behavior among adolescents designed to show their peers that they are not cowards. The police are also believed to be unfair in their designations of the crimes for which they arrest adolescents, counting similar behavior as more serious when carried out by blacks.

A variety of studies have sought to document police bias in their encounters with juveniles. Results have been mixed and conclusions inconsistent, perhaps because of variations over time and in location. Some of the earliest studies reported disparities in the treatment of white and black suspects, to the disadvantage of the latter. These disparities were attributed to factors other than race itself, such as to the more frequently disrespectful demeanor of black (or other minority) suspects (Black, 1971), or to the more frequently proarrest preferences of black complainants (Black and Reiss, 1970; Lundman et al., 1978). In a reanalysis of his earlier work, Black (1980:107-108) reconsidered his earlier conclusion about racial bias, finding that black offenders were more likely to be treated in a punitive fashion by the police even though they were not more likely to be arrested. In subsequent analyses, Smith and Visher (1981) and Mastrofski et al. (1995) showed that race had an effect on police behavior, independent of other factors. Research has not consistently shown that minorities are treated more harshly than whites in terms of arrest (Mastrofski et al., 1995) or the use of force (Friedrich, 1980).

Smith and colleagues (1984) found that the effect of citizens' race on police arrest decisions was contingent on other factors. In police encounters with suspects only (and no victims), white and black men were (with other factors held constant) at equal risk of arrest, while white women were at much lower risk than black women. Furthermore, in encounters involving both suspects and victims, police were more likely to arrest if the victim was white and the crime was a property offense. While the police were more likely to comply with the preference of a white victim for arrest, the race of the suspect had no effect. Again, to illustrate the complexity of studying this problem, Mastrofski et al. (1995) failed to replicate these findings in a subsequent study.

The two most widely cited analyses of police encounters with juveniles (Black and Reiss, 1970; Lundman et al., 1978) were based on data collected for large-scale observational studies in 1966 and 1970, respectively. Since that time, the implementation of the due-process revolution[4]

---

[4]*Due process* refers to the basic rights of a defendant in criminal proceedings and the requisites for a fair trial. The basic due process rights are embodied in the 5th and 14th Amendments to the U.S. Constitution. The *due process revolution* refers to the expansion of these rights and requirements by the Supreme Court to include timely notice of a hearing or trial which informs the accused of the charges against him or her; the opportunity to confront accusers and to present evidence on one's own behalf before an impartial jury or judge; the right of an accused to be warned of constitutional rights at the earliest stage of the criminal process; and the guarantee that an individual will not be tried more than once for the same offense (Black et al., 1990).

and changes in the composition of police forces (better educated and more diverse) have altered the context of policing and, perhaps, the attitudes and values that police officers bring to their work. With the advent of community policing, police act more frequently on their own initiative. This is especially so in their handling of less serious, so-called quality-of-life offenses. Under these circumstances, police might initiate more encounters with juveniles, and one might expect a relatively large proportion of cases of minor legal gravity. In addition, in an era of community policing, law enforcement officers may use a wide repertoire of responses with correspondingly greater chances of biased decision making.

The Project on Policing Neighborhoods, described in Chapter 5, involved systematic social observations of patrol officers in the field by trained observers who accompanied officers during their entire work shifts (Worden and Myers, 1999).

Worden and Myers reported that 62 percent of the juvenile suspects encountered by police were minority, and 95 percent of these were black. Most were males and most appeared to be of lower socioeconomic status. According to these reports, few of the youth showed any indication of alcohol or other drug use, and few were found to have a weapon in their possession. Minority suspects were 43 percent more likely to be arrested than white suspects (13 versus 9 percent) and twice as likely to be judged as having shown disrespect (14 versus 7 percent).

Table 6-3 shows analyses from Worden and Myers (1999) predicting the arrest of juvenile suspects. In the first analysis, all of the police encounters with juveniles were included (n = 612). For the total encounters, being a minority was not a significant predictor of arrest, although

TABLE 6-3 Prediction of Juvenile Arrest in Police Encounters

	Odds of Arrest					
	All Encounters with Juvenile Suspects (N = 612)			Police Initiated Cases Only (N = 319)		
Male (vs. female)	2.08*	2.63	2.33	3.85*	8.33*	7.69*
Minority (vs. white)	1.43	1.27	1.19	3.27*	2.22	2.09
Crime serious (vs. not)		1.95*	1.93*		2.55*	2.59*
Evidence (vs. none)		6.11*	5.82*		12.81*	12.19*
Disrespect (vs. none)			2.17			1.46

* p<.05
Source: Worden and Myers (1999).

being a male suspect, the seriousness of the crime, the amount of evidence, and the level of disrespect shown to the police were significant predictors of the odds of being arrested. The second set of figures in Table 6-3 shows a similar analysis for only those encounters that were officer initiated (n = 319). In contrast to the previous analyses, in officer-initiated cases, in which there is considerable police discretion, the minority status of the juvenile was a significant predictor of arrest. When the seriousness of the crime and the presence of evidence were taken into account, the effect of minority status was no longer statistically significant, although the odds of being arrested remained twice as high for minority juveniles compared with white juveniles.

Observational studies of police behavior have typically examined police actions in specific cities. Bachman (1996), however, used the national data collected for NCVS from 1987 to 1992 in order to address issues regarding the role of race in initial police responses to robbery and aggravated assault. Analyses focused only on crimes for which there were single offenders, thus eliminating 36 percent of the robberies and 16 percent of the aggravated assaults. A total of 52 percent of the remaining robberies and 54 percent of the assaults by single offenders were reported to police. Police responded more quickly to crimes committed by blacks with white victims than to white on white or black on black or white on black crimes. In addition, police put more effort into obtaining evidence for black on white crimes. Thus, blacks would have been more likely to be arrested and subsequently convicted, given that whites and blacks committed the same crime.

Police also exercise discretion in deciding what charges to make for particular crime events. Using data from the National Youth Survey sample of 11- to 17-year-olds, Huizinga and Elliott (1987) compared self-reported criminal behavior with official charges. They found that a slightly larger proportion of blacks reported involvement in general delinquency and that blacks and Hispanics reported more felony assaults than did whites. There were no consistent differences in rates of felony thefts. Among both nonserious and serious offenders, blacks were much more likely than whites to be arrested on a charge for an index offense. The racial differences could not be attributed to either the seriousness of the offense or to the frequency of offending.

Despite the fact that police tend to concentrate patrols in poor neighborhoods, they also appear to respond more slowly to client calls from inner-city residents than in more affluent neighborhoods (Bachman, 1996). In addition, inner-city black residents distrust the largely white police (Anderson, 1997; Russell, 1998) and believe the police are unlikely to be available when they are most needed (Pinderhughes, 1999). Many residents therefore believe that they must defend themselves.

In sum, evidence from this review of the research and analysis of a recent study of police encounters with youth reveals some evidence of bias, although also some inconsistency in the evidence. Such inconsistencies may arise from variations in police practice by location (e.g., particular city or rural area), variation in police practice over time as policies and administrations change, or even as a consequence of alterations in police behavior when they are under research observation. Methodological problems in this research are a difficult issue, as the problem of potential influence of observation on police behavior is nearly insurmountable, and problems of racial bias in the observations of investigators are also hard to control or assess.

Referrals to Juvenile Justice Intake Units

After the police have encountered youth and have made decisions about whether to continue to process or to divert them, others become involved in the decision-making process. Table 6-4 presents a number of studies that have examined racial disparities at various points in the processing of youth through the juvenile justice system. Despite the fact that existing evidence is fairly limited in quantity and studies vary in methodological rigor, the studies listed in Table 6-4 present a fairly consistent picture. Disparities exist in arrest (6 of 7 studies), intake (4 of 4), detention (6 of 7), counsel (1 of 1), and placement (7 of 7). Adjudication reveals a different pattern, with only one of the studies showing disparity and three not showing disparity.

In one of the largest studies of this topic undertaken so far, Frazier and Bishop (1995) analyzed data from all cases referred to juvenile justice intake units (N = 137,028) in Florida between January 1, 1985, and December 31, 1987. Frazier and Bishop looked at processing at four points—intake (case closure versus formal processing), detention (detention versus release), court referral (prosecutor files petition versus no petition filed), and judicial disposition (community treatment versus residential facilities or transferred to criminal court). In simple bivariate analyses, Frazier and Bishop found that nonwhites were more likely than whites to be (1) referred by intake for formal processing, (2) held in secure detention facilities, and (3) petitioned to court by prosecutors. However, in trying to interpret findings regarding racial disproportionality, it is commonly recognized that analyses need to control for certain factors that influence the decision-making process. For example, the seriousness of a crime obviously affects the decision-making process. Similarly, a youth's prior record would be something that judges and others involved in the decision-making process might take into account. Other factors about the life circumstances of the juvenile, such as living with a single parent or school

TABLE 6-4 A Summary of Findings Regarding Racial Disparity in the Juvenile Justice System

Study	Sample	Self-report of delinquency
Pope and Feyerherm (1992)[a]	National Juvenile Court Data Archives California and Florida, 1985	
Elliott (1994a)	National Youth Survey National Sample, 1976-1989	No
Elliott (1995)	National Youth Survey National Sample, 1976-1989	No
Austin (1995)[a]	Aggregate level multiple sources California, 1991	
Wordes and Bynum (1995)	Nine jurisdictions in Michigan, 1990	
Feld (1995)	Hennepin County, Minnesota, 1986	
Frazier and Bishop (1995)	Florida, 1985-1987	
Leonard and Sontheimer (1995)	Counties in Pennsylvania, 1989	
Poupart (1995)[b]	Counties in Wisconsin, 1985-1991	
Hamparian et al. (1997)[a]	States, 1980s and 1990s	
Bridges and Steen (1998)	Three counties in Washington state, 1990-1991	
Cook and Laub (1998)	Uniform Crime Reports, National Crime Victimization Survey, Supplemental Homicide Reports, 1976-1995	
DeComo (1998)	36 states, 1995	
Greenfeld (1999)	National Crime Victimization Survey Aggravated Assault Robbery	

[a]Does not control for important covariates. No determination can be made regarding whether the disparities are justified or unjustified.
[b]The race comparison is white versus American Indian.
[c]Only in misdemeanor model.

Victim Reporting	Arrest	Intake	Detention	Counsel	Adjudication	Placement
		Yes	Yes		Yes	Yes
	Yes					
	Yes		Yes			Yes
	Yes		Yes^c			
			Yes	Yes		Yes
		Yes	No		No	
		Yes			No	
		Yes	Yes		No	Yes
	Yes		Yes			Yes
						Yes
	Yes					
						Yes
Yes	Yes	Yes			Yes	Yes
No	No	No			No	No

failure, may also influence the decision about how to handle a juvenile. Thus, analyses need to control for some of these factors to better reveal the importance of race or ethnicity in the disproportionality. As indicated in Table 6-4, only a few studies include controls for important covariates.

Using this more rigorous test of the disproportionality hypothesis involving multivariate analyses, Frazier and Bishop (1995) found that being nonwhite significantly increased the likelihood of an intake decision of formal processing, despite controls for gender, age, prior record, offense severity, and contempt status. Being nonwhite did not seem to affect decisions at other points in the process.

Waiver to Adult Courts

In an analysis of transfer decisions in Boston, Detroit, Newark, and Phoenix, Fagan et al. (1987a) found that blacks were 75 percent more likely to be waived to criminal court than whites (1.4 versus 0.8 percent of cases, respectively). Juveniles who were older at the time of the offense, juveniles with an earlier age of delinquency onset, and juveniles charged with murder were most often transferred. Although Fagan et al. (1987a) found that minority juveniles were transferred more often, race was not a statistically independent influence on the decision to transfer. However, these authors suggested that race may indirectly affect transfer decisions through factors such as dress, demeanor, quality of defense representation, verbal abilities of the minor, and status in the community.

Podkopacz and Feld (1995, 1996) closely scrutinized court processing variables and reported no race effects in waiver decisions after appropriate controls were added. In contrast, the General Accounting Office (1995) reported substantial racial effects when controlling only for present offense. Again, though there is little empirical information on which to draw conclusions, the evidence that exists suggests a complicated picture of decision making affected by multiple factors, including a number that are relatively subjective. The possibility that race may play a role in those waiver decisions in which substantial discretion is granted decision makers cannot be completely discarded.

Decision Making in the Courts and Institutions

By necessity, court officials classify youth and make judgments about character, and these decisions influence the outcome of legal proceedings. Since the 1960s, studies of racial bias in juvenile courts have examined whether court officials treat minority youth more severely than white youth (Aday, 1986; Arnold, 1971; Bishop and Frazier, 1988; Bortner and Reed, 1985; Carter and Wilkins, 1970; Fagan et al., 1987a, 1987b; Horowitz and Pottieger, 1991; Piliavin and Briar, 1964). Bridges and Steen (1998) point out that, although these studies call attention to racial discrimination in the juvenile courts, few have examined the mechanisms by which this process might take place. That is, how might court officials' perceptions of juvenile offenders contribute to racial differences in legal dispositions? Bridges and Steen (1998) argue that differential perceptions of youth and their crimes may act to "legitimate" racial disparities associated with official assessments of a youth's dangerousness and risk of future criminal behavior.

Bridges and Steen (1998) studied juvenile offenders and their probation officers' written accounts of the decisions made about their cases. Using these written accounts from reports and other information about the offenders, they examined the link between the offender's race and the probation officer's assessments of the youth, his or her crime, the perceived likelihood of future criminal behavior, and sentence recommendations. Bridges and Steen used information from 233 narrative reports written by probation officers in three counties in a western state, drawn from a larger sample of juvenile court cases processed through the courts between 1990 and 1991(Bridges and Steen, 1998). Probation officers write these reports for the court at the disposition of the case, typically following conviction.

Many other scholars believe that race is a marker of social status that influences how officials evaluate the offender's case and character. For example, Cicourel's (1968) analysis of juvenile courts suggests that minorities are more likely than whites to be seen as disrespectful of authority and, in particular, disrespectful of court officials. Other studies have reported similar findings: that minorities are perceived differently from whites, despite having similar offense histories and characteristics, and often are seen as threatening and dangerous (Bridges et al., 1995, 1987; Farrell and Swigert, 1978; Tonry, 1995). The first question Bridges and Steen asked is whether court officials perceived and judged minority offenders differently from whites with similar characteristics. They also asked whether officials perceive minorities as more likely than white youths to commit future crimes. If court officials perceive minorities as more threatening, then they will be more likely to recommend greater punishment and control (Farrington et al., in press).

Bridges and Steen (1998) found pronounced differences in officers' attributions about the causes of crime committed by white and minority youth. For black children, crime was attributed to negative attitudinal traits and personality defects. Among white children, their offenses were thought to be primarily caused by external environmental factors (e.g., family dysfunction, drug abuse, negative peer influence). Furthermore, they found that these differences contributed significantly to differential assessments of the risk of reoffending and to sentence recommendations, even after adjusting for legally relevant case and offender characteristics. These differences tended to shape the probation officers' evaluation of how likely the child would be to commit crime in the future and how amenable the child would be to treatment. Since juvenile court judges typically follow the sentencing recommendations of probation officers, these findings are important.

This study also provided insight into the factors that influence preadjudication detention. Bridges and Steen (1998) found that race indirectly influenced decisions to detain through factors like performance in school and family situation. This was the case regardless of the nature and severity of the offense. When school performance and family were viewed as positive and stable, juveniles were more likely to be viewed as amenable to the court's influence and control. The perceived ability of the family to supervise the juvenile may affect the court's decision about whether or not to detain. Black juveniles are more likely than whites or Hispanics to live in single-parent families (62 percent, 27 percent, and 36 percent, respectively) (U.S. Census Bureau, 1999). To the extent that court decision makers believe that single-parent families provide less supervision of youngsters than two-parent families, black juveniles are at higher risk of being detained. Being detained before adjudication negatively affects sentencing outcomes (e.g., whether or not to incarcerate as well as the length of a sentence).

Petersen and Hagan (1984) have suggested that research must consider context-specific conceptions of race and realize that race and minority status can act in combination with other variables to produce differential outcomes. For example, using a sample of 2,329 felony offenders sentenced from July 1977 to June 1978 in Minnesota, Miethe and Moore (1986) tested and compared additive (main effects) and race-specific models of analysis. While the additive model was not sensitive to race differences, the interactive model was. Black offenders receiving the most severe sentences tended to be single, from urban areas, had a previous felony record, and committed multiple and more serious offenses. For white offenders, this combination of characteristics revealed little effect on sentencing outcome. Race remained a major source of differential treatment in criminal processing when it was considered in conjunction with other social, legal, and case factors (Miethe and Moore, 1986).

Research pertaining to the use of the death penalty indicates possible racial biases. For example, Baldus and colleagues (1983) reported that black offenders found guilty of murdering whites were at highest risk for the death penalty, whereas offenders of any race who were found guilty of murdering blacks were least likely to receive the death penalty. Some evidence, too, indicates that blacks are likely to serve a higher proportion of their sentences (Carroll and Mondrick, 1976). Time served also would contribute to racial disproportionality.

Blacks are not the only minority at risk for unequal treatment by the justice system. Alvarez and Bachman (1996) examined racial disparity comparing American Indians to whites in Arizona. After accounting for previous felony convictions and several other factors, American Indians were found to receive longer sentences than whites for the relatively common crimes of robbery and burglary and relatively shorter sentences for the less common crime of homicide (Alvarez and Bachman, 1996). Commenting on the study, Stone (1999) suggested that both types of discrepancies may indicate bias. The longer sentences could be evidence of harsher treatment of American Indian offenders for crimes against strangers, but lesser punishments for homicides, which largely involve acquaintances. Stone further suggested that there may be both under- and over-enforcement in some communities and that these two kinds of bias may cancel each other out in studies that do not take interactions into account.

Despite the lack of an extensive literature on this topic, the review by Bridges and colleagues (1987) suggests that the bias in the juvenile justice system may be subtle, indirect, and difficult to detect. This makes it difficult, in turn, for policy makers to justify changes in policies to remedy the disparate treatment of youth in the juvenile justice system. Liska and Tausig (1979) reexamined 17 juvenile justice studies that considered the relationship between social class, race, and legal decision making. They found race differences that produced a cumulative effect that changed a racially heterogeneous prearrest population into a nonwhite, homogeneous institutionalized population. Initial race differences were compounded at successive stages of the juvenile justice system. Accumulated racial differences were also found by Feyerherm (1981) in his examination of status offenders.

Risk is a limiting concept to the extent that it fails to make explicit the degree to which enduring features of racial stratification and discrimination interact with and compound problems related to individual decision making, family dysfunction, school failure, community context, crime, and contact with the juvenile justice system. Hawkins et al. (1998) highlighted the important connections between race and risk when they wrote: "the social and developmental life courses of African Americans and whites in the United States are products of not only their specific individual experiences but also their membership in historically distinct and unequal social and economic groupings" (p. 40).

To reduce racial disparities, many jurisdications have undertaken the imposition of sentencing guidelines. In a study to determine effects of using sentencing guidelines, Ulmer and Kramer (1996) studied three counties in Pennsylvania. They discovered that race, sex, and age continued to have an impact on sentencing differences, even though legal factors, such as severity of crime or number of prior offenses, accounted for much of the impact.

COMPOUND RISK

So far this chapter has examined the racial disparity evident in the juvenile justice system as a function of differences in behavior on the part of the black and white youth and biases in the juvenile justice system. The evidence adduced has not, of course, provided a complete account of why or how the disparities occur. Yet our review has shown that both behavior and biases contribute to the racial disparities.

Compound effects, even of small disparities, can produce large differences. The degree to which such effects can magnify disparities has been calculated using information from the UCR (Federal Bureau of Investigation, 1997), Snyder and Finnegan's *Easy Access to FBI Arrest Statistics 1994-1997* (1999), and Stahl et al.'s *Juvenile Court Statistics, 1996* (1999). Figure 6-3 shows the numbers in each category and the probabilities that a juvenile will reach a point in the juvenile justice process separately for black and white juveniles.[5] The probabilities that appear on the outside of Figure 6-3 are the proportion of the population under age 18 that reach each stage of the process, shown separately for blacks and whites. (These are referred to as compound probabilities because they are also the product of transitional probabilities.) For example, the probability of a white juvenile being handled formally by the courts is:

$$\frac{620,200}{54,700,000} = 0.011$$

and the probability of a black juvenile being handled formally by the courts is:

$$\frac{326,500}{10,700,000} = 0.031$$

The probabilities that appear on the inside of Figure 6-3 are the transitional probabilities, computed as the proportion of people at one stage

---

[5]The panel expresses appreciation to Jane Costello and Alaattin Erkanli of Duke University Medical School and Nancy Crowell of the National Research Council staff for providing the results of this analysis.

255

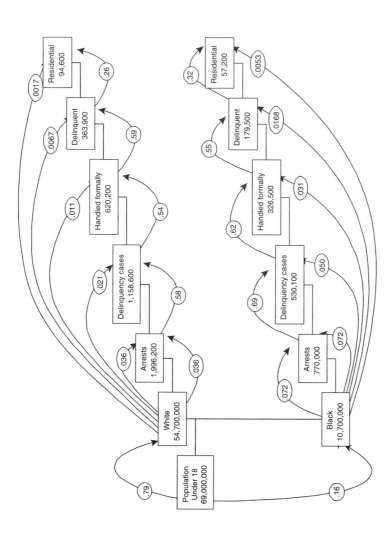

FIGURE 6-3 Compounding of risk through the juvenile justice system, by race. Source: Population data from Bureau of the Census, online at http://www.census.gov/population/estimates; arrest data from Snyder and Finnegan (1999) and Federal Bureau of Investigation (1997); court and placement data from Stahl et al. (1999).

who show up at the next one. Transitional probabilities for juveniles being handled formally, for example, are calculated as the proportion of delinquency cases who were handled formally in the courts, calculated separately for whites and blacks. For whites, the transitional probability of being handled formally is:

$$\frac{620,200}{1,586,000} = 0.54$$

For blacks, it is:

$$\frac{326,500}{530,100} = 0.62$$

Table 6-5 compares the transitional and compound probabilities of blacks to whites. The first column shows relative risk, which takes into account the proportions of blacks to whites. The relative risk for a black juvenile being handled formally, in relation to that for a white juvenile is the ratio of the transitional probabilities:

$$\frac{0.62}{0.54} = 1.15$$

TABLE 6-5 Compounding of Racial Disparity in the Juvenile Justice System

Risk of:	Relative Black to White Risk	Relative Compound Black to White Risk
Being arrested	2.00:1.00	2.00:1:00
Referred to court for delinquency case	1.19:1.00	2.38:1:00
Case being handled formally	1.15:1.00	2.82:1:00
Being adjudicated delinquent or found guilty	0.93:1.00	2.51:1:00
Being put in residential placement	1.23:1.00	3.12:1:00

Source: Arrest data from Federal Bureau of Investigation (1997) and Snyder and Finnegan (1999); court and placement data from Stahl et al. (1999).

The second column of Table 6-5 shows relative compound risk, which is the ratio of the compound probabilities. The relative compound risk for a black juvenile being handled formally in relation to a white is:

$$\frac{0.031}{0.011} = 2.82$$

As this example shows, the relative risk for being handled formally in the courts by blacks is 1.15 to 1; it rises to 2.82 to 1 when compounding is taken into account.

Black juveniles are at greater risk than white juveniles of being arrested, charged for delinquency, and handled formally. They are not at greater risk, given formal handling, for being adjudicated delinquent or found guilty. Thus, at almost every stage in the juvenile justice process the racial disparity is clear, but not extreme. However, because the system operates cumulatively the risk is compounded and the end result is that black juveniles are three times as likely as white juveniles to end up in residential placement (see Table 6-5). Even among those juveniles who are arrested, blacks are more than one and a half times as likely as whites to end up in residential placement.

Some of this overrepresentation of blacks in correctional institutions and justice system residential placements may be accounted for by differences in treatment of blacks and whites at various stages of juvenile justice system processing. Other forms of differential treatment, too, may contribute to the overrepresentation of blacks in secure juvenile justice facilities. For example, some juveniles who steal or commit assault are sent to mental hospitals for treatment of their behavior; others who exhibit similar behaviors are confined in the juvenile justice system.

A comparison of two samples of adolescents, one sent to a correctional facility and the other admitted to a state psychiatric hospital, in one urban area during a one-year time period found that the most powerful distinguishing factor between the two groups was race: 71 percent of the hospitalized youth were white, whereas 67 percent of the incarcerated adolescents were black. The authors noted that "clinical and epidemiological findings indicate clearly that many seriously psychiatrically disturbed, aggressive African American adolescents are being channeled to correctional facilities while their equally aggressive white counterparts are directed toward psychiatric treatment facilities" (Lewis et al., 1980:1216).

Three additional considerations should be noted in accounting for the overrepresentation of blacks in the criminal justice system. Hawkins (1998) has suggested that one of the reasons for the disproportionate presence of blacks in the nation's justice system may be the geographic and social marginalization of the white underclass. The vast majority of poor blacks live in cities. Poor whites are more likely to be distributed in rural areas and small towns, which may shield them from some forms of crime detection and social control found in large cities.

The second consideration is that laws governing drug offenses result in a much greater likelihood of incarceration for blacks (Hawkins, 1998). Not only are there longer mandatory sentences for the less expensive form of cocaine that is more likely to be used by blacks, but also the distribution system for inner-city purchases is under far greater surveillance than is the suburban distribution system. Snyder et al. (1996:142) reported that during 1992, of all black juveniles in the United States who were processed through the justice system for varying offenses, 25 percent were detained. This compares with 18 percent of white cases and 22 percent of cases involving juveniles of other races. In contrast, the rates of confinement for juveniles charged with drug offenses were 47 percent for blacks, 26 percent for whites, and 19 percent for others. At the same time, surveys of the public have shown white adults to be major users of drugs, including cocaine, and have found unexpectedly low rates of drug use among black adolescents (Bachman et al., 1991; Lockwood et al., 1995; National Institute of Drug Abuse, 1991; Rebach, 1992).

Other potential consequences associated with discriminatory treatment may affect the development of youth from different racial and ethnic minority backgrounds. The effect of these experiences on the individual may be to create barriers to obtaining such resources as jobs, housing, and health care. Furthermore, when a person is exposed to persistent discriminatory experiences, the consequences may involve perceptions of the unfairness of the system (Bobo, 2001, Crocker and Major, 1989), reactive coping strategies (Spencer, 1999), hostile attributions (Graham, 1997), and psychological disengagement (Crocker et al., 1998).

CONCLUSIONS AND RECOMMENDATIONS

Overrepresentation of blacks, Hispanics, and American Indians in the juvenile justice system requires immediate attention. The existence of disproportional racial representation in the juvenile justice system raises concerns about differential exposure to risks and the fairness and equal treatment of youth by the police, courts, and other players in the juvenile justice system. Given the importance of the problem of race, crime, and juvenile justice in the United States, the scant research attention that has been paid to understanding the factors contributing to racial disparities in the juvenile justice system is shocking.

Recommendation: The panel recommends that a comprehensive, systematic, and long-term agenda for acquiring empirical knowledge to understand and meaningfully reduce problems of unwarranted racial disparity in the juvenile justice system is a critical priority and that new funding should be set aside for this effort.

- Research should focus on the entirety of the juvenile justice system by examining multiple decision-making points and processing stages. This report demonstrates how small biases in one part of the system may have an unforeseen and dramatic outcome at later points in the juvenile justice system process. The links across each of the decision-making points, as well as the decisions themselves, should be scrutinized.
- Research is needed to examine the role of organizational policy and practice in the production of juvenile arrest, adjudication, and confinement rates and the organizational policy/practice and the decisions of individual officials. Research should especially target police-juvenile encounters, prosecutorial practices, and correctional processes. Challenges to the research community should be issued to develop creative ways to overcome methodological limitations of much existing research.
- Research on bias should take into account the fact that problems may appear on a local level that do not show up when state-aggregated data provide the only source for information. We need information about private as well as public facilities. Research should also take into account sample selection biases as the screening process operates to filter youth in different directions within the system.
- Research is needed to examine how juvenile justice system decisions are influenced by the characteristics of the communities in which different youth live.
- Research should move beyond traditional emphasis on black-white differences to include other minorities and should recognize the diversity within racial and ethnic groups.
- Research should move beyond the traditional focus on urban jurisdictions to include rural and suburban jurisdictions as well.

The Office of Juvenile Justice and Delinquency Prevention has been instrumental in the process of collecting data to establish the existence of racial disproportionality among juveniles involved in the juvenile justice system. There remains a need for ongoing data collection and an expansion of the effort in order to track whether progress is being made in reducing unwarranted racial and ethnic disproportionality at all stages of juvenile justice system processing.

> **Recommendation: Changes are needed in data collection, monitoring, and juvenile justice administration to address racial disproportionality in the juvenile justice system. Suggested changes include:**

- Developing a systematic monitoring procedure to determine the percentage of minority youth being processed through each stage of the juvenile justice system, from initial police contact through confinement release.
- Developing and implementing training workshops focusing on race and juvenile justice system processing. At a minimum, diversity training for justice system employees and officials must focus on beliefs and attitudes that shape assessments.

References

Aber, J.L., J.L. Brown, N. Chaudry, S.M. Jones, and F. Samples
  1996 The evaluation of the Resolving Conflict Creatively program: An overview. *American Journal of Preventive Medicine* 12(Supp. 5):82-90.
Aber, J.L., S.M. Jones, J.L. Brown, N. Chaudry, and F. Samples
  1998 Resolving conflict creatively: Evaluating the development effects of a school-based violence prevention program in neighborhood and classroom context. *Development and Psychopathology* 10:187-213.
Abramovitch, R., M. Peterson-Badali, and M. Rohan
  1995 Young people's understanding and assertion of their rights to silence and legal counsel. *Canadian Journal of Criminology* 37:1-18.
Acoca, L., and K. Dedel
  1998 *No Place to Hide: Understanding and Meeting the Needs of Girls in the California Juvenile Justice System*. San Francisco: National Council on Crime and Delinquency.
Aday, D.P.Jr.
  1986 Court structure, defense attorney use, and juvenile court decisions. *Sociological Quarterly* 27:107-119.
Agnew, R.
  1999 A general strain theory of community differences in crime rates. *Journal of Research in Crime and Delinquency* 36:123-155.
Ahlstrom, W., and R.J. Havighurst
  1982 The Kansas City work/study experiment. Pp. 259-275 in *School Programs for Disruptive Adolescents*, D.J. Safer, ed. Baltimore, MD: University Park Press.
Altschuler, D.M., and T.L. Armstrong
  1991 Intensive aftercare for the high-risk juvenile parolee: Issues and approaches in reintegration and community supervision. Pp. 45-84 in *Intensive Interventions With High Risk Youths: Promising Approaches in Juvenile Probation and Parole*, T.L. Armstrong, ed. Monsey, NY: Criminal Justice Press.

1994a *Intensive Aftercare for High-Risk Juveniles: A Community Care Model*, Office of Justice Programs, Office of Juvenile Justice and Delinquency Prevention. Washington, DC: U.S. Department of Justice.

1994b *Intensive Aftercare for High-Risk Juveniles: Policies and Procedures*, Office of Juvenile Justice and Delinquency Prevention. Washington, DC: U.S. Department of Justice.

Altschuler, D.M., T.L. Armstrong, and D.L. MacKenzie
1999 Reintegration, Supervised Release, and Intensive Aftercare. *Juvenile Justice Bulletin*, July, Office of Justice Programs, Office of Juvenile Justice Delinquency Prevention. Washington, DC: U.S. Department of Justice.

Alvarez, A., and R.D. Bachman
1996 American Indians and sentencing disparity: An Arizona test. *Journal of Criminal Justice* 24:549-561.

Anderson, C., and K.E. Dill
2000 Video games and aggressive thoughts, feelings, and behavior in the laboratory and in life. *Journal of Personality and Social Psychology* 78(4):772-790.

Anderson, D.R.
1998 Educational television is not an oxymoron. *Annals of the American Academy of Political and Social Sciences: Children and Television* 557(May):24-38.

Anderson, E.
1990 *Streetwise: Race, Class, and Change in an Urban Community.* Chicago: University of Chicago Press.
1994 The code of the streets. *Atlantic Monthly* (May):81-94.
1997 Violence and the inner city code of the streets. Pp. 1-30 in *Violence and Childhood in the Inner City*, J. McCord, ed. New York: Cambridge University Press.

Andrews, D.A., and J. Bonta
1994 *The Psychology of Criminal Conduct.* Cincinnati, OH: Anderson Publishing Company.

Andrews, D.A., J. Bonta, and I. Hoge
1990a Classification for effective rehabilitation: Rediscovering psychology. *Criminal Justice and Behavior* 17(1):19-52.

Andrews, D.A., I. Zinger, R.D. Hoge, J. Bonta, P. Gendreau, and F.T. Cullen
1990b Does correctional treatment work? A clinically relevant and psychologically-informed meta-analysis. *Criminology* 28(3):369-404.

Andrews, R.H., and A.H. Cohn
1974 Ungovernability: The unjustifiable jurisdiction. *Yale Law Journal* 83:1383-1409.

Arbuthnot, J., and D.A. Gordon
1986 Behavioral and cognitive effects of a moral reasoning development intervention for high-risk behavior-disordered adolescents. *Journal of Consulting and Clinical Psychology* 54:208-216.

Armstrong, T.L.
1991 Introduction. Pp. 1-26 in *Intensive Interventions With High-Risk Youths: Promising Approaches in Juvenile Probation and Parole*, T.L. Armstrong, ed. Monsey, NY: Criminal Justice Press.

Arnold, J.E., A.G. Levine, and G.R. Patterson
1975 Changes is sibling behavior following family intervention. *Journal of Consulting and Clinical Psychology* 43(5):683-688.

Arnold, W.R.
1971 Race and ethnicity relative to other factors in juvenile court dispositions. *American Journal of Sociology* 77:211-227.

Arum, R., and I.R. Beattie
   1999   High school experience and the risk of adult incarceration. *Criminology* 37:515-537.
Austin, J.
   1995   The overrepresentation of minority youths in the California juvenile justice system: Perceptions and realities. Pp. 153-178 in *Minorities in Juvenile Justice*, K.K. Leonard, C.E. Pope, and W.H. Feyerherm, eds. Thousand Oaks, CA: Sage Publications, Inc.
Austin, J., B. Krisberg, R. DeComo, S. Rudenstine, D. Del Rosario, and National Council on Crime and Delinquency
   1995   *Juveniles Taken Into Custody: Fiscal Year 1993 Statistics Report*, September, Office of Juvenile Justice and Delinquency Prevention, Office of Justice Programs. Washington, DC: U.S. Department of Justice.
Austin, R.L.
   1978   Race, father-absence, and female delinquency. *Criminology* 15:487-504.
Bachman, J.G., J.M. Wallace, P.M. O'Malley, L.D. Johnston, C.L. Kurth, and H.W. Neighbors
   1991   Racial/ethnic differences in smoking, drinking, and illicit drug use among American high school seniors, 1976-1989. *American Journal of Public Health* 81:372-377.
Bachman, R.
   1996   Victim's perceptions of initial police responses to robbery and aggravated assault: Does race matter? *Journal of Quantitative Criminology* 12(4):363-390.
Bain, A., and A. MacPherson
   1990   An examination of the system-wide use of exclusion with disruptive students. *Australia and New Zealand Journal of Developmental Disabilities* 16(2):109-123.
Baird, A.A., S.A. Gruber, D.A. Fein, L.C. Mass, R.J. Steingard, P.F. Renshaw, B.M. Cohen, and D.A. Yurgelun-Todd
   1999   Functional magnetic resonance imaging of facial affect recognition in children and adolescents. *Journal of the American Academy of Child and Adolescent Psychiatry* 38(2):195-199.
Baird, C.S.
   1991   Intensive supervision programs for high-risk juveniles: Critical issues of program evaluation. Pp. 295-315 in *Intensive Interventions With High-Risk Youths: Promising Approaches in Juvenile Probation and Parole*, T.L. Armstrong, ed. Monsey, NY: Criminal Justice Press.
Baldus, D.C., C. Pulaski, and G. Woodworth
   1983   Comparative review of death sentences: An empirical study of the Georgia experience. *The Journal of Criminal Law and Criminology* 74:661-673.
Ball, D.W., J.M. Newman, and W.J. Scheuren
   1984   Teachers' generalized expectations of children of divorce. *Psychological Reports* 54:347-353.
Bandura, A.
   1962   Social learning through imitation. Pp. 211-269 in *Nebraska Symposium on Motivation*, M.R. Jones, ed. Lincoln: University of Nebraska Press.
   1965   Vicarious processes: A case of no-trial learning. Pp. 1-55 in *Advances in Experimental Social Psychology*, L. Berkowitz, ed. New York: Academic Press.
   1986   *Social Foundations of Thought and Action: A Social Cognitive Theory*. Englewood Cliffs, NJ: Prentice-Hall.
Barnett, W.S.
   1995   Long-term effects of early childhood programs on cognitive and school outcomes. *The Future of Children* 5(3):25-50.

Barton, W.H., and J.A. Butts
    1990   Viable options: Intensive supervision programs for juvenile delinquents. *Crime & Delinquency* 36(2):238-256.
    1991   Intensive supervision alternatives for adjudicated juveniles. Pp. 317-340 in *Intensive Interventions With High-Risk Youths: Promising Approaches in Juvenile Probation and Parole*, T.L. Armstrong, ed. Monsey, NY: Criminal Justice Press.
Battin, S.R., K.G. Hill, R.D. Abbott, R.F. Catalano, and J.D. Hawkins
    1998   The contribution of gang membership to delinquency beyond delinquent friends. *Criminology* 36(1):93-115.
Bazemore, G., and M. Umbreit
    1995   Rethinking the sanctioning function in juvenile court: Retributive or restorative responses to youth crime. *Crime and Delinquency* 41(3):296-316.
Beck, A.J., and B.E. Shipley
    1987   Recidivism of young parolees. *Criminal Justice Archive Information Network*
Belknap, J.
    1996   *Invisible Woman: Gender, Crime, and Justice.* Belmont, CA: Wadsworth Publishing Co.
Bell, C.C., and E.J. Jenkins
    1993   Community violence and children on Chicago's Southside. *Psychiatry: Interpersonal and Biological Processes* 45:46-54.
Bender, L.
    1947   Psychopathic behavior disorders in children. Pp. 360-377 in *Handbook of Correctional Psychology*, R. Lindner and R. Seliger, eds. New York: Philosophical Library.
Bennett, W.J., J.J. DiIulio, and J.P. Walters
    1996   *Body Count: Moral Poverty and How to Win America's War Against Crime and Drugs.* New York: Simon and Schuster.
Berends, M.
    1995   Educational stratification and students' social bonding to school. *British Journal of Sociology of Education* 16(3):327-351.
Berger, R.J., J.E. Crowley, M. Gold, J. Gray, and M.S. Arnold
    1975   *Experiment in a Juvenile Court: A Study of a Program of Volunteers Working With Juvenile Probationers.* Ann Arbor: Institute for Social Research at the University of Michigan.
Bergsmann, I.
    1994   Establishing a foundation: Just the facts. *1994 National Juvenile Female Offender Conference: A Time for Change*, American Correctional Association. Laurel, MD: American Correctional Association.
Bernard, T.J.
    1990   Angry aggression among the 'truly disadvantaged'. *Criminology* 28(1):73-95.
Beyth-Marom, R., and B. Fischhoff
    1997   Adolescents' decisions about risks: A cognitive perspective. *Health Risks and Developmental Transaction During Adolescence*, J. Schulenberg, J. Maggs, and K. Hurnelmans, eds. New York: Cambridge University Press.
Biddle, B.J., B.J. Bank, and M.J. Marlin
    1980   Social determinants of adolescent drinking. *Journal of Studies on Alcohol* 41:215-240.
Bishop, D.M., and C.E. Frazier
    1988   The influence of race in juvenile justice processing. *Journal of Research in Crime and Delinquency* 25:242-263.

1991 Transfer of juveniles to criminal court: A case study and analysis of prosecutorial waiver. *Notre Dame Journal of Law, Ethics, and Public Policy* 5(2):281-302.

1992 Gender bias in juvenile justice processing: Implications of the JJDP Act. *The Journal of Criminal Law and Criminology* 82(4):1162-1186.

2000 Consequences of waiver. In *The Changing Borders of Juvenile Justice: Transfer of Adolescents to the Criminal Court*, J. Fagan and F.E. Zimring, eds. Chicago: University of Chicago Press.

Bishop, D.M., C.E. Frazier, L. Lanza-Kaduce, and L. Winner

1996 The transfer of juveniles to criminal court: Does it make a difference? *Crime and Delinquency* 42(2):171-191.

Bjorkqvist, K., K.M.J. Lagerspetz, and A. Kaukiainen

1992 Do girls manipulate and boys fight? Developmental trends in regard to direct and indirect aggression. *Aggressive Behavior* 18:117-127.

Black, D.

1971 The social organization of arrest. *Stanford Law Review* 23:1087-1111.

1980 *The Manners and Customs of the Police.* New York: Academic Press.

Black, D., and A.J. Reiss, Jr.

1970 Police control of juveniles. *American Sociological Review* 35(February):63-77.

Black, H.C., J.R. Nolan, J.M. Nolan-Haley, M.J. Connolly, S.C. Hicks, and M.N. Alibrandi

1990 *Black's Law Dictionary*, 6th edition. St. Paul, MN: West Publishing Co.

Block, J.H., J. Block, and P.F. Gjerde

1986 The personality of children prior to divorce: A prospective study. *Child Development* 57:827-840.

Blumstein, A.

1995 Youth violence, guns and the illicit-drug industry. *The Journal of Criminal Law and Criminology* 86(1):10-36.

Blumstein, A., and D. Cork

1996 Linking gun availability to youth gun violence. *Law and Contemporary Problems* 59(1):5-37.

Blumstein, A., and R. Rosenfeld

1998 Explaining recent trends in U.S. homicide rates. *The Journal of Criminal Law and Criminology* 88(4):1175-1216.

Blumstein, A., D.P. Farrington, and S. Moitra

1984 Delinquency careers: Innocents, amateurs, and persisters. *Crime and Justice: A Review of Research* 6:187-219.

Bobo, L.D.

2001 Racial attitudes and relations at the close of the twentieth century. Pp 264-301 in *America Becoming: Racial Trends and Their Consequence*, Vol. I, National Research Council. Washington, D.C.: National Academy Press.

Bock, G.R., and J.A. Goode, ed

1996 *Genetics of Criminal and Antisocial Behavior.* Toronto: Wiley & Sons.

Bordua, D.J.

1958 Juvenile delinquency and anomie: An attempt at replication. *Social Problems* 6:230-238.

Borduin, C.M., L.T. Cone, B.J. Mann, S.W. Henggeler, B.R. Fucci, D.M. Blaske, and R.A. Williams

1995 Multisystemic treatment of serious juvenile offenders: Long-term prevention of criminality and violence. *Journal of Consulting and Clinical Psychology* 63(4):569-578.

Bortner, M.A., and W.L. Reed
    1985   The preeminence of process: An example of refocused justice research. *Social Science Quarterly* 66:413-425.
The Boston Globe
    1998   Study shows why teenagers often react without thinking. By M.C. Sanchez. *The Boston Globe* 1 (June 12).
Bottoms, A.E., and P. Wiles
    1986   Housing tenure and residential community crime careers in Britain. Pp. 101-163 in *Communities and Crime*, A.J. Reiss and M. Tonry, eds. Chicago: University of Chicago Press.
Bourgois, P.
    1995   *In Search of Respect: Selling Crack in El Barrio.* New York: Cambridge University Press.
Bowlby, J.
    1940   The influence of early environment on neurosis and neurotic character. *International Journal of Psychoanalysis* 21:154-178.
Brannigan, A.
    1997   Self control, social control and evolutionary psychology: Towards an integrated perspective on crime. *Canadian Journal of Criminology* 39(4):403-431.
Brennan, P.A., and S.A. Mednick
    1997   Medical histories of antisocial individuals. *Handbook of Antisocial Behavior*, D. Stoff, J. Breiling, and J.D. Maser, eds. New York: Wiley.
Brewer, D.D., J.D. Hawkins, R.F. Catalano, and H.J. Neckerman
    1995   Preventing serious, violent, and chronic juvenile offending: A review of evaluations of selected strategies in childhood, adolescence, and the community. Pp. 61-141 in *A Sourcebook: Serious, Violent, and Chronic Juvenile Offenders*, J.C. Howell, B. Krisberg, J.D. Hawkins, and J.J. Wilson, eds. Thousand Oaks, CA: Sage.
Bridges, G.S., and S. Steen
    1998   Racial disparities in official assessments of juvenile offenders: Attributional stereotypes as mediating mechanisms. *American Sociological Review* 63(August):554-570.
Bridges, G.S., R.D. Crutchfield, and E.E. Simpson
    1987   Crime, social structure, and criminal punishment: White and nonwhite rates of imprisonment. *Social Problems* 34(4):345-361.
Bridges, G.S., D.J. Conley, R.L. Engen, and T. Price-Spratlen
    1995   Racial disparities in the confinement of juveniles: Effects of crime and community social structure on punishment. Pp. 128-152 in *Minorities in Juvenile Justice*, K.K. Leonard, C.E. Pope, and W.H. Feyerherm, eds. Thousand Oaks, CA: Sage Publications, Inc.
Broman, S.H., P.L. Nichols, and W.A. Kennedy
    1975   *Preschool IQ: Prenatal and Early Developmental Correlates.* Hillsdale, NJ: Erlbaum.
Brooks, B.D.
    1975   Contingency management as a means of reducing school truancy. *Education* 95:206-211.
Brown, J.M., and P.A. Langan
    1998   *State Court Sentencing of Convicted Felons, 1994*, Bureau of Justice Statistics. NCJ 164614. Washington, DC: U.S. Department of Justice.
Brown, R., C.D. Coles, I.E. Smith, K.A. Platzman, J. Silverstein, S. Erickson, and A. Falek
    1991   Effects of prenatal alcohol exposure at school age. *Neurotoxicology and Teratology* 13:369-376.

Brown, W.K., T.P. Miller, R.L. Jenkins, and W.A. Rhodes
1989 The fallacy of radical nonintervention. *International Journal of Offender Therapy and Comparative Criminology* 33:177-182.

Bry, B.H.
1982 Reducing the incidence of adolescent problems through preventive intervention: One- and five-year follow-up. *American Journal of Community Psychology* 10:265-276.

Bureau of Justice Statistics
2000 Crime and Victim Statistics. Available: http://www.ojp.usdoj.gov/bjs/cvict.htm (accessed March 8, 2000).

Bureau of Labor Statistics
1998 *Handbook of Labor Statistics*. Washington, DC: U.S. Government Printing Office.

Bursik, R.J., and J. Webb
1982 Community change and patterns of delinquency. *American Journal of Sociology* 88:24-42.

Byrne, J., and M. Brewster
1993 Choosing the future of American corrections: Punishment or reform? *Federal Probation* 57(4):3-9.

Byrne, J.M., and L. Kelly
1989 *Restructuring Probation As an Intermediate Sanction: An Evaluation of the Massachusetts Intensive Probation Supervision Program.* Washington, D.C.: United States Department of Justice.

California Youth Authority
1997- *Population Movement Summary: Fiscal Year 1997-98*. Online. Available: http://
1998 www.cya.ca.gov/facts/pop_mov_9798.html.

Campbell, S.B.
1990a *Behavior Problems in Preschool Children: Clinical and Developmental Issues*. New York: Guilford Press.
1990b Longitudinal studies of active and aggressive preschoolers: individual differences in early behavior and in outcome. Pp. 57-90 in *Internalizing and Externalizing Expressions of Dysfunction*, D. Cicchetti and S.L. Toth, eds. Hillsdale, NJ: Erlbaum.

Canada, G.
1995 *Fist, Knife, Stick, Gun.* Boston: Beacon.

Capaldi, D.M., and G.R. Patterson
1991 Relation of parental transitions to boys' adjustment problems: I. A linear hypothesis. II. Mothers at risk for transitions and unskilled parenting. *Developmental Psychology* 27(3):489-504.
1996 Can violent offenders be distinguished from frequent offenders? Prediction from childhood to adolescence. *Journal of Research in Crime and Delinquency* 33:206-231.

Carnegie Task Force on Meeting the Needs of Our Youngest Children
1994 *Starting Points*. New York: Carnegie Corporation of New York.

Carroll, L., and M.E. Mondrick
1976 Racial bias and the decision to grant parole. *Law and Society* 11:93-107.

Carter, R.M., and L.T. Wilkins
1970 *Probation and Parole: Selected Readings*. New York, NY: J. Wiley.

Caspi, A., T.E. Moffitt, P.A. Silva, M. Stouthamer-Loeber, R.F. Krueger, and P.S. Schmutte
1994 Are some people crime-prone? Replications of the personality-crime relationship across countries, genders, races, and methods. *Criminology* 32:163-194.

Catalano, R.F., M.W. Arthur, J.D. Hawkins, L. Berglund, and J.J. Olson
  1998   Comprehensive community- and school-based interventions to prevent antisocial behavior. Pp. 248-283 in *Serious and Violent Juvenile Offenders: Risk Factors and Successful Interventions*, R. Loeber and D.H. Farrington, eds. Thousand Oaks, CA: Sage.

Catterall, J.S.
  1987   An intensive group counseling drop-out prevention intervention: Some cautions on isolating at-risk adolescents within high schools. *American Educational Research Journal* 24:521-540.

Centers for Disease Control and Prevention
  1990   Homicide among young Black males—United States, 1978-1987. *Morbidity and Mortality Weekly Report* 39:869-873.
  1991   Weapon carrying among high school students—United States, 1990. *Morbidity and Mortality Weekly Report* 40:681-684.
  1993   Violence-related attitudes and behaviors of high school students—New York City, 1992. *Morbidity and Mortality Weekly Reviews* 42:773-777.
  1995   Youth risk behavior surveillance: United States, 1993. *Morbidity and Mortality Weekly Report* 44(SS-1):1-25.

Chamberlain, P.
  1998   Treatment foster care. *OJJDP Juvenile Justice Bulletin*, December, Office of Juvenile Justice and Delinquency Programs, Office of Justice Programs. Washington, D.C.: U.S. Department of Justice.

Chamberlain, P., and S.F. Mihalic
  1998   Multidimensional treatment foster care. Pp. Book Eight in *Blueprints for Violence Prevention*, D.S. Elliott, ed. Boulder, CO: Center for the Study and Prevention of Violence, University of Colorado at Boulder.

Chamberlain, P., and J.B. Reid
  1998   Comparison of two community alternatives to incarceration for chronic juvenile offenders. *Journal of Consulting and Clinical Psychology* 66:624-633.

Cherlin, A.J., F.F. Furstenberg, Jr., P.L. Chase-Lansdale, K.E. Kiernan, P.K. Robins, D.R. Morrison, and J.O. Teitler
  1991   Longitudinal studies of effects of divorce on children in Great Britain and the United States. *Science* 252:1386-1389.

Chesney-Lind, M.
  1973   Judicial enforcement of the female sex role. *Issues in Criminology* 8:51-70.
  1989   Girls' crime and woman's place: Toward a feminist model of female delinquency. *Crime and Delinquency* 35:5-30.
  1997   *The Female Offender: Girls, Women, and Crime*. Thousand Oaks, CA: Sage Publications.

Chesney-Lind, M., and R.G. Shelden
  1998   *Girls, Delinquency, and Juvenile Justice*. Belmont, CA: Wadsworth Publishing Co.

Chiles, J.A., M.L. Miller, and G.B. Cox
  1980   Depression in an adolescent delinquent population. *Archives of General Psychiatry* 37:1179-1184.

Chilton, R.J.
  1964   Continuity in delinquency area research: A comparison of studies for Baltimore, Detroit, and Indianapolis. *American Sociological Review* 28:71-83.

Chilton, R.J., and G.E. Markle
  1972   Family disruption, delinquent conduct and the effect of subclassification. *American Sociological Review* 37:93-99.

Chin, K.
1996 *Chinatown Gangs: Extortion, Enterprise, and Ethnicity.* New York: Oxford University Press.

Chou, C.P., S. Montgomery, M.A. Pentz, L.A. Rohrbach, C.A. Johnson, B.R. Flay, and D.P. MacKinnon
1998 Effects of a community-based prevention program on decreasing drug use in high-risk adolescents. *American Journal of Public Health* 88(6):944-948.

Cicourel, A.
1968 *The Social Organization of Juvenile Justice.* New York, NY: John Wiley.

Clarke, E.E.
1996 A case for reinventing juvenile transfer. *Juvenile and Family Court Journal* 47(4):3-21.

Clarke, J.W.
1998 *The Lineaments of Wrath: Race, Violent Crime, and American Culture.* Somerset, NJ: Transaction Publishers.

Clarke, S.H., and G.C. Koch
1980 Juvenile court: Therapy and crime control, and do lawyers make a difference? *Law and Society Review* 14:263-308.

Clayton, R.R., A.M. Cattarello, and B.M. Johnstone
1996 The effectiveness of Drug Abuse Resistance Education (Project DARE): Five-year follow-up results. *Preventive Medicine* 25:307-318.

Clear, T.R.
1991 Juvenile intensive probation supervision: Theory and Rationale. Pp. 29-44 in *Intensive Interventions With High-Risk Youths: Promising Approaches in Juvenile Probation and Parole,* T.L. Armstrong, ed. Monsey, NY: Criminal Justice Press.

Clear, T.R., and A.A. Braga
1995 Community corrections. Pp. 421-444 in *Crime,* J.Q. Wilson and J. Petersilia, eds. San Francisco, CA: ICS Press.

Coalition for Juvenile Justice
1998 *A Celebration or a Wake? The Juvenile Court After 100 Years.* Washington, DC: Coalition for Juvenile Justice.
1999 *Ain't No Place Anybody Would Want to Be: Conditions of Confinement. 1999 Annual Report.* Washington, DC: Coalition for Juvenile Justice.

Coates, R.B., and J. Gehm
1989 An empirical assessment. *Mediation and Criminal Justice,* M. Wright and B. Galaway, eds. London: Sage.

Coe, C.
1999 Psychosocial processes and psychoneuroimmunology within a lifespan perspective. Pp. 201-219 in *Developmental Health and the Wealth of Nations: Social, Biological, and Educational Dynamics,* D. Keating and C. Hertzman, eds. New York: Guilford Press.

Cohen, A.
1955 *Delinquent Boys.* New York: Free Press of Glencoe.

Cohen, J., and J.A. Canela-Cacho
1994 Incarceration and violent crime: 1965-1988. *Understanding and Prevention Violence, Volume 4, Consequences and Controls,* A.J. Reiss Jr. and J.A. Roth, eds. Washington, DC: National Academy Press.

Cohen, L.E., and K.C. Land
1987 Age structure and crime: Symmetry versus asymmetry and the projection of crime rates through the 1990s. *American Sociological Review* 52:170-183.

Cohen, L.E., and J.R. Kluegel
    1979 Selecting delinquents for adjudication. *Journal of Research in Crime and Delinquency* 16:143-163.
Cohen, M.A.
    1998 The monetary value of saving a high-risk youth. *Journal of Quantitative Criminology* 14(1):5-33.
Cohen, P., and J. Cohen
    1996 *Life Values and Adolescent Mental Health.* Mahwah, NJ: Erlbaum.
Cohn, L.D., S. MacFarlane, C. Yanez, and W.K. Imai
    1995 Risk perception: Differences between adolescents and adults. *Health Psychology* 14(3):217-222.
Coie, J.D., and K.A. Dodge
    1998 Aggression and antisocial behavior. Pp. 779-862 in *Handbook of Child Psychology, Volume 3: Social, Emotional, and Personality Development,* 5th edition, W. Damon and N. Eisenberg, eds. New York: Wiley & Sons.
Coleman, J.S.
    1990 *Foundations of Social Theory.* Cambridge, MA: Harvard University Press.
Conduct Problems Prevention Research Group
    1999a Initial impact of the Fast Track prevention trial for conduct problems I: The high-risk sample. *Journal of Consulting and Clinical Psychology* 67(5):631-647.
    1999b Initial impact of the Fast Track prevention trial for conduct problems II: Classroom effects. *Journal of Consulting and Clinical Psychology* 67(5):648-657.
Conley, D.J.
    1994 Adding color to a black and white picture: Using qualitative data to explain racial disproportionality in the juvenile justice system. *Journal of Research in Crime and Delinquency* 31(2):135-148.
Connell, J.P., A.C. Kubisch, L.B. Schorr, and C.H. Weiss, eds
    1995 *New Approaches to Evaluating Community Initiatives: Concepts, Methods, and Contexts.* Washington, DC: The Aspen Institute.
Conseur, A., F.P. Rivara, R. Barnoski, and I. Emanuel
    1997 Maternal and perinatal risk factors for later delinquency. *Pediatrics* 99(6):785-790.
Conway, A., and C. Bogdan
    1977 Sexual delinquency: The persistence of the double standard. *Crime and Delinquency* 23:131-135.
Cook, P.J.
    1987 Robbery violence. *Journal of Criminal Law and Criminology* 78:357-376.
Cook, P.J., and J.H. Laub
    1998 The unprecedented epidemic in youth violence. Pp. 27-64 in *Youth Violence, Crime and Justice,* vol. 24, M. Tonry and M.H. Moore, eds. Chicago: University of Chicago Press.
Cooper, J., and D. Mackie
    1986 Video games and aggression in children. *Journal of Applied Social Psychology* 16:726-744.
Cottle, T.
    1975 A case of suspension. *National Elementary Principal* 55:4-9.
Covington, S.
    1998 The relational theory of women's psychological development: Implications for the criminal justice system. *Female Offenders: Critical Perspectives and Effective Interventions,* R.T. Zaplin, ed. Gaithersburg, MD: Aspen Publishers.

Crick, N.R., and J.K. Grotpeter
    1995   Relational aggression, gender, and social-psychological adjustment. *Child Development* 66:710-722.
Criminal Justice Policy Council
    1997   *Determinate Sentencing: Examining the Growing Use of the Tougher Juvenile Incarceration Penalty.* Austin, TX: Criminal Justice Policy Council.
    1999   *Average Length of Stay in the Texas Youth Commission for Violent Juveniles, Fiscal Years 1995 and 1999.* Online. Available: http://www.cjpc.state.tx.us.
Crocker, J., and B. Major
    1989   Social stigma and self-esteem: The self-protective properties of stigma. *Psychological Review* 96:608-630.
Crocker, J., B. Major, and C. Steele
    1998   Social stigma. Pp. 504-553 in *The Handbook of Social Psychology*, 4th edition, D.T. Gilbert, S.T. Fiske, and L. Gardner, eds. Boston, MA: McGraw-Hill.
Crockett, L.J., D.J. Eggebeen, and A.J. Hawkins
    1993   Father's presence and young children's behavioral and cognitive adjustment. *Journal of Family Issues* 14(3):355-377.
Crouch, B.
    1993   Is incarceration really worse? Analysis of offenders' preferences for prisons over probation. *Justice Quarterly* 10:67-88.
Curry, G.D., and I.A. Spergel
    1988   Gang homicide, delinquency, and community. *Criminology* 26(3):381-405.
Datesman, S., and F. Scarpitti
    1977   Unequal protection for males and females in the juvenile court. *Juvenile Delinquency: Little Brother Grows Up*, T.N. Ferdinand, ed. Newbury Park, CA: Sage.
Davis, D.L., G.J. Bean, J.E. Schumacher, and T.L. Stringer
    1991   Prevalence of emotional disorders in a juvenile justice institutional population. *American Journal of Forensic Psychology* 9:5-17.
Davis, M., and E.K. Emory
    1995   Sex differences in neonatal stress reactivity. *Child Development* 66:14-27.
Dawson, R.O.
    1990   The future of juvenile justice: Is it time to abolish the system? *Journal of Criminal Law and Criminology* 81:136-155.
    2000   Judicial waiver in practice and theory. In *The Changing Borders of Juvenile Justice: Transfer of Adolescents to the Criminal Court*, J. Fagan and F.E. Zimring, eds. Chicago: University of Chicago Press.
Deci, E.L.
    1971   Effects of externally mediated rewards on intrinsic motivation. *Journal of Personality and Social Psychology* 18:105-155.
Decker, S.H., and B. Van Winkle
    1996   *Life in the Gang: Family, Friends, and Violence.* Cambridge, UK: Cambridge University Press.
DeComo, R.E.
    1998   Estimating the prevalence of juvenile custody by race and gender. *Crime and Delinquency* 44(4):489-506.
Dedel, K.
    1997   *Assessing the Education of Incarcerated Youth.* San Francisco, CA: National Council on Crime and Delinquency.
DeFrances, C.J., and G. Steadman
    1998   *Prosecutors in State Courts, 1996*, July, Bureau of Justice Statistics. NCJ 170092. Washington, DC: U.S. Department of Justice.

Deschenes, E.P., P.W. Greenwood, and G. Marshall
1996   *The Nokomis Challenge Program Evaluation.*   Santa Monica, CA: The RAND Corporation.
Devine, P., K. Coolbaugh, and S. Jenkins
1998   Disproportionate minority confinement: Lessons learned from five states. *Juvenile Justice Bulletin*, December , Office of Juvenile Justice and Delinquency Prevention. Washington, DC: U.S. Department of Justice.
Dicken, C., R. Bryson, and N. Kass
1977   Companionship therapy: A replication in experimental community psychology. *Journal of Consulting and Clinical Psychology* 45:637-646.
DiPietro, J.A., D.M. Hodgson, K. Costigan, S. Hilton, and T.R. Johnson
1996   Fetal neurobehavioral development. *Child Development* 67:2553-2567.
Dishion, T.J., and D.W. Andrews
1995   Preventing escalation in problem behaviors with high-risk young adolescents: Immediate and 1-year outcomes. *Journal of Consulting and Clinical Psychology* 63(4):538-548.
Dishion, T.J., D.W. Andrews, K. Kavanagh, and L.H. Soberman
1996   Preventive interventions for high-risk youth: The Adolescent Transitions Program. Pp. 184-214 in *Preventing Childhood Disorders, Substance Abuse, and Delinquency*, R.D. Peters and R.J. McMahon, eds. Thousand Oaks, CA: Sage Publications.
Dishion, T.J., D. Capaldi, K.M. Spracklen, K.M. Spracklen, and F. Li
1995   Peer ecology of male adolescent drug use. *Development and Psychopathology* 7:803-824.
Dishion, T.J., J.M. Eddy, E. Haas, F. Li, and K. Spracklen
1997   Friendships and violent behavior during adolescence. *Social Development* 6:207-223.
Dishion, T.J., J. McCord, and F. Poulin
1999   When interventions harm: Peer groups and problem behavior. *American Psychologist* 54(9):755-764.
Dishion, T.J., K.M. Spracklen, D.W. Andrews, and G.R. Patterson
1996   Deviancy training in male adolescent friendships. *Behavior Therapy* 27:373-390.
Dodge, K.A., J.E. Bates, and G.S. Pettit
1990   Mechanisms in the cycle of violence. *Science* 250:1678-1683.
Dodge, K., J.E. Lochman, J.D. Harnish, and J.E. Bates
1997   Reactive and proactive aggression in school children and psychiatrically impaired chronically assaultive youth. *Journal of Abnormal Psychology* 106(1):37-51.
Dornbusch, S.M., J.M. Carlsmith, S.J. Bushwall, P.L. Ritter, H. Leiderman, A.H. Hastorf, and R.T. Gross
1985   Single parents, extended households, and the control of adolescents. *Child Development* 56:326-341.
Drillien, C.M., A.J.M. Thomson, and K. Burgoyne
1980   Low birthweight children at early school-age: A longitudinal study. *Developmental Medicine and Child Neurology* 22:26-47.
Dryfoos, J.
1990   *Adolescents at Risk: Prevalence and Prevention.* New York: Oxford University Press.
Eggert, L.L., E.A. Thompson, J.R. Herting, L.J. Nicholas, and B.G. Dicker
1994   Preventing adolescent drug abuse and high school dropout through an intensive school-based social network development program. *American Journal of Health Promotion* 8:202-215.

Eisenberg, N., and P.H. Mussen
1989   *The Roots of Prosocial Behavior in Children*. Cambridge, UK: Cambridge University Press.

Elder, G.H., Jr.
1986   Military times and turning points in men's lives. *Developmental Psychology* 22:233-245.

Elliott, D.S.
1994a Longitudinal research in criminology: Promise and practice. Pp. 189-201 in *Cross-National Longitudinal Research on Human Development and Criminal Behavior*, E.G.M. Weitekamp and H.-J. Kerner, eds. Boston: Kluwer Academic Publishers.

1994b Serious violent offenders: Onset, developmental course, and termination. *Criminology* 32(1):1-21.

1995   *Lies, Damn Lies, and Arrest Statistics: The Sutherland Award Presentation*. Boulder: University of Colorado.

1999   Alternative Perspectives on Trends. Paper presented to the National Research Council Panel on Juvenile Crime: Prevention, Treatment, and Control, Washington, DC, June 29.

Elliott, D.S., and S.S. Ageton
1980   Reconciling race and class differences in self-reported and official estimates of delinquency. *American Sociological Review* 45:95-110.

Elliott, D.S., and S. Menard
1996   Delinquent friends and delinquent behavior. *Delinquency and Crime*, J.D. Hawkins, ed. New York: Cambridge University Press.

Elliott, D.S., and H.L. Voss
1974   *Delinquency and Dropout*. Lexington, MA: Lexington Books.

Elliott, D.S., F.W. Dunford, and B. Knowles
1978   *Diversion: A Study of Alternative Processing Practices: An Overview of Initial Study Findings*. Boulder: Behavioral Research Institute, University of Colorado.

Elliott, D.S., D. Huizinga, and S.S. Ageton
1985   *Explaining Delinquency and Drug Use*. Beverly Hills, CA: Sage.

Elliott, D., W.J. Wilson, D. Huizinga, R. Sampson, A. Eddiot, and B. Rankin
1996   The effects of neighborhood disadvantage on adolescent development. *Journal of Crime and Delinquency* 33:389-426.

Emory, E.K., and J.R. Noonan
1984   Fetal cardiac responding: A correlate of birthweight and newborn behavior. *Child Development* 55:1651-1657.

Emory, E.K., R. Patillo, E. Archibold, M. Bayorh, and R. Sung
1999   Neurobehavioral effects of low-level lead exposure in human neonates. *Journal of Obstetrics & Gynecology* 188:S2-S11.

Emory, E., L.J. Schlackman, and K. Fiano
1996   Drug-hormone interactions on neurobehavioral responses in human neonates. *Infant Behavior and Development* 19:312-221.

Ennett, S.T., N.S. Tobler, C.L. Ringwalt, and R.L. Flewelling
1997   How effective is drug abuse resistance education?: A meta-analysis of project DARE outcome evaluations. Pp. 60-67 in *Drug Use and Drug Policy*, M. McShane and F.P. Williams, eds. New York: Garland Publishing.

Ensminger, M.E., S.G. Kellam, and B.R. Rubin
1983   School and family origins of delinquency: Comparisons by sex. Pp. 73-97 in *Prospective Studies of Crime and Delinquency*, K.T. Van Dusen and S.A. Mednick, eds. Boston: Kluwer-Nijhoff.

Eppright, T.D., J.H. Kashani, B.D. Robison, and J.C. Reid
   1993   Comorbidity of conduct disorder and personality disorders in an incarcerated
          juvenile population. *American Journal of Psychiatry* 150:1233-1236.
Eron, L.D., and L.R. Huesmann
   1986   The role of television in the development of prosocial and antisocial behavior.
          Pp. 285-314 in *Development of Antisocial and Prosocial Behavior*, D. Olweus, J. Block,
          and M. Radke-Yarrow, eds. New York: Academic Press.
Esbensen, F.-A., and D.W. Osgood
   1999   Gang Resistance Education and Training (GREAT): Results from the national
          evaluation. *Journal of Research in Crime and Delinquency* 36(2):194-225.
Esbensen, F., D. Huizinga, and A.W. Weiher
   1993   Gang and non-gang youth: Differences in explanatory factors. *Journal of Contem-
          porary Criminal Justice* 9(2):94-116.
Fagan, J.
   1995   Separating the men from the boys: The comparative advantage of juvenile versus
          criminal court sanctions on recidivism among adolescent felony offenders. Pp.
          238-261 in *A Sourcebook: Serious, Violent, and Chronic Juvenile Offenders*, J.C. Howell,
          B. Krisberg, J.D. Hawkins, and J.J. Wilson, eds. Thousand Oaks, CA: Sage.
Fagan, J., and M. Guggenheim
   1996   Preventive detention and the judicial prediction of dangerousness for juveniles:
          A natural experiment. *Journal of Criminal Law and Criminology* 86(2):415-448.
Fagan, J.A., and C. Reinarman
   1991   The social context of intensive supervision: Organizational and ecological influ-
          ences on community treatment of violent adolescents. Pp. 341-394 in *Intensive
          Interventions With High-Risk Youths: Promising Approaches in Juvenile Probation and
          Parole*, T.L. Armstrong, ed. Monsey, NY: Criminal Justice Press.
Fagan, J., and D.L. Wilkinson
   1998   Guns, youth violence, and social identity. Pp. 105-188 in *Youth Violence: Crime
          and Justice, Vol. 24*, M. Tonry and M.H. Moore, eds. Chicago: University of
          Chicago Press.
Fagan, J., M. Forst, and T.S. Vivona
   1987a Racial determinants of the judicial transfer decision: Prosecuting violent youth in
          criminal court. *Crime and Delinquency* 33(2):259-286.
Fagan, J., E. Slaughter, and E. Hartstone
   1987b Blind justice?: The impact of race on the juvenile justice process. *Crime and
          Delinquency* 33(2):224-258.
Farrell, A.D., and S.E. Bruce
   1997   Impact of exposure to community violence on violent behavior and emotional
          distress among urban adolescents. *Journal of Clinical Child Psychology* 26:2-14.
Farrell, A.D., and A.L. Meyer
   1997   The effectiveness of a school based curriculum for reducing violence among urban
          sixth grade students. *American Journal of Public Health* 87(6):979-984.
Farrell, R., and V.L. Swigert
   1978   Prior offense as a self-fulfilling prophecy. *Law and Society Review* 12:437-453.
Farrington, D.P.
   1983   Offending from 10 to 25 years of age. Pp. 17-37 in *Prospective Studies of Crime and
          Delinquency*, K.T. VanDusen and S.A. Mednick, eds. Boston: Kluwer-Nijhoff.
   1985   Predicting self-reported and official delinquency. Pp. 105-173 in *Predictions in
          Criminology*, D.P. Farrington and R. Tarling, eds. New York: State University of
          New York Press.
   1986a Age and crime. *Crime and Justice: An Annual Review of Research* 7:29-90.

1986b Stepping stones to adult criminal careers. Pp. 359-384 in *Development of Antisocial and Prosocial Behavior*, D. Olweus, J. Blockland, and M.R. Yarrow, eds. New York: Academic Press.

1987 Early precursors of frequent offending. Pp. 27-50 in *From Children to Citizens (Vol. III). Families, Schools and Delinquency Prevention.*, J.Q. Wilson and G.C. Loury, eds. New York: Springer-Verlag.

1989 Early predictors of adolescent aggression and adult violence. *Violence and Victims* 4:79-100.

1991 Childhood aggression and adult violence: Early precursors and life outcomes. Pp. 5-29 in *Development and Treatment of Childhood Aggression*, D.J. Pepler and K.H. Rubin, eds. Hillsdale, NJ: Erlbaum.

1998 Predictors, causes, and correlates of male youth violence. Pp. 421-475 in *Youth Violence*, Crime and Justice, vol. 24, M. Tonry and M.H. Moore, eds. Chicago: University of Chicago Press.

Farrington, D.P., and J.D. Hawkins
1991 Predicting participation, early onset, and later persistence in officially recorded offending. *Criminal Behavior and Mental Health* 1:1-33.

Farrington, D.P., and R. Loeber
1999 Transatlantic replicability of risk factors in the development of delinquency. Pp. 299-329 in *Historical and Geographical Influences on Psychopathology*, P. Cohen, C. Slomkowski, and L.N. Robins, eds. Mahwah, NJ: Lawrence Erlbaum Associates.

Farrington, D.P., and D.J. West
1995 Effects of marriage, separation, and children on offending by adult males. *Current Perspectives on Aging and the Life Cycle. Vol. 4: Delinquency and Disrepute in the Life Course*, Z.B. Smith and J. Hagan, eds. Greenwich, CT: JAI Press.

Farrington, D.P., and P.-O.H. Wikstrom
1994 Criminal careers in London and Stockholm: A cross-national comparative study. Pp. 65-89 in *Cross-National Longitudinal Research on Human Development and Criminal Behavior*, E.G.M. Weitekamp and H.-J. Kerner, eds. Boston: Kluwer Academic Publishers.

Farrington, D.P., R. Loeber, M. Stouthamer-Loeber, W.B. Van Kammen, and L. Schmidt
1996 Self-reported delinquency and a combined delinquency seriousness scale based on boys, mothers, and teachers: Concurrent and predictive validity for African-Americans and Caucasians. *Criminology* 34(4):493-517.

Farrington, D.P., R. Loeber, and M. Stouthamer-Loeber
in How can the relationship between race and violence be explained? *Violent Crimes:*
press *The Nexus of Ethnicity, Race, and Class*, D.F. Hawkins, ed. New York: Cambridge University Press.

Federal Bureau of Investigation
1971 *Crime in the United States 1970.*   Washington, DC: U.S. Department of Justice.
1972 *Crime in the United States 1971.*   Washington, DC: U.S. Department of Justice.
1973 *Crime in the United States 1972.*   Washington, DC: U.S. Department of Justice.
1974 *Crime in the United States 1973.*   Washington, DC: U.S. Department of Justice.
1975 *Crime in the United States 1974.*   Washington, DC: U.S. Department of Justice.
1976 *Crime in the United States 1975.*   Washington, DC: U.S. Department of Justice.
1977 *Crime in the United States 1976.*   Washington, DC: U.S. Department of Justice.
1978 *Crime in the United States 1977.*   Washington, DC: U.S. Department of Justice.
1979 *Crime in the United States 1978.*   Washington, DC: U.S. Department of Justice.
1980 *Crime in the United States 1979.*   Washington, DC: U.S. Department of Justice.
1981 *Crime in the United States 1980.*   Washington, DC: U.S. Department of Justice.
1982 *Crime in the United States 1981.*   Washington, DC: U.S. Department of Justice.

1983   *Crime in the United States 1982.*   Washington, DC: U.S. Department of Justice.
1984   *Crime in the United States 1983.*   Washington, DC: U.S. Department of Justice.
1985   *Crime in the United States 1984.*   Washington, DC: U.S. Department of Justice.
1986   *Crime in the United States 1985.*   Washington, DC: U.S. Department of Justice.
1987   *Crime in the United States 1986.*   Washington, DC: U.S. Department of Justice.
1988   *Crime in the United States 1987.*   Washington, DC: U.S. Department of Justice.
1989   *Crime in the United States 1988.*   Washington, DC: U.S. Department of Justice.
1990   *Crime in the United States 1989.*   Washington, DC: U.S. Department of Justice.
1991   *Crime in the United States 1990.*   Washington, DC: U.S. Department of Justice.
1992   *Crime in the United States 1991.*   Washington, DC: U.S. Department of Justice.
1993   *Crime in the United States 1992.*   Washington, DC: U.S. Department of Justice.
1994   *Crime in the United States 1993.*   Washington, DC: U.S. Department of Justice.
1995   *Crime in the United States 1994.*   Washington, DC: U.S. Department of Justice.
1996   *Crime in the United States 1995.*   Washington, DC: U.S. Department of Justice.
1997   *Crime in the United States 1996.*   Washington, DC: U.S. Department of Justice.
1998   *Crime in the United States 1997.*   Washington, DC: U.S. Department of Justice.
1999   *Crime in the United States 1998.*   Washington, DC: U.S. Department of Justice.

Feld, B.C.
1993   *Justice for Children: The Right to Counsel and the Juvenile Courts.* Boston: North-
       eastern University Press.
1995   The social context of juvenile justice administration: Racial disparities in an urban
       juvenile court. Pp. 66-97 in *Minorities in Juvenile Justice*, K.K. Leonard, C.E. Pope,
       and W.H. Feherherm, eds. Thousand Oaks, CA: Sage Publications, Inc.
1997   Abolish the juvenile court: Youthfulness, criminal responsibility, and sentencing
       policy. *The Journal of Criminal Law and Criminology* 88(1):68-136.
1999   *Bad Kids: Race and the Transformation of the Juvenile Court.* New York: Oxford
       University Press.

Feldman, R.A.
1992   The St. Louis experiment: Effective treatment of antisocial youths in prosocial
       peer groups. Pp. 233-252 in *Preventing Antisocial Behavior: Interventions From
       Birth Through Adolescence,* J. McCord and R.E. Tremblay, eds. New York: Guilford
       Press.

Feldman, R.A., T.E. Caplinger, and J.S. Wodarski
1983   *The St. Louis Conundrum: The Effective Treatment of Antisocial Youths.* Englewood
       Cliffs, NJ: Prentice-Hall, Inc.

Fergusson, D.M., and L.J. Horwood
1995   Predictive validity of categorically and dimensionally scored measures of disrup-
       tive behavior adjustment and juvenile offending. *Journal of the American Academy
       of Child and Adolescent Psychiatry* 34:477-485.

Fergusson, D.M., and M.T. Lynskey
1997   Early reading difficulties and later conduct problems. *Journal of Child Psychology
       and Psychiatry* :899-908.

Feyerherm, W.
1981   Juvenile court dispositions of status offenders: An analysis of case decisions. *Race,
       Crime, and Criminal Justice*, R.L. McNeely and C.E. Pope, eds. Thousand Oaks,
       CA: Sage Publications.

Field, T., S. Widmayer, M.A. Greenberg, and S. Stoller
1982   Effects of parent training on teenage mothers and their infants. *Pediatrics* 69:703-
       707.

Figueira-McDonough, J.
  1986 School context, gender, and delinquency. *Journal of Youth and Adolescence* 15:79-98.
Finkelhor, D., G. Hotaling, and A. Sedlak
  1990 *Missing, Abducted, Runaway, and Thrownaway Children in America: Numbers and Characteristics.* Washington, D.C.: Office of Juvenile Justice and Delinquency Prevention, U.S. Department of Justice.
Fo, W.S., and C.R. O'Donnell
  1974 The Buddy System: Relationship and contingency conditions in a community intervention program for youth with nonprofessionals as behavior change agents. *Journal of Consulting and Clinical Psychology* 2:163-169.
Fox, J.A.
  1978 *Forecasting Crime Data: An Econometric Analysis.* Lexington, MA: Lexington Books.
  1996 *Trends in Juvenile Violence: A Report to the United States Attorney General on Current and Future Rates of Juvenile Offending,* March. Washington, DC: Bureau of Justice Statistics, U.S. Department of Justice.
Frazier, C.E., and D.M. Bishop
  1985 The pretrial detention of juveniles and its impact on case dispositions. *The Journal of Criminal Law and Criminology* 76(4):1132-1152.
  1995 Reflections on race effects in juvenile justice. Pp. 16-46 in *Minorities in Justice,* K.K. Leonard, C.E. Pope, and W.H. Feyerherm, eds. Thousand Oaks, CA: Sage Publications, Inc.
Frazier, C.E., and J.K. Cochran
  1986a Detention of juveniles: Its effects on subsequent juvenile court processing decisions. *Youth and Society* 17(3):286-305.
  1986b Official intervention, diversion from the juvenile justice system, and dynamics of human services work: Effects of a reform goal based on labeling theory. *Crime & Delinquency* 32(2):157-176.
Freeman, R.
  1992 Crime and the economic status of disadvantaged young men. *Urban Labor Markets and Job Opportunities,* G. Peterson and W. Vroman, eds. Washington, DC: Urban Institute Press.
Friedlander, D., and P. Robins
  1994 Estimating the Effect of Employment and Training Programs: An Assessment of Some Nonexperimental Techniques. Manpower Demonstration Research Corporation Working Paper (February). New York: Manpower Demonstration Research Corporation.
Friedrich, R.J.
  1980 Police use of force: Individuals, situations, and organizations. *Annals of the American Academy of Political and Social Science* 452:82-97.
Furano, K., P.A. Roaf, M.B. Styles, and A.Y. Branch
  1993 *Big Brothers/Big Sisters: A Study of Program Practices.* Philadelphia: Public/Private Ventures.
Furstenberg, F.F., J. Brooks-Gunn, and S.P. Morgan
  1987 *Adolescent Mothers in Later Life.* New York: Cambridge University Press.
Furstenburg, F.F., T.D. Cook, J. Eccles, G.H. Elder, Jr., and A. Sameroff
  1999 *Managing to Make It: Urban Families and Adolescent Success.* Chicago: University of Chicago Press.

Gallagher, C.A.
   1999   Juvenile Offenders in Residential Placement, 1997. *OJJDP Fact Sheet, #96*, March, Office of Juvenile Justice and Delinquency Prevention, Office of Justice Programs. Washington, DC: U.S. Department of Justice.
Gamoran, A.
   1992   The variable effects of high school tracking. *American Sociological Review* 57:812-828.
Gendreau, P., and R.R. Ross
   1979   Effective correctional treatment: Bibliotherapy for cynics. *Crime and Delinquency* 25(4):463-489.
Gibbons, D., and M.J. Griswold
   1957   Sex differences among juvenile court referrals. *Sociology and Social Research* 42:106-110.
Gittelman, R., S. Mannuzza, R. Shenker, and N. Bonagura
   1985   Hyperactive boys almost grown up. *Archives of General Psychiatry* 42:937-947.
Glueck, S., and E.T. Glueck
   1950   *Unraveling Juvenile Delinquency.* New York: Commonwealth Fund.
Gold, M., and D. Mann
   1972   Delinquency as defense. *American Journal of Orthopsychiatry* 42(3):463-479.
Goldfarb, W.
   1945   Psychological privation in infancy and subsequent adjustment. *American Journal of Orthopsychiatry* 15:247-255.
Goldstein, J.
   1960   Police discretion not to invoke the criminal process: Low visibility decisions in the administration of justice. *Yale Law Journal* 69(March):543-594.
Goodenough, F.L.
   1931   *Anger in Young Children.* Westport, CT: Greenwood Press.
Goodman, G.
   1972   *Companionship Therapy: Studies in Structured Intimacy.* San Francisco: Jossey-Bass.
Gorman-Smith, D., P.H. Tolan, and D. Henry
   1999   The relation of community and family to risk among urban-poor adolescents. Pp. 349-367 in *Historical and Geographical Influences on Psychopathology*, P. Cohen, C. Slomkowski, and L.N. Robins, eds. Mahwah, NJ: Lawrence Erlbaum Associates.
Gottschalk, R., W.S. Davidson II, J. Mayer, and L.K. Gensheimer
   1987   Behavioral approaches with juvenile offenders: A meta-analysis of long-term treatment efficacy. Pp. 399-423 in *Behavioral Approaches to Crime and Delinquency*, E.K. Morris and C.J. Braukmann, eds. New York: Plenum Press.
Gottfredson, D.C.
   1986   An empirical test of school-based environmental and individual interventions to reduce the risk of delinquent behavior. *Criminology* 24:705-731.
   1987   An evaluation of an organization development approach to reducing school disorder. *Evaluation Review* 11:739-763.
   1997   School-based crime prevention. Pp. 5-1-5-74 in *Preventing Crime: What Works, What Doesn't, What's Promising*, L.W. Sherman, D.C. Gottfredson, D. MacKenzie, J. Eck, P. Reuter, and S. Bushway, eds. Washington, D.C.: U.S. Department of Justice.
Gottfredson, D.C., and G.D. Gottfredson
   1992   Theory-guided investigation: Three field experiments. Pp. 311-329 in *Preventing Antisocial Behavior: Interventions From Birth Through Adolescence*, J. McCord and R.E. Tremblay, eds. New York: Guilford Press.

Gottfredson, D.C., G.D. Gottfredson, and S. Skroban
1998   Can prevention work where it is needed most? *Evaluation Review* 22(3):315-340.
Gottfredson, G.D.
1987   Peer group interventions to reduce the risk of delinquent behavior: A selective review and a new evaluation. *Criminology* 25:671-714.
Gragg, F.
1986   *Juveniles in Adult Court: A Review of Transfers at the Habitual Serious and Violent Juvenile Offender Program Sites*, American Institutes for Research. Washington, DC: U.S. Department of Justice.
Graham, S.
1997   Using attribution theory to understand academic and social motivations in African American youth. *Educational Psychologist* 31:167-180.
Granovetter, M.
1974   *Getting a Job: A Study of Contacts and Careers*. Cambridge, MA: Harvard University Press.
Greenberg, M.T., and C.A. Kusché
1996   *The PATHS Project: Preventive Intervention for Children*. Final report to the National Institute of Mental Health, Grant No. R01MH42131.
1998   Promoting Alternative Thinking Strategies. Book ten in *Blueprints for Preventing Violence*, D.S. Elliott, ed. Boulder, CO: Center for the Study and Prevention of Violence, University of Colorado.
Greene, Peters and Associates
1998   *Guiding Principles for Promising Female Programming: An Inventory of Best Practices*. Washington, DC: U.S. Department of Justice. Available online: http://www.ojjdp.ncjrs.org/pubs/principles/contents.html.
Greenfeld, L.A.
1999   Juvenile Offending as Reported by Victims of Violence. Unpublished paper presented at the NRC Workshop on Racial Disparity in the Juvenile Justice System, Washington, DC, 99.
Greenfeld, L.A., and M.W. Zawitz
1995   *Weapons Offenses and Offenders*. Washington, DC: Bureau of Justice Statistics, U.S. Department of Justice.
Greenwood, P., A. Lipson, A. Abrahamse, and F. Zimring
1983   *Youth Crime and Juvenile Justice in California: A Report to the Legislature*. Santa Monica, CA: Rand.
Greenwood, P.W., E.P. Deschenes, and J. Adams
1993   *Chronic Juvenile Offenders: Final Results From the Skillman Aftercare Experiment*. MR-220-SKF. Santa Monica, CA: Rand.
Griffin, P., P. Torbet, and L. Szymanski
1998   *Trying Juveniles As Adults in Criminal Courts: An Analysis of State Transfer Provisions*, December. Office of Juvenile Justice and Delinquency Prevention, Office of Justice Programs Washington, DC: U.S. Department of Justice.
Grisso, T.
1980   Juveniles' capacities to waive *Miranda* rights: An empirical analysis. *California Law Review* 68(6):1134-1166.
1981   *Juveniles' Waiver of Rights: Legal and Psychological Competence*. New York: Plenum Press.
1997   The competence of adolescents as trial defendants. *Psychology, Public Policy, and Law* 3(1):3-32.

Grogger, J.
    1995 The effects of arrest on the employment and earnings of young men. *Quarterly Journal of Economics* 110:51-72.
    1997 Incarceration-related costs of early childbearing. In *Kids Having Kids: Economic Costs and Social Consequences of Teen Pregnancy*, R.A. Maynard, ed. Washington, DC: Urban Institute Press.
Grossman, D.C., H.J. Neckerman, T.D. Koepsell, L. Ping-Yu, K.N. Asher, K. Beland, K. Frey, and F.R. Rivera
    1997 Effectiveness of a violence prevention curriculum among children in elementary school: A randomized controlled trial. *Journal of the American Medical Association* 277(20):1605-1611.
Hagan, J.
    1991 Destiny and drift: Subcultural preferences status attainments and the risks and rewards of youth. *American Sociological Review* 56:567-582.
    1993 The social embeddedness of crime and unemployment. *Criminology* 31(4):465-491.
Hagan, J., and H. Foster
    2000 Making corporate and criminal America less violent: Public norms and structural reforms. *Contemporary Sociology* 29(1):44-53.
Hagan, J., and B. McCarthy
    1997 *Mean Streets: Youth Crime and Homelessness*. New York: Cambridge University Press.
Hagan, J., and A. Palloni
    1990 The social reproduction of a criminal class in working class London, circa 1950-80. *American Journal of Sociology* 96:265-99.
Haller, M.H.
    1989 Bootlegging: The business and politics of violence. Pp. 146-162 in *Violence in America, Volume 1: The History of Crime*, T.R. Gurr, ed. Newbury Park, CA: Sage.
Hamparian, D., M.J. Leiber, R. Morton, and Community Research Associates
    1997 *Disproportionate Confinement of Minority Juveniles in Secure Facilities: 1996 National Report*, December, Office of Juvenile Justice and Delinquency Prevention State Relations and Assistance Division. Washington, DC: U.S. Department of Justice.
Hansen, W.B., and J.W. Graham
    1991 Preventing alcohol, marijuana, and cigarette use among adolescents: Peer pressure resistance training versus establishing conservative norms. *Preventive Medicine* 20:414-430.
Hare, R.D., L.M. McPherson, and A.E. Forth
    1988 Male psychopaths and their criminal careers. *Journal of Consulting and Clinical Psychology* 56(5):710-714.
Hart, T.C., and B.A. Reaves
    1999 *Felony Defendants in Large Urban Counties, 1996*, October, Bureau of Justice Statistics. NCJ 176981. Washington, DC: U.S. Department of Justice.
Hawkins, D.F.
    1998 The nations within: Race, class, region, and American lethal violence. *Colorado Law Review* 69(4):905-926.
Hawkins, D.F., J.H. Laub, and J.L. Lauritsen
    1998 Race, ethnicity, and serious juvenile offending. Pp. 30-46 in *Serious & Violent Juvenile Offenders: Risk Factors and Successful Interventions*, R. Loeber and D. Farrington, eds. Thousand Oaks, CA: Sage Publications.

Hawkins, J.D.
  1997 Preventing Violence, Alcohol Misuses, and Teen Pregnancy Using the Social De-
        velopment Strategy: Results from a Twelve-Year Field Experiment. 12th Interna-
        tional Workshop on Research into Juvenile Criminology, Leeuwenhorst, The
        Netherlands,
Hawkins, J.D., M.W. Arthur, and R.F. Catalano
  1995 Preventing substance abuse. Pp. 343-427 in *Building a Safer Society: Strategic
        Approaches to Crime Prevention: Volume 19, Crime and Justice: A Review of the
        Research*, M. Tonry and D.P. Farrington, eds. Chicago: University of Chicago
        Press.
Hawkins, J.D., M.W. Arthur, and J.J. Olson
  1997 Community interventions to reduce risk and enhance protection against antiso-
        cial behavior. Pp. 365-374 in *Handbook of Antisocial Behaviors*, D.S. Stoff, J. Breling,
        and J.D. Masters, eds. New York: NIMH/John Wiley.
Hawkins, J.D., R.F. Catalano, and D.D. Brewer
  1995 Preventing serious, violent, and chronic juvenile offending: Effective strategies
        from conception to age 6. Pp. 47-60 in *A Sourcebook: Serious, Violent, and Chronic
        Juvenile Offenders*, J.C. Howell, B. Krisberg, J.D. Hawkins, and J.J. Wilson, eds.
        Thousand Oaks, CA: Sage.
Hawkins, J.D., R.F. Catalano, R. Kosterman, R.D. Abbott, and K.G. Hill
  1999 Preventing adolescent health-risk behaviors by strengthening protection during
        childhood. *Archives of Pediatric and Adolescent Medicine* 153(3):226-234.
Hawkins, J.D., R.F. Catalano, J.M. Morrison, J. O'Donnell, R.D. Abbott, and L.E. Day
  1992 The Seattle Social Development Project: Effects of the first four years on protec-
        tive factors and problem behaviors. Pp. 139-161 in *Preventing Antisocial Behavior:
        Interventions From Birth Through Adolescence*, J. McCord and R.E. Tremblay, eds.
        New York: Guilford.
Hawkins, J.D., D.P. Farrington, and R.F. Catalano
  1998a Reducing violence through the schools. *Violence in American Schools: A New
        Perspective*, D.S. Elliott, B.A. Hamburg, and K.R. Williams, eds. New York: Cam-
        bridge University Press.
Hawkins, J.D., T. Herrenkohl, D.P. Farrington, D. Brewer, R.F. Catalano, and T.W. Harachi
  1998b A review of predictors of youth violence. Pp. 106-146 in *Serious and Violent Juve-
        nile Offenders: Risk Factors and Successful Interventions*, R. Loeber and D.P.
        Farrington, eds. Thousand Oaks, CA: Sage.
Hayden, D., and D. Ward
  1996 Faces behind the figures: Interviews with children excluded from primary school.
        Children & Society 10(4):255-266.
Hechtman, L., G. Weiss, T. Perlman, and R. Amsel
  1984 Hyperactives as young adults: Initial predictors of adult outcome. *Journal of the
        American Academy of Child Psychiatry* 23:250-260.
Helmer, J.
  1975 *Drugs and Minority Oppression*. New York: The Seabury Press.
Hemenway, D., D. Prothrow-Smith, J.M. Bergstein, R. Ander, and B.P. Kennedy
  1996 Gun carrying among adolescents. *Law and Contemporary Problems* 59(1):39-53.
Henggeler, S.W.
  1999 Multisystemic therapy. *Paradigm* 2(4):12-13.
Henggeler, S.W., G.B. Melton, L.A. Smith, S.K. Schoenwald, and J.H. Hanley
  1993 Family preservation using multisystemic treatment: Long-term follow-up to a
        clinical trial with serious juvenile offenders. *Journal of Child and Family Studies*
        2(4):283-293.

Hindelang, M.J., T. Hirschi, and J.G. Weis
1981   *Measuring Delinquency*. Beverly Hills, CA: Sage.
Hirschi, T.
1969   *Causes of Delinquency*. Berkeley, CA: University of California Press.
Hoge, R.D., D.A. Andrews, and A.W. Leschied
1994   Tests of three hypotheses regarding predictors of delinquency. *Journal of Abnormal Child Psychology* 22:547-559.
Hollander, H.E., and F.D. Turner
1985   Characteristics of incarcerated delinquents: Relationship between development disorders, environmental and family factors, and patterns of offense and recidivism. *Journal of the American Academy of Child and Adolescent Psychiatry* 24:221-226.
Hollister, R.G., and J. Hill
1995   Problems in the evaluation of community-wide initiatives. Pp. 127-172 in *New Approaches to Evaluating Community Initiatives: Concepts, Methods, and Contexts*, J.P. Connell, A.C. Kubisch, L.B. Schorr, and C.H. Weiss, eds. Washington, D.C.: The Aspen Institute.
Honig, A.S.
1977   The Children's Center and the Family Development Research Program. Pp. 81-99 in *Infant Education: A Guide for Helping Handicapped Children in the First Three Years*, B.M. Caldwell and D.J. Stedman, eds. New York: Walker & Co.
Honig, A.S., and J.R. Lally
1982   The Family Development Research Program: Retrospective review. *Early Child Development and Care* 10:41-62.
Hope, T.
1995   Community crime prevention. Pp. 21-89 in *Building a Safer Society: Strategic Approaches to Crime Prevention*, M. Tonry and D.P. Farrington, eds. Chicago: The University of Chicago Press.
Hopkins, D.D., J.A. Grant-Worley, and D.W. Fleming
1995   Fatal and nonfatal suicide attempts among adolescents—Oregon, 1988-1993. *Morbidity and Mortality Weekly Report* 44(16):312-315,321.
Horney, J., D.W. Osgood, and I.H. Marshall
1995   Criminal careers in the short-term: Intra-individual variability in crime and its relation to local life circumstances. *American Sociological Review* 60:655-673.
Horowitz, R.
1987   Community tolerance of gang violence. *Social Problems* 34(5):437-450.
Horowitz, R., and Pottieger
1991   Gender bias in juvenile justice handling of seriously crime-involved youths. *Journal of Research in Crime and Delinquency* 28:75-100.
Houghtalin, M., and G.L. Mays
1991   Criminal dispositions of New Mexico juveniles transferred to adult court. *Crime and Delinquency* 37(3):393-407.
Hudley, C., and S. Graham
1993   An attributional intervention to reduce peer-directed aggression among African-American boys. *Child Development* 64:124-138.
Huesmann, L.R.
1988   An information processing model for the development of aggression. *Aggressive Behavior* 14(1):13-24.
Huesmann, L.R., L.D. Eron, M.M. Lefkowitz, and L.O. Walder
1984   Stability of aggression over time and generations. *Developmental Psychology* 20:1120-1134.

Huff, C.R.
  1998   *Comparing the Criminal Behavior of Youth Gangs and At-Risk Youths*, National Insti-
         tute of Justice. NCJ 172852. Washington, DC: U.S. Department of Justice. Avail-
         able online: http://www.ncjrs.org/pdffiles/172852.pdf.
Huizinga, D., and D.S. Elliott
  1986   Reassessing the reliability and validity of self-reported data. *Journal of Quantita-
         tive Criminology* 2(4):293-327.
  1987   Juvenile offenders: Prevalence, offender incidence, and arrest rates by race. *Crime
         and Delinquency* 33(2):206-223.
Huizinga, D., and C. Jakob-Chien
  1998   The contemporaneous co-occurrence of serious and violent offending and other
         problem behavior. Pp. 47-67 in *Serious and Violent Juvenile Offenders: Risk Factors
         and Successful Interventions*, R. Loeber and D.P. Farrington, eds. Thousand Oaks:
         Sage.
Human Rights Watch
  1995   *Children in Confinement in Louisiana.* New York: Human Rights Watch.
Hunt, G., S. Riegel, T. Morales, and D. Waldorf
  1993   Changes in prison culture: Prison gangs and the case of the "Pepsi Generation".
         Social Problems 40:398-409.
Hurst, H.
  1985   *Confidentiality of Juvenile Justice Records and Proceedings: A Legacy Under Siege.*
         Pittsburgh, PA: National Center for Juvenile Justice.
Huston, A., and J.C. Wright
  1998   Television and the informational and educational needs of children. *Annals of the
         American Academy of Political and Social Sciences: Children and Television* 557(May):9-
         23.
Institute of Medicine
  1990   *Broadening the Base of Treatment for Alcohol Problems.* Committee for the Study of
         Treatment and Rehabilitation Services for Alcoholism and Alcohol Abuse, Divi-
         sion of Mental Health and Behavioral Medicine. Washington, DC: National
         Academy Press.
  1994   *Reducing Risks for Mental Disorders: Frontiers for Preventive Intervention Research.*
         Committee on Prevention of Mental Disorders, P.J. Mrazek and R.J. Haggerty,
         eds. Division of Biobehavioral Sciences and Mental Disorders. Washington, DC:
         National Academy Press.
  1996   *Fetal Alcohol Syndrome: Diagnosis, Epidemiology, Prevention, and Treatment.* Com-
         mittee to Study Fetal Alcohol Syndrome, K. Stratton, C. Howe, and F. Battaglia,
         eds. Division of Biobehavioral Sciences and Mental Disorders. Washington, DC:
         National Academy Press.
  1997   *Dispelling the Myths About Addiction: Strategies to Increase Understanding and
         Strengthen Research.* Committee to Identify Strategies to Raise the Profile of Sub-
         stance Abuse and Alcoholism Research, Division of Neuroscience and Behavioral
         Health and Division of Health Promotion and Disease Prevention. Washington,
         DC: National Academy Press.
Irwin, J., and J. Austin
  1994   *It's About Time.* Belmont, CA: Wadsworth.
Jackson, K.T.
  1985   *Crabgrass Frontier: The Suburbanization of the United States.* New York: Oxford
         University Press.
Jensen, E.L., and L.K. Metsger
  1994   A test of the deterrent effect of legislative waiver on violent juvenile crime. *Crime
         and Delinquency* 40(1):96-104.

Jensen, G.F.
  1972 Parents, peers, and delinquent action: A test of the differential association perspective. *American Journal of Sociology* 78:562-575.
Jeter, H.R.
  1922 *The Chicago Juvenile Court*. Washington, DC: U.S. Government Printing Office.
Jimerson, S., E. Carlson, E. Rotert, B. Egeland, and A.L. Sroufe
  1997 A prospective, longitudinal study of the correlates and consequences of early grade retention. *Journal of Social Psychology* 35(1):3-25.
Johnson, B.D., E.D. Wish, J. Schmeidler, and D. Huizinga
  1991 Concentration of delinquent offending: Serious drug involvement and high delinquency rates. *Journal of Drug Issues* 21:205-291.
  1993 Concentration of delinquent offending: Serious drug involvement and high delinquency rates. Pp. 1-25 in *Drugs and Crime*, R. Dembo, ed. Lanham, MD: University Press of America.
Johnson, C.A., M.A. Pentz, M.D. Weber, J.H. Dwyer, N.A. Baer, D.P. MacKinnon, W.B. Hansen, and B.R. Flay
  1990 Relative effectiveness of comprehensive community programming for drug abuse prevention with high-risk and low-risk adolescents. *Journal of Consulting and Clinical Psychology* 58:447-456.
Johnson, D.L., and T. Walker
  1987 Primary prevention of behavior problems in Mexican American children. *American Journal of Community Psychology* 15(4):375-385.
Johnson, D.R., and L.K. Scheuble
  1991 Gender bias in the disposition of juvenile court referrals: The effects of time and location. *Criminology* 29(4):677-699.
Johnson, R.
  1987 Mother's versus father's role in causing delinquency. *Adolescence* 22:305-315.
Johnston, L.D., P.M. O'Malley, and J.G. Bachman
  1998 *National Survey Results on Drug Use From The Monitoring the Future Study, 1975-1997*, Volume 1, Secondary School Students, National Institute on Drug Abuse. Washington, DC: U.S. Department of Health and Human Services.
Jones, M.B., and D.R. Offord
  1989 Reduction of antisocial behavior in poor children by nonschool skill development. *Journal of Child Psychology and Psychiatry* 30(5):737-750.
Jordan, B.K., W.E. Schlenger, J.A. Fairbank, and J.M. Caddell
  1996 Prevalence of psychiatric disorders among incarcerated women. *Archives of General Psychiatry* 53(6):513-519.
Juby, H., and D.P. Farrington
  2001 Disentangling the link between disrupted families and delinquency. *British Journal of Criminology* 41:22-40.
Kachur, S.P., L.B. Potter, and S.P.P.K.E. James
  1995 *Suicide in the United States, 1980-1992*. Atlanta, GA: National Center for Injury Prevention and Control.
Kaeser, S.
  1979 Suspensions in school discipline. *Education and Urban Society* 11:465-484.
Kammer, J.J., K.I. Minor, and J.B. Wells
  1997 An outcome study of the Diversion Plus program for juvenile offenders. *Federal Probation* 61(2):51-56.
Kandel, D.B.
  1980 Drug and drinking behavior among youth. *Annual Review of Sociology* 6:235-285.

Kandel, D.B., and K. Andrews
1987 Process of adolescent socialization by parents and peers. *The International Journal of the Addictions* 22:319-342.

Kandel, D.B., R.C. Kessler, and R.Z. Margulies
1978 Antecedents of adolescent initiation into stages of drug use: A developmental analysis. *Journal of Youth and Adolescence* 7(1):13-40.

Kandel, E., P.A. Brennan, S.A. Mednick, and N.M. Michelson
1989 Minor physical abnormalities and recidivistic adult violent criminal behavior. *Acta Psychiatrica Scandinavia* 79:103-107.

Kandel, E., and S.A. Mednick
1991 Perinatal complications predict violent offending. *Criminology* 29:519-520.

Kaplan, H.B., and R.J. Johnson
1991 Negative social sanctions and juvenile delinquency: Effects of labeling in a model of deviant behavior. *Social Science Quarterly* 72(1):97-122.

Karoly, L.A., P.W. Greenwood, S.S. Everingham, J. Hoube, M.R. Kilburn, C.P. Rydell, M. Sanders, and J. Chiesa
1998 *Investing in Our Children: What We Know and Don't Know About the Costs and Benefits of Early Childhood Interventions.* Santa Monica, CA: Rand Corporation. Online at http://www.rand.org/publications/MR/MR898 (3/25/99).

Karr-Morse, R., and M.S. Wiley
1997 *Ghosts From the Nursery: Tracing the Roots of Violence.* New York: Grove Atlantic.

Katz, L.F., J.R. Kling, and J.B. Liebman
2000 Moving to Opportunity in Boston: Early Results of a Randomized Mobility Experiment. Working Paper #441, Industrial Relations Section, Princeton University. [Online.] Available: http://www.irs.princeton.edu/pubs/working_papers.html Accessed October 10, 2000.

Kaufman, J.G., and C.S. Widom
1999 Childhood victimization, running away, and delinquency. *Journal of Research in Crime and Delinquency* 36(4):347-370.

Kazdin, A.E.
1997 Parent management training: Evidence, outcomes, and issues. *Journal of the American Academy of Child and Adolescent Psychiatry* 36(10):1349-1356.

Kellam, S.G., X. Ling, R. Merisca, C.H. Brown, and N. Ialongo
1998 The effect of the level of aggression in the first grade classroom on the course and malleability of aggressive behavior into middle school. *Development and Psychopathology* 10:165-185.

Kelley, B.T., D. Huizinga, T. Thornberry, and R. Loeber
1997 Epidemiology of serious violence. Juvenile Justice Bulletin. Washington, DC: Office of Juvenile Justice and Delinquency Prevention, U.S. Department of Justice.

Kelly, D.H.
1971 School failure, academic self-evaluation, and school avoidance and deviant behavior. *Youth and Society* 2:489-502.

Kenney, D.J., and T.S. Watson
1996 Reducing fear in the schools: Managing conflict through student problem solving. *Education and Urban Society* 28:436-455.

Kerr, M., R.E. Tremblay, L. Pagani-Kurtz, and F. Vitaro
1997 Boys' behavioral inhibition and the risk of later delinquency. *Archives of General Psychiatry* 54(9):809-816.

Keyes, L.C.
  1992   *Strategies and Saints: Fighting Drugs in Public Housing.* Washington, DC: The Urban Institute Press.
Kilgore, S.B.
  1991   The organizational context of tracking in schools. *American Sociological Review* 56:189-203.
Kinder, K., C. Veneziano, M. Fichter, and H. Azuma
  1995   A comparison of the dispositions of juvenile offenders certified as adults with juvenile offenders not certified. *Juvenile and Family Court Journal* 46:37-42.
Kitzman, H., D.L. Olds, C.R. Henderson, C. Hanks, R. Cole, R. Tatelbaum, K.M. McConnochie, K. Sidora, D.W. Luckey, D. Shaver, K. Engelhardt, D. James, and K. Barnard
  1997   Effect of prenatal and infancy home visitation by nurses on pregnancy outcomes, childhood injuries, and repeated childbearing: A randomized controlled trial. *Journal of the American Medical Association* 278(8):644-652.
Klein, M.W.
  1971   *Street Gangs and Street Workers.* Englewood Cliffs, NJ: Prentice-Hall.

  1995   *The American Street Gang: Its Nature, Prevalence, and Control.* New York: Oxford University Press.
Klein, N.C., J.F. Alexander, and B.V. Parsons
  1977   Impact of family systems intervention on recidivism and sibling delinquency: A model of primary prevention and program evaluation. *Journal of Consulting and Clinical Psychology* 45:469-477.
Kochanska, G., T.L. Tjebkes, and D.R. Forman
  1998   Children's emerging regulation of conduct: Restraint, compliance, and internalization from infancy to the second year. *Child Development* 69(5):1378-1389.
Kolvin, I., R.F. Garside, A.R. Nicole, A. MacMillen, F. Wolstenhome, and I.M. Leitch
  1981   *Help Starts Here.* New York: Tavistock.
Kolvin, I., F.J.W. Miller, D.M. Scott, S.R.M. Gatzanis, and M. Fleeting
  1990   *Continuities of Deprivation? The Newcastle Thousand-Family Survey.* Aldershot, England: Avebury.
Kopp, C.B., and J.B. Krakow
  1983   The developmentalist and the study of biological risk: A view of the past with an eye toward the future. *Child Development* 54:1086-1108.
Korbin, J., and C.J. Coulton
  1997   *Understanding the Neighborhood Context for Children and Families.* New York: Russell Sage Foundation Press.
Kovacs, M.
  1996   Presentation and course of major depressive disorder during childhood and later years of the life span. *Journal of the American Academy of Child and Adolescent Psychiatry* 35:705-715.
Kramer, J.H., and D.J. Steffensmeier
  1978   The differential detention/jailing of juveniles: A comparison of detention and nondetention courts. *Peperdine Law Review* 5(3):795-807.
Krisberg, B., and J.C. Howell
  1998   The impact of the juvenile justice system and prospects for graduated sanctions in a comprehensive strategy. Pp. 346-366 in *Serious and Violent Juvenile Offenders: Risk Factors and Successful Interventions,* R. Loeber and D.P. Farrington, eds. Thousand Oaks, CA: Sage Publications.
Krisberg, B., and I. Schwartz
  1983   Rethinking juvenile justice. *Crime and Delinquency* (July):333-364.

Kruglanski, A.W., I. Friedman, and G. Zeevi
  1971   The effects of extrinsic incentives on some qualitative aspects of task performance. *Journal of Personality* 39:606-617.
Lab, S.P., and R.B. Allen
  1984   Self-report and official measures: A further examination of the validity issue. *Journal of Criminal Justice* 12:445-455.
Lab, S.P., and J.T. Whitehead
  1990   From 'nothing works' to 'the appropriate works': The latest stop on the search for the secular grail. *Criminology* 28(3):405-417.
Lahey, B.B., I.D. Waldman, and K. McBurnett
  1999   Annotation: The development of antisocial behavior, an integrative causal model. *Journal of Child Psychology and Psychiatry* 40(5):669-682.
Lally, J.R., and A.S. Honig
  1977   The Family Development Research Program: A program for prenatal, infant and early childhood enrichment. Pp. 147-194 in *The Preschool in Action: Exploring Early Childhood Programs*, M.C. Day & R.D. Parker, eds. Boston: Allyn & Bacon.
Lally, J.R., P.L. Mangione, and A.S. Honig
  1988   The Syracuse University Family Development Research Program: Long-range impact of an early intervention with low-income children and their families. Pp. 79-104 in *Advances in Applied Developmental Psychology. Parent Education As Early Childhood Intervention: Emerging Directions in Theory, Research, and Practice*, D.R. Powell, ed. Norwood, NJ: Ablex Publishing.
Land, K., P.L. McCall, and L.E. Cohen
  1990   Structural covariates of homicide rates: Are there any invariances across time and social space. *American Journal of Sociology* 95:922-963.
Land, K.C., P.L. McCall, J.R. Williams, and M. Ezell
  1992   Intensive supervision of status offenders: Evidence on continuity of treatment effects for juveniles and a ""Hawthorne Effect"" for counselors. Pp. 339-349 in *Preventing Antisocial Behavior: Interventions From Birth Through Adolescence*, J. McCord and R. Tremblay, eds. New York: Guilford.
  1998   *Alternatives to Detention Study: Final Report*, Administrative Office of the Courts, Juvenile Services Division. Raleigh, NC: North Carolina Administrative Office of the Courts.
Land, K.C., P.L. McCall, and J.R. Williams
  1990   Something that works in juvenile justice: An evaluation of the North Carolina court counselors' intensive protective supervision randomized experimental project, 1987-1989. *Evaluation Review* 14(6):574-606.
Lander, B.
  1954   *Toward an Understanding of Juvenile Delinquency*. New York: Columbia University Press.
Lane, R.
  1986   *Roots of Violence in Black Philadelphia 1860-1900*. Cambridge, MA: Harvard University Press.
Langan, P.A., and D.P. Farrington
  1998   *Crime and Justice in the United States and in England and Wales, 1981-96*, October. Washington, D.C.: U.S. Department of Justice. Online at http://www.ojp.usdoj.gov/bjs/abstract/cjusew96.htm (3/25/99).
Larson, R., and C. Lampman-Petraitis
  1989   Daily emotional states as reported by children and adolescents. *Child Development* 60:1250-1260.

Larson, R., and M. Richards
1994 Family emotions: Do young adolescents and their parents experience the same states? *Journal of Research on Adolescence* 4(4):567-583.
Larson, R., M. Csikszemtmihalyi, and R. Graef
1980 Mood variability and the psychosocial adjustment of adolescents. *Journal of Youth and Adolescence* 9(6):469-490.
Larzelere, R.E., and G.R. Patterson
1990 Parental management: Mediator of the effect of socioeconomic status on early delinquency. *Criminology* 28(2):301-323.
Lasley, J.R.
1996 *Using Traffic Barriers to Design Out Crime: A Program Evaluation of LAPD's Operation Cul-De-Sac.* Report to the National Institute of Justice. California State University, Fullerton.
Laub, J.H., and R.J. Sampson
1988 Unraveling families and delinquency: A reanalysis of the Gluecks' data. *Criminology* 26(3):355-380.
1995 The long-term effects of punitive discipline. Pp. 247-258 in *Coercion and Punishment in Long-Term Perspectives*, J. McCord, ed. New York: Cambridge University Press.
Laub, J.H., D.S. Nagin, and et al.
1998 Trajectories of change in criminal offending: Good marriages and the desistance process. *American Sociological Review* 63(2):225-238.
Lawrence, R.
1983 The role of legal counsel in juveniles' understanding of their rights. *Juvenile and Family Court Journal* 34:49-58.
Leonard, K.K., and H. Sontheimer
1995 The role of race in juvenile justice in Pennsylvania. Pp. 98-127 in *Minorities in Juvenile Justice*, K.K. Leonard, C.E. Pope, and W.H. Feyerherm, eds. Thousand Oaks, CA: Sage Publications, Inc.
Lepper, M.R., S. Sethi, D. Dialdin, and M. Drake
1997 Intrinsic and extrinsic motivation: A developmental perspective. *Developmental Psychopathology: Perspectives on Adjustment, Risk, and Disorder*, S.S. Luthar, J.A. Burack, D. Cicchetti, and J.R. Weisz, eds. New York: Cambridge University Press.
Lepper, M.R.
1983 Social-control processes and the internalization of social values: An attributional perspective. Pp. 294-330 in *Social Cognition and Social Development*, E.T. Higgins, D.N. Ruble, and W.W. Hartup, eds. New York: Cambridge University Press.
Lerman, P.
1977 Discussion of differential selection of juveniles for detention. *Journal of Research in Crime and Delinquency* 14(2):166-172.
Lester, B.M., E.K. Emory, S. Hoffman, and D.V. Eitzman
1976 A multivariate study of the effects of high-risk factors on performance on the Brazelton Neonatal Assessment Scale. *Child Development* 47:515-517.
Levitt, S.D.
1998 Juvenile crime and punishment. *Journal of Political Economy* 106(6):1156-1185.
Lewis, D.O., J.H. Pincus, R. Lovely, E. Spitzer, and E. Moy
1987 Biopsychosocial characteristics of matched samples of delinquents and non-delinquents. *Journal of the American Academy of Child and Adolescent Psychiatry* 26:744-752.

Lewis, D.O., S.S. Shanok, R.J. Cohen, M. Kligfeld, and G. Frisone
  1980 Race bias in the diagnosis and disposition of violent adolescents. *American Journal of Psychiatry* 137(10):1211-1216.
Lincoln, S.B.
  1976 Juvenile referral and recidivism. Pp. 321-328 in *Back on the Street: Diversion of Juvenile Offenders*, R.M. Carter and M.W. Klein, eds. Englewood Cliffs, NJ: Prentice-Hall.
Lipsey, M.W.
  1992 Juvenile delinquency treatment: A meta-analytic inquiry into the variability of effects. *Meta-Analysis of Explanation: A Casebook*, T. Cook and et al., eds. New York: Russell Sage Foundation Press.
  1995 What do we learn from 400 research studies on the effectiveness of treatment with juvenile delinquents. Pp. 63-78 in *What Works: Reducing Reoffending: Guidelines From Research and Practice*, J. McGuire, ed. New York: John Wiley & Sons.
Lipsey, M.W., and D.B. Wilson
  1998 Effective intervention for serious juvenile offenders: A synthesis of research. Pp. 313-345 in *Serious and Violent Juvenile Offenders: Risk Factors and Successful Interventions*, R. Loeber and D.P. Farrington, eds. Thousand Oaks, CA: Sage.
Lipsey, M.W., and J.H. Derzon
  1998 Predictors of violent or serious delinquency in adolescence and early adulthood: A synthesis of longitudinal research. Pp. 86-105 in *Serious and Violent Juvenile Offenders: Risk Factors and Successful Interventions*, R. Loeber and D. Farrington, eds. Thousand Oaks, CA: Sage.
Liska, A.E., and M.D. Reed
  1985 Ties to conventional institutions and delinquency: Estimating reciprocal effects. *American Sociological Review* 50(August):547-560.
Liska, A.E., and M. Tausig
  1979 Theoretical interpretations of social class and racial differentials in legal decision-making for juveniles. *Sociological Quarterly* 20(2):197-207.
Lockwood, D., A.E. Pottieger, and J.A. Inciardi
  1995 Crack use, crime by crack users, and ethnicity. *Ethnicity, Race, and Crime: Perspectives Across Time and Place.*, D.F. Hawkins, ed. Albany, NY: State University of New York Press.
Loeber, R.
  1988 Behavioral precursors and accelerators of delinquency. Pp. 51-67 in *Explaining Delinquency*, W. Buikhuisen and S.A. Mednick, eds. Leiden, Holland: Brill.
Loeber, R., and D. Hay
  1997 Key issues in the development of aggression and violence from childhood to early adulthood. *Annual Review of Psychology* 48:371-410.
Loeber, R., and K. Keenan
  1994 Interaction between conduct disorder and its comorbid conditions: Effects of age and gender. *Clinical Psychology Review* 14:497-523.
Loeber, R., and M. Stouthamer-Loeber
  1986 Family factors as correlates and predictors of juvenile conduct problems and delinquency. Pp. 29-149 in *Crime and Justice*, M. Tonry, N. Morris, et al., eds. Chicago: University of Chicago Press.
Loeber, R., D.P. Farrington, M. Stouthamer-Loeber, and Van Kammen
  1998a *Antisocial Behavior and Mental Health Problems: Explanatory Factors in Childhood and Adolescence.* Mahwah, NJ: Lawrence Erlbaum.

Loeber, R., D.P. Farrington, and D.A. Waschbusch
　1998b Serious and violent juvenile offenders. Pp. 13-29 in *Serious and Violent Juvenile Offenders: Risk Factors and Successful Interventions*, R. Loeber and D.P. Farrington, eds. Thousand Oaks, CA: Sage.
Loeber, R., D.P. Farrington, M. Stouthamer-Loeber, T.E. Moffitt, and A. Caspi
　1998c The development of male offending: Key findings from the first decade of the Pittsburgh Youth Study. *Studies on Crime and Crime Prevention* 7(2):141-172.
Loftin, C.
　1986 The validity of robbery-murder classifications in Baltimore. *Violence and Victims* 1:191-204.
Loney, J., J. Kramer, and R.S. Milich
　1982 The hyperactive child grows up: Predictors of symptoms, delinquency, and achievement at follow-up. Pp. 381-415 in *Psychosocial Aspects of Drug Treatment for Hyperactivity*, K.D. Gadow and J. Loney, eds. Boulder, CO: Westview.
Lundman, R.J.
　1993 *Prevention and Control of Delinquency*. New York: Oxford University Press.
Lundman, R.J., E. Sykes, and J.P. Clark
　1978 Police control of juveniles: A replication. *Journal of Research in Crime and Delinquency* 15(January):74-91.
Luntz, B., and C.S. Widom
　1994 Antisocial personality disorder in abused and neglected children grown up. *American Journal of Psychiatry* 151:670-674.
Lynam, D., T.E. Moffitt, and M. Stouthamer-Loeber
　1993 Explaining the relationship between IQ and delinquency: Class, race, test motivation, school failure, or self control? *Journal of Abnormal Psychology* 102:187-196.
Macallair, D., and M. Males
　1998 The Impact of Juvenile Curfew Laws in California. Justice Policy Institute, San Francisco, Calif. Available online: http://www.cjcj.org/curfew.html [1998 June 25].
Maccoby, E.E.
　1958 Effects upon children of their mothers' outside employment. *National Manpower Council, Work in the Lives of Married Women*. New York: Columbia University Press.
　1964 Effects of the mass media. Pp. 323-348 in *Review of Child Development Research*, M.L. Hoffman and L.W. Hoffman, eds. New York: Russell Sage Foundation.
　1980 *Social Development*. New York: Harcourt Brace Jovanovich.
MacKenzie, D.L.
　1997 Criminal justice and crime prevention. Pp. 9,1-9,76 in *Preventing Crime: What Works, What Doesn't, What's Promising*, L.W. Sherman, D. Gottfredson, D. MacKenzie, J. Eck, P. Reuter, S. Bushway, and University of Maryland Department of Criminology and Criminal Justice, eds. Washington, DC: U.S. Department of Justice.
Magnusson, D., and L.R. Bergman
　1990 A pattern approach to the study of pathways from childhood to adulthood. Pp. 101-115 in *Straight and Devious Pathways From Childhood to Adulthood*, L. Robins and M. Rutter, eds. Cambridge, UK: Cambridge University Press.
Maguin, E., and R. Loeber
　1996 Academic performance and delinquency. Pp. 145-264 in *Crime and Justice: A Review of Research, Volume 20*, M. Tonry, ed. Chicago: University of Chicago Press.

Maguire, K., and A.L. Pastore, eds.
  1999 *Sourcebook of Criminal Justice Statistics,* 1994-1998 Annual Editions (on CD Rom). NCJ-178912. Bureau of Justice Statistics. Washington, D.C.: U.S. Department of Justice.
  1998 Sourcebook of Criminal Justice Statistics 1998. *U.S. Department of Justice, Bureau of Justice Statistics.* Washington, DC: USGPO, 1999

Maltz, M.D.
  1999 *Bridging Gaps in Police Crime Data.* Bureau of Justice Statistics NCJ 176365. September. Washington, DC: U.S. Department of Justice.

Mannuzza, S., R.G. Klein, A. Bessler, P. Malloy, and M. LaPadula
  1993 Adult outcome of hyperactive boys. Educational achievement, occupational rank, and psychiatric status. *Archives of General Psychiatry* 50:565-576.

Mannuzza, S., R.G. Klein, N. Bonagura, P. Malloy, T.L. Giampino, and D.A. Addalli
  1991 Hyperactive boys almost grown up. Replications of psychiatric status. *Archives of General Psychiatry* 48:77-84.

Marshall, T.F., and S. Merry
  1990 *Crime and Accountability: Victim Offender Mediation in Practice.* London: The Home Office.

Massey, D.S.
  2000 Residential segregation and neighborhood conditions in U.S. metropolitan areas. *America Becoming: Racial Trends and Their Consequence,* National Research Council. Washington, D.C.: National Academy Press.

Massey, D.S., and N.A. Denton
  1993 *American Apartheid: Segregation and the Making of the Underclass.* Cambridge, MA: Harvard University Press.

Mastrofski, S.D., W.E. Worden, and J.B. Snipes
  1995 Law enforcement in a time of community policing. *Criminology* 33(November):539-563.

Matsueda, R.L., and K. Heimer
  1987 Race, family structure, and delinquency: A test of differential association and social control theories. *American Sociological Review* 52(December):826-840.

Mauer, M.
  1997 Americans Behind Bars: U.S. and International Use of Incarceration, 1995. Washington, DC: The Sentencing Project.

Maughan, B., and M. Lindelow
  1997 Secular change in psychosocial risks: The case of teenage motherhood. *Psychological Medicine* 27:1129-1144.

Maxfield, M.G.
  1989 Circumstances in supplementary homicide reports: Variety and validity. *Criminology* 26(4):123-155.
  1999 The National Incidence-Based Reporting System: Research and policy applications. *Journal of Quantitative Criminology* 15(2):119-149.

Maxfield, M.G., and C.S. Widom
  1996 The cycle of violence: Revisited 6 years later. *Archives of Pediatric and Adolescent Medicine* 150:390-395.

Maxfield, M.G., B.L. Weiler, and C.S. Widom
  2000 Comparing self-reports and official records of arrests. *Journal of Quantitative Criminology* 16(1):87-110.

Maxson, C.L., M.A. Gordon, and M.W. Klein
  1985 Differences between gang and non-gang homicides. *Criminology* 23:209-222.

Mayer, J.P., L.K. Gensheimer, W.S. Davidson II, and R. Gottschalk
    1986   Social learning treatment within juvenile justice: A meta-analysis of the impact in
           the natural environment. Pp. 24-38 in *Youth Violence Program and Prospects*, S.J.
           Apter and A. Goldstein, eds. Elmsford: Pergamon Press.
Mayer, G.R., T.W. Butterworth, M. Nafpaktitis, and B. Sulzer-Azaroff
    1983   Preventing school vandalism and improving discipline: A three-year study. *Jour-
           nal of Applied Behavior Analysis* 16:355-369.
Mayhew, P., and P. White
    1997   The 1996 International Crime Victimisation Survey. *Research Findings, No. 57.*
           London: Home Office Research and Statistics Directorate.
Maynard, R.A.
    1997   *Kids Having Kids: Economic Costs and Social Consequences of Teen Pregnancy.* Wash-
           ington, DC: Urban Institute Press.
McBride, D.C., C.J. VanderWaal, Y.M. Terry, and H. VanBuren
    1999   *Breaking the Cycle of Drug Use Among Juvenile Offenders*, November, National Insti-
           tute of Justice.   NCJ 179273. Washington, DC: U.S. Department of Justice.
           Online only. Available: http://www.ojp.usdoj.gov/nij/pubs-sum/179273.htm
           (Accessed 1/12/00).
McCarthy, B.R., and B.L. Smith
    1986   The conceptualization of discrimination in the juvenile justice process: The im-
           pact of administrative factors and screening decisions on juvenile court disposi-
           tions. *Criminology* 24(1):41-64.
McCord, J.
    1978   A thirty-year follow-up of treatment effects. *American Psychologist* 33:284-289.
    1979   Some child-rearing antecedents of criminal behavior in adult men. *Journal of
           Personality and Social Psychology* 37:1477-1486.
    1981   Consideration of some effects of a counseling program. Pp. 394-405 in *New Direc-
           tions in Rehabilitation of Criminal Offenders*, S.E. Martin, L.B. Sechrest, and R.
           Redner, eds. Washington, DC: National Academy Press.
    1982   A longitudinal view of the relationship between paternal absence and crime. Pp.
           113-128 in *Abnormal Offenders, Delinquency and the Criminal Justice System*, J. Gunn
           and D.P. Farrington, eds. Chichester, England: Wiley.
    1983   A forty year perspective on effects of child abuse and neglect. *Child Abuse and
           Neglect* 7:265-270.
    1990   Getting a Handle on Co-offending and Criminal Careers. Paper presented at the
           Criminal Careers and the Control of Crime Conference, Rutgers University,
           Newark, New Jersey, July 26-27.
    1991   The cycle of crime and socialization practices. *The Journal of Criminal Law and
           Criminology* 82(1):211-228.
    1992   The Cambridge-Somerville Study: A pioneering longitudinal experimental study
           of delinquency prevention. Pp. 196-206 in *Preventing Antisocial Behavior: Inter-
           ventions from Birth through Adolescence*, J. McCord and R.E. Tremblay, eds. New
           York: Guilford Press.
    1997a He did it because he wanted to... Pp. 1-43 in *Motivation and Delinquency, Volume
           44 of the Nebraska Symposium on Motivation*, D.W. Osgood, ed. Lincoln, NE: Uni-
           versity of Nebraska Press.
    1997b On discipline. *Psychological Inquiry* 8(3):215-217.
    1997c Placing American urban violence in context. Pp. 78-115 in *Violence and Childhood
           in the Inner City*, J. McCord, ed. New York: Cambridge University Press.
    1999   Understanding childhood and subsequent crime. *Aggressive Behavior* 25(4):241-
           253.

2000 Developmental trajectories and intentional actions. *Journal of Quantitative Criminology* 16(2):237-253.

2001 Alcohol and dangerousness. Pp. 195-215 in *Clinical Assessment of Dangerousness: Empirical Contributions*, G.F. Pinard and L. Pagani, eds. Cambridge, England: Cambridge University Press.

McCord, J., and K. Conway

2000 Unpacking Age, Co-offending, and Crime Relationships. Paper presented at the annual meeting of the American Society of Criminology, San Francisco, CA, November 15-18.

McCord, J., and M. Ensminger

1997 Multiple risks and comorbidity in an African American population. *Criminal Behavior and Mental Health* 7:339-352.

In Racial discrimination and violence: A longitudinal perspective. *Violent Crimes:*
press *The Nexus of Ethnicity, Race, and Class*, D. Hawkins, ed. New York: Cambridge University Press.

McCord, J., R.E. Tremblay, F. Vitaro, and L. Desmarais-Gervais

1994 Boys' disruptive behavior, school adjustment, and delinquency: The Montreal Prevention Experiment. *International Journal of Behavioral Development* 17:739-752.

McFadden, A., G. March, B. Price, and Y. Hwang

1992 A study of race and gender bias in the punishment of school children. *Education and Treatment of Children* 15:140-146.

McLloyd, V.C.

1990 The impact of economic hardship on black families and children: Psychological distress, parenting, and socioemotional development. *Child Development* 61:311-346.

McManus, M., N.E. Alessi, W.L. Grapentine, and A. Brickman

1984a Psychiatric disturbance in serious delinquents. *Journal of the American Academy of Child and Adolescent Psychiatry* 23:602-615.

McManus, M., A. Brickman, N.E. Alessi, and W.L. Grapentine

1984b Borderline personality in serious delinquents. *Comprehensive Psychiatry* 25:446-454.

McPartland, J.M., and S.M. Nettles

1991 Using community adults as advocates or mentors for at-risk middle school students: A two-year evaluation of Project RAISE. *American Journal of Education* 99:568-586.

Mecartney, C.A., M.B. Styles, and K.V. Morrow

1994 *Building Relationships with Youth in Program Settings: Findings from Two Pilot Programs*. Philadelphia: Public/Private Ventures.

Messner, S.F., L.E. Raffalovich, and R. McMillan

2000 Macroeconomic deprivation and changes in juvenile arrest rates, 1968-1998: A national time-series analysis. Seventieth Annual Meeting of the Eastern Sociological Society, Baltimore, MD, March 2-5.

Miethe, T.D., and C.A. Moore

1986 Racial differences in criminal processing: The consequences of model selection on conclusions about differential treatment. *Sociological Quarterly* 27(2):217-237.

Miller, M.L., J.A. Chiles, and V.E. Barnes

1982 Suicide attempters within a delinquent population. *Journal of Consulting and Clinical Psychology* 50:491-498.

Miller, P., and N. Eisenberg

1988 The relation of empathy to aggression and externalizing/antisocial behavior. *Psychological Bulletin* 103:324-344.

Miller, W.B.
   1982   Gangs, groups, and youth crime. Pp. 311-328 in *Juvenile Delinquency: A Book of Readings*, R. Giallarnbardo, ed. New York: John Wiley and Sons.
Minor, K.L., and H.P. Elrod
   1990   The effects of a multi-faceted intervention on the offense activities of juvenile probationers. *Journal of Offender Counseling, Service and Rehabilitation* 15(2):87-108.
Mischel, W., Y. Shoda, and M.L. Rodriguez
   1989   Delay of gratification in children. *Science* 244:933-938.
Moffitt, T.E.
   1990   The neuropsychology of delinquency: A critical review of theory and research. Pp. 99-169 in *Crime and Justice, Volume 12*, N. Morris and M. Tonry, eds. Chicago: University of Chicago Press.
   1993   Adolescence-limited and life-course-persistent antisocial behavior: A developmental taxonomy. *Psychological Review* 100(4):674-701.
   1997   Neuropsychology, antisocial behavior, and neighborhood context. Pp. 116-170 in *Violence and Childhood in the Inner City*, J. McCord, ed. Cambridge, UK: Cambridge University Press.
Moffitt, T.E., D. Lynam, and P.A. Silva
   1994   Neuropsychological tests predict persistent male delinquency. *Criminology* 32:101-124.
Moore, J.
   1978   *Homeboys*. Philadelphia: Temple University Press.
   1991   *Going Down to the Barrio: Homeboys and Homegirls in Change*. Philadelphia: Temple University Press.
Moore, M.H.
   1995   Public health and criminal justice approaches to prevention. Pp. 237-262 in *Crime and Justice: A Review of Research. Building a Safer Society: Strategic Approaches to Crime Prevention.*, M. Tonry and D.P. Farrington, eds. Chicago: University of Chicago Press.
Moore, M.H., and S. Wakeling
   1997   Juvenile justice: Shoring up the foundations. Pp. 253-301 in *Crime and Justice, Vol. 22*, M. Tonry, ed. Chicago: University of Chicago Press.
Morrison, G.M., and B. D'Incau
   1997   The web of zero-tolerance: Characteristics of students who are recommended for expulsion from school. *Education and Treatment of Children* 20(3):316-335.
Nagin, D.S., G. Pogarsky, and D.P. Farrington
   1997   Adolescent mothers and the criminal behavior of their children. *Law and Society Review* 31(1):137-162.
Nagin, D., and R.E. Tremblay
   1999   Trajectories of boys' physical aggression, opposition, and hyperactivity on the path to physically violent and non-violent juvenile delinquency. *Child Development* 70(5):1181-1196.
National Institute of Drug Abuse
   1991   *National Household Survey on Drug Abuse: Population Estimates.*, National Institute of Drug Abuse. Rockville, MD: National Institute on Drug Abuse, U.S. Department of Health and Human Services.
National Institute of Justice
   1999   *1998 Annual Report on Drug Use Among Adult and Juvenile Arrestees*, April. NCJ 175656. Washington, DC: U.S. Department of Justice.

National Research Council
  1982 *Neither Angels Nor Thieves: Studies in Deinstitutionalization of Status Offenders*, J.F. Handler and J. Zatz, eds. Panel on the Deinstitutionalization of Children and Youth Assembly of Behavioral and Social Sciences. Washington, DC: National Academy Press.
  1986 *Criminal Careers and Career Criminals*, A. Blumstein, J. Cohen, J.A. Roth, and C.A. Visher, eds. Washington, DC: National Academy Press.
  1993a *Losing Generations: Adolescents in High Risk Settings.* Panel on High Risk Youth, Commission on Behavioral and Social Sciences and Education. Washington, DC: National Academy Press.
  1993b *Understanding and Preventing Violence.* Panel on the Understanding and Control of Violent Behavior. A.J. Reiss, Jr., and J.A. Roth, eds. Commission on Behavioral and Social Sciences and Education. Washington, DC: National Academy Press.
  1998 *Violence in Families: Assessing Prevention and Treatment Programs*, R. Chalk and P.A. King, eds. Committee on the Assessment of Family Violence Interventions, Commission on Behavioral and Social Sciences and Education and Institute of Medicine. Washington, DC: National Academy Press.
National Youth Gang Center
  1997 *The 1995 National Youth Gang Survey*, Office of Juvenile Justice and Delinquency Prevention. Washington, DC: U.S. Department of Justice.
Needels, K.
  1996 Go directly to jail and do not collect? A long-term study of recidivism, employment, and earnings patterns among prisons releasees. *Journal of Research in Crime and Delinquency* 33:471-496.
Neimeyer, M., and D. Shichor
  1996 A preliminary study of a large victim offender reconciliation program. *Federal Probation* 60(3):30-34.
The New York Times
  1998 Louisiana boys' prison is epitome of neglect and abuse. By F. Butterfield. *The New York Times* July 15.
Oakes, J.
  1987 Tracking in secondary schools: A contextualist perspective. *Educational Psychologist* 22:129-153.
Obeidallah, D.A., and F.J. Earls
  1999 Adolescent girls: The role of depression in the development of delinquency. *NIJ Research Preview*, July, National Institute of Justice, Office of Justice Programs. Washington, DC: U.S. Department of Justice.
O'Donnell, C.R., T. Lydgate, and W.S.O. Fo
  1979 The buddy system: Review and follow-up. Child Behavior Therapy 1(2):161-169.
Office of Juvenile Justice and Delinquency Prevention
  1997 *OJJDP Guide to Good Juvenile Detention Practice.* Washington, DC: U.S. Department of Justice.
Office of Juvenile Justice and Delinquency Prevention
  1998 Guide for implementing the balanced and restorative justice model. *OJJDP Report*, December, Office of Juvenile Justice and Delinquency Prevention, Office of Justice Programs. NCJ 167887. Washington, D.C.: U.S. Department of Justice.
Offord, D.R.
  1982 Family backgrounds of male and female delinquents. Pp. 129-151 in *Abnormal Offenders: Delinquency and the Criminal Justice System*, J. Gunn and D.P. Farrington, eds. Chichester, England: Wiley.

Offord, D.R., R.J. Adler, and M.H. Boyle
  1986   Prevalence and sociodemographic correlates of conduct disorder. *American Journal of Social Psychiatry* 4(272-278).
Olds, D.L.
  1998   Prenatal and infancy home visitation by nurses. Book seven in *Blueprints for Violence Prevention*, D.S. Elliott, ed. Boulder, CO: Center for the Study and Prevention of Violence, University of Colorado.
Olds, D.L., J. Eckenrode, C.R. Jr. Henderson, H. Kitzman, J. Powers, R. Cole, K. Sidora, P. Morris, L.M. Pettitt, and D. Luckey
  1997a Long-term effects of home visitation on maternal life course and child abuse and neglect: Fifteen-year follow-up of a randomized trial. *Journal of the American Medical Association* 278:637-643.
Olds, D.L., H. Kitzman, R. Cole, and J. Robinson
  1997b Theoretical foundations of a program of home visitation for pregnant women and parents of young children. *Journal of Community Psychology* 25:9-25.
Olds, D., C.R. Henderson, Jr., R. Cole, J. Eckenrode, H. Kitzman, D. Luckey, L. Pettitt, K. Sidora, P. Morris, and J. Powers
  1998   Long-term effects of Nurse Home Visitation on children's criminal and antisocial behavior: 15-year follow-up of a randomized controlled trial. *Journal of the American Medical Association* 280(14):1238-1244.
Olweus, D.
  1991   Bully/victim problems among school children: Basic facts and effects of a school-based intervention program. *The Development and Treatment of Childhood Aggression*, D.J. Pepler and K.H. Rubin, eds. Hillsdale, NJ: Lawrence Erlbaum.
  1992   Bullying among school children: Intervention and prevention. *Aggression and Violence Throughout the Life Span*, R.D. Peters, R.J. McMahon, and V.L. Quinsey, eds. Newbury Park, CA: Sage.
Olweus, D., and F.D. Alsaker
  1991   Assessing change in a cohort-longitudinal study with hierarchical data. *Problems and Methods in Longitudinal Research: Stability and Change*, D. Magnusson, L.R. Bergman, G. Rudinger, and B. Torestad, eds. Cambridge: Cambridge University Press.
Osofsky, J.D., S. Wewers, D.M. Hann, and A.C. Fick
  1993   Chronic community violence: What is happening to our children. *Psychiatry* 56:36-45.
Padilla, F.M.
  1992   *The Gang as an American Enterprise*. New Brunswick, NJ: Rutgers University Press.
Pajer, K.A.
  1998   What happens to "bad" girls? A review of the adult outcomes of antisocial adolescent girls. *American Journal of Psychiatry* 155(7):862-870.
Palmer, T.
  1975   Martinson revisited. *Journal of Research and Crime and Delinquency* 12(2):133-152.
Parent, D.G., V. Lieter, S. Kennedy, L. Livens, D. Wentworth, and S. Wilcox
  1994   *Conditions of Confinement: Juvenile Detention and Corrections Facilities*, Office of Juvenile Justice and Delinquency Prevention. NCJ 145793. Washington, DC: U.S. Department of Justice.
Patterson, G.R.
  1976   The aggressive child: Victim and architect of a coercive system. Pp. 267-316 in *Behavior Modification and Families: Vol. 1. Theory and Research*, E.J. Marsh, L.C. Handy, and L.A. Hamerlynck, eds. New York: Brunner/Mazel.

1995   Coercion as a basis for early age of onset for arrest. Pp. 81-105 in *Coercion and Punishment in Long-Term Perspectives*, J. McCord, ed. New York: Cambridge University Press.

Patterson, G.R., and K. Yoerger
1997   A developmental model for late-onset delinquency. Pp. 119-177 in *Motivation and Delinquency*, D.W. Osgood, ed. Lincoln, NE: University of Nebraska Press.

Patterson, G.R., D. Capaldi, and L. Bank
1991   An early starter model for predicting delinquency. Pp. 139-168 in *The Development and Treatment of Childhood Aggression*, D.J. Pepler and K.H. Rubin, eds. Hillsdale, NJ: Lawrence Erlbaum.

Patterson, G.R., T.J. Dishion, and L. Bank
1984   Family interaction: A process model of deviancy training. *Aggressive Behavior* 10:253-267.

Patterson, G.R., J.B. Reid, R.R. Jones, and R.E. Conger
1975   *A Social Learning Approach to Family Intervention: Families With Aggressive Children, Volume 1.* Eugene, OR: Castalia Publishing Company.

Pawlak, E.J.
1977   Differential selection of juveniles for detention. *Journal of Research in Crime and Delinquency* 14(2):152-165.

Pentz, M.A., B.R. Brannon, V.L. Charlin, E.J. Barrett, D.P. MacKinnon, and B.R. Flay
1989a   The power of policy: The relationship of smoking policy to adolescent smoking. *American Journal of Public Health* 79:857-862.

Pentz, M.A., J.H. Dwyer, D.P. MacKinnon, B.R. Flay, W.B. Hansen, E.Y.I. Wang, and C.A. Johnson
1989b   A multi-community trial for primary prevention of adolescent drug abuse: Effects on drug use prevalence. *Journal of the American Medical Association* 261:3529-3266.

Pentz, M.A., D.P. MacKinnon, B.R. Flay, W.B. Hansen, C.A. Johnson, and J.H. Dwyer
1989c   Primary prevention of chronic diseases in adolescence: effects of the Midwestern Prevention Project on tobacco use. *American Journal of Epidemiology* 130:713-724.

Pepler, D.J., and W.M. Craig
1995   A peek behind the fence: Naturalistic observations of aggressive children with remote audiovisual recording. *Developmental Psychology* 31:548-553.

Perry, C.L., S.H. Kelder, and K.-I. Klepp
1994   Community-wide cardiovascular disease prevention in young people: Long-term outcomes of the Class of 1989 Study. *European Journal of Public Health* 4:188-194.

Perry, C.L., C.L. Williams, S. Veblen-Mortenson, T.L. Toomey, K.A. Komro, P.S. Anstien, P.G. McGovern, J.R. Finnegan, J.L. Forster, A.C. Wagenaar, and M. Wolfson
1996   Project Northland: Outcomes of a community-wide alcohol use prevention program during early adolescence. *American Journal of Public Health* 86(7):956-965.

Petersen, R.D., and J. Hagan
1984   Changing conceptions of race: Towards an account of anomalous findings of sentencing research. *American Sociological Review* 49(1):56-70.

Peterson, R.D., L.J. Krivo, and M.A. Harris
2000   Disadvantage and neighborhood crime: Do local institutions matter? *Journal of Research in Crime and Deliquency* 31(1): 31-63.

Petersilia, J.
1997   Probation in the United States: Practices and challenges. *National Institute of Justice Journal* September:2-8.

Petersilia, J., and E.P. Deschenes
  1994 Perceptions of punishment: Inmates and staff rank the severity of prison versus intermediate sanctions. *Prison Journal* 74:306-328.
Petersilia, J., and S. Turner
  1993 Intensive probation and parole. Pp. 281-335 in *Crime and Justice*, vol. 17, M. Tonry, ed. Chicago: University of Chicago Press.
Pettit, G.S., J.E. Bates, K.A. Dodge, and D.W. Meece
  1999 The impact of after-school peer contact on early adolescent externalizing problems is moderated by parental monitoring, perceived neighborhood safety, and prior adjustment. *Child Development* 70(3):768-778.
Petrosino, A., C. Turpin-Petrosino, and J.O. Finckenauer
  2000 Well-meaning programs can have harmful effects! Lessons from experiments of programs such as Scared Straight. *Crime & Delinquency* 46(3):354-379.
Pfeiffer, C.
  1998 Juvenile crime and juvenile violence in European countries. Pp. 255-328 in *Crime and Justice: A Review of Research*, Vol. 23, M. Tonry, ed. Chicago: University of Chicago Press.
Piliavin, I., and S. Briar
  1964 Police encounters with juveniles. *American Journal of Sociology* 70:206-214.
Pinderhughes, H.
  1997 *Race in the Hood: Conflict and Violence Among Urban Youth*. Minneapolis: University of Minnesota Press.
Pinderhughes, H.
  1999 Presentation to the Panel on Juvenile Crime: Treatment, Prevention, and Control. Racial Disparity Workshop. Washington, D.C., 99.
Platt, A.
  1977 *The Child Savers: The Invention of Delinquency*. 2nd edition. Chicago: University of Chicago Press.
Podkopacz, M.R., and B.C. Feld
  1995 Judicial waiver policy and practice: Persistence, seriousness, and race. *Law and Inequality* 14:74-178.
Podkopacz, M.R., and B.C. Feld
  1996 The end of the line: An empirical study of judicial waiver. *Journal of Criminal Law and Criminology* 86(2):449-492.
Pogrebin, M.R., E.D. Poole, and R.M. Regoli
  1984 Constructing and implementing a model juvenile diversion program. *Youth and Society* 15(3):305-324.
Polk, K.
  1975 Schools and the delinquency experience. *Criminal Justice and Behavior* 2:315-338.
Pope, C.E., and W.H. Feyerherm
  1982 Gender bias in juvenile court dispositions. *Social Service Research* 6:1-16.
Poorjak, H., and C. Bockelman
  1973 The impact of community volunteers on delinquency prevention. *Sociology and Sociological Research* 57:335-341.
Poulos, T.M., and S. Orchowsky
  1994 Serious juvenile offenders: Predicting the probability of transfer to criminal court. *Crime and Delinquency* 40(1):3-17.
Poupart, L.M.
  1995 Juvenile justice processing of American Indian youths: Disparity in one rural county. *Minorities in Juvenile Justice*, K.K. Leonard, C.E. Pope, and W.H. Feyerherm, eds. Thousand Oaks, CA: Sage Publications.

Power, T.G., and M.L. Chapieski
1986 Childrearing and impulse control in toddlers: A naturalistic investigation. Developmental Psychology 22(2):271-275.

Poyner, B., and B. Webb
1987 *Successful Crime Prevention: Case Studies.* London: Tavistock Institute of Human Relations.

Pulkkinen, L., and R.E. Tremblay
1992 Patterns of boys' social adjustment in two cultures and at different ages: A longitudinal perspective. *International Journal of Behavioral Development* 15(4):527-553.

Pumariega, A.J., L. Atkins, and et al.
1996 Psychopathology and symptomatology in incarcerated versus hospitalized youth. The 8th Annual Research Conference Proceedings: A System of Care for Children's Mental Health: Expanding the Research Base., Tampa, Florida, University of Florida, Florida Mental Health Institute, Research and Training Center for Children's Mental Health.

Quadrel, M.J., B. Fischhoff, and W. Davis
1993 Adolescent (in)vulnerability. *American Psychologist* 48(2):102-116.

Quinton, D., A. Pickles, et al.
1993 Partners, peers and pathways: Assortative pairing and continuities in conduct disorder. *Development and Psychopathology* 5:763-783.

Quinton, D., and M. Rutter
1988 *Parenting Breakdown: The Making and Breaking of Intergenerational Links.* Aldershot, England: Avebury.

Radecki, C.M., and J. Jaccard
1995 Perceptions of knowledge, actual knowledge, and information search behavior. *Journal of Experimental Social Psychology* 31:107-118.

Raine, A., P. Brennan, and S.A. Mednick
1994 Birth complications combined with early maternal rejection at age 1 year predispose to violent crime at age 18 years. *Archives of General Psychiatry* 53:544-549.
1997 Interaction between birth complications and early maternal rejection in predisposing individuals to adult violence: Specificity to serious, early-onset violence. *American Journal of Psychiatry* 154:1265-1271.

Rausch, S.
1983 Court processing versus diversion of status offenders: A test of deterrence and labeling theories. *Journal of Research in Crime and Delinquency* 20:39-54.

Rebach, H.
1992 Alcohol and drug use among American minorities. *Drugs and Society* 6:23-57.

Reiss, A.J.
1986 Co-offender influences on criminal careers. Pp. 121-160 in *Criminal Careers and Career Criminals, Volume II*, A. Blumstein, J. Cohen, J.A. Roth, and C.A. Visher, eds. Washington, DC: National Academy Press.

Reiss, A.J., Jr.
1988 Co-offending and criminal careers. Pp. 117-170 in *Crime and Justice*, vol. 7, N. Morris and M. Tonry, eds. Chicago: University of Chicago Press.

Reiss, A.J., and D.P. Farrington
1991 Advancing knowledge about co-offending: Results from a prospective longitudinal survey of London males. *Journal of Criminal Law and Criminology* 82(2):360-395.

Renouf, A.G., and S. Harter
1990 Low self-worth and anger as components of the depressive experience in young adolescents. *Development and Psychopathology* 2:293-310.

Restoin, A., H. Montagner, D. Rodriguez, J.J. Girardot, D. Laurent, F. Kontar, V. Ullmann, C. Casagrande, and B. Talpain
    1985   Chronologie des comportements de communication et profils de comportement chez le jeune enfant. Pp. 93-130 in *Ethologie Et Developpement De L'Enfant*, R.E. Tremblay, M.A. Provost, and F.F. Strayer, eds. Paris, France: Editions Stock/ Laurence Pernoud.
Rhodes, A.L., and A.J. Reiss
    1969   Apathy, truancy, and delinquency as adaptations to school failure. *Social Forces* 48:12-22.
Richman, N., J. Stevenson, and P.J. Graham
    1982   *Preschool to School: A Behavioral Study.* London: Academic Press.
Richters, J.E., and J.E. Martinez
    1993   The NIMH Community Violence Project: Children as victims of and witnesses to violence. *Psychiatry* 56:7-21.
Roberts, D.J.
    1997   *Implementing the National Incident-Based Reporting System: A Project Status Report*, Bureau of Justice Statistics. Washington, DC: U.S. Department of Justice.
Robin Hood Foundation
    1996   *Kids Having Kids: A Special Report on the Cost of Adolescent Childbearing.* New York: Robin Hood Foundation.
Robins, L.N.
    1974   Deviant Children Grown Up. Huntington, NY: *Krieger*
Robins, L.N.
    1978   Sturdy childhood predictors of adult antisocial behavior: Replications from longitudinal studies. *Psychological Medicine* 8:611-622.
Robinson, C.D.
    1993   The production of black violence in Chicago. Pp. 279-333 in *Crime and Capitalism: Readings in Marxist Criminology*, D.F. Greenberg, ed. Philadelphia: Temple University Press.
Roderick, M.
    1994   Grade retention and school dropout: Investigating the association. *American Educational Research Journal* 31:729-759.
Rojek, D.G., and M.L. Erickson
    1982   Reforming the juvenile justice system: The diversion of status offenders. *Law and Society Review* 16(2):241-264.
Roncek, D.W., and P. Maier
    1991   Bars, blocks, and crime revisited: Linking the theory of routine activities to the empiricism of "hot spots." *Criminology* 29:725-753.
Rosenbaum, D.P., R.L. Flewelling, S.L. Bailey, C.L. Ringwalt, and D.L. Wilkinson
    1994   Cops in the classroom: A longitudinal evaluation of drug abuse resistance education (DARE). *Journal of Research in Crime and Delinquency* 31:3-31.
Rosenbaum, D.P., and G.S. Hanson
    1998   Assessing the effects of school-based drug education: A six-year multilevel analysis of Project D.A.R.E. *Journal of Research in Crime and Delinquency* 35(4):381-412.
Rosenbaum, D.P., D.A. Lewis, and J.A. Grant
    1986   Neighborhood-based crime prevention: Assessing the efficacy of community organization in Chicago. Pp. 109-133 in *Community Crime Prevention: Does It Work?*, D.P. Rosenbaum, ed. Beverly Hills, CA: Sage.
Rosenbaum, J.E.
    1976   The stratification of the socialization process. *American Sociological Review* 40:48-54.

Rosenheim, M.K.
    1983   Juvenile justice: Organization and process. Pp. 969-977 in *Encyclopedia of Crime and Justice, Vol. 3*, S. Kadish, ed. New York: Free Press.

Rotherman, M.J.
    1982   Social skills training with underachievers, disruptive, and exceptional children. *Psychology in the Schools* 19:532-539.

Rowe, D.C., and D.P. Farrington
    1997   The familial transmission of criminal convictions. *Criminology* 35:177-201.

Rowland, R.G.
    1992   An evaluation of the effects of a mentoring program on at-risk students in selected elementary schools in the North East Independent School District (Doctoral dissertation, Texas A&M University). *Dissertation Abstracts International* 52(1A):30.

Russell, K.
    1998   *The Color of Crime: Racial Hoaxes, White Fear, Black Protectionism, Police Harassment, and Other Macroaggressions.* New York: New York University Press.

Rust, B.
    1999   Juvenile jailhouse rocked. *Advocasey* Fall/Winter:1-16. Annie E. Casey Foundation.

Rutter, M.
    1983   School effects on pupil progress: Research findings and policy implications. *Child Development* 54:1-19.

Rutter, M., and H. Giller
    1983   *Juvenile Delinquency: Trends and Perspectives.* Harmondsworth, England: Penguin.

Rutter, M., H. Giller, and A. Hagell
    1998   *Antisocial Behavior by Young People.* New York: Cambridge University Press.

Sameroff, A.J., and J.M. Chandler
    1975   Reproductive risk and the continuum of caretaker casualty. Pp. 187-244 in *Review of Child Development Research*, F.D. Horowitz, E.M. Hetherington, S. Scarr-Salapatek, and G. Siegel, eds. Chicago: University of Chicago Press.

Sampson, R.J.
    1986   The effects of urbanization and neighborhood characteristics on criminal victimization. Pp. 3-25 in *Metropolitan Crime Problems*, R.M. Figlio, S. Kakim, and G.F. Rengert, eds. New York: Criminal Justice Press.
    1987   Urban black violence: The effect of male joblessness and family disruption. *American Journal of Sociology* 93(2):348-382.
    1992   Family management and child development: Insights from social disorganization theory. Pp. 63-93 in *Facts, Frameworks, and Forecasts: Advances in Criminological Theory*, J. McCord, ed. New Brunswick: Transaction Press.
    1997   The embeddedness of child and adolescent development: A community-level perspective on urban violence. *Violence and Childhood in the Inner City*, J. McCord, ed. Cambridge, UK: Cambridge University Press.

Sampson, R.J., and J.B. Groves
    1989   Community structure and crime: Testing social disorganization theory. *American Journal of Sociology* 94:774-802.

Sampson, R.J., and J.L. Lauritsen
    1997   Racial and ethnic disparities in crime and criminal justice in the United States. Pp. 311-374 in *Ethnicity, Crime, and Immigration: Comparative and Cross-National Perspective*, M. Tonry, ed. Volume 21 of *Crime and Justice, A Review of Research.* Chicago: University of Chicago Press.

Sampson, R.J., and J.H. Laub
    1990   Crime and deviance over the life course: The salience of adult social bonds.
           American Sociological Review 55:609-627.
    1993   *Crime in the Making: Pathways and Turning Points Through Life.* Cambridge, MA:
           Harvard University Press.
    1996   Socioeconomic achievement in the life course of disadvantaged men: Military
           service as a turning point, circa 1940-1965. *American Sociological Review* 61:347-
           367.
Sampson, R.J., S.W. Raudenbush, and F. Earls
    1997   Neighborhoods and violent crime: A multilevel study of collective efficacy. *Sci-
           ence* 277:918-924.
Sand, E.A.
    1966   *Contribution a L'Etude Du Developpement De L'Enfant. Aspects Medico-Sociaux et
           Psychologiques.* Bruxelles: Editions de l'Institut de sociologie de l'Unversite libre
           de Bruxelles.
Sanson, A., D. Smart, M. Prior, and F. Oberklaid
    1993   Precursors of hyperactivity and aggression. *Journal of the American Academy of
           Child and Adolescent Psychiatry* 32:1207-1216.
Sarnecki, J.
    1986   *Delinquent Networks.* Stockholm: The National Council for Crime Prevention.
Satterfield, J.M., C.M. Hoppe, and A.M. Schell
    1982   A prospective study of delinquency in 110 adolescent boys with attention deficit
           disorder and 88 normal adolescent boys. *American Journal of Psychiatry* 139:795-
           798.
Schlossman, S.
    1977   *Love and the American Delinquent: The Theory and Practice of "Progressive" Juvenile
           Justice, 1825-1920.* Chicago, IL: University of Chicago Press.
    1983   Juvenile justice: History and philosophy. Pp. 961-969 in *Encyclopedia of Crime and
           Justice, Vol. 3*, S. Kadish, ed. New York: Free Press.
    1989   *The California Experience in American Juvenile Justice: Some Historical Perspectives*,
           Bureau of Criminal Statistics and Special Services, Department of Justice. Sacra-
           mento, CA: State of California.
Schneider, A.L.
    1984a Deinstitutionalization of status offenders: The impact on recidivism and secure
           confinement. *Criminal Justice Abstracts* 16:410-432.
    1984b Divesting status offenses from juvenile court jurisdiction. *Crime and Delinquency*
           30(3):347-370.
    1986   Restitution and recidivism rates of juvenile offenders: Results from four experi-
           mental studies. *Criminology* 24(3):533-552.
Schochet, P.Z., J. Burghardt, and S. Glazerman
    2000   *National Job Corps Study: The Short-Term Impacts of Job Corps on Participants' Em-
           ployment and Related Outcomes. Executive Summary.* Report submitted to the U.S.
           Department of Labor. Mathematica Policy Research, Princeton, NJ. [Online.]
           Available: http://www.mathematica-mpr.com/publications/publications.asp
           Accessed September 14, 2000.
Schuerman, L., and S. Kobrin
    1986   Community careers in crime. Pp. 67-100 in *Communities and Crime*, A.J. Reiss and
           M. Tonry, eds. Chicago: University of Chicago Press.
Schwartz, I.M.
    1989   *(In)Justice for Juveniles.* Lexington, MA: Lexington Books

Schwartz, R., and J. Skolnick
  1964   Two studies of legal stigma. Pp. 103-117 in *The Other Side: Perspectives on Deviance*, H. Becker, ed. New York: Free Press.
Schweinhart, L.J., and D.P. Weikart
  1993   Success by empowerment: The High/Scope Perry Preschool study through age 27. *Young Children* 49(1):54-58.
  1997   *Lasting Differences: The High/Scope Preschool Curriculum Comparison Study Through Age 23.* Ypsilanti, Mich.: High/Scope Press.
Schweinhart, L.L., H.V. Barnes, and D.P. Weikart
  1993   *Significant Benefits. The High/Scope Perry School Study Through Age 27.* Ypsilanti, MI: High/Scope Press.
Schweinhart, L.J., D.P. Weikart, and M.B. Larner
  1986   Consequences of three preschool curriculum models through age 15. *Early Childhood Research Quarterly* 1:15-45.
Sealock, M.D., and S.S. Simpson
  1998   Unraveling bias in arrest decisions: The role of juvenile offender type-scripts. *Justice Quarterly* 15(3):427-457.
Sealock, M.D., D.C. Gottfredson, and C.A. Gallagher
  1995   Addressing Drug Use and Recidivism in Delinquent Youth: An Examination of Residential and Aftercare Treatment Programs. Annual Meeting of the American Society of Criminology, Boston, MA,
  1997   Drug treatment for juvenile offenders: Some good and bad news. *The Journal of Research in Crime and Delinquency* 34(2):210-236.
Seguin, J.R., R.O. Pihl, P.W. Harden, R.E. Tremblay, and B. Boulerice
  1995   Cognitive and neuropsychological characteristics of physically aggressive boys. *Journal of Abnormal Psychology* 104(4):614-624.
Selner-O'Hagan, M.B., D.J. Kindlon, S.J. Buka, S.W. Raudenbush, and F.J. Earls
  1998   *Journal of Child Psychology and Psychiatry and Allied Professions.*
Serbin, L.A., J.M. Cooperman, P.L. Peters, P.M. Lehoux, D.M. Stack, and A.E. Schwartzman
  1998   Intergenerational transfer of psychosocial risk in women with childhood histories of aggression, withdrawal, or aggression and withdrawal. *Developmental Psychology* 34(6):1246-1262.
Shannon, L.W.
  1986   Ecological effects of the hardening of the inner city. Pp. 27-53 in *Metropolitan Crime Patterns*, R.M. Figlio, S. Hakim, and G.F. Rengert, eds. Monsey, NY: Criminal Justice Press.
  1988   *Criminal Career Continuity.* New York: Human Sciences Press.
Shannon, L., J. McKim, J. Curry, and L. Haffner
  1988   *Criminal Career Continuity: Its Social Context.* New York, N.Y.: Human Sciences Press, Inc.
Shaw, C.R.
  1930   *The Jack-Roller: A Delinquent Boy's Own Story.* Chicago: University of Chicago Press.
Shaw, C.R., and H.D. McKay.
  1969   *Juvenile Delinquency and Urban Areas*, revised edition. Chicago: University of Chicago Press.
Shaw, C., and H. McKay
  1942   *Juvenile Delinquency and Urban Areas.* Chicago: University of Chicago Press.

Shelden, R.G.
  1999 Detention diversion advocacy: An evaluation. *Juvenile Justice Bulletin*, Septem-
        ber, Office of Justice Programs, Office of Juvenile Justice and Delinquency Pre-
        vention. Washington, DC: U.S. Department of Justice.
Sheley, J.F., and J.D. Wright
  1998 High school youths, weapons, and violence: A national survey. *Research in Brief*,
        October, National Institute of Justice. Washington, DC: U.S. Department of
        Justice.
Shelton, D.
  1998 *Estimates of Emotional Disorder in Detained and Committed Youth in the Maryland
        Juvenile Justice System.* Baltimore: University of Maryland School of Nursing.
Shepard, L.A., and M.L. Smith
  1990 Synthesis of research on grade retention. *Educational Leadership* 47:84-88.
Sherman, L.W.
  1997a Policing for crime prevention. In *Preventing Crime: What Works, What Doesn't,
        What's Promising*, L.W. Sherman, D. Gottfredson, D. MacKenzie, J. Eck, P. Reuter,
        and S. Bushway. Washington, DC: U.S. Department of Justice.
  1997b Family-based crime prevention. In *Preventing Crime: What Works, What Doesn't,
        What's Promising*, L.W. Sherman, D. Gottfredson, D. MacKenzie, J. Eck, P. Reuter,
        and S. Bushway. Washington, DC: U.S. Department of Justice.
Short, J.F.
  1997 *Poverty, Ethnicity, and Violent Crime.* Boulder, CO: Westview Press.
Short, J.F., Jr., and F.L. Strodtbeck
  1965 *Group Process and Gang Delinquency.* Chicago: University of Chicago Press.
Sickmund, M., H. Snyder, and E. Poe-Yamagata
  1997 *Juvenile Offenders and Victims: 1997 Update on Violence.* Washington, D.C.: Office
        of Juvenile Justice and Delinquency Prevention, U.S. Department of Justice.
Sickmund, M., A.L. Stahl, T.A. Finnegan, H.N. Snyder, and J.A. Butts
  1998 Juvenile Court Statistics 1995. May, Office of Juvenile Justice and Delinquency
        Prevention. Washington, DC: U.S. Department of Justice.
Sigler, R.T., and G.B. Talley
  1995 Drug Abuse Resistance Training program effectiveness. *American Journal of Police*
        14(3/4):111-121.
Simcha-Fagan, O., and J.E. Schwartz
  1986 Neighborhood and delinquency: An assessment of contextual effects. *Criminol-
        ogy* 24(4):667-699.
Simmons, R., L. Whitbeck, R. Conger, and K. Conger
  1991 Parenting factors, social skills, and value commitments as precursors to school
        failure, involvement with deviant peers, and delinquent behavior. *Journal of Youth
        and Adolescence* 20:645-664.
Simons, R.L., C. Wu, R.D. Conger, and F.O. Lorenz
  1994 Two routes to delinquency: Differences between early and late starters in the
        impact of parenting and deviant peers. *Criminology* 32:247-275.
Singer, M., T.M. Anglin, L.Y. Song, and L. Lunghofer
  1995 Adolescents' exposure to violence and associated symptoms of psychological
        trauma. *Journal of the American Medical Association* 273:477-492.
Singer, S., and D. McDowall
  1988 Criminalizing delinquency: The deterrent effects of the New York Juvenile
        Offender Law. *Law and Society Review* 22:521-535.

Slaby, R.G.

1997 Development of psychological mediators of violence in urban youth. Pp. 171-206 in *Violence and Childhood in the Inner City*, J. McCord, ed. New York: Cambridge University Press.

Slavin, R.E.

1987 Ability grouping and student achievement in elementary schools: A best-evidence synthesis. *Review of Educational Research* 57:293-336.

1990 *Achievement Effects of Ability Grouping in Secondary Schools: A Best Evidence Synthesis*. Madison: Wisconsin Center for Education Research.

Slicker, E.K., and D.J. Palmer

1993 Mentoring at-risk high school students: Evaluation of a school-based program. *School Counselor* 40:327-334.

Smith, B.

1998 Children in custody: 20-year trends in juvenile detention, correctional, and shelter facilities. *Crime and Delinquency* 44(4):526-543.

Smith, C., and T.P. Thornberry

1995 The relationship between childhood maltreatment and adolescent involvement in delinquency. *Criminology* 33:451-481.

Smith, M.L., and L.A. Shepard

1987 What doesn't work: Explaining policies of retention in the early grades. *Phi Delta Kappan* 69:129-134.

Smith, D.A., and C.A. Visher

1981 Street-level justice: Situational determinants of police arrest decisions. *Social Problems* 29(2):167-177.

Smith, D.A., C.A. Visher, and L.A. Davidson

1984 Equity and discretionary justice: The influence of race on police arrest decisions. *Journal of Criminal Law and Criminology* 75(1):234-249.

Snyder, H.N.

1998 Juvenile arrests 1997. *Juvenile Justice Bulletin*. December. Office of Juvenile Justice and Delinquency Prevention, Office of Justice Programs. Washington, D.C.: U.S. Department of Justice.

1999a Juvenile arrests 1998. *Juvenile Justice Bulletin*. December. Office of Justice Programs, Office of Juvenile Justice and Delinquency Prevention. NCJ 179064. Washington, DC: U.S. Department of Justice.

1999b Juvenile Male and Female Arrest Rates: 1981-1997. Unpublished data. National Center for Juvenile Justice, Pittsburgh, PA.

Snyder, H.N., and T. Finnegan

1999 Easy Access to FBI Arrest Statistics 1994-1997 (data presentation package). Pittsburgh, PA: National Center for Juvenile Justice. [Online]. Available: http://www.ojjdp.ncjrs.org/facts/ezaccess.html#UCR Accessed June 19, 2000.

Snyder, H.N., and M. Sickmund

1999 *Juvenile Offenders and Victims: 1999 National Report*, September, Office of Juvenile Justice and Delinquency Prevention. NCJ 178257. Washington, DC: U.S. Department of Justice.

Snyder, H.N., M. Sickmund, and E. Poe-Yamagata

1996 *Juvenile Offenders and Victims: 1996 Update on Violence*. Washington D.C.: Office of Juvenile Justice and Delinquency Program, U.S. Department of Justice.

Sontheimer, H., and L. Goodstein

1993 An evaluation of juvenile intensive aftercare probation: Aftercare versus system response effects. *Justice Quarterly* 10(2):197-227.

Spencer, M.B.
    1999 Social and cultural influences on school adjustment: The application of an iden-
          tity-focused cultural ecological perspective. *Educational Psychologist* 34(1):43-57.
Spergel, I.A.
    1995 *The Youth Gang Problem: A Community Approach.* New York: Oxford University
          Press.
Spicer, J.W., and G.D. Hampe
    1975 Kinship interaction after divorce. *Journal of Marriage and the Family* 37:113-119.
Stahl, A.L., M. Sickmund, T.A. Finnegan, H.N. Snyder, R.S. Poole, and N. Tierney
    1999 *Juvenile Court Statistics 1996* . Washington, D.C.: Office of Juvenile Justice and
          Delinquency Prevention.
Stanton, M.D., and W.R. Shadish
    1997 Outcome, attrition, and family-couples treatment for drug abuse: A meta-analysis
          and review of the controlled, comparative studies. *Psychological Bulletin*
          122(2):170-191.
Stattin, H., and I. Klackenberg-Larsson
    1993 Early language and intelligence development and their relationship to future
          criminal behavior. *Journal of Abnormal Psychology* 102(3):369-378.
Stattin, H., and D. Magnusson
    1989 The role of early aggressive behavior in the frequency, seriousness and types of
          later crime. *Journal of Counseling and Clinical Psychiatry* 57:710-718.
Staub, E.
    1979 *Positive Social Behavior and Morality: Socialization and Development, Vol. 2.* New
          York: Academic Press.
Steffensmeier, D., and M.D. Harer
    1987 Is the crime rate really falling? *Journal of Research in Crime and Delinquency* 24:23-
          48.
    1999 Making sense of recent U.S. crime trends, 1980-96/8: Age-composition effects
          and other explanations. *Journal of Research in Crime and Delinquency* 36(3).
Steinberg, L.
    1987 Single parents, stepparents, and the susceptibility of adolescents to antisocial peer
          pressure. *Child Development* 58:269-275.
    2000 Youth violence: Do parents and families make a difference? *National Institute of
          Justice Journal* April:30-38.
Steiner, H., I.G. Garcia, and Z. Mathews
    1997 Posttraumatic stress disorder in incarcerated juvenile delinquents. *Journal of the
          American Academy of Child and Adolescent Psychiatry* 36:357-365.
Stern, M., J.E. Northman, and M.R. Van Slyck
    1984 Father absence and adolescent problem behaviors: Alcohol consumption, drug
          use, and sexual activity. *Adolescence* 14:301-312.
Stone, C.
    1999 Race, crime, and the administration of justice: A summary of the available facts.
          National Institute of Justice Journal (April):26-32.
Stone, W.L., R.D. Bendell, and T.M. Field
    1988 The impact of socioeconomic status on teenage mothers and children who
          received early intervention. *Journal of Applied Developmental Psychology* 9:391-408.
Strassberg, Z., K.A. Dodge, G. Pettit, and J.E. Bates
    1994 Spanking in the home and children's subsequent aggression toward kindergarten
          peers. *Development and Psychopathology* 6(3):445-461.

Strom, K.J.
  2000   *Profile of State Prisoners Under Age 18*, Bureau of Justice Statistics. NCJ 176989. Washington, DC: U.S. Department of Justice.
Stuart, R.B., S. Jayaratne, and T. Tripodi
  1976   Changing adolescent deviant behavior through reprogramming the behavior of parents and teachers: An experimental evaluation. *Canadian Journal of Behavioral Science* 8:132-144.
Sullivan, M.
  1983   Youth crime: New York's two varieties. *New York Affairs* 8:31-48.
  1989   *Getting Paid: Youth Crime and Employment in the Inner City*. Ithaca, NY: Cornell University Press.
  1996   Neighborhood social organization: A forgotten object of ethnographic study? Pp. 205-224 in *Ethnography and Human Development*, R. Jessor, A. Colby, and R.A. Schweder, eds. Chicago: University of Chicago Press.
  1998   Evaluating the effects of community development corporations on conditions and perceptions of safety. *Security Journal* 11:51-60.
  1998   Integrating qualitative and quantitative methods in the study of developmental psychopathology in context. *Development and Psychopathology* 10:377-393.
Suttles, G.D.
  1968   *The Social Order of the Slum: Ethnicity and Territory in the Inner City*. Chicago: University of Chicago Press.
Tanenhaus, D.
  2000   The evolution of waiver in the juvenile court. In *The Changing Borders of Juvenile Justice: Transfer of Adolescents to the Criminal Court*, J. Fagan and F.E. Zimring, eds. Chicago: University of Chicago Press.
Teilmann, K., and P. Landry
  1981   Gender bias in juvenile justice. *Journal of Research in Crime and Delinquency* 18:47-80.
Teplin, L.A., K.M. Abram, and G.M. McClelland
  1996   Prevalence of psychiatric disorders among incarcerated women. I. Pretrial jail detainees. *Archives of General Psychiatry* 53:505-512.
Thompson, P.M., J.N. Gledd, R.P. Woods, D. MacDonald, A.C. Evans, and A.W. Toga
  2000   Growth patterns in the developing brain detected by using continuum mechanical tensor maps. *Nature* 404(6774):190-193.
Thornberry, T.P.
  1998   Membership in youth gangs and involvement in serious and violent offending. Pp. 147-166 in *Serious & Violent Juvenile Offenders: Risk Factors and Successful Interventions*, R. Loeber and D.P. Farrington, eds. Thousand Oaks, CA: Sage.
Thornberry, T.P., D. Huizinga, and R. Loeber
  1995   The prevention of serious delinquency and violence: Implications from the Program of Research on the Causes and Correlates of Delinquency. Pp. 213-237 in *A Sourcebook: Serious, Violent, and Chronic Juvenile Offenders*, J.C. Howell, B. Krisberg, J.D. Hawkins, and J.J. Wilson, eds. Thousand Oaks, CA: Sage.
Thornberry, T.P., M.D. Krohn, A.J. Lizotte, and D. Chard-Wierschem
  1993   The role of juvenile gangs in facilitating delinquent behavior. *Journal of Research in Crime and Delinquency* 30(1):55-87.
Thornberry, T.P., A. Lizotte, M. Krohn, M. Farnsworth, and S. Jang
  1994   Delinquent peers, beliefs, and delinquent behavior: A longitudinal test of interactional theory. *Criminology* 32:47-83.
Thornberry, T., and R.L. Christenson
  1984   Unemployment and criminal involvement: An investigation of reciprocal causal structures. *American Sociological Review* 49:398-411.

Thrasher, F.M.
    1927 *The Gang*. Chicago: University of Chicago Press.
Tierney, J.P., and A.Y. Branch
    1992 *College Students as Mentors for At-Risk Youth: A Study of Six Campus Partners in
          Learning Programs*. Philadelphia: Public/Private Ventures.
Tierney, J.P., J.B. Grossman, and N.L. Resch
    1995 *Making a Difference: An Impact Study of Big Brothers/Big Sisters*. Philadelphia:
          Public/Private Ventures.
Timmons-Mitchell, J., C. Brown, S.C. Schulz, S.E. Webster, L.A. Underwood, and W.E.
Semple
    1997 Comparing the mental health needs of female and male incarcerated juvenile
          delinquents. *Behavioral Sciences and the Law* 15:195-202.
Tittle, C.R., and D.J. Curran
    1988 Contingencies for dispositional disparities in juvenile justice. *Social Forces* 67:23-
          58.
Tolan, P., and N. Guerra
    1998 *What Works in Reducing Adolescent Violence: An Empirical Review of the Field*. Boul-
          der, CO: Center for the Study and Prevention of Violence, University of Colo-
          rado.
Tonry, M.H.
    1995 *Malign Neglect: Race, Crime, and Punishment in America*. New York, NY: Oxford
          University Press.
Tonry, M., L.E. Ohlin, and D.P. Farrington
    1991 *Human Development and Criminal Behavior: New Ways of Advancing Knowledge*.
          New York: Springer-Verlag.
Torbet, P.Mc.
    1996 Juvenile probation: The workhorse of the juvenile justice system. *Juvenile Justice
          Bulletin*, March, Office of Justice Programs, Office of Juvenile Justice and Delin-
          quency Prevention. Washington, DC: U.S. Department of Justice.
Torbet, P., and L. Szymanski
    1998 State Legislative Responses to Violent Juvenile Crime: 1996-97 Update. *Juvenile
          Justice Bulletin*, November, Office of Juvenile Justice and Delinquency Prevention,
          Office of Justice Programs. Washington, D.C.: Office of Juvenile Justice and
          Delinquency Prevention.
Torbet, P., R. Gable, I.H. Hurst, I. Montgomery, L. Szymanski, and D. Thomas
    1996 *State Responses to Serious and Violent Juvenile Crime: Research Report*. Washing-
          ton, D.C.: Office of Juvenile Justice and Delinquency Prevention, U.S. Depart-
          ment of Justice.
Torbet, P.
    1990 *Organization and Administration of Juvenile Services: Probation, Aftercare, and Delin-
          quent Institutions*. Pittsburgh, PA: National Center for Juvenile Justice.
Towbin, A.
    1978 Cerebral dysfunctions related to perinatal organic damage: Clinical neuro-
          pathologic correlations. *Journal of Abnormal Psychology* 87(6):617-635.
Tracy, P.E.
    1987 Race and class differences in official and self-reported delinquency. Pp. 87-121 in
          From Boy to Man, From Delinquency to Crime, M.E. Wolfgang, T.P. Thornberry, and
          R.M. Figlio, eds. Chicago: University of Chicago Press.
Tremblay, R.E.
    1995 Kindergarten behavioral patterns, parental practices, and early adolescent antiso-
          cial behavior. Pp. 139-153 in *Coercion and Punishment in Long Term Perspectives*, J.
          McCord, ed. Cambridge: Cambridge University Press.

2000 The development of aggressive behavior during childhood: What have we learned in the past century? *International Journal of Behavioral Development* 24(2):129-141.

Tremblay, R.E., and W. Craig
1995 Developmental crime prevention. Pp. 151-236 in *Building a Safer Society, Crime and Justice, Vol. 19*, M. Tonry and D.P. Farrington, eds. Chicago: University of Chicago Press.

Tremblay, R.E., B. Boulerice, P. Harden, P. McDuff, D. Perusse, R. Pihl, and M. Zoccolillo
1996a Do children in Canada become more aggressive as they approach adolescence? Pp. 127-137 in *Growing Up in Canada: National Longitudinal Survey of Children and Youth*, Human Resources Development Canada and Statistics Canada, eds. Ottawa: Statistics Canada.

Tremblay, R.E., C. Japel, D. Perusse, M. Boivin, M. Zoccolillo, J. Montplaisir, and P. McDuff
1999a The search for age of "onset" of physical aggression: Rousseau and Bandura revisited. *Criminal Behavior and Mental Health* 9:8-23.

Tremblay, R.E., D. LeMarquand, and F. Vitaro
1999b The prevention of ODD and CD. Pp. 525-555 in *Handbook of Disruptive Behavior Disorders*, H.C. Quay and A.E. Hogan, eds. New York: Kluwer Academic/ Plenum Publishers.

Tremblay, R.E., B. Masse, D. Perron, M. LeBlanc, A.E. Schwartzman, and J.E. Ledingham
1992a Early disruptive behavior, poor school achievement, delinquent behavior and delinquent personality: Longitudinal analyses. *Journal of Consulting and Clinical Psychology* 60:64-72.

Tremblay, R.E., L.C. Masse, L. Pagani, and F. Vitaro
1996b From childhood physical aggression to adolescent maladjustment: The Montreal prevention experiment. Pp. 268-298 in *Preventing Childhood Disorders, Substance Abuse, and Delinquency*, R.D. Peters and R.J. McMahon, eds. Thousand Oaks, CA: Sage.

Tremblay, R.E., L. Pagani-Kurtz, L.C. Mâsse, F. Vitaro, and R.O. Pihl
1995 A bimodal preventive intervention for disruptive kindergarten boys: Its impact through mid-adolescence. *Journal of Consulting and Clinical Psychology* 63(4):560-568.

Tremblay, R.E., R. Pihl, F. Vitaro, and P. Dobkin
1994 Predicting early onset of male antisocial behavior from preschool behavior. *Archives of General Psychiatry* 51:732-739.

Tremblay, R.E., F. Vitaro, L. Bertrand, M. LeBlanc, H. Beauchesne, H. Boileau, and L. David
1992b Parent and child training to prevent early onset of delinquency: The Montreal longitudinal experimental study. Pp. 117-138 in *Preventing Antisocial Behavior: Interventions From Birth Through Adolescence*, J. McCord and R.E. Tremblay, eds. New York: Guilford Press.

Ulmer, J.T., and J.H. Kramer
1996 Court communities under sentencing guidelines: Dilemmas of formal rationality and sentencing disparity. *Criminology* 34(3):383-408.

Umbreit, M.S., and J. Greenwood
1998 *National Survey of Victim Offender Mediation Programs in the U.S.* St. Paul, MN: Center for Restorative Justice and Peacemaking, University of Minnesota. Online. Available: http://ssw.che.umn.edu/rjp/Resources/Documents/UmbGre97.PDF (Accessed 2/1/00).

Umbreit, M.S.
1990 The meaning of fairness to burglary victims. *Criminal Justice, Restitution, and Reconciliation*, B. Galaway and J. Hudson, eds. Monsey, NY: Criminal Justice Press.

Umbreit, M.S., and R.B. Coates
    1992   *Executive Summary: Victim Offender Mediation—An Analysis of Programs in our
            States of the U.S.* St. Paul, MN: Center for Restorative Justice and Peacemaking,
            University of Minnesota. Online. Available: http://sss.che.umn.edu/rjp/
            Resources/Documents/umbcoa92.PDF (Accessed 2/1/00).
    1993   Cross-site analysis of victim offender mediation in four states. *Crime and Delin-
            quency* 39:565-585
U.S. Census Bureau
    1977   *Statistical Abstract of the United States, 1977.* Washington, DC: U.S. Government
            Printing Office.
    1982   *Preliminary Estimates of the Population of the United States, by Age, Sex, and Race:
            1970 to 1981.* Series P-25, No. 917. Washington, D.C. U.S. Department of Com-
            merce.
    1999   *Statistical Abstract of the United States, 1999,* 119th edition. Washington, DC: U.S.
            Government Printing Office.
U.S. Department of Health and Human Services
    1998   *Trends in the Well-Being of America's Children and Youth, 1998.* Washington, D.C.:
            U.S. Government Printing Office.
U.S. General Accounting Office
    1995a   *Juvenile Justice: Juveniles Processed in the Criminal Court and Case Dispositions.*
            GAO/GGD-95-170. U.S. Government Printing Office.
    1995b   *Juvenile Justice: Representation Rates Varied as did Counsel's Impact on Court Out-
            comes.* GAO/GGD-95-139. U.S. Government Printing Office.
    1995c   *Juvenile Justice: Minimal Gender Bias Occurred in Processing Noncriminal Juveniles.*
            GAO/GGD-95-56. Washington, DC: U.S. General Accounting Office.
Vandell, D.L., and J. Posner
    1999   Conceptualization and measurement of children's after-school environments. Pp.
            167-197 in *Assessment of the Environment Across the Lifespan,* S.L. Friedman and
            T.D. Wachs, eds. Washington, DC: American Psychological Association Press.
Van Waters, M.
    1927   The juvenile court from the child's viewpoint. Pp. 217-237 in *The Child, The Clinic,
            and The Court,* J. Addams, ed. New York: New Republic, Inc.
Vigil, J.D.
    1988   *Barrio Gangs.* Austin: University of Texas Press.
Vigil, J.D., and S.C. Yun
    1990   Vietnamese youth gangs in southern California. Pp. 146-162 in *Gangs in America,*
            R. Huff, ed. Thousand Oaks, CA: Sage.
Vitaro, F., R.E. Tremblay, and W.M. Bukowski
    in   Friends, friendships, and conduct disorders. *Conduct Disorders in Childhood,* J.
    press   Hill and B. Maughan, eds. Cambridge: Cambridge University Press.
Wade, R.C.
    1972   Violence in the cities. Pp. 475-491 in *Cities in American History,* K.T. Jackson and
            S.K. Schultz, eds. New York: Alfred A. Knopf.
Wakschlag, L.S., B.B. Lahey, R. Loeber, S.M. Green, R.A. Gordon, and B.L. Leventhal
    1997   Maternal smoking during pregnancy and the risk of conduct disorder in boys.
            Archives of General Psychiatry 54(7):670-676.
Wallace, R., and D. Wallace
    1990   Origins of public health collapse in New York City: The dynamics of planned
            shrinkage, contagious urban decay and social disintegration. *Bulletin of the New
            York Academy of Medicine* 66:391-434.

Walker, S., C. Spohn, and M. DeLone
1996   *The Color of Justice: Race, Ethnicity, and Crime in America*. Belmont, CA: Wadsworth Publishing Company.

Walmsley, R.
1999   World prison population list. *Research Findings No. 88*.   London: Home Office Research, Development, and Statistics Directorate.

Ward, D., and C. Tittle
1993   Deterrence or labeling: The effects of informal sanctions. *Deviant Behavior* 14:43-64.

Warner, B.D., and G.L. Pierce
1993   Reexamining social disorganization theory using calls to the police as a measure of crime. *Criminology* 31(4):493-517.

Warr, M.
1993   Age, peers, and delinquency. *Criminology* 31:17-40.
1998   Life-course transitions and desistance from crime. *Criminology* 36(2):183-216.

The Washington Post
1999   Top juvenile officials ousted: Maryland probe shows teens abused at boot camps. By D. LeDuc. *The Washington Post* December 16:B1, B4.

Wasserman, G.A., and L. Miller
1998   The prevention of serious and violent juvenile offending.   Pp. 197-247 in *Serious and Violent Juvenile Offenders: Risk Factors and Successful Interventions*, R. R. Loeber and D.P. Farrington, eds. Thousand Oaks, CA: Sage.

Webster-Stratton, C.
1998   Preventing conduct problems in Head Start children. *Journal of Consulting and Clinical Psychology* 66(5):715-730.

Weikart, D.P., and others
1970   *Longitudinal Results of the Ypsilanti Perry Preschool Project. Final Report*. Ypsilanti, MI: High/Scope Press.

Weinberg, K.M., and E.Z. Tronick
1997   Maternal depression and infant maladjustment: A failure of mutual regulation. *The Handbook of Child and Adolescent Psychiatry*, J. Noshpitz, ed. New York: Wiley.

Weitekamp, E. G. M., H.-J. Kerner, and G. Trueg
1999   International Comparison of Juvenile Justice Systems.   Paper prepared for the National Research Council Panel on Juvenile Crime: Prevention, Treatment, and Control.

Wells, L.E., and J.H. Rankin
1991   Families and delinquency: A meta-analysis of the impact of broken homes. *Social Problems* 38:71-93.

Werner, E.E., J.M. Bierman, and F.E. French
1971   *The Children of Kauai: A Longitudinal Study From the Prenatal Period to Age Ten*. Honolulu: University of Hawaii Press.

West, D.J., and D.P. Farrington
1977   *The Delinquent Way of Life*. London, England: Heinemann.

Westbury, B.
1994   The effect of elementary grade retention on subsequent school achievement and ability. *Canadian Journal of Education* 19:241-250.

White, J.L., T.E. Moffitt, A. Caspi, D.J. Bartusch, D.J. Needles, and M. Stouthamer-Loeber
1994   Measuring impulsivity and examining its relationship to delinquency. *Journal of Abnormal Psychology* 103(2):192-205.

White, J.L., T.E. Moffitt, F. Earls, L. Robins, and P.A. Silva
  1990   How early can we tell? Predictors of childhood conduct disorder and adolescent
         delinquency. *Criminology* 28:507-533.
Whyte, W.F.
  1943   *Street Corner Society.* Chicago: University of Chicago Press.
Widom, C.S.
  1989   The cycle of violence. *Science* 244:160-166.
Widom, C.S., and S. Morris
  1997   Accuracy of adult recollections of childhood victimization: Part 2. Childhood
         sexual abuse. *Psychological Assessment* 9(1):34-46.
Wilkinson, D.L., and J. Fagan
  1996   The role of firearms in violence 'scripts': The dynamics of gun events among
         adolescent males. *Law and Contemporary Problems* 59(Winter):55-90.
Williams, J.
  1989   Reducing the disproportionately high frequency of disciplinary actions against
         minority students: An assessment-based approach. *Equity and Excellence* 24:31-
         37.
Wilson, B.J., D. Kinkel, D. Linz, J. Potter, E. Donnerstein, S.L. Smith, E. Blumenthal, and
M. Berry
  1998   Part 1. Violence in television programming overall: University of California,
         Santa Barbara study. Pp. 3-204 in *National Television Violence Study, Part 2*, Uni-
         versity of California at Santa Barbara. Center for Communication and Social
         Policy, ed. Thousand Oaks, Ca: Sage.
Wilson, J.Q.
  1995   Crime and public policy. *Crime*, J.Q. Wilson and J. Petersilia, eds. San Francisco:
         Institute for Contemporary Studies Press.
Wilson, J.Q., and R.J. Herrnstein
  1985   *Crime and Human Nature.* New York: Simon & Schuster.
Wilson, J.Q., and G.L. Kelling
  1982   Broken windows. *Atlantic Monthly* 249(3):29-38.
Wilson, W.J.
  1985   The urban underclass in advanced industrial society. Pp. 129-160 in *The New
         Urban Reality*, P.E. Peterson, ed. Washington, D.C.: The Brookings Institution.
  1987   *The Truly Disadvantaged: The Inner-City, the Underclass, and Public Policy.* Chicago:
         University of Chicago Press.
Winner, L., L. Lanza-Kaduce, D.M. Bishop, and C.E. Frazier
  1997   The transfer of juveniles to criminal court: Reexamining recidivism over the long
         term. *Crime and Delinquency* 43(4):548-563.
Wolfgang, M.E., M. Figlio, and T. Sellin
  1972   *Delinquency in a Birth Cohort.* Chicago: University of Chicago Press.
Worden, R.E., and S.M. Myers
  1999   *Police Encounters With Juvenile Suspects.* Unpublished paper Commissioned by
         the Panel of Juvenile Crime: Prevention, Treatment, and Control..
Wordes, M., and S.M. Jones
  1998   Trends in juvenile detention and steps toward reform. *Crime and Delinquency*
         44(4):544-560.
Wordes, M., and T.S. Bynum
  1995   Policing juveniles: Is there bias against youths of color? Pp. 47-65 in *Minorities in
         Juvenile Justice*, K.K. Leonard, C.E. Pope, and W.H. Feyerherm, eds. Thousand
         Oaks, CA: Sage Publications, Inc.

Wu, S., R. Pink, R. Crain, and O. Moles
1982   Student suspension: A critical reappraisal. *The Urban Review* 14:245-325.

Yamamoto, K., and D.A. Byrnes
1984   Classroom social status, ethnicity, and ratings of stressful events. *Journal of Educational Research* 77(5):283-286.

Yin, R.K.
1989   *Case Study Research: Design and Methods.* Newbury Park, CA: Sage Publications.

Yoshikawa, H.
1994   Prevention as cumulative protection: Effects of early family support and education on chronic delinquency and its risks. *Psychological Bulletin* 115:28-54.

1995   Long-term effects of early childhood programs on social outcomes and delinquency. *The Future of Children* 5(3):51-76.

Zhang, L., J.W. Welte, and W.F. Wieczorek
1999   Youth gangs, drug use, and delinquency. *Journal of Criminal Justice* 27(2):101-109.

Zimring, F.E.
1981   Kids, groups, and crime: Some implications of a well-known secret. *Journal of Criminal Law and Criminology* 72:867-885.

1982   *The Changing Legal World of Adolescence.* New York: Free Press.

1996   Kids, guns, and homicide: Policy notes on an age-specific epidemic. *Law and Contemporary Problems* 59(1):25-37.

1998   *American Youth Violence.* New York: Oxford University Press.

Zingraff, M.T., J. Leiter, K.A. Myers, and M.C. Johnsen
1993   Child maltreatment and youthful problem behavior. *Criminology* 31:173-202.

Zoccolillo, M., A. Pickles, D. Quinton, and M. Rutter
1992   The outcome of conduct disorder: Implications for defining adult personality disorder and conduct disorder. *Psychological Medicine* 22:1-16.

Appendix A

Definition of Offenses Used in Uniform Crime Reporting

The following definitions are taken directly from *Crime in the United States 1997* (Federal Bureau of Investigation, 1998) and are listed in the order that the Federal Bureau of Investigation lists offenses in all reports based on the Uniform Crime Reports. The offenses are broken into Part I, the offenses from which the FBI calculates its Crime Index. These offenses are, therefore, often referred to as index crimes. The first four are the index violent crimes; the second four are the index property crimes. Part II offenses cover the rest of the crimes recorded in the Uniform Crime Reports.

PART I OFFENSES

Criminal homicide (murder and nonnegligent manslaughter): The willful (nonnegligent) killing of one human being by another. Excluded are deaths caused by negligence, attempts to kill, assaults to kill, suicides, accidental deaths, traffic fatalities, and justifiable homicides. Justifiable homicides are limited to the killing of a felon by a law enforcement officer in the line of duty and the killing of a felon, during the commission of a felony, by a private citizen.

Note: This appendix is adapted from Federal Bureau of Investigation (1998:407).

Forcible rape: The carnal knowledge of a female forcibly and against her will. Included are rapes by force and attempts or assaults to rape. Excluded are statutory offenses (no force used, but victim under the age of consent).

Robbery: The taking or attempting to take anything of value from the care, custody, or control of a person or persons by force or threat of force or violence and/or by putting the victim in fear.

Aggravated assault: An unlawful attack by one person upon another for the purpose of inflicting severe or aggravated bodily injury. This type of assault is usually accompanied by the use of a weapon or by means likely to produce death or great bodily harm.

Burglary/breaking and entering: The unlawful entry of a structure to commit a felony or theft. Attempted forcible entry is included.

Larceny/theft: The unlawful taking, carrying, leading, or riding away of property from the possession or constructive possession of another. Examples are thefts of bicycles or automotive accessories, shoplifting, pocket-picking, or stealing of any property or article which is not taken by force and violence or by fraud. Attempted larcenies are included. Motor vehicle thefts are excluded, as are embezzlement, confidence games, forgery, worthless checks, etc.

Motor vehicle theft: The theft or attempted theft of a motor vehicle. A motor vehicle is self-propelled and runs on the surface and not on rails. Specifically excluded from this category are motorboats, construction equipment, airplanes, and farming equipment.

Arson: Any willful or malicious burning or attempt to burn, with or without intent to defraud, a dwelling house, public building, motor vehicle or aircraft, personal property of another, etc.

PART II OFFENSES

Other assaults (simple): Assaults and attempted assaults where no weapon is used and which do not result in serious or aggravated injury to the victim.

Forgery and counterfeiting: Making, altering, uttering, or possessing, with intent to defraud, anything false in the semblance of that which is true. Attempts are included.

Fraud: Fraudulent conversion and obtaining money or property by false pretenses. Included are confidence games and bad checks, except forgeries and counterfeiting.

Embezzlement: Misappropriation or misapplication of money or property entrusted to one's care, custody, or control.

Stolen property; buying, receiving, possessing: Buying, receiving, and possessing stolen property, including attempts.

Vandalism: Willful or malicious destruction, injury, disfigurement, or defacement of any public or private property, real or personal, without consent of the owner or persons having custody or control.

Weapons; carrying, possessing, etc.: All violations of regulations or statutes controlling the carrying, using, possessing, furnishing, and manufacturing of deadly weapons or silencers. Included are attempts.

Prostitution and commercialized vice: Sex offenses of a commercialized nature, such as prostitution, keeping a bawdy house, procuring, or transporting women for immoral purposes. Attempts are included.

Sex offenses (except forcible rape, prostitution, and commercialized vice): Statutory rape and all offenses against chastity, common decency, morals, and the like. Attempts are included.

Drug abuse violations: State and/or local offenses relating to the unlawful possession, sale, use, growing, and manufacturing of narcotic drugs. The following drug categories are specified: opium or cocaine and their derivatives (morphine, heroin, codeine); marijuana; synthetic narcotics— manufactured narcotics that can cause true addiction (demerol, methadone); and dangerous nonnarcotic drugs (barbiturates, benzedrine).

Gambling: Promoting, permitting, or engaging in illegal gambling.

Offenses against the family and children: Nonsupport, neglect, desertion, or abuse of family and children.

Driving under the influence: Driving or operating any vehicle or common carrier while drunk or under the influence of liquor or narcotics.

Liquor laws: State and/or local liquor law violations, except "drunkenness" and "driving under the influence." Federal violations are excluded.

Drunkenness: Offenses relating to drunkenness or intoxication. Excluded is "driving under the influence."

Disorderly conduct: Breach of the peace.

Vagrancy: Vagabondage, begging, loitering, etc.

All other offenses: All violations of state and/or local laws, except those listed above and traffic offenses.

Suspicion: No specific offense; suspect released without formal charges being placed.

Curfew and loitering laws (persons under age 18): Offenses relating to violations of local curfew or loitering ordinances where such laws exist.

Runaways (persons under age 18): Limited to juveniles taken into protective custody under provisions of local statutes.

REFERENCE

Federal Bureau of Investigation
  1998   *Crime in the United States 1997*. Washington, DC: U.S. Department of Justice.

Appendix B

The Indeterminacy of Forecasts of Crime Rates and Juvenile Offenses

Kenneth C. Land and Patricia L. McCall

How much crime will there be in the United States in the next 5 or 10 years? Will crime rates go up or down or remain about the same? Since juvenile crime often is a leading edge of crime problems to come, how many juvenile offenses will there be? Will the number of juvenile serious violent offenders/homicide perpetrators increase? What will be the resulting demands on the juvenile and criminal justice systems? Over the past three decades, criminologists have made a number of attempts to address these and related questions. These usually have taken the form of efforts to explain past variations or to project future levels of crime by applying techniques of demographic and statistical analysis. These techniques typically consist of:

- the application of demographic age standardization methods to combine relatively accurate estimates of the age structure of the American population with age-specific arrest rates for various types of crimes and categories of the population to calculate expected numbers of criminal offenses or crime rates or
- the construction of an explanatory time-series regression or structural equation models to explain or predict variations in crime rates over time.

Kenneth C. Land is John Franklin Crowell Professor of Sociology, Duke University. Patricia L. McCall is Associate Professor of Sociology, North Carolina State University.

Such analyses may be useful exercises with respect to explaining past experiences in the ups and downs of observed crime or the projection of recent trends in order to anticipate future problems and needs for levels of resources in the juvenile and criminal justice systems. Yet even a casual review of the various projections of crime rates or offenses that have been made over the years suggests that they contain large amounts of uncertainty. That is, the mere fact that a projection indicates that, say, juvenile homicide offenders may increase (or decrease) by some specific percentage over the next 5 or 10 years does not mean that the rates will, in fact, exhibit such an increase (or decrease).

The purposes of this paper are twofold. First, we review a number of extant demographic projections of crime rates and offenses that have been made for the United States over the past few decades, with a special focus on projections of juvenile crime rates and offenses. We commence in the next section with a brief summary of demographic analyses of the crime wave in the 1960s based on the coming of age of the baby boomers. This is followed by a review of projections of downturns in crime rates in the 1980s based on the smaller "baby bust" birth cohorts. More recently, following the rise in delinquent and criminal offenses by adolescents and teenagers in the 1985-1993 period, criminologists have produced some scary projections, which we next describe, of increasing numbers of violent criminal offenses expected in the period 1995-2005, as the "echo-boomers" enter their teenage years.

It will be seen that one characteristic of most extant projections of juvenile and criminal offenses is that, until recently, they have produced only expected or average values of future levels of crime rates or offenses. But temporal variability of age-specific crime rates has been a key characteristic of offending patterns, especially for juveniles, in recent years. Yet most projections of criminal and juvenile offending rates and numbers of offenses disregard the uncertainty associated with such projections. To emphasize the significance of the uncertainty of projections of criminal and juvenile offenses, a second objective of the paper is to describe some exercises in the construction of plausible national projections of expected numbers of male juvenile homicide offenders—as well as upper and lower bounds for the expected numbers—for each year from 1998 to 2007. A final section contains a statement of the major conclusions from our review and analyses.

THE BABY BOOMERS COME OF AGE IN THE 1960s AND 1970s

One of the first attempts to examine the impact of a changing demographic age composition of the population on numbers of criminal offenses reported to the police was made during the 1960s—when the

United States was stunned by skyrocketing crime rates. On the heels of the relatively low levels of criminal and juvenile offending in the 1950s, scholars and politicians began searching for reasons behind the dramatic increase in crime rates during the 1960s. Criminologists were well aware of the fact that the Uniform Crime Reports (UCR) published annually by the Federal Bureau of Investigation (FBI), the primary measure of national crime levels and rates at that time, was at best a politically influenced undercount and a weak indicator of the extent of criminal activity in the United States (see, e.g., Biderman, 1966). This was an unsettling notion especially in light of the growing magnitude of crime. One of the outcomes of this crime wave was the development of the annual National Crime Victimization Survey (NCVS) beginning in 1973.[1] This survey was introduced as a new tool to determine the extent of criminal activity in the United States by surveying individual households in the population regarding the victimization status of their members in the past year.

Criminologists attempted to determine the impetus behind the crime surge of the 1960s. Philip Sagi and Charles Wellford, in their 1967 report to the President's Commission on Law Enforcement and the Administration of Justice, identified the centrality of shifts in the age composition of the population as an explanation. Using a variety of demographic techniques, they attempted to accurately estimate the extent to which the increasing crime rate was due to an increase in individuals' crime proneness versus the changing composition of the population with respect to age, race, and geographic location.

In particular, Sagi and Wellford (1968) cited the contribution that the post-World War II baby boom generation was making to the crime wave in the 1960s.[2] They argued that, during the early 1960s, individuals born in the early years of the baby boom hit peak criminal offending ages, i.e., their late teens and early 20s. Using techniques of demographic age standardization, Sagi and Wellford demonstrated that the population increase in these young ages between 1958 (the low point of national crime rates in the late 1950s) and 1964 (the most recent year's data available at the time of their study), in and of itself, accounted for 24 percent of the increase in

---

[1]The NCVS was originally called the National Crime Survey. It was redesigned and renamed in 1992 (see Bureau of Justice Statistics, 1995).

[2]Demographers have defined baby boomers in the United States as individuals born in the 18 high birth rate years from 1946 to 1964 (see, e.g., Crispell, 1993). Birth cohorts from these years are relatively large compared with those both earlier and later, and their movement through the age structure has been associated with various social movements and changes in social institutions. Sometimes "early boomers" born in 1946-1955 are further distinguished from "late boomers" born 1956-1964 (Gibson, 1993).

FBI Index (or UCR Part I) offenses. They further demonstrated that changes in population race, age, and place of residence in combination accounted for 46 percent of that increase (President's Commission on Law Enforcement and Administration of Justice, 1967:208; see also Sagi and Wellford, 1968).

Wellford (1973) followed up this analysis by extending the time series to include annual index crime rates through 1969. He first computed age- and crime-specific arrest rates. Then Wellford computed the age-standardized total offense rate by adjusting for the underrepresentation of the total U.S. population in the UCR. He estimated that the percentage increases in person or violent (homicide, aggravated assault, and robbery) and property (burglary, larceny-theft, and motor vehicle theft) crimes were 148 and 92 percent (age-standardized crime rates) as opposed to 165 and 117 percent (as indicated by the crude crime rates reported in the UCR), respectively. Even though the increase in offending rates during the 1960s was not as large as the official crime rates would lead one to believe, the disconcerting news was that the rate of violent crimes rose more than that of property crimes among youth during this period. The other disturbing results of Wellford's cohort analysis showed that, with one exception, each cohort born during the baby boom was exhibiting crime rates higher than the one before. The main point made in his research was that "minimally, age composition effects must be controlled in attempting to estimate crime increase" rather than relying solely on "rates reflecting only the changes in the size of the total population" (Wellford, 1973:63).

Sagi and Wellford did not attempt to project the crime rates past the 1960s. But they noted that it is possible to forecast fairly accurately the size and age composition of the juvenile and adult populations for one or two decades into the future and, thereby, to project the extent of crime for that period. Beside noting the problems inherent in attempting to make these estimates, they also warned of the necessity to obtain arrest information for each sex and age group within each race and geographic location category in order to better account for the impact that the changing population composition has on crime trends and "to make much better judgments as to how much of any particular increase or decrease in crime rates was due to a change in the criminality of the persons involved" (President's Commission on Law Enforcement and Administration of Justice, 1967:210). To a large extent, data readily available from the FBI today still possess the shortcomings identified by Sagi and Wellford over three decades ago.

DECREASING CRIME RATES FOR THE BABY BUSTERS
IN THE 1980S

During the years after Sagi and Wellford conducted their initial study, the United States saw an increasing crime trend through the 1970s and into the early 1980s, at which time the crime rates began falling. With an additional 10 to 15 years of crime data at their disposal, James A. Fox (1978), Lawrence E. Cohen and Kenneth C. Land (1987), and Darrell Steffensmeier and Miles Harer (1987) reexamined the impact of age composition on crime trends. The question posed by the latter two groups of investigators was whether the decline in crime rates in the 1980s was due to the baby boomers aging out of those crime prone ages—adolescence and young adulthood.

Steffensmeier and Harer (1987) studied changes in crime rates among index crimes between 1980 and 1984. Echoing Sagi and Wellford's concern with the changes in crime trends reported in the UCR and the National Crime Survey, they noted that the official "crime figures are not age specific but are crude rates based on the U.S. population as a whole" (Steffensmeier and Harer, 1987:29). Using methods similar to Sagi and Wellford's, Steffensmeier and Harer applied the demographic technique of indirect standardization of crime rates on age-specific arrest rates adjusted for the proportions of the U.S. population not covered in the annual UCR series. By applying this age-adjustment method to data derived from the UCR and the National Crime Survey reports, they compared percentage changes between 1980 and 1984 in unadjusted crude rates (the traditional measure of change) with their adjusted percentage change that corrects for the changes in the age structure. They showed that the age composition accounted for approximately 30 to 70 percent of declines in property and robbery crime rates, since the baby boomers had aged past the property crime prone ages of adolescence and the early twenties. Violent crimes had not enjoyed such a large decline as the baby boomers had not quite reached the ages where the violent criminal offending tends to drop—that is, the late 20s and early 30s.

Based on those findings, Steffensmeier and Harer (1987) used age-specific estimates of the U.S. population produced by the Bureau of the Census through the end of the 20th century to forecast reductions in the nation's crime rate from 1980 to 2000. The forecasts assumed that age-specific offending rates would remain constant into the future and thus were based solely on changes in age composition. Specifically, they noted that the proportion of young people (ages 15-24), those at high risk for property crime, was estimated to decline sharply into the early 1990s and the proportion of youth and young adults (ages 15-35), those at high risk for person crime, were expected to decline steadily into and even beyond the year 2000. This was due to the arrival of the "baby busters" at these high crime-prone ages.[3] The projections made by Steffensmeier and Harer (1987) showed a steadily declining violent crime rate until the year 2000 and a somewhat steeper declining property crime rate until the mid-1990s, when the rate would plateau and begin a slight increase in the late 1990s. More precisely, they forecasted that violent crime rates would fall about 13 percent compared with about 20 percent for property crime rates during the 1980 to 2000 period.

The projections of crime rates in the 1980s and 1990s of Steffensmeier and Harer (1987) based on demographic standardization can be compared with those of two studies, Fox (1978) and Cohen and Land (1987), based on regression models of crime rate time series. Fox was the first researcher to publish forecasts of U.S. crime rates based on this type of analysis.[4] Using national crime rate data for the years 1950 through 1974, he studied the impact the baby boomers had on the surge in crime rates during the 1960s and 1970s. This led to a conclusion similar to that of Steffensmeier and Harer (1987)—that crime rates would fall during the 1980s when the baby boomers matured out of the crime prone ages and were replaced by the baby busters. Fox constructed structural equation models that estimated not only the impact that race and age composition had on crime trends, but also that of socioeconomic characteristics of the population as well as police activities and expenditures. Based on his study, Fox concluded (1978:51): "The crime rate forecasts reveal a general reduction in upward trend during the 1980s and a trend increase during the 1990s. In fact, the violent crime rate . . . should decline in the 1980s before increasing once again in the 1990s." These projections were based primarily on age- and race-specific population estimates and projections published by the Census Bureau for the last quarter of the century.

Cohen and Land (1987) also conducted an analysis of crime trends in the United States through the mid-1980s based on a time-series regression analysis for a somewhat longer post-World War II period, 1946 through 1984, to determine the extent to which changes in the age structure influenced the crime trends. By relating their analysis to the question of the relationship between age and crime then debated by Hirschi and Gottfredson (1983) and Greenberg (1985), they attempted to answer whether the decline in crime rates beginning in the mid-1980s would continue to

---

[3]Demographers generally refer to individuals in the United States born in the relatively low birth rate years from 1965 through 1976 that followed the baby boom years as *baby busters* (Crispell, 1993). Members of the baby buster birth cohorts also have been labeled in the popular press as "Generation X."

[4]See also Cohen et al. (1980) for a time-series regression analysis of U.S. property crime rates, 1947-1974, with projections to the mid-1980s.

decrease symmetrically (i.e., proportionally to the declining population in the high crime-prone ages) versus asymmetrically (whereby cohort-specific effects produce non decreasing crime propensities throughout the life courses of high crime-prone cohorts as argued by Greenberg [1985], as well as suggested in the crime patterns displayed by the cohort analysis conducted by Wellford [1973]).

Cohen and Land (1987) focused specifically on homicide and motor vehicle theft rates and controlled for other social forces affecting crime rates: trends in business cycles as well as in criminal opportunity and the rate of imprisonment. They first identified the peak ages of offending for homicide and motor vehicle theft—15 to 29 and 15 to 24, respectively. By overlaying the trends in graphic form, Cohen and Land demonstrated that the homicide and motor vehicle trends mirrored the trends in age structure for these two youthful groups (see Figures B-1 and B-2, which reprint Figures 3 and 4 from their 1987 report). In their time-series regression analysis, they included the percentage of the population ages 15 to 29 as the age composition control in the homicide model and the percentage ages 15 to 24 in the motor vehicle theft model. In addition, they introduced measures for age-proneness shifts among the cohorts computed as

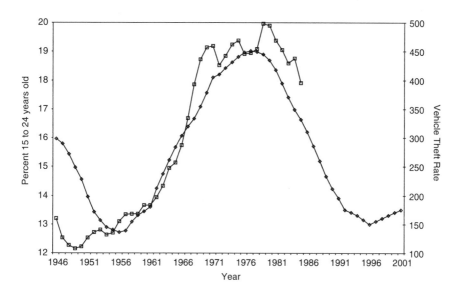

FIGURE B-1 Annual estimates of vehicle theft rate and the percentage of the population ages 15 to 24, United States, 1946-1984, with projections of the latter to 2001. Reproduction of Figure 3 from Cohen and Land (1987). Reprinted with permission.

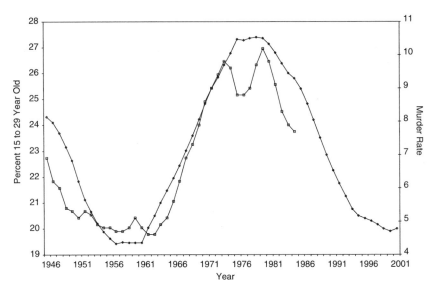

FIGURE B-2 Annual estimates of the murder rates and the percentage of the population ages 15 to 29, United States, 1946-1984, with projections of the latter to 2001. Reproduction of Figure 4 from Cohen and Land (1987). Reprinted with permission.

the product of a dummy variable, equal to one for the years 1966-1984 and zero for 1947-1965, times the natural logarithm of the age structure index. This variable was "incorporated in order to test for the time series signifi-cance of changes in the levels of the age-specific crime rates in the later as compared to the earlier part of the sample period" (Cohen and Land, 1987:178). The results of their time-series analyses showed that the age structure variables in both homicide and motor vehicle theft models were significant, but that the age proneness shift measure was not (contrary to the finding of Wellford's 1973 study). They argued that whatever cohort changes have occurred are not of sufficient magnitude net of those cohort differences transmitted through the other causal measures included in their models: unemployment rate, unemployment fluctuations, criminal opportunity, and imprisonment rate variables. They concluded from their analyses that the age structure-crime relationship, at least as evident in the homicide and motor vehicle theft rates series up to the mid-1980s, appeared to be symmetric.

Cohen and Land (1987) compared their findings to those of Steffensmeier and Harer (1987), noting that the latter's use of age-standardized arrest rates focused on the offender population and attributed all variation either to changes in the entire age composition of the population or to changes in offending rates. Cohen and Land argued that by using a single age composition index for each crime model, they concentrated exclusively on the relative frequency of adolescents and young adults in the population, which takes into account the pool of potential victims as well as offenders. Whereas Steffensmeier and Harer's techniques accounted for about two-thirds of the decline in motor vehicle theft and none of the decline in homicide, Cohen and Land's analysis accounted for about 26 percent of the year-to-year change in the vehicle theft series and about 58 percent of the change in the homicide series.

Based on Census Bureau projections of the U.S. population age composition into the 21st century, Cohen and Land cautiously forecasted generally declining homicide and vehicle theft rates for the post-1985 period into the mid-1990s to be followed by increases into the next decade. Noting that increases already had occurred in the homicide and motor vehicle theft rates for 1985 and 1986 after they concluded their analysis of crime trends in the 1946-1984 period, Cohen and Land (1987) further conjectured that these increases could be explained by three possible scenarios. One was that the increases were due to a short-term illegal "drugs/crime bubble," which their models were not designed to capture. This conjecture proved somewhat prophetic relative to recent explanations of the high levels of crime reported in the late 1980s and the early 1990s.

SCARY PROJECTIONS OF INCREASING VIOLENT CRIME RATES FOR THE ECHO-BOOMERS IN THE 1990s

Instead of the predicted drop in crime trends through the 1980s, the American public enjoyed only a five-year hiatus from the surging crime trends of the previous two decades. The increasing violent crime rates in 1985 and 1986 noted by Cohen and Land (1987) continued to climb until 1993. Violent crime rates particularly spiked for teenage males. Since males ages 15-19 in, say, 1990 were born in the 1971-1975 period, they were members of the baby buster birth cohorts who, according to both the demographic standardization and the time-series analyses cited above, were expected to have relatively low crime rates. Yet it became evident in the late 1980s and early 1990s that these members of the tail end of the baby buster cohorts were not behaving with respect to participation in index crimes, especially violent crimes, as had been expected.

Responding to these increases, some criminologists projected that the age-specific violent crime trends of young offenders (ages 14-24) would continue to rise throughout the latter part of the 1990s and into the next decade (Fox, 1996). This trend in violence among adolescents—particularly shocking to the public—raised serious concerns about the potential harm posed by these youths. In addition, some analysts argued that what had typically been only a threat to lower-class, inner-city dwellers, might become a reality for the rest of society. "Americans are sitting on a demographic crime bomb . . . . Despite the recent decline in murder rates, homicides committed by 14- to 17-year-olds between 1985 and 1993 increased by 165 percent (more for minority males). The next wave of homicidal and near-homicidal violence among urban youth is bound to reach adjacent neighborhoods, inner-ring suburbs, and even the rural heartland" (DiIulio, 1995a:15).

Prominent criminologists and policy scientists such as John J. DiIulio (1997), James A. Fox (1996), and James Q. Wilson (1995) also warned that rising violent crime trends would only worsen as the echo boomers aged into their crime-prone years—a phenomenon that would begin during the first two decades of the 21st century.[5] Census Bureau population projections supported this contention (U.S. Bureau of the Census, 1985; 1995; 1996). The numbers of teenage males in America were due to climb by 1 million from 1995 to 2000. Based on extant cohort studies that estimated that 6 percent of the youthful population become high rate, repeat offenders, Wilson estimated that there would be 30,000 more serious offenders on the streets by the turn of the century. "Get ready," he warned (Wilson, 1995:507).

Heeding Wilson's warning and expanding his depiction of this growing tide of youthful offenders, DiIulio coined the term "superpredators"—noting that today's offenders are worse than yesterday's and that tomorrow's will be worse than today's. "According to Professor Wolfgang, . . . each male cohort has been about three times as violent as the one before it. We concur" (Bennett et al., 1996:29). DiIulio's (as well as Wilson's) characterization of the 21st century youthful offenders is nothing short of scary (Bennett et al., 1996:27):

> America is now home to thickening ranks of juvenile "super-predators"—radically impulsive, brutally remorseless youngsters, including ever more preteenage boys, who murder, assault, rape, rob, burglarize, deal deadly drugs, join gun-toting gangs, and create serious communal disorders. They do not fear the stigma of arrest, the pains of imprisonment,

---

[5]Due to the large size of the baby boomer cohorts, even with lower birth rates than their parents, the number of children they bore is larger than the number of children in the baby buster years. Because these *baby boomlet* birth cohorts, born 1977-1995, thus reflect their parents' large cohorts, they often are referred to as *echo boomers* (Crispell, 1993). In the popular press, following the labeling of the cohorts who were born just before them as Generation X, the echo boomers have been dubbed "Generation Y."

or the pangs of conscience. They perceive hardly any relationship between doing right (or wrong) now and being rewarded (or punished) for it later. To these mean-street youngsters, the words "right" and "wrong" have no fixed moral meaning.

Touting the success of tougher law enforcement efforts against adult offenders especially during the war on drugs (DiIulio, 1995b) and demanding the incarceration of youthful offenders as a minimum require-ment for curbing the tide of violence among youthful offenders, DiIulio (1997) stated that most juvenile criminals still received no punishment for their crimes and that prosecutors and judges are unduly burdened with caseloads, which leaves them impotent against this struggle to bring jus-tice to and incarcerate juvenile offenders. The bottom line for DiIulio (DiIulio, 1995a:16) is that "we must remain deadly serious about targeting hardened adult and juvenile criminals for arrest, prosecution, and incar-ceration."[6]

IS AN IMPENDING EXPLOSION IN
YOUTH VIOLENCE REALISTIC?

Besides the projected "baby boomerang" effect of the echo boomers on violent crime rates of the 21st century (Fox, 1996:1), there is little hard evidence that changes in other social and economic forces would exacer-bate or relieve the forecasted explosion in youth violence. To be sure, the demographic force of increasing numbers of echo boomer adolescents and teenagers up to about the year 2010 is inexorable. Assuming further that age-specific delinquent and crime rates, especially violent crime rates, remain constant at the high levels experienced in the 1985-1993 period, it would appear inevitable that juvenile crimes would increase substan-tially, especially in the years 1996-2005. Assuming also that a constant proportion of birth cohorts become high rate, repeat offenders, Wilson's conclusion that the numbers of such offenders in the youth population— and the associated numbers of offenses they commit—will increase dra-matically and disturbingly during these years also appears indisputable.

With the benefit of several additional years of data, however, it is clear that the age-specific delinquent and crime rates of adolescents and teenagers rose dramatically in the 1985 to 1993 years (relative to the rates

---

[6]In spite of his call for enhanced law enforcement efforts, DiIulio (1997: A23) argues that the superpredators—"these more savage than salvageable young criminals could not and should not be punished into submission. Instead, the only responsible option is to try and save these typically abused, neglected, fatherless, Godless and impoverished children before it's too late, working mainly through the youth outreach efforts of local churches."

that had been observed through the 1960-1985 period) and then began falling. This decline continued through 1996 and, evidently, based on preliminary UCR estimates, through 1997 and 1998 as well (Bureau of Justice Statistics, 1998). The reasons behind recently shrinking crime rates are as obscure today as were the reasons for the booming crime rates of the late 1980s and early 1990s circa 1990. Criminologists and politicians have speculated on the impetus behind the fluctuations in crime trends— each side of the liberal/conservative stance taking advantage of the numbers as providing support for their ideologies. Explanations offered for the 1985-1993 climb in youth violence include:

- the reluctance of juvenile justice agencies to incarcerate youths (DiIulio, 1997);
- prevalence of drug use and drug trafficking, especially crack cocaine (Blumstein, 1995);
- availability of deadly weapons, especially firearm possession by youths (Blumstein, 1995);
- casual attitudes about violence—resulting from "cumulative, de-sensitizing effects of media-glamorized violence" (Fox, 1996:2); and
- ineffective socializing efforts of family, school, religion, and neighborhood, the absence of parental supervision, and the diminished role of the family (Bennett et al., 1996).

And what accounts for the declines in crime rates, especially violent and juvenile crime rates since 1994? Steffensmeier and Harer (1999) recently reviewed the effects of age composition and other forces on crime rates. They noted the following plausible explanatory factors:

- reductions in drug use and stabilization of drug markets;
- tougher laws and enforcement that have deterred and incapacitated offenders;
- changes in crime opportunities—e.g., due to shifts in the population age structure towards more elderly, who rarely are exposed or have their property exposed to crime risk, improvements in domestic and commercial security, and changes from cash to credit card and electronic transactions;
- a strong economy in the mid- to late 1990s and improvements in social and economic conditions;
- greater police visibility and effectiveness through wide improvements in problem-oriented or community-oriented policing;
- gang abatement programs; and,
- with the aging of the boomers, a collective conscience shift toward greater civility and mediation.

What are the implications of these trends for crime rates in the first decade of the 21st century? Steffensmeier and Harer (1999) observed that other analysts (such as Fox, DiIulio, and Wilson in the publications cited above) have concentrated on the effects of the projected increase in the number of teenagers by 20 percent from 1995 to 2005—to roughly 30 million—on expected crime increases. They argued, however, that these scary forecasts considered only the changes in the size of the youth population and ignored projected shifts in the size of the middle-aged and elderly populations that are at low risk for crime. Again assuming that age-specific rates of offending remain constant through the forecast period, Steffensmeier and Harer updated their 1987 age-standardization analyses using the whole age structure of the population. This yielded projections of violent crimes that rise very slowly to the year 2010, rising about 5 percent from 1996 levels; see Figure B-3, which reproduces Figure 14 from Steffensmeier and Harer (1999). They similarly projected values for property crime rates that rise even more slowly, to about 4 percent from 1996 levels to the year 2010. Steffensmeier and Harer (1999) specifically rejected the forecast of a crime explosion in the first decade of the 21st century.

As with the other crime rate forecasts reviewed above, however, these projections assumed that age-specific arrest rates for juveniles continue at the levels observed in 1996 to the year 2010. This is the reason that

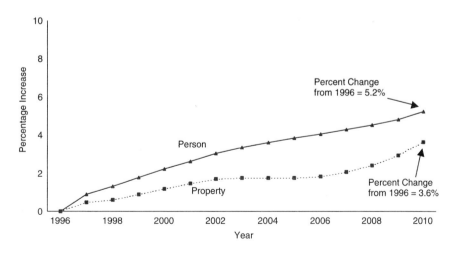

FIGURE B-3 Projected age-adjustment effects for person and property crimes to year 2010 (base year is 1996). Reproduction of Figure 14 from Steffensmeier and Harer (1999). Reprinted with permission.

Steffensmeier and Harer's projected increases for 1997 and 1998 already are inconsistent with UCR estimates of declines in violent and property crimes for 1997 and (preliminarily) 1998. If, in fact, these age-specific rates continue to decline, then the modest increases in violent and property crime rates projected by Steffensmeier and Harer could become even more modest or even turn into decreases. In any event, it almost surely will be the case that the age-specific arrest rates for juveniles will vary over these years. Accordingly, these projections should be considered expected values only, and some account should be taken of the uncertainly surrounding the production of the expected values.

THE NEED TO RECOGNIZE UNCERTAINTY IN FORECASTS OF CRIME AND JUVENILE OFFENSES

Based on the foregoing review of various efforts to forecast levels of crime, it is evident that the typical forecast consists of a "point estimate" (i.e., a specific number) of expected crime rates or numbers of offenders for each of a sequence of years in some forecast period. Furthermore, all of these forecasts either explicitly or implicitly assumed fixed curves of age-specific rates of offending—that is, they assumed that the rates of offending will remain fixed at each age across an age range from childhood to the eldest age group in the population.[7] When the age-specific schedules in fact remains relatively fixed, as in the 1970s with the baby boomers aging through the teenage and young adult years of relatively high criminal offending, then such point estimates can be relatively accurate. The reason is straightforward—under such circumstances, the main forecasting task is to trace out the implications of changes in the age distribution of the population as projected by the Census Bureau. When, however, there are significant turning points or points at which age-specific rates of offending rise or fall significantly, then crime forecasts based on the assumption of fixed age-specific offending rates may be substantially off the mark. This occurred during the 1985-1993 period when age-specific offending rates for teenagers and young adults, due to what Cohen and Land (1987) labeled a short-term "drug bubble," rose rapidly to historically high levels. The consequence was that the forecasts for the 1985-1995 period of Fox (1978), Cohen and Land (1987), and Steffensmeier and Harer (1987) for crime rates and numbers of offenses were far too low.

---

[7]Demographers refer to this as the *age-specific schedule* of event occurrence of a specific type, in this case criminal offending.

But offense rates for juveniles and young adults also changed rapidly in the 1994-1998 period—this time falling to levels not seen in some cases since the early 1970s. This rapid fall in age-specific offense rates again confounded analysts, who forecasted a scary wave of juvenile and young adult offending to begin in the mid-1990s. A case in point is the 1996 Bureau of Justice Statistics report, *Trends in Juvenile Violence: A Report to the United States Attorney General on Current and Future Rates of Juvenile Offending* by James A. Fox. This report focuses on trends in homicide, especially teenage homicide, from 1976 through 1994 and thus embodies the frightening rise in teenage homicide in the period 1985 to 1994. The Executive Summary (Fox, 1996) of the report notes the following "key statistical findings" (among others):

- From 1985 to 1994, the rate of murder committed by teens, ages 14-17, increased 172 percent. The rate of killing rose sharply for both black and white male teenagers, but not for females.
- By the year 2005, the number of teens, ages 14-17, will increase by 20%, with a larger increase among blacks in this age group (26%).
- Even if the per-capita rate of teen homicide remains the same, the number of 14-17 year-olds who will commit murder should increase to nearly 5,000 annually because of changing demographics. However, if offending rates continue to rise because of worsening conditions for our nation's youth, the number of teen killings could increase even more.

Figure B-4, which reproduces Figure 15 from the report (Fox, 1996), illustrates this last point. Specifically, the lower bound of projected numbers of homicide offenders to the year 2005 (as shown by the lower dotted line in the figure), which is based on the assumption of no change in offending rates from those of 1994, rises to about 5,000. By contrast, the upper bound projection to 2005 in the figure (also shown by a dotted line), which is based on the assumption that the "recent trend" (i.e., the trend observed in 1985-1994) of increases in the homicide rate for 14- to 17-year-olds persists, rises to nearly 9,000.

As noted, however, the rising trend in the teenage homicide offending rate of 1985-1993 did not persist. The downturn in the teenage homicide rate in 1994 continued through 1995 and 1996. This fact was noted by Fox (1997) in his follow-up Bureau of Justice Statistics report, *Trends in Juvenile Violence: 1997 Update*. Remaining cautious, however, Fox (1997:1) states that "it is premature to suggest that the problem of teen violence has disappeared." Nonetheless, the continuing downturn of teenage homicide rates through the mid-1990s brought the number of offenders to a level of about 3,000 by 1996—well below the lower bound of about 4,000

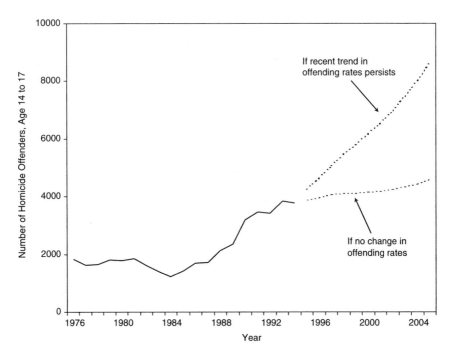

FIGURE B-4 Forecast of homicide offenders, ages 14-17. Reproduction of Figure 15 from Fox (1996).

projected for 1996 in Fox (1996), as reproduced in Figure B-4. Accordingly, Fox (1997) presented a revised forecast of teenage homicide offenders, which is reproduced in Figure B-5. This revised forecast of the numbers of teen perpetrators of homicide assumes constant levels of age/race/sex-specific offending rates at the 1994-1996 average. It can be seen from Figure B-5 that the upper and lower bounds of Figure B-4 again are replaced by a single projection series. Regarding the forecast in Figure B-5, Fox (1997:1) states: "If only because of demographic shifts, the annual number of teen killers could once again surpass 4,000, just as it did in the early 1990s in the midst of the last youth crime wave."

The purpose of citing this latest round of crime forecasts by James Fox is not to dwell on their relative accuracy. Rather, the objective is to use them to make two points about extant forecasts of crime levels in the United States. First, forecasts into the future must depart from some base or jump-off year. As such, they may embody continuity biases or a ten-

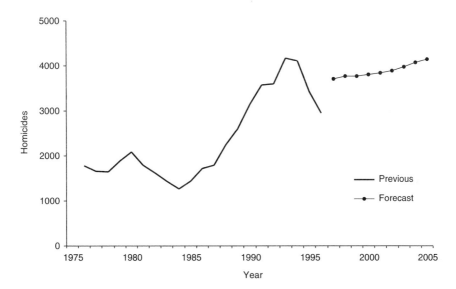

FIGURE B-5 Forecast of teen homicide offenders. Reproduction of Figure 1 from Fox (1997). Counts include both known perpetrators and an estimate of unidentified perpetrators.

dency to be unduly influenced by, and to project into the future, the most recent trends in crime levels and rates observed in the years immediately prior to the base year of the forecasts.[8] This is evident, for example, in crime forecasts from the 1980s, which assumed that the relatively low age-specific offense rates of the mid-1980s would continue into the future. It also is evident in the forecasts in Fox (1996), and even those of Fox (1997), which did not anticipate the continued downturn of juvenile violent offending rates in the mid-1990s. Second, the focus on point forecasts ignores the uncertainty in crime forecasts, or the fact that the eventually observed crime rates almost surely will not track along the paths of expected values described in the forecasts. On this subject, criminologists can learn from demographers, who long have recognized uncertainty in their forecasts. We now turn to some illustrations of how this can be done and what the implications are for forecasting levels of juvenile crime offenders into the next decade.

---

[8]Continuity biases in forecasts are not unique to crime forecasts; for evidence of this in demographic projections, see Stoto (1983) and Lutz et al. (1999).

SOME HIGH AND LOW BOUNDS ON JUVENILE HOMICIDE
OFFENSES TO THE YEAR 2007

Demographers have been in the business of producing demographic forecasts or projections longer than criminologists. And they also have had their share of forecasting blunders. After World War II, demographers failed to anticipate the baby boom. At the end of the baby boom in the mid-1960s, they then failed to anticipate how rapidly and far fertility would fall in the 1970s (see, e.g., Lee, 1999, for a review of past major forecasting errors by demographers). On the mortality side, demographic forecasts in the early 1970s tended to assume that period of stable adult and elderly death rates from the late 1950s to the late 1960s would continue indefinitely into the future. Adjusting to these forecasting errors, however, demographers have begun to recognize that large-scale social systems are governed by complex nonlinear interactions like those for weather, climate, and ecology (Land and Schneider, 1987; see, e.g., Lutz et al., 1999). As such, these systems may have chaotic elements and intrinsic limits to predictability. Accordingly, for some time, demographers have been developing various ways to incorporate uncertainty into their forecasts. Criminologists can learn from studying these approaches to dealing with uncertainty.

Both forecasters and users of forecasts would like to know how much confidence to place in different forecasts. As noted by Ahlburg and Lutz (Ahlburg and Lutz, 1999:10), there are three main approaches to the presentation of the degree of uncertainty in demographic forecasts: (1) variants and scenarios, (2) stochastic forecasts, and (3) the combination of statistical approaches with expert judgment.[9]

The variants approach is the conventional method applied by demographers to produce high, medium, and low projections of expected population size (usually by age, sex, and race) by year into the future (usually 50 to 100 years). The variants approach—often with several variations on high, medium, and low series—still is the methodology employed by the Bureau of the Census for projections of the U.S. population into the 21st century. This method consists of choosing a combination of assumptions about the components of demographic change (fertility, mortality, and migration) that are internally consistent and represent paths of likely outcomes for population under certain conditions without specifying any probabilities of occurrence.

---

[9]For surveys of the state of the art of demographic forecasting methods as of the 1980s and early 1990s, see Land (1986) and Ahlburg and Land (1992); Lutz et al. (1999) present a collection of articles on more recent contributions.

If the variants are designed to demonstrate the future consequences of certain specified conditions, then they are called scenarios. A set of scenarios can be chosen to predict the most likely outcome (usually designated the "middle" variant) and also less likely but possible outcomes (usually designated "high" and "low" variants). The scenarios correspond to particular sets of conditions determined in part by policies and in part by possible outcomes of uncontrolled societal conditions or trends. In this way, scenarios are like simulations: they show the effects of changing a policy or the working out of societal conditions or trends.[10] The high and low projection series also can be viewed as forming projection cones (since they typically expand in width with successive years into the future from the base or jump-off year of the projection series), within which it is considered highly likely that the actual historically observed population numbers of future years will lie.[11] A methodological problem in the use of scenarios is that choices of certain values for some assumptions can imply unreasonable values for others, and the approach can give probabilistically inconsistent indications of uncertainty (Lee, 1999).

Statistical or stochastic approaches to the incorporation of uncertainty into population forecasting tend to be of two general types: forecasts that include probability distributions and forecasts generated by probabilistic population renewal (also called stochastic population forecasts). Lee (1999) argues that only fully probabilistic population forecasts from stochastic renewal models are capable of producing internally consistent probability distributions. Examples of the stochastic approach to population forecasting are Ahlo (1990), Lee (1993), Lee and Carter (1992), and Lee and Tuljapurkar (1994). The main drawbacks to the widespread use of the stochastic approach are its substantial data requirements and the levels of expertise they require of both the forecaster and the user.

A third approach to population forecasting that has emerged in the 1990s is the use of expert opinion to calculate uncertainty by combining

---

[10]Indeed, it is for this reason that demographers typically refer to their numbers as "projections," reserving the term "forecast" for the particular scenario or variant a user chooses as most plausible.

[11]Just how likely is it that an observed historical population series will fall within a typical demographic high and low projection series? Do they correspond to the conventional + 2 sigma (i.e., 95 percent) confidence intervals of statistics? Stoto (1983) compared projected and actual U.S. population totals and differences in projected and observed growth rates for Bureau of the Census high-low projection series made every five years for jump-off years 1945 through 1970 for target years 1950 through 1975. He concluded that the high-low projection series corresponded to two-thirds rather than 95 percent confidence intervals. That is, the observed population growth rates for each of these target years were within the respective high-low bounds about two-thirds of the time.

statistical approaches with expert judgment. One variation of this approach consists of asking a group of interacting experts to give both a point estimate and a range for fertility, mortality, and migration (Lutz et al., 1999). Another variation applies a formal Bayesian statistics framework to the combination of expert judgments in demographic forecasting (Daponte et al., 1997). One advantage of this general approach is that the combination of subjective probability distributions of a number of experts to form one joint predictive probability distribution diminishes the danger of individual bias. This approach may be particularly useful for forecasting when structural changes or unanticipated events need to be factored into the forecasts. Its main drawback is the difficulty of eliciting the necessary input from experts.

A careful and sophisticated application of the stochastic and combined stochastic-expert judgment approaches to the production of forecasts of crime levels and rates for a decade or two into the future clearly requires a large research project (or projects) and is beyond the scope of this paper. However, the application of the variants/scenarios forecasting recipe combined with a dash of expert judgment can be illustrated. For this, we focused on the construction of plausible national projections of expected numbers of male teenage (ages 14-17) homicide offenders—as well as upper and lower bounds for the expected numbers—for each year from 1998 to 2007.[12] This is the age group and the crime that led to the scary projections of DiIulio, (1995b), Fox (1996), and Wilson (1995) reviewed above. It thus is an instructive exercise to examine the plausibility of the assumptions necessary to produce the high-level wave of teenage homicide offenders cited by these analysts. Since the last year for which official estimates of homicide offending rates for this age group are available is 1997, we used 1997 as a jump-off year for the projection series and constructed high and low projection series annually for 10 years from 1998 to the year 2007.

To generate the high and low projection series, we first accessed homicide offending rate time series for the 14-17 age group provided in

---

[12]Only the results of our projection exercises for annual numbers of teenage homicide offenders are reported here. However, we also have produced high and low projection series of numbers of offenders for the years 1998 to 2007 for the following crimes and population-age groups: white male homicide offenders (ages 18-24, 25-59), black male homicide offenders (ages 18-24, 25-59), all violent offenders (ages 10-17, 18-24, and 25-59), all property offenders (ages, 10-17, 18-24, 25-59), white violent offenders (ages 0-17), black violent offenders (ages 0-17), white property offenders (ages 0-17), and black property offenders (ages 0-17). Generally, the results from the projection cones for these other crimes are comparable to those for teenage homicide as reported in Figures B-6 and B-7. They are available from the authors on request.

Fox (1997) for the years 1980 through 1997.[13] These rates were estimated by Fox from FBI Supplementary Homicide Reports and include both known perpetrators as well as an estimated share of unidentified perpetrators computed by a statistical imputation procedure. Since almost all teenage homicide offenders are males, we focused on projections for males only. Furthermore, since the white male and black male rates are quite different, we constructed projections for these two groups separately. Second, we examined the ages 14-17 black male and white male homicide rates for the years 1980-1997 to determine the highest and lowest rates observed during this period. These are:

Population Category	Year and Low Homicide Rate	Year and High Homicide Rate
Black males, 14-17 years old	1984 - 47.6 per 100,000	1993 - 244.1 per 100,000
White males, 14-17 years old	1984 - 9.4 per 100,000	1994 - 22.4 per 100,000

Consistent with previous characterizations of trends in crime over the past two decades reviewed above, it can be seen that 1984 was the low year for homicide rates for both race groups in the 1980-1997 period—just before the 1985-1993 upsurge in young male homicide rates. By comparison, the high years occurred in 1993 for black male teenagers and 1994 for white male teens.

As a third step, we next conjectured about the highest and lowest bounds that these rates could plausibly attain in the 10 years 1998-2007— given (1) the "observed" time series of homicide offending rates for the observation period 1980-1997 and (2) the high and low rates noted above. In doing so, we had the advantage, compared to Fox (1997), of information about the teenage homicide offending rates for 1997 as well as preliminary UCR data on aggregate homicide levels for 1998. These preliminary data indicate overall declines in homicide of about 7 percent from 1997 to 1998. These overall homicide trends have not yet been transformed into age-specific offending rates (as in Fox, 1997). However, we know from Fox's (1997) data that homicide declines for teenagers in the mid-1990s were on the order of 2 to 2.5 times larger than the declines in the overall homicide levels.

---

[13]Fox actually provides estimates of homicide offending rates by age back to 1976. But, for consistency with high and low projection series, we generated for other crime categories, we used Fox's data series only back to 1980. We also used the update for 1997 of teenage homicide offending rates provided by the Federal Bureau of Investigation at the Internet address: http://www.fbi.gov/ucr/prelim98.pdf.

Assuming this pattern has continued, these overall homicide rate declines suggest that homicide offending rates for black and white males ages 14-17 continued to decline by 15 to 20 percent in 1998. Although informal observations suggest the declines in overall and teenage homicide offending have continued through mid-1999 (the date of construction of our projections), it is impossible to know how long this downward trend in teenage homicides will continue. But it is clear that the lower bound of a plausible projection cone for the annual numbers of homicides for these two teenage populations must accommodate the continuing rapid decline in 1998 and possibly for a few additional years into the future. Accordingly, we chose a lower bound to which the homicide offending rates could decline of 25 percent of the lowest rate observed during the 1980-1997 period. Furthermore, since the declines in the 1997 and 1998 offending rates have continued the rapid pace of the mid-1990s, we chose to allow the lower bound for the projection cones to decline linearly to this rate within five years from the jump-off year, i.e., from 1998 to 2002, and then remain fixed for the years 2003 to 2007.

With respect to plausible upper bounds for the homicide offending rates, we conjectured that if teenage homicide offending rates were to reach 125 percent of the highest rates observed during the 1980-1997 period, the public outcry would be so strong that all sorts of societal homeostatic mechanisms—from even more active policing to more active involvement of school, religious, community, and civic organizations in juvenile crime prevention programs—would come into play to stabilize the rates and pressure them down again. And yet the possibility of a new wave of teenage homicide offending associated with the coming of age of the echo boomers—like that of the 1985-1993 period—should not entirely be ruled out of a projection cone designed to contain with a high probability the possible range of future teen homicide offending. Accordingly, we set the upper bound for our projection series to 125 percent of the highest rates reported above for each race group, 1980-1997. We also chose to allow the high bound for the projection cones to increase linearly to this level over a five-year period beginning in 1998 and then remain fixed for 2003 to 2007.

The fourth step in the calculation of our projection cones consisted of multiplying the projected homicide offending rates for the entire 1998 through 2007 period by Census Bureau population race-specific projections for the 14-17 age group (U.S. Census Bureau, 1996). The results of the projected upper and lower bounds for the years 1998-2007 are displayed in Figures B-6 (black males) and B-7 (white males) together with the observed series (based on the rates provided in Fox, 1997) for the years 1980 to 1997.

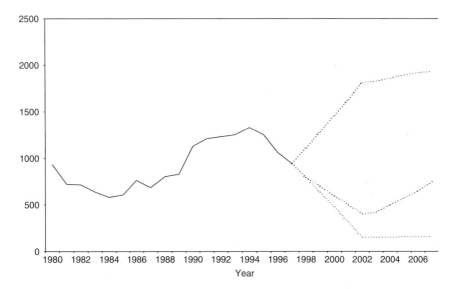

FIGURE B-6 Black male homicide offenders, ages 14-17: Observed series 1980 to 1997 with projected upper and lower bounds to 2007.

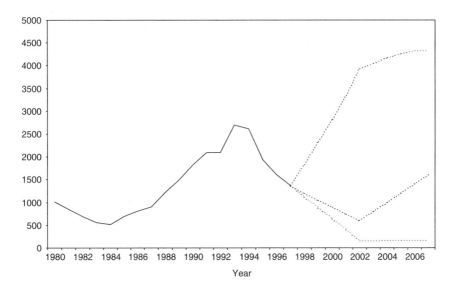

FIGURE B-7 White male homicide offenders, ages 14-17: Observed series 1980 to 1997 with projected upper and lower bounds to 2007.

Several observations can be made about these projection cones. First, it can be seen that the projection cones widen fairly rapidly from the jump-off year of 1997 to the year 2002. This is consistent with our decision to allow the projected lower and upper bounds of homicide offending rates for these two populations to reach the respective limits in five years. Second, at the same time, on the basis of the preliminary evidence regarding homicide trends from 1997 to 1998, and evidently from 1998 to 1999, cited above, the lower bounds of the projection cones decline just rapidly enough to envelop the expected numbers of teenage homicide offenders for these two years. Third, if indeed these declines are on the order of magnitude we expect, this will reduce the numbers of teenage black and white male homicide offenders to levels last seen in the middle 1980s. Fourth, it is evident that the effects of allowing the teenage homicide offending rates to grow to a maximum of 125 percent of the highest rates observed in the 1980-1997 period by the year 2002 are to produce upper bounds that increase by 2002 to about 3,800 for black males and about 1,800 for white males. Fifth, after 2002, the lower and upper bounds for both population groups continue to exhibit slow growth to 2007. Since the homicide offending rates are held constant for these years, these increases are due to continuing growth in the teenage populations at risk during this remaining five years of the forecast period.

Since we approached this projections exercise primarily from a variants/scenarios perspective rather than as an attempt at the formal combination of stochastic forecasting with expert judgment, we have not sampled expert opinion about the probabilities that should be attached to the high and low bounds of our projection cones. However, based on the historical record of juvenile homicide offending rates, we believe they would contain future numbers of teenage homicide offenders with a high (.9 or .95) probability.

Within the confines of the broad upper and lower bounds for the projection cones plotted in Figures B-6 and B-7, we also can describe the trajectories of expected values as well as the probability surfaces for various paths of juvenile homicide offenders across the years shown in the graphs. For us, these probability densities initially are highest along ridges—corresponding to the paths of expected values of the series (i.e., the paths of the annual numbers of offenders we consider most likely)—running close to the lower bounds of the graphs. This is necessary in order to accommodate what evidently are continuing declines in juvenile homicide offenses in 1998 and 1999 (despite highly visible and shocking mass shootings in public middle and high schools during these years). Nonetheless, because of the inherent unpredictability of the series plotted in the figures, we also allow for small but nonzero probability densities (corresponding to the possibility that they could occur) of numbers of offenders in the middle and upper reaches of the projection cones for these two years.

For the years 2000 through 2002, we then allow the ridges containing our most likely scenarios/expected values of juvenile homicide offenders to continue to decline, but at decelerating rates. Because of greater uncertainty with increasing years into the forecast period, however, we concentrate the probability densities somewhat less in this region of the projection cones. For the years 2003 to 2007, we then locate the probability ridges along slightly increasing lines toward the middle part of the projection cones, due to the larger numbers of echo-boomer juveniles at risk of homicide offending in these years. We also flatten the probability surface for our forecasts for these years even more—allowing for somewhat higher probabilities that there may be another upsurge in juvenile homicide offenders later in the 10-year forecast horizon.

These exercises in the calculation of expected values, probability density surfaces, and high and low rate projection bounds for juvenile homicide offenders also can be used to assess the plausibility of the forecasts of homicide and other crimes by Fox (1996, 1997) and Steffensmeier and Harer (1999) summarized above in Figures B-3 and B-5. As noted earlier, the forecasts by these analysts were in the form of single expected values for each of a series of years into the first decade of the 21st century. In contrast, the forecast cones exhibited in Figures B-6 and B-7 are in the spirit of the conventional demographic high-medium-low projection scenarios or variants. As such, they provide lower and upper bounds within which the expected values of single-series forecasts should be contained. Recall that the forecasts of Steffensmeier and Harer (1999) did not focus on teenage homicides specifically but pertained to the general categories of person and property index crimes. Assume, however, that the slow increases in the person index crime rate that they expect over the years 1997 to 2010 (to a maximum increase of about 5 percent by 2010) also imply slow increases in teenage homicide offending rates. Then it clearly is the case that the Steffensmeier and Harer forecasts would fall well within the upper and lower projection series exhibited in Figures B-6 and B-7. In fact, this even would be true if teenage homicide rates over the projection period grow at twice the general rate of increase Steffensmeier and Harer expect for person crimes.

A somewhat more direct comparison can be made between Fox's single-expected-value forecast series and the projection cones in Figures B-6 and B-7 by summing the bounds in these figures to compare with the non-race-specific forecasts of total teenage homicide offenders reproduced in Figures B-4 and B-5 above. Specifically, the upper bounds of our projection cones in 2005 sum to a total number of teenage homicide offenders of about 6,200, which is well below the approximately 8,500 upper bound of Fox's (1996) forecast reproduced above in Figure B-4. Our upper bound for 2005 does, however, contain Fox's (1997) forecast for this year of approximately 4,000. But it also is the case that even the latter forecast requires a considerable growth in homicide offending rates for the two teenage groups in Figures B-6 and B-7. Put otherwise, Fox's (1997) forecast lies in the upper regions of the projection cones of Figures B-6 and B-7. Thus, his 1997 forecasts are not entirely implausible, but, in view of the apparent continuing declines in homicide in 1997 and 1998, perhaps not as plausible as forecasts that fall further within our upper and lower bounds projection series.

CONCLUSIONS

Criminologists have engaged in a number of attempts to forecast both numbers of criminal offenders and crime rates in the United States over the past three decades. In addition to their sheer intellectual interest, there are other reasons for an increasing interest in crime forecasts, such as the policy need to plan for resources for the juvenile and criminal justice systems. Our review of several existing contributions to the crime forecasting literature suggests, first of all, that these forecasts often contain continuity biases, i.e., are heavily influenced by recent trends in crime rates in the years just prior to the period for which the forecasts are made. Admittedly, forecasts of crime rates/offenses have various purposes, one of which could be the projection of recent trends into the future in order to draw out their implications (as in the case of the Fox, 1996, projections). However, to the extent that crime forecasts are meant to go beyond drawing out the implications of recent trends to represent likely paths that crime rates and offenses may take, they should attempt to minimize, or at least be cognizant of, the effects of continuity bias on the forecasts.

A second characteristic of existing crime forecasts is that they typically produce only single-expected-value projections of juvenile or adult crime rates into the future and fail to recognize the uncertainty surrounding such forecasts. It is clear, however, that just because the projection of recent levels of crime rates or trends therein into the immediate future suggests that, say, juvenile crime will rise by a certain percentage does not mean that juvenile crime will in fact rise by that amount. In other words, there is a lot of indeterminancy or, in statistical terminology, uncertainty in crime forecasts. Future efforts in crime forecasting should recognize this and attempt to provide bounds on levels of uncertainty in the forecasts.

We have illustrated some ways in which this can be done by adapting and applying the high-medium-low scenarios approach widely employed in demography to the projection of annual numbers of juvenile homicide offenders for the years 1998 to 2007. Based on the high-low projection cones reported above, we concluded that scary forecasts of a new wave of juvenile homicide offenders in the first decade of the 21st century are relatively implausible. Rather, it is more likely that the numbers of juvenile male homicide offenders will continue to decline during the period 1998 to 2002 and then increase slightly thereafter to the year 2007. However, the possibility that members of the relatively large echo-boomer birth cohorts will develop—as they age into their teen and young adult years—a new fad or fashion related to dangerous and violent interpersonal activities (such as a new attachment to illegal drugs) and, accordingly, that the annual numbers of teenage homicide offenders will again increase in the 1998-2007 period cannot be entirely ruled out.

Our exercise in forecasting juvenile homicide offenders also illustrates two additional implications of uncertainty in forecasts of crime rates and offenders. These are that the periods over which crime forecasts are made should be as short as possible and that the forecasts should be updated as often as possible (i.e., when new or updated data are available). As noted above, large-scale social systems have elements of complexity or nonlinear dynamics and chaos that militate against the accuracy of long-term forecasts. In practical terms, this means that forecasting cones (upper and lower bounds) for enveloping the ranges within which crime forecasts are likely to fall with a high probability will grow very rapidly from the base year into the future. For instance, the forecasting cones for juvenile homicide offenders developed herein lose their informative content very rapidly (i.e., the probability surfaces of the projections become less and less concentrated around the expected values). By the fifth year into the forecasting period, the probability density surfaces for these forecasts have diffused quite extensively. This corresponds to the fact that juvenile homicide offending rates can change very rapidly. To take this into account, the time periods of the forecasts should be relatively short and the forecasts should be revised when new information becomes available. For most police, court, and penal components of the juvenile and criminal justice systems, this is not particularly problematic, as forecasts typically are necessary only for one- or two-year government budgeting cycles. Only occasionally are projections more that five years into the future required for budgeting and/or planning purposes.

In sum, future forecasts of crime rates/offenders should:

- guard against continuity biases or at least recognize their presence in projections the objective of which is to draw out implications of recent trends;

- take into account uncertainty in the forecasts by developing upper and lower bounds within which paths of crime rates and offenses are expected to lie;
- shorten the forecast time period as much as the purpose for which the forecasts are produced will allow; and
- be updated as often as possible.

The incorporation of these characteristics into crime forecasts should result in more realistic uses and assessments of the forecasts.

REFERENCES

Ahlburg, D.A., and K.C. Land
  1992   Special issue: Population forecasting. *International Journal of Forecasting* 8:289-542.
Ahlburg, D.A., and W. Lutz
  1999   Introduction: The need to rethink approaches to population forecasts. Pp. 1-14 in *Frontiers of Population Forecasting*, Supplement to Volume 24, 1998, W. Lutz, J. Vaupel, and D. Ahlburg, eds.
Ahlo, J.M.
  1990   Stochastic methods in population forecasting. *International Journal of Forecasting* 6:521-530.
Bennett, W.J., J.J. DiIulio, and J.P. Walters
  1996   *Body Count: Moral Poverty and How to Win America's War Against Crime and Drugs.* New York: Simon and Schuster.
Biderman, A.D.
  1966   Social indicators and goals. Pp. 68-153 in *Social Indicators*, R.A. Bauer, ed. Cambridge, MA: MIT Press.
Blumstein, A.
  1995   Youth violence, guns and the illicit-drug industry. *The Journal of Criminal Law and Criminology* 86(1):10-36.
Bureau of Justice Statistics
  1995   *National Crime Victimization Survey Redesign.* Fact Sheet.
  1998   Serious violent crime levels continued to decline in 1997. *Four Measures of Serious Violent Crime.* [Online.] Available: http://www.ojp.usdoj.gov/bjs/glance.cv2.htm
Cohen, L.E., M. Felson, and K.C. Land
  1980   Property crime rates in the United States: A macrodynamic analysis, 1947-1974, with ex ante forecasts for the mid-1980s. *American Journal of Sociology* 86:90-118.
Cohen, L.E., and K.C. Land
  1987   Age structure and crime: Symmetry versus asymmetry and the projection of crime rates through the 1990s. *American Sociological Review* 52(170-183).
Crispell, D.
  1993   Where generations divide: A guide. *American Demographics* 15(May):9-10.
Daponte, B.O., J.B. Kadane, and L.J. Wolfson
  1997   Bayesian demography: Projecting the Kurdish population, 1977-1990. *Journal of the American Statistical Association* 92:1256-1267.
DiIulio, J.J., Jr.
  1995a Arresting ideas: Tougher law enforcement is driving down urban crime. *Policy Review* 74:12-16.
  1995b Why violent crime rates have dropped. *The Wall Street Journal* (September 6):A19.

1997 Jail alone won't stop juvenile super-predators. *The Wall Street Journal* (June 11):A23.

Fox, J.A.
1978 *Forecasting Crime Data: An Econometric Analysis.* Lexington, MA: Lexington Books.

1996 *Trends in Juvenile Violence: A Report to the United States Attorney General on Current and Future Rates of Juvenile Offending,* March. Washington, DC: Bureau of Justice Statistics.

1997 *Update on Trends in Juvenile Violence: A Report to the United States Attorney General on Current and Future Rates of Juvenile Offending.* Washington, DC: Bureau of Justice Statistics.

Gibson, C.
1993 The four baby booms. *American Demographics* 15(November):36-40.

Greenberg, D.
1985 Age, crime and social explanation. *American Journal of Sociology* 91:1-21.

Hirschi, T., and M. Gottfredson
1983 Age and the explanation of crime. *American Journal of Sociology* 89:552-584.

Land, K.C.
1986 Methods for national population forecasts: A review. *Journal of the American Statistical Association* 81:888-901.

Land, K.C., and S.H. Schneider
1987 Forecasting in the social and natural sciences: An overview and analysis of isomorphisms. Pp. 7-31 in *Forecasting in the Social and Natural Sciences,* K.C. Land and S.H. Schneider, eds. Boston: D. Reidel Publishing.

Lee, R.E.
1993 Modeling and forecasting the times series of U.S. fertility: Age patterns, range, and ultimate level. *International Journal of Forecasting* 9:187-202.

1999 Probabilistic approaches to population forecasting. Pp. 156-191 in *Frontiers of Population Forecasting,* Supplement to Volume 24, 1998, W. Lutz, J. Vaupel, and D. Ahlburg, eds.

Lee, R.E., and L. Carter
1992 Modeling and forecasting the time series of U.S. mortality. *Journal of the American Statistical Association* 87:659-671.

Lee, R.E., and S. Tuljapurkar
1994 Stochastic population projections for the United States: Beyond high, medium, and low. *Journal of the American Statistical Association* 89:1175-1189.

Lutz, W., W. Sanderson, and S. Scherbov
1999 Expert-based population projections. Pp. 139-155 in *Frontiers of Population Forecasting,* Supplement to Volume 24, 1998, W. Lutz, J. Vaupel, and D. Ahlburg, eds.

President's Commission on Law Enforcement and Administration of Justice
1967 *Task Force Report: Crime and its Impact: An Assessment.* Washington, DC: U.S. Government Printing Office.

Sagi, P.C., and C.F. Wellford
1968 Age composition and patterns of change in criminal statistics. *The Journal of Criminal Law, Criminology and Police Science* 59(1):29-36.

Steffensmeier, D., and M.D. Harer
1987 Is the crime rate really falling? *Journal of Research in Crime and Delinquency* 24:23-48.

1999 Making sense of recent U.S. crime trends, 1980-96/8: Age-composition effects and other explanations. *Journal of Research in Crime and Delinquency* 36(3).

Stoto, M.A.
    1983   The accuracy of population projections. *Journal of the American Statistical Association* 78:13-20.
U.S. Census Bureau
    1985   Estimates of the population of the United States and components of change by age, sex, and race: 1980 to 1984. *Current Population Reports*, Series P-25, No. 965. Washington, DC: U.S. Government Printing Office.
    1995   National and state population estimates: 1990 to 1994. *Current Population Reports*, Series P-25, No. 1127. Washington, DC: U.S. Government Printing Office.
    1996   Population Projections of the United States by Age, Sex, Race, and Hispanic Origin: 1995 to 2050. *Current Population Reports*, Series P-25, No. 1130. Washington, DC: U.S. Government Printing Office.
Wellford, C.
    1973   Age composition and the increase in recorded crime. *Criminology* 11(1):61-70.
Wilson, J.Q.
    1995   Crime and public policy. *Crime*, J.Q. Wilson and J. Petersilia, eds. San Francisco, CA: Institute for Contemporary Studies Press.

Appendix C

Workshop Agendas

WORKSHOP ON EDUCATION AND DELINQUENCY

October 2, 1998

8:00-8:15 a   Welcoming Remarks
          Joan McCord, Workshop Chair

School Environment and Social Climate

8:15-9:00 a   *School Environment and Effects on Learning*
          John Devine, New York University
          Q&A/Discussion
9:00-10:00 a   *School Safety Security Measures (e.g., metal detectors,*
          guards, etc.)
          Kenneth Trump, National School Safety and Security
          Services
          Q&A/Discussion
10:00-10:15 a   Break
10:15-11:00 a   *Tracking, Social Promotions, and Other Educational*
          Organizational Issues
          Mark Berends, RAND Corporation
          Q&A/Discussion
11:00-11:45 a   High-Risk Young Adolescents in Learning Environments
          Thomas Dishion, University of Oregon
          Q&A/Discussion

11:45-12:30 p	**Lunch (Lunch to be served in meeting room)**
12:30-1:15 p	*Using the Framework of Risk and Resilience to Understand the Developmental Trajectories of Students who are Expelled from School*

Gale Morrison, University of California, Santa Barbara
Q&A/Discussion

School Performance, Intervention, and Delinquency

1:15-2:00 p   *Overview of Educational Performance and Delinquency*
Rolf Loeber, University of Pittsburgh Medical Center
Q&A/Discussion

2:00-2:45 p   *Approaches to Improve School Performance*
Margaret Beale Spencer, University of Pennsylvania
Q&A/Discussion

2:45-3:00 p   Break

3:00-3:45 p   Motivation, School Readiness, and Teacher Preparation
Carol Dweck, Columbia University
Q&A/Discussion

3:45-4:15 p   *Commentary*
Doris Entwisle, Johns Hopkins University

4:15-5:00 p   **General Discussion**

5:00 p   Meeting Adjourns

**JUVENILE JUSTICE SYSTEM WORKSHOP:
FROM ENTRY TO AFTER CARE**

DAY ONE   **January 21, 1999**

8:00-8:15 a   Welcoming Remarks
Cathy Spatz Widom, Workshop Chair

8:15-9:00 a   Theory and Scope of the Juvenile Court
Jay Blitzman, Judge, Juvenile Court, Middlesex County, Massachusetts
Q&A/Discussion

9:00-9:45 a   Breaking the Cycle of Youth Violence: Problem Solving Approaches
David Kennedy, Kennedy School of Government, Harvard University
Q&A/Discussion

9:45-10:00 a   Break

10:00-10:45 a	Policing of Juveniles
	Robert Worden and Stephanie Myers, The University at Albany
	Q&A/ Discussion
10:45-11:30 a	Race, Ethnicity, and Gender Issues in Pretrial Detention of Juveniles
	Kimberly Kempf-Leonard, University of Missouri, St. Louis
	Q&A/Discussion
11:30 a-12:45 p	Lunch
12:45-2:15 p	Transfer Mechanisms: Issues, Practices, and Consequences
	Legal Overview: Jeff Fagan, School of Public Health, Columbia University
	Waivers: Consequences and Empirical Issues: Donna Bishop, University of Central Florida
	Policy, Law, and Theory: Jeff Fagan, School of Public Health, Columbia University
	Q&A/Discussion
2:15-2:30 p	Break
2:30-3:15 p	Sentencing Issues and Correctional Consequences
	Barry Feld, University of Minnesota
	Q&A/Discussion
3:15-4:00 p	Effectiveness of Programs for Institutionalized Delinquents
	Mark Lipsey, Vanderbilt University
	Q&A/Discussion
4:00-4:45 p	The Effects of Incarceration on Juveniles
	Lee Underwood, The Pines Residential Treatment Center
	Q&A/Discussion
5:00 p	Reception and Dinner will follow the meeting for panel members and workshop speakers

DAY TWO	**January 22, 1999**
8:15-8:30 a	Opening remarks
8:30-9:15 a	Alternatives to Incarceration
	Phil Harris, Temple University
	Q&A/Discussion
9:15-10:00 a	What Happens After Incarceration? Issues Regarding Aftercare
	David Altschuler, Institute for Policy Studies, Johns Hopkins University
	Q&A/Discussion
10:00-10:15 a	Break

10:15-11:00 a   The Federal Role in the Juvenile Justice System: The
                Policy Debate
                Federal Legislation
                Mary Didier, U.S. Sentencing Commission
                Juveniles in the Federal System
                Holly MacKay, U.S. Sentencing Commission
                Q&A/Discussion
11:00-11:45 a   Decriminalizing Status Offenders and the "Hidden
                System"
                Ira Schwartz, University of Pennsylvania
                Q&A/Discussion
11:45 a-12:15 p General Discussion
12:15 p   Workshop Adjourns

WORKSHOP ON DEVELOPMENTAL ISSUES

May 3, 1999

8:30-9:00 a   Welcome and Opening Remarks
                Joan McCord, Workshop Chair
9:00-10:00 a   Development of Language and Cognition
                Ellen Markman, Stanford University
                Q&A/Discussion
10:00-11:00 a   Development of Self Perceptions
                Daphna Oyserman, University of Michigan
                Q&A/Discussion
11:00-11:15 a   Break
11:15 a-12:15 p Development of Family Interactions and Peer Relationships
                Gregory Pettit, Auburn University
                Q&A/Discussion
12:15-1:30 p   Lunch and Luncheon speaker
                Laurence Steinberg, Temple University
                Director, Research Network on Adolescent Development
                and Juvenile Justice, John D. and Catherine T.
                MacArthur Foundation
1:30-2:35 p   Developmental Issues on Motivation
                Mark Lepper, Stanford University
                Q&A/Discussion
2:30-3:30 p   Emergence of Skills to Regulate Emotions
                Cynthia Stifter, Pennsylvania State University
                Q&A/Discussion

3:30-3:45 p	Break
3:45-4:45 p	Critical Points for Successful Development
	Kenneth Maton, University of Maryland Baltimore County
	Q&A Discussion
4:45-5:45 p	Developmental Perspectives on Deviance
	Rolf Loeber, Western Psychiatric Institute
	Q&A/Discussion
5:45-6:00 p	General Discussion
6:00 p	Meeting adjourns

RACIAL DISPARITY WORKSHOP

June 29, 1999

8:30 am	Opening Remarks
9:00- 9:45 a	Economic and Social Inequality
	Robert Bursik, University of Missouri, St. Louis (canceled)
	Steven Messner, University of Albany, State University of New York
	Ted Chiricos, Florida State University
9:45-10:30 a	Discussion
10:30-10:45 a	Break
10:45-11:30 a	Values, Beliefs and Situational Determinants of Offending
	Howard Pinderhughes, University of California at San Francisco
	William Oliver, Indiana University
	Philip Cook, Duke University
11:30 a-12:15 p	Discussion
12:15-12:45 p	Pick up lunch
12:45-1:30 p	Assessing Racial Disparity in Juvenile Residential Placements and in Sentencing: Factors Affecting Data Quality
	Laurie Schwede, U.S. Bureau of the Census
	Q&A
1:30-2:00 p	Alternative Perspectives on Trends
	Delbert Elliott, University of Colorado, Boulder
	Lawrence Greenfeld, Bureau of Justice Statistics
2:00-2:30 p	Discussion
2:30-2:45 p	Break

2:45-3:15 p	Differential Processing and Establishing Bias
	George Bridges, University of Washington
	David Harris, University of Toledo College of Law
3:15-3:45 p	Discussion
3:45-4:30 p	Implications for Future Research
4:30 p	Workshop Adjourns

APPENDIX D

Biographical Sketches

Joan McCord (*Cochair*) is professor of criminal justice at Temple University. She is an expert in adolescent development and juvenile justice, criminological theory, and social science research methodology. The winner of numerous fellowships and awards throughout her distinguished career, she is a past president of the American Society of Criminology and past chair of the section on crime, law and deviance of the American Sociological Association. She is a former vice chair of the National Research Council's Committee on Law and Justice. Her recent publications include *Integrating Crime Prevention Strategies: Propensity and Opportunity* and *Contemporary Masters of Criminology*. She has B.A., M.A., and Ph.D. (sociology) degrees from Stanford University and an Ed.M. from Harvard University.

Cathy Spatz Widom (*Cochair*) is professor of psychiatry and university professor in the Department of Psychiatry at the New Jersey Medical School. She is a former professor of criminal justice and psychology at the University of Albany, as well as a former faculty member in psychology and social relations at Harvard University and in criminal justice and psychology at Indiana University. She has published extensively on topics that include child abuse and neglect, juvenile delinquency, female criminality, and violence. Her current research interests focus on the intergenerational transmission of violence and the long-term consequences of early childhood abuse and neglect. She received the 1989 behavioral research prize from the American Association for the Advancement of

355

Science and was elected a fellow of the American Psychological Association in 1993. She has served on National Research Council committees on child abuse and family violence interventions and is currently a member of the Committee on Law and Justice. She has Ph.D. (psychology) and M.S. degrees from Brandeis University and a B.S. from Cornell University.

Patricia Cohen is a social psychologist-psychiatric epidemiologist at the New York State Psychiatric Institute and a faculty member at the Center for Young Children and Families, Teachers College, with a long-term interest in methodological issues. Cohen's methodological work includes the popular text *Applied Multiple Regression/Correlation for the Behavioral Sciences*, written with Jacob Cohen. Among her widely cited methodological articles are "To Be or Not To Be: The Control and Balancing of Type 1 And Type 2 Errors in Research" and "The Clinician's Illusion," which demonstrates the biasing effects of sampling on one's understanding of the nature and course of disease. Her current work focuses on an empirical comparison of children in the mental health, special education, substance abuse, juvenile abuse, and social service (foster care) programs in Westchester County, NY, with regard to emotional and behavioral problems, demographic factors, and the course of their problems. She has a B.A. from Hamline University and a Ph.D. in social psychology from New York University.

Elizabeth Jane Costello is associate professor of medical psychology in the Department of Psychiatry and Behavioral Sciences at Duke University Medical Center and has been a faculty member of the department since 1988. She has served as director for the Psychiatric Epidemiology Training Program at the University of Pittsburgh School of Medicine. She is a member of the American College of Epidemiology and has served as council member and chair in the mental health section of the American Public Health Association. Costello's areas of research interest include developmental epidemiology, life-span developmental psychopathology, mental health services for children and adolescents, and clinical decision making. She has also published numerous works in refereed journals on developmental psychology and epidemiology. She has a Ph.D. in psychology from the University of London, an M.Phil. and a B.Sci. from the London School of Economics, and an M.A. from Oxford University.

Nancy A. Crowell (*Study Director*) is staff officer with the Commission on Behavioral and Social Sciences and Education in the National Research Council/National Academy of Sciences. She serves on the staff of the Committee of Law and Justice and the Board on Children, Youth, and Families. She was the study director for a study of the health and safety implications of child labor, which produced the report *Protecting Youth at Work*. She previously staffed studies on violence against women, family violence, risk communication, and policy implications of greenhouse warming. Trained as a pediatric audiologist, she worked in a demonstration project for preschool hearing-impaired children and their families at Ball State University. She also worked on several political campaigns and for a political polling and consulting firm prior to joining the National Research Council staff. She holds B.S. from St. Lawrence University in mathematics and French and an M.A. in audiology from Vanderbilt University.

Eugene K. Emory is a professor of psychology at Emory University who specializes in clinical psychology, neuropsychology, and behavioral perinatology. His research focus is on the effects of early stress on behavior, fetal and infant development, and human neuroscience. He was a recipient of the research scientist development award from the National Institute of Mental Health. An editorial board member of the *International Journal of Psychophysiology* and *Child Development* since 1984, he has published numerous research materials including *Psychophysiological Responses to Stress During Pregnancy* and *Salivary Caffeine and Neonatal Behavior*. He has a B.S. from Edward Waters College and an M.Ed. and a Ph.D. in clinical and developmental psychology from the University of Florida, Gainesville.

Tony Fabelo is the executive director of the Texas Criminal Justice Policy Council, a state agency that conducts research, program evaluations, and strategic planning in criminal justice for the governor and the legislature. He has been with the agency since 1984 and has assisted four governors and six Texas legislatures in the development of criminal justice policies. He has numerous publications to his credit in academic and professional journals and is a well-known keynote speaker in criminal justice forums nationwide. He has Ph.D. and M.S. degrees from the University of Texas at Austin and a B.A. from Loyola University.

Lawrence Gary is professor in the School of Social Work at Howard University, where he has been on the social work faculty for 27 years. His long list of publications include five (5) books and monographs, most notably the classic work, *Black Men*, and has over 90 research articles and chapters in scholarly journals and books. He is the recipient of numerous awards, including the 1993 outstanding leadership and community service award of the National Association of Black Social Workers. He has a B.S. degree (with high honors) from Tuskegee Institute and M.P.A., M.S.W., and Ph.D. degrees from the University of Michigan.

Sandra Graham is a professor in the Department of Education at the University of California, Los Angeles. Her research interests include the cognitive approaches to motivation, the development of attributional process, motivation in African Americans, and peer-directed aggression. She was a Ford Foundation postdoctoral minority fellow and was elected to fellow status in the American Psychological Association. She has a B.A. (with honors) from Barnard College, an M.A. in history from Columbia University, and a Ph.D. in education from University of California, Los Angeles.

John Hagan is professor of sociology at Northwestern University and research fellow at the American Bar Foundation in Chicago. He is a former professor of sociology and law and Killam research fellow at the University of Toronto. His current research focuses on the causes and consequences of delinquency and crime in the life course and on the professional and personal lives of lawyers. In addition to more than 120 published papers on criminological and sociological topics, he has published seven books, one of which, *Structural Criminology* (1989), received awards from the Society for the Study of Social Problems and the American Sociological Association. He is a fellow of the Royal Society of Canada and the American Society of Criminology, a former president of the American Society of Criminology, a research fellow of Statistics Canada, and a fellow of the Canadian Institute of Advanced Research. He served on the National Research Council's Panel on High Risk Youth. He has a B.A. degree from the University of Illinois and M.A. and Ph.D. degrees in sociology from the University of Alberta.

Darnell Hawkins is professor of African-American studies and sociology and a faculty affiliate in the Department of Criminal Justice at the University of Illinois, Chicago. He has previously served on the faculty of the University of North Carolina and has taught grades three and four in the Detroit public schools. He is currently a member of the National Research Council's Committee on Law and Justice and served on its study of family violence interventions. His publications have featured research on homicide among young African Americans and press coverage of homicide. He has a J.D. from the University of North Carolina at Chapel Hill, a Ph.D. in sociology from the University of Michigan, an M.A.T. from Wayne State University, and a B.A. from Kansas State University.

Kenneth Land is the John Franklin Crowell professor of sociology at Duke University. He is a social statistician with substantive research interests in criminology, demography, and social indicators/trends. His research contributions to criminology include participation in the articulation and testing of crime opportunity/routine activities theory, the specification and testing of models of crime rate distributions both in cross-sections and over time, and the development and application of the semiparametric mixed Poisson regression approach to models of delinquent/criminal careers. In addition, he has participated in a number of projects to evaluate juvenile justice programs. He has a Ph.D. in sociology with a minor in mathematics and an M.A. in sociology from the University of Texas at Austin and a B.A. from Texas Lutheran College.

Honorable Cindy Lederman (*Liaison Member*) is the Administrative Judge of the Juvenile Court in Dade County, Florida. Previously, she was a leader of the team that created the Dade County Domestic Violence Court and served as the court's first Administrative Judge. Her expertise is in family law. With Susan Schechter she conceived the idea of the Dependency Court Intervention Program for Family Violence, a national demonstration project funded by the U.S. Department of Justice, Violence Against Women Grants Office. She is a co-principal investigator of the Miami Safe Start Initiative, a community collaboration to prevent exposure to violence for children under age 6. She has served on numerous commissions of the Florida Supreme Court investigating bias and fairness and was a member of the National Research Council's Committee on Family Violence Interventions. She now serves on the Board of Children, Youth, and Families of the National Research Council and Institute of Medicine. In 1997 she received the Florida governor's peace at home award for her work in the field of domestic violence and in 1999 the William E. Gladstone award, the state's highest honor for children's advocacy. She has a J.D. from the University of Miami School of Law.

Daniel S. Nagin (*Liaison Member*) is a professor of management at the H.J. Heinz III School of Public Policy and Management, Carnegie Mellon University, and the research director of the National Consortium on Violence Research. He has written widely on deterrence, developmental trajectories and criminal careers, tax compliance, and statistical methodology. He is a member of the National Research Council's Committee on Law and Justice and is also a coeditor of the widely cited report *Deterrence and Incapacitation: Estimating the Effect of Criminal Sanctions on Crime Rate* (1978). He is on the editorial board of five academic journals and a fellow of the American Society of Criminology. He has a B.S. in administrative and managerial sciences, an M.S. in industrial administration, and a Ph.D. in urban and public affairs from Carnegie Mellon University.

Steven Schlossman is professor and head of the history department and director of the Center for History and Policy at Carnegie Mellon University. His interests include education and criminal justice, particularly issues of race and gender in juvenile justice systems. He also has served as manager of the office of research for the California State Assembly. He has a B.A. (magna cum laude) in history and political science from Queens College, an M.A. in history from University of Wisconsin, an M.A. in education from Teachers College, Columbia University, and a Ph.D. in history from Columbia University.

Mercer Sullivan is associate professor of criminal justice at Rutgers University and senior research fellow at the Vera Institute of Justice in New York. His research interests include the impact of social context on adolescent development and youth crime and the integration of qualitative and quantitative methods. He is a member of the American Anthropological Association and the American Society of Criminology. He has a B.A. from Yale College and a Ph.D. in anthropology from Columbia University.

Honorable Viola Taliaferro is a judge for the Monroe Circuit Court VII, where she handles many juvenile cases. In 1996 she received a service award and the Harrison Centennial Award from the Indiana State Bar Association. She serves on numerous panels and forums, speaking to both professional and community organizations on a wide array of legal issues, including disposition of juvenile court cases. Her published work includes articles on juvenile offenders and waivers of juveniles to adult courts. She has a B.S. from the Virginia State College, an M.L.A. from Johns Hopkins University, and a J.D. from Indiana University School of Law.

Richard Tremblay holds a chair in child development and is professor in the Departments of Psychiatry and Psychology at the University of Montréal, and director of the Research Unit on Children's Psychosocial Maladjustment of the University of Montréal, Laval University, and McGill University. He is a member of the National Consortium on Violence Research, Molson fellow of the Canadian Institute for Advanced Research, and fellow of the Royal Society of Canada. For the past 12 years he has directed a program of longitudinal studies addressing the physical, cognitive, emotional, and social development of children from conception onward, in order to gain a better understanding of the development of antisocial behavior. He has also tested the long-term effects of an intervention program to prevent violent and antisocial behavior. He has a B.A. from the University of Ottawa, an M.Psed. from the University of Montréal, and a Ph.D. in child development and educational psychology from the University of London.

Franklin Zimring is William G. Simon professor of law and director of the Earl Warren Legal Institute at the University of California, Berkeley. His major research interest is the empirical study of law and legal institutions, with special emphasis on criminal violence. He is a member of the American Academy of Arts and Sciences. He is author or coauthor of *The Changing Legal World of Adolescence* (1982), *Capital Punishment and the American Agenda* (1987), *The Scale of Imprisonment* (1991), *The Search for Rational Drug Control* (1992), *Incapacitation: Penal Confinement and the Restraint of Crime* (1995), and *Crime Is Not the Problem* (1997). He has a B.A. from Wayne State University and a J.S. from the University of Chicago, where he served on the law faculty from 1967 to 1985.

Index

HV
9104
.J832
2001

Juvenile crime,
  juvenile justice.

DATE			